LAW FOR
SOCIAL WORKERS

A Canadian Guide

FOURTH EDITION

Rachel Birnbaum   Janet E. Mosher

formerly written by

Elaine J. Vayda   Mary T. Satterfield

THOMSON
™
CARSWELL

Library and Archives Canada Cataloguing in Publication

Birnbaum, Rachel
  Law for social workers: A Canadian guide.

A cataloguing record for this publication is available from Library and Archives Canada.

ISBN: 978-0-7798-1470-1

Composition: Computer Composition of Canada Inc.

One Corporate Plaza
2075 Kennedy Road
Toronto, Ontario
M1T 3V4

Customer Relations:
Toronto: 1-416-609-3800
Elsewhere in Canada/U.S.: 1-800-387-5164
Fax: 1-416-298-5094
E-mail: carswell.orders@thomson.com
Internet: www.carswell.com

Acknowledgements

This book would not have been possible to complete without the support of many individuals. We would like to thank our families for their support and patience as we completed this work. We are most grateful to Dean Melamed, law student at Queens University for his research assistance, Carol Pollack for her editing and Christine Galea, law student at Osgoode Hall Law School for her excellent editorial assistance throughout the drafting and editing process. We are indebted to our many colleagues who took time out from their busy schedules to review and comment on various chapters. We benefited enormously from their input; mistakes are of course our own.

Finally, we thank Gail Armstrong for her support and Carswell Publishing for their financial assistance.

Preface

As the new authors of this fourth edition we are indebted to the work undertaken over many years by the book's original authors, Elaine Vayda and Mary Satterfield. When they first published this book in 1984 they were truly pioneers; in many respects well ahead of their time in recognizing the important links between law and social work. They were among the first in the disciplines of law and social work to begin to explore not only the multiple ways in which law insinuated itself into the lives of the clients of social workers—for the better sometimes, but often for the worse—but also the potential for cross-disciplinary collaboration not only in relation to individual clients but also in broader advocacy on behalf of disenfranchised communities. In approaching this fourth edition we wanted to not only update the cases and legislation, but also frame this edition in the spirit of collaboration between law and social work. We have tried to keep the essence of our colleagues work in this edition, but add our comments and perspectives. Vayda and Satterfield coined the term "social law" to capture those areas of law which deal with many aspects of human social activity on both an individual, family, and community level and which act to define, limit, protect, remedy, and punish, both at the time of life's transitional events and unanticipated, critical events. The former include birth, school entry, marriage, retirement, and planning for aging and death, while the latter include separation, divorce, loss of employment or shelter, need for financial and social assistance, involvement in criminal activity, and physical and mental illness and incapacity.

Law atttempts to regulate, at some level, virtually every one of these life events, be they transitional or unexpected and critical. The legal frameworks which are imposed upon these life events are of crucial importance. These frameworks—created by legislation, its administration and judicial decision-making—are not of a single character. Rather they reflect the values, interests and ideas of those who have had access to the institutions of law-making, law's interpretation and law's application at given times and in given places. These legal frameworks may create important rights and protections, yet be virtually inaccessible to the vast majority of citizens;

they may restrict the options available or conversely generate new ones; and their impact may vary dramatically depending upon the social location of those subject to them. While law is often portrayed as fixed, its boundaries clearly drawn and its application readily discernible, in fact, it is often in flux, its boundaries very unclear, and its application in particular contexts vigorously contested.

While many turn to law as a vehicle to facilitate social change, and while many examples exist of where law has played an important role in this regard, law often struggles to keep apace of shifting social, economic and political changes and evolving knowledge in other disciplines. We examine instances where law has played a significant role in fostering important structural changes that impact importantly on many of the issues clients of social workers face. We also provide examples of the many difficult issues legislatures and courts struggle with, including how to define the family, how to select those factors that should be given weight in assessing the best interests of children, how to deal with young people who come into contact with the law, how to discern what rights people ought to have in regard to anticipating how they wish to be treated if they should fall ill and lose the ability to participate in decision-making, and how to draw the appropriate boundaries regarding the right of persons with mental illness to refuse treatment. In order to focus on these issues, we adopt a collaborative approach and structure, and to highlight the strain between social complexities and law, we have added new material, rearranged and redefined sections, and cited new case law and legislation.

Finally, we hope to foster a critical analysis of both law and social work theory and practice. Postmodernists would argue that laws and theories can be deconstructed to reveal presuppositions or a world view that is biased to favour the privileged in any society. Those who are marginalized on account of their race, gender, ethnicity, social class, age, or physical or mental disability can be at risk from those same laws or practices. Equity, justice, and mutual caring are requisites for a healthy society. To achieve these goals, society requires ongoing challenge from those who work at the interface between social work and law. Both social workers and lawyers are advocates for achieving justice and fair treatment amid competing and colliding interests and perceptions. Both professions have a responsibility to practice with a critical focus, to use advocacy to redress inequity, and to promote general awareness of inequity. This means that both professions are obligated to look beyond the "problem." We will attempt to address these responsibilities and the questions they raise throughout the book.

A unifying aspect of both social work and legal education is the use of a case approach to clients' problems and remedies. Whenever possible, cases will be used for illustration. It is assumed the reader is aware of the psycho-social issues which need attention. The legal issues arising from the situation will be emphasized, rather than the social work perspective. The legal cases presented throughout this book are included to give the reader a sense of how decisions are reached. The details in the cases will be similar in some respects to situations affecting the reader's clients. Published legal cases identify by name the parties to the dispute, a practice which may cause discomfort to social workers who are required to protect the identity of clients.

Our intent is not to suggest that social workers can replace legal counsel. Rather, our hope is to encourage social workers to help clients identify their rights and responsibilities, decide when legal assistance should be sought, locate appropriate assistance and to provide informed support for clients involved in legal proceedings.

Table of Contents

Part I—Fundamentals

Chapter 1

Law's Interface with Social Work

Chapter 2

A Primer on Law for Social Workers

Chapter 3

Human Rights

Chapter 4

Confronting the Courts

Chapter 5

The Litigation Process

Chapter 6

Alternative Dispute Resolution

Chapter 7

Finding and Using Legal Services

Chapter 8

The Social Worker and the Court: Evidentiary Issues

Part II—Children, Families and Law

Chapter 9

The Social and Legal Dynamics of Families

Chapter 10

Structure of the Court System in Family Law

Chapter 11

Marriage and Divorce

Chapter 12

Spousal and Child Support

Chapter 13

Family Property

Chapter 14

Enforcement of Family Court Orders

Chapter 15

Child Custody and Access in Separation and Divorce: In Whose Best Interest?

Chapter 16

Rethinking Child Welfare Issues

Chapter 17

Child Protection

Chapter 18

Adoption

Part III—Criminal Law

Chapter 19

Structure of a Crime

Chapter 20

A Field Guide to the *Criminal Code* and Related Statutes

Chapter 21

Youths in Conflict with the Law

Part IV—Selected Topics in "Social Law"

Chapter 22

Consent, Capacity, and Substitute Decision-Makers

Part V—Legal and Regulatory Issues for Social Workers

Chapter 26

Legal Accountability of Social Workers

Chapter 27

Self-Regulation of Social Workers

PART I

FUNDAMENTALS

1

Law's Interface with Social Work

(1) INTRODUCTION

The interface between law and social work is multi-faceted, complex and dynamic. Here we examine several—but by no means all—of these facets. Inevitably the perspectives we offer are derived from a particular time and place. The law itself is constantly in flux and the practices of both lawyers and social workers continuously evolving and shifting. Although these categories are somewhat artificial, we explore the interface of law and social work under four broad categories: law's impact upon the practices of social work; law's presence in the lives of the clients of social workers; the tensions and synergies between the practices of law and of social work; and collaborative practices.

(2) LAW'S IMPACT UPON SOCIAL WORK PRACTICE

Law shapes the practice of social work in significant ways. Many social workers, for example, practice in agencies or environments where they are carrying out a mandate that is defined by statute. It is the law that shapes their responsibilities and duties. Social workers employed by child welfare agencies are, for instance, carrying out duties and responsibilities created by statute. Ontario's *Child and Family Services Act*,[1] for example, provides that the functions of a children's aid society are to,

> (a) investigate allegations or evidence that children who are under the age of 16 years or are in the society's care or under its supervision may be in need of protection;

 (b) protect, where necessary, children who are under the age of 16 years or are in the society's care or under its supervision;

 (c) provide guidance, counselling and other services to families for protecting children or for the prevention of circumstances requiring the protection of children;

 (d) provide care for children assigned or committed to its care under this *Act*;

 (e) supervise children assigned to its supervision under this *Act*;

 (f) place children for adoption under Part VII; and

 (g) perform any other duties given to it by this or any other *Act*.[2]

Law operates in further ways to shape social work practice. The law regulates such matters as record-keeping, confidentiality and access to personal information of clients, all of which impact the day-to-day practices of social work. Additionally, the potential of professional liability operates as a constant backdrop in the practice of social work. Social workers must maintain the minimum standards of practice expected by the profession, understand and respect the law of consent, and respect the fiduciary duties they owe their clients (the duties that arise as a result of the relationship of trust between a social worker and his or her client and which require loyalty, good faith, and protection of the client's interests) or they risk a civil suit or professional sanction by the governing professional body.

Moreover, law creates the framework within which the profession of social work is itself regulated. By statute, in seven Canadian provinces, the profession of social work is given authority to regulate its members; in the other three provinces responsibility for regulation of the profession has been delegated to a social work regulatory body that is independent of the provincial association of social workers.[3] It is the governing statute that creates the authority of the profession to, for example, determine criteria for admission to the profession, set standards of practice, and define professional misconduct.

(3) LAW'S PRESENCE IN THE LIVES OF THE CLIENTS OF SOCIAL WORKERS

Law is a pervasive presence in the lives of the clients of social workers. Many clients seek out, or are directed to, social workers at points of crisis in their lives, be it marital breakdown, declining loss of mental capacity, involvement with the criminal justice system as an accused or victim, resettlement in Canada, or an experience with discrimination. At these points of crisis, the law is invariably present, shaping in some manner the issues and the options.

Quite apart from these defined moments of crisis, the law is an ubiquitous presence in the lives of those who are marginalized. As we discuss in Chapter 7, a survey conducted in March, 2004 of some 4,500 low and middle-income Canadians revealed that the distribution of legal problems is anything but equitable. Rather, single parents, persons with disabilities, persons between the ages of 18 and 29, those who were unemployed and those in receipt of social assistance benefits showed the greatest likelihood of experiencing one or more legal problems. Aboriginal people and members of visible minority groups were slightly more likely than others to report at least one problem.[4]

As Stephen Wexler observed more than 30 years ago, "[p]oor people are not just like rich people without money."[5] Rather, their relationship to the law is both qualitatively and quantitatively different.

> Poor people do not lead settled lives into which the law seldom intrudes; they are constantly involved with the law in its most intrusive forms. For instance, poor people must go to government officials for many of the things which non-poor people get privately. Life would be very difficult for the non-poor person if he had to fill out an income tax return once or twice a week. Poverty creates an abrasive interface with society; poor people are always bumping into sharp legal things.[6]

Whether at a moment of crisis, or as a persistent feature of daily life, law is inextricably bound up with other non-legal issues, shaping and being shaped by them. Indeed, it is "a rare legal problem that is in fact purely "legal". . . nearly all disputes involve complex emotional and interpersonal dynamics and most involve "industries" other than law."[7] Moreover, the roots of many of these legal issues cannot be resolved by a legal intervention alone and failing to address the root causes may result in ongoing involvement with the legal system.

Robin Steinberg illustrates this effectively in her description of one particular case in which she represented Lisa, a young woman accused of robbery who was addicted to heroin. While confident that she had performed well her role as a zealous advocate devoted to the advancement of her client's interest in the context of the criminal proceeding, Steinberg expressed concern about the limits of that representation.

> Because while I addressed the needs of her criminal case effectively, I did nothing to change her life—to address, in other words, her human needs. Those needs, left unaddresse, would eventually drive her back into the criminal justice system and into that same prison cell from which she narrowly escaped the first time. Looking back, what Lisa needed was an advocate who could look beyond her criminal case, to her drug addiction, to her homelessness, and to her psychological needs (which stemmed from years of trauma

and abuse). Lisa needed an advocate who regarded her as a "whole client," rather than as a case. . . .[8]

Indeed, for many clients, the legal issues may not be the most pressing and the legal remedies, even if available and accessible, not particularly helpful. For example, over the past few decades there has been a tremendous focus upon criminal justice intervention in cases of women abused in their intimate relationships. While criminal justice intervention will assist some women, for others it creates more harm than good. This is particularly true for women who are economically and/or racially marginalized. For low-income women, pressing and oppressive poverty may be exacerbated by a criminal justice intervention; adequate food and shelter more effective in making them safe.[9] For women who are racialized, engagement with the criminal justice system may strain, if not break, their relationships with others in their communities.[10]

Similarly, Margaret Barry notes that elder law advocates "have cautioned against approaching client legal problems in isolation from financial, psychological, medical and religious issues since loneliness, fear, anxieties about aging, financial problems, and family concerns, often accompany the elderly client's legal problems."[11] Similar observations could be made across a wide range of legal issues.

It is clear then, that in many instances, an approach which is narrowly focused upon legal processes and remedies will be less than satisfactory; so too will be an approach grounded in social work practices that fails to appreciate the legal issues and the potential legal risks and opportunities at play. Social workers need a basic understanding of law to practice effectively, and social workers and lawyers both need to find ways of working together collaboratively. Clients need the assistance of both lawyers and social workers—working collaboratively—to address the legal problems they face, both at the individual level and at a systems level.[12] In many instances, lawyers and social workers require the assistance and expertise of the other in order to function optimally in the service of the client's best interests. These critical situations where law and social need intersect define what the original authors of this text, Vayda and Satterfield, have termed the terrain of social law.

Many lawyers are aware of the inadequacy of narrow remedies for complex socio-legal problems. For the social work profession, practitioners and educators have recognized that the traditional delivery of service has not created significant change in the lives of many recipients. A new generation of social workers is not content to rely on the assessment and treatment of individual and family psychopathology. Instead, these social workers have argued for a holistic approach, one in which assessment of a problem demands an ecological scan that not only includes individual and family systems but also a structural analysis of the influence of societal institutions on the definition of problems. For example, institutionalized racism, sexism, and power inequities may be reflected in laws. The client's reaction may be powerlessness flowing from these structural defects. This enlarged view requires a broad range of knowledge and strategies for service that can be undertaken with the fullest possible participation of the client. Change in attitude and behaviour of clients may depend upon a perception that internal and external resources are interrelated. Many lawyers also appreciate the need to examine underlying structures, and law's role in upholding—but also potentially in dismantling—those structures.

(4) SYNERGIES AND TENSIONS BETWEEN THE PRACTICES OF LAW AND SOCIAL WORK

How we understand the synergies and tensions between the practices of law and social work depends, of course, upon how we understand the practices of each profession. This is made more complex by the reality that there is no single vision of practice of either law or social work. In fact, there are a multiplicity of practice visions and on-the-ground practices in both law and social work.

That said, we can identify some general commonalities between law and social work, as well as some possible tensions. As the above discussion makes clear, lawyers and social workers are frequently working with the very same clients, on the same issues, but often independently rather than collaboratively. As Anderson *et al.* note,

> Both lawyers and social workers identify as helping professionals. Both serve as counselors, advisors and advocates for their clients. Both attempt to facilitate conflict resolution, while respecting client self-determination and confidentiality. In addition, both strive to uphold fundamental societal values and promote public service. These values are at the core of each profession's orientation to practice.[13]

Like social workers, many lawyers involved in the practice of "social law" seek ways to work with, rather than on behalf of, their clients. And many in both professions seek to find ways to empower not only individuals, but communities, through community development approaches. Each aims to provide advocacy for individuals, and to encourage groups to participate as advocates. Both use a case-by-case approach to situations and place a high value on the dignity of the individual. Both participate in activities designed to exert pressure and influence to seek broader change through the formulation of policy.

An obstacle to co-operation between social work and law resides in the distorted and stereotyped views each profession has maintained about the other. It is tempting to disclaim simplistic thinking, but elements of exaggeration are manifest in the respective attitudes of lawyers and social workers. Lawyers have been seen by social workers as rigid, technical, precise, interested in logic and facts but uncomfortable when confronted with human ambiguity. Because many social workers are employed by agencies, lawyers are unwilling to accept them as professionals with a direct accountability to their clients. Social workers are believed to be emotional and imprecise, relying too much on subjective impressions.

Anderson *et al.* have identified several perceived tensions between law and social work, and we explore briefly several of them here.[14] Lawyering is frequently identified with the undivided zeal and commitment to client autonomy (*i.e.* the individual), while social work identifies with the larger social community and with social justice. This clash may exist in some instances while be absent in others. The model of the lawyer as zealous partisan advocate who knows but one duty in the world—that owed to his or her client—has given way to a more complex model, where the nature of the lawyering demanded varies with context. So, for example, the Law Society of Upper Canada "Guidelines for Lawyers Acting in Cases Involving Claims of Residential School Abuses" provides, among other things, that lawyers should understand that the harms experienced include those that result from being cut off from Aboriginal society, culture and traditions, should appreciate the client's cultural roots and customs and should be able to identify and refer clients to appropriate community resources, including counselling.[15] The Rules of Professional Conduct for lawyers in Ontario note, for example, that counsel for corporate interests,

> are in a central position to encourage organizations to comply with the law and to advise that it is in the organizations' and the public's interest that organizations do not violate the law. Lawyers acting for organizations are often in a position to advise the executive officers of the organization not only about the technicalities of the law but about the public relations and public policy concerns that motivated the government or regulator to enact the law. Moreover, lawyers for organizations, particularly in-house counsel, may guide organizations to act in ways that are legal, ethical, reputable, and consistent with the organization's responsibilities to its constituents and to the public.[16]

Thus, while lawyers in some contexts may defend the interests of their clients zealously and in what may seem to be an exceedingly partisan way, in other contexts a very different approach will be taken. The Rules governing lawyers' conduct clearly contemplate a range of duties beyond that owed to the client.

Another tension is one that derives from a portrayal of law as an adversarial process, while social work is cast as embracing a co-operative process and a broader problem-solving approach.[17] Again, this may be true in some instances, but the comparison belies the common use of non-adversarial processes in law, as well as the evolution of broader problem-solving approaches in legal practice. So, for example, there is often an assumption that lawyers are devoutly wedded to adversarial litigation and concerned only with the zealous and partisan advocacy of their clients. This may be true of some lawyers, in some contexts—particularly in criminal defence work—but not true in others. Many lawyers acknowledge the limitations of, and indeed harms that can be worked by, adversarial proceedings in some contexts, but appreciate that in other contexts adversarialism is the best mechanism to protect important interests. Particularly in the family law context there has been a growing recognition that the problems of family breakup cannot be left to the judiciary, or entirely to the marital therapists, for resolution. The social and emotional costs to all concerned far outweigh the considerable legal costs of adversarial resolutions to questions of custody, access, and support. It has been noted by responsible members of the legal profession that in family law matters the adversary system does not function to the benefit of anyone except perhaps to inflate legal fees, and that the conflict has destructive consequences. In a working paper, the Law Reform Commission of Canada observed that ". . .in general the adversary approach promotes a ritualistic and unrealistic approach to family problems."[18] Mediation has become an effective instrument to help many families through the crisis of separation and divorce with the least damage to children, parents, and extended family members. Conciliation is a natural climate for lawyers and social workers to develop a working relationship based on mutual respect for each other's expertise. A broad approach to problem-solving is particularly reflected in multi-disciplinary practices, or multi-service centres, but may also be found simply in the way individual legal practitioners approach his or her work.

Law is frequently associated with the protection of client rights and social work, the safeguarding of a client's best interests.[19] A British lawyer, writing on law addressed to social workers, observed that, "[i]n general, rights, duties, and remedies characterize legal thinking while social workers may think first of needs and relationships."[20] For example, a man, terminally ill, is living with a woman, but is legally married to another woman from whom he has been separated for many years. A social worker might not introduce the subject of his will or suggest that he may want to get legal advice on this matter because the focus of concern would be on the psychological aspects of the situation. In another instance, a social worker may be working toward the rehabilitation of an accident victim, helping that person to accept the residual physical disability and adjust to an altered life, but that worker may never bring up the question of adequate financial compensation that legal intervention may be able to secure. A focus upon effective counselling through the establishment of a therapeutic, helping relationship may obscure the possibility of concurrently pursuing the concrete needs of clients through legal channels.[21]

No doubt lawyers do work to protect and advance clients' rights. However, as we review in Chapter 7, a disturbingly large segment of the Canadian population has no access to legal representation to enforce their rights, and commonly no knowledge of their rights. Many "rights" that exist on paper, including Constitutional rights, are simply not respected in practice. Social workers can and should play an important role in providing clients with knowledge of their rights, in making legal information accessible to a wider audience and in helping to protect client rights. In other words, while social workers are indeed frequently concerned with a client's best interests, they are also concerned with respect for their rights.

As Steinberg's discussion of her own lawyering reviewed earlier suggests, lawyers are frequently focused upon the legal problem, rather than addressing the underlying cause. While it may be argued that the lawyer's expertise is such that it is precisely in relation to the legal solution that lawyers have something to offer clients, it does not follow that lawyers should therefore be oblivious to the underlying roots of the problem. As Steinberg's example illustrates, neglect of the underlying problem will often lead to re-engagement with the legal system, and all too frequently to a proliferation of legal problems. Secondly, attention to the underlying cause often reveals patterns over several cases and points to a structural root; one that systemic advocacy might address. Lawyers and social workers share an interest in identifying and attempting to remove the root causes underlying client problems.[22]

Social work has embraced systems theory for more than a decade and social workers are expected to act as an advocate for and with individuals confronting hostile systems, as well as an advocate on behalf of persons sharing similar life situations. More recent social work theory has suggested other models that focus on social justice, on identification and utilization of client strengths rather than pathology, and on methods of enabling clients to develop empowerment strategies. Another model works with individual or family narratives or life stories that encourage these stories to be perceived differently by acknowledging the authenticity of specific systemic inequities in order that persons may choose to act for appropriate social change.[23]

(5) COLLABORATION

As the above discussion suggests, there are many compelling reasons not only for social workers to have a basic knowledge and understanding of the law, but for the active collaboration between lawyers and social workers. It is suggested that the combined knowledge and assistance of social workers and lawyers is necessary to help alleviate client distress and/or advocate on their behalf. Bronstein aptly describes interdisciplinary collaboration as an effective means to address the range of problems presented by an individual, family, and the broader community.[24]

Social work has a long tradition of working collaboratively with other disciplines to help advocate and alleviate social problems. This is less true of law, but practices have begun to change. The idea of collaborative lawyering in the family and poverty law contexts is starting to take hold, and as Steinberg indicates, even in the criminal context there is receptivity to collaboration. Indeed, Steinberg illustrates how the crisis of the criminal case may present,

> an ideal time for social workers, psychologists, mental health professionals, and other advocates to work with clients to help them gain a better disposition and a better life outcome. Such collaborations include: (a) helping clients maintain health treatments that may have been interrupted by the arrest; (b) securing counseling to help a client cope with any past trauma or abuse that may have, directly or indirectly, led to the arrest, and; (c) charting out a service plan to help the client secure employment, gain remedial services, and fulfill court mandated programs."[25]

Attempts have been made to reconcile or rationalize legal and social work thought within a common framework. A modern critique of legal thought seeks to import into legal reasoning a moral reasoning similar to social work thought. Gilligan demonstrates that the "logic of justice" approach, typical of lawyers' and judges' reasoning, solves dilemmas by a choice of principles such as "life is more important than property." An "ethic of care" approach, more characteristic of social workers yet increasingly advocated as an approach for lawyers, sees dilemmas rooted in persons and situations and seeks to find resolutions to partially satisfy both needs. Each presents a problem-solving approach which may frequently produce the same result, and are essentially remedial and libertarian in nature. Both approaches also require the assistance and expertise of the other in order to function optimally in the service of the client's best interest. Critical situations where law and social need intersect define the terrain of social law. In the final analysis, it is maintained that social work and law combined have a unique role to play and contribute to the resolution of legal/social problems.

In the following chapters, we explore important legal and social issues that have been addressed by the courts and established legal principles affecting social work clients. Special consideration is given to examining legislation, regulations and other organizational practices[26] to assist the reader regarding the judicial and legal context of social policy, social service provision and social work practice.[27] In doing so, we hope to provide social workers with knowledge of the law and the implications of social work practice with individuals, families and the broader community. For the lawyer, we hope to provide the social contextual issues that affect social work clients.

SELECTED READINGS

Aiken, Jane & Stephen Wizer, "Law as Social Work" (2003) 11 Wash. U.J.L. & Pol'y 63.

Albert, Raymond, *Law and Social Work Practice. A Legal Systems Approach*, 2d ed. (New York: Springer Publishing Company, Inc., 2000).

Anderson, Alexis, Lynn Barenbery and Paul R. Tremblay, "Professional Ethics in Interdisciplinary Collaborations: Zeal, Partisanship and Mandatory Reporting" (2007) 13 Clinical L. Rev. 659.

Daley, Barbara J., "Learning and Professional Practice: A Study of Four Professions" (2001) 52(1) Adult Education Quarterly 39.

Krouse, Kate, "Lawyers Should Be Lawyers: But What Does That Mean?: A Response to Aiken, Wizner and Smith" (2004) 14 Wash. U.J.L. & Pol'y 49.

Madden, Robert, "Legal Content in Social Work Education: Preparing Students for Interprofessional Practice" in Raymond Albert, ed., *Law and Social Work Practice: A Legal Systems Approach*, 2d ed. (New York: Springer Publishing Company, Inc., 2000) 333.

Minow, Martha, "Lawyering for Human Dignity" (2002) 11 Am. U.J. Gender Soc. Pol'y & L. 143.

Molina, Olga, "A Joint Legal/Social Work Services Program Helps Working Women Through the Divorce Process" (2001) 35(3/4) Journal of Divorce and Remarriage 169.

Spakes, P., "Social Workers and the Courts: Education, Practice, and Research Needs" (1987) 23(2) Journal of Social Work Education 30.

Stein, Theodore J., *The Role of Law in Social Work Practice and Administration* (New York: Columbia University Press, 2004).

Steinberg, Robin G., "Beyond Lawyering: How Holistic Representation Makes for Good Policy, Better Lawyers, and More Satisfied Clients" (2006) 30 N.Y.U. Rev. L. & Soc. Change 625.

Taylor, Sarah, "Educating Future Practitioners of Social Work and Law: Exploring the Origins of Inter-Professional Misunderstanding" (2005) 28 Children and Youth Services Review 638.

ENDNOTES

1. *Child and Family Services Act*, R.S.O. 1990, c. C.11, s. 15(3).
2. *Ibid.* at s. 15(3).
3. For a fuller discussion see Chapter 27.
4. Ab Currie, *A National Survey of the Civil Justice Problems of Low and Moderate Income Canadians: Incidence and Patterns* (Ottawa: Research and Statistics Division, Department of Justice, December, 2005).
5. Stephen Wexler, "Practicing Law for Poor People" (1970) 79(6) Yale L.J. 1049.
6. *Ibid.* at 1049-50.
7. Alexis Anderson, Lynn Barenberg & Paul R. Tremblay, "Professional Ethics in Interdisciplinary Collaborations: Zeal, Partisanship and Mandatory Reporting" (2007) 13 Clinical L. Rev. 659 at 660.
8. Robin G. Steinberg, "Beyond Lawyering: How Holistic Representation Makes for Good Policy, Better Lawyers, and More Satisfied Clients" (2006) 30 N.Y.U. Rev. L. & Soc. Change 625 at 626; see generally this volume for a discussion of collaborative approaches between law and social work when working with those caught up in the criminal justice system.
9. Janet Mosher & Pat Evans, "Welfare Policy—A Critical Site of Struggle for Women's Safety" (2006) 25 (1&2) Canadian Woman Studies 162.
10. Dianne Martin & Janet Mosher, "Unkept Promises: Experiences of Immigrant Women with the Neo-Criminalization of Wife Abuse" (1995) 8 C.J.W.L. 3; and Anannya Bhattacharjee, "Private Fists and Public Force: Race, Gender and Surveillance" in Joel Sillinian & Anannya Bhattacharjee, eds., *Policing the National Body: Race, Gender and Criminalization* (Cambridge: South End Press, 2002).
11. Margaret Martin Barry, Jon C. Dubin & Peter A. Joy, "Clinical Education for this Millennium: The Third Wave" (2000-01) 7 Clinical L. Rev. 1.

12. Louise G. Trubek & Jennifer J. Farnham, "Social Justice Collabora-
    tives: Multidisciplinary Practices for People" (2000) 7 Clinical L. Rev.
    227; see also *supra* note 7.
13. See *supra* note 7 at 665.
14. *Ibid.* at 66.
15. *Guidelines for Lawyers Acting in Cases Involving claims of Aboriginal
    Residential School Abuses,* online: Law Society of Upper Canada
    <http://www.lsuc.on.ca/media/guideline_aboriginal_res.pdf>.
16. *Rules of Professional Conduct, Rule 2.02(5.2),* online: Law Society of
    Upper Canada <http://www.lsuc.on.ca/regulation/a/profconduct/>.
17. See *supra* note 7 at 666.
18. Law Reform Commission of Canada, *The Family Court* (Working
    Paper No. 1) (Ottawa, 1977) at 11.
19. See *supra* note 7 at 666.
20. Andrew Philips, "Social Work and the Delivery of Legal Services"
    (1979) 42 Mod. L. Rev. 29.
21. John D. McClean, *The Legal Context of Social Work* (Toronto: Butter-
    worths, 1975) at 2.
22. See *supra* note 7 at 666. Other tensions identified by the authors are
    analytic versus synthetic; focus on outcome versus focus on process;
    and the valuing of professional autonomy versus professional collab-
    oration.
23. See Dennis Saleeby, ed., *The Strengths Perspective in Social Work
    Practice* (New York: Longman, 1990).
24. Laura R. Bronstein, "Index of Interdisciplinary Collaboration" (2002)
    26(2) Social Work Research 113.
25. See *supra* note 8 at 627.
26. Rufus Sylvester Lynch & Edward Allan Brawley, "Social workers and
    the judicial system: Looking for a better fit" (1994) 10(1/2) Journal of
    Teaching in Social Work 65.
27. John Allen Lemmon, "Legal content in the social work curriculum"
    (1983) 19(2) Journal of Education for Social Work 71.

2

A Primer on Law for Social Workers

(1) INTRODUCTION

Both social work and law deal with words as the primary instrument of their professions. Words can be ambiguous and the exact meaning is sometimes difficult to convey. Social workers are not distressed unduly by the imprecision of language which they accept as a fact of human discourse. The law, however, must be concerned with exactness of meaning, particularly with the language used in the construction of statutes. The framers of statutes are not always successful in achieving clarity, and consequently revisions and amendments are often required. Legal writing is commonly an irritation for social workers, the general public and indeed, even lawyers. There seems to be a preoccupation with form and ritual, with repetition, ponderous phrases and qualifying clauses. All this is true, but careful legal drafting provides safeguards against ambiguity of content and limits what is included or excluded by that particular statute or document. Nevertheless, there are instances where the statutory language is purposively ambiguous in order to permit some interpretive variation. Most likely, however, it is unintentional.[1]

Anyone wishing to gain some confidence in comprehending statutory language must, of course, confront the statute itself. Although this may seem self-evident, it is not unusual for social workers to be so intimidated by the form and wording of a statute that they rely on a summary of the provisions of an Act provided by the media, their agency, or the government. They also may not know that the statute itself, as well as regulations made pursuant to it, are readily available on government web sites or through government bookstores. To non-lawyers, the legal language of documents such as wills and contracts may be unintelligible at first reading, and appear to be filled with unnecessary words that are designed to obscure their intent. Most often, the reason behind the precise form required, aside from mere custom, is to ensure that a proper legal document fulfils its specific purpose. That said, in many instances "legalise" may obscure meaning, and render it difficult for lay persons to access important legal information. Through the influence of what is often described as the "plain language movement," many involved in community legal education have effectively "translated" legalise into plain language without compromising the meaning or nuances of legal documents. The plain language movement has also had some influence upon statutory drafting.

(2) HOW LAW IS DEFINED

The law, like social work, does not lend itself to a ready and exacting definition and countless volumes have been dedicated to philosophical explorations of the question, "what is law?" However, for our purposes, it is important to note points of widespread agreement on "what law is." The following definition, which bears remarkable similarity to some definitions of social work, highlights law's role in resolving basic tensions in human society. S. M. Waddams states, for example, that "the law in any society is the society's attempt to resolve the most basic of human tensions, that between the needs of the person as an individual, and her needs as a member of a community."[2] Gerald Gall suggests that law addresses these tensions in at least two ways: by ordering or regulating the actions, relationships and affairs of all "persons" (individuals, corporations and governments); and as a standard of conduct and morality.[3] Philip S. James describes law as "a body of rules for the guidance of human conduct which are imposed upon and enforced among members of a given state."[4]

Similarly, Black's Law Dictionary defines law in this way:

> Law in its generic sense is a body of rules of action or conduct prescribed by controlling authority, and having binding legal force. . . . The term is also used in opposition to "fact."[5]

This definition is positivistic; that is, it describes the law from a functional point of view. There are some who feel that there are overriding moral values which make some laws unjust and that such laws should be opposed.[6] The danger here is obvious, for who is to determine which moral values shall prevail? Yet, at the same time, we can all quickly bring to mind examples of laws that are profoundly unjust: laws unholding racial segregation or apartheid for example. Critics of social work theory and practice have identified a similar dilemma by pointing out that social welfare policies, services, and practices are not neutral but based on moral and political bias. The constant tension between the functional, positivistic definition of law and a search for a definition approaching a concept of universal justice provides some guarantee against complacency, both for law and for social work.

(3) THE RULE OF LAW

The concept of the rule of law originated early in the 17th century when the British Chief Justice held that even the King could not interfere with the processes of justice. Under our modern parliamentary system, the government itself cannot make law outside of those powers given to it by law. Moreover, no person stands above the law, rather all members of society, including government officials, are equally subject to it. The rule of law is an attempt to protect society from personal whims of those in power or the politics of the moment. We, as a people, submit to decisions made impartially within the four corners of rational, general principles which have been accepted as binding. Although an ideal of western democratic society, the rule of law is never totally achieved.[7]

The principle of the rule of law is illustrated by the case of *Roncarelli v. Duplessis*.[8] In that case, the liquor license for Mr. Roncarelli's Montreal restaurant was forever revoked. However, he was not in violation of any liquor licensing regulation nor any other law. The Supreme Court of Canada characterized the revocation as an arbitrary and foundation-less act motivated by the then Premier Duplessis' efforts to punish Mr. Roncarelli for his support of the Jehovah's Witnesses. The state had acted outside the law, in an arbitrary fashion, violating the rule the law. As Frederick Morton notes, the decision of the Court affirmed that ". . . in Canada there is a general right not to be punished by the arbitrary exercise of government power. A government, federal or provincial, can only move against an individual in accordance with known rules, and the Duplessis government had failed to meet this threshold."[9]

(4) SOURCES OF LAW

(a) Common Law

The term "common law" has a variety of meanings. Often the concept of "common law" is used to describe a system of law based primarily on judicial decisions in contrast to a system based on Roman law, in which the law is codified. The Province of Quebec, the State of Louisiana and many countries in the world function under a civil code based on Roman law. The remaining Canadian provinces, all other American states, England, Australia, and New Zealand are common law jurisdictions.[10]

The term "common law," within common law jurisdictions, is often used to denote those areas of substantive law governed by law derived through judicial decisions (the law of torts or contract, for example) from those areas of law that are statute-based (social assistance benefits or income tax, for example). None of these delineations are static, but rather evolve over time, and thus some areas of law once governed by the common law are now governed by statute. It is also important to appreciate that although an area of law may be governed by statute, frequently disputes arise regarding the interpretation and/or application of its provisions. As some of these disputes wind their way through court processes and are ultimately subject to judicial decision-making, over time a body of judge-made law (precedent) evolves regarding the interpretation and application of the applicable statute.

In defining common law, Jowitt states:

> It is sometimes used in contradistinction to statute law, and then denotes the unwritten law, whether legal or equitable in its origin, which does not derive its authority from any express declaration of the will of the legislature. This unwritten law has the same force and effect as the statute law. It depends for its authority upon the recognition given by the courts to principles, customs and rules of conduct previously existing among the people. This recognition was formerly enshrined in the memory of legal practitioners and suitors in the courts; it is now recorded in the law reports which embody the decisions of the judges together with the reasons which they assigned for their decisions.[11]

The pattern of laws that create common law has evolved over 1,000 years of English history. Mr. Justice Estey, formerly a judge of the Supreme Court of Canada, referred to the three-fold magic of the common law as:

(a) The judgment in the settlement of each dispute arising in the community itself becomes part of our principles or concepts for the legal governance of the community.

(b) Because the body of concepts is thus ever growing and because the concepts arise out of actual differences within the community, the law, as the body of concept is called, is flexible and adaptable to the changing community.

(c) As the principles or concepts are those visibly evolving from the life of the community itself, the body of the law so produced is accepted by the inhabitants as their own and not resisted as the imposed will of others.[12]

Finally, the concept of the "common law" is also used in contradistinction to that of "equity." Historically there evolved two separate courts: those of the common law; and those of equity. Originally one could apply to the Court of Equity in order to seek discretionary relief, on the grounds of fairness, from the rigidity of the common law. In other words, the results of law were in some instances regarded as unfair or unjust, and these results could be avoided through a favourable decision of the Court of Equity. While the separate courts were fused in 1881, the concepts of law and equity were not and the distinction between the two continues to be relevant in some instances. An important equitable doctrine that emerged is the "trust." For example, the courts have found that in some circumstances, unmarried women will be entitled to a share of the property of their partners upon separation, and this is based on the construct of a "trust."[13] It is also important to note that the concept of equity has created certain significant remedies that are unavailable at common law.[14]

(i) The Meaning of Precedent

In reaching decisions, courts rely on decided cases based on the principle of *stare decisis* which means "to stand by what has been decided." In so far as possible, similar cases must be decided similarly if law is to provide guidance, predictability, and stability. The application of *stare decisis* requires two steps: first, the governing or controlling legal principle of an existing decision must be discerned; and second, the court must determine whether, in all material respects, the case currently being considered is sufficiently similar to the existing decision so that the same principle must be applied. The controlling legal principle behind a decision is called the *ratio decidendi* (or often simply the *ratio*). While one might assume that the ratio of each case would be obvious, in reality, lawyers often argue strenuously over what the ratio of any particular case is. As for determining the similarity between cases, the courts method of reasoning is, for the most part, through analogy. The court will consider whether the case at hand is sufficiently analogous to a prior case that the same ratio ought to apply and thus a similar result to follow. Conversely, the court will consider whether there is a distinguishing fact that so weakens the analogy, that logic does not dictate that the same result need follow.

Judicial opinions about the law, which are not necessary to decide the issues in a particular case (that is, that are not part of the *ratio*), are called *obiter dicta* or that which is said "by the way." While only the *ratio* is binding for the purpose of establishing a governing precedent, the *obiter*, especially that of the Supreme Court of Canada, may be both valuable and persuasive in other cases.

Throughout this book you will find citations of relevant cases. Legal argument and judicial decisions are built upon the search for relevant cases. Two judges considering the same set of facts and relevant cases may reach different conclusions using equally compelling and persuasive reasoning as the basis for their findings. The value of reading these decisions lies in the realization that law is not hardened, but remains flexible, and is always subject to the limitations of human understanding.

Judges may also take note of decisions made in co-ordinate courts, or common law jurisdictions such as the United States or Commonwealth countries, for their persuasive value. However, judges are bound only by the decisions of higher courts in their own province. All courts in Canada are bound by the Supreme Court of Canada. The Supreme Court of Canada is not bound by its own decisions and indeed, has overruled itself on many occasions.

To understand a judicial opinion, it is instructive to read or brief an actual case report. In order to identify the essential elements of an opinion, one should look to answer the following questions:

- Who are the parties to the dispute? What does each want?
- What are the facts as the court describes them? Is this an appeal from a lower court finding?
- What is the legal issue or question that the court is being asked to decide?
- What cases does the court canvass as precedents (cited as considerations) in reaching its decision?
- What is the court's decision or holding; the decision will often include a phrase such as "Held that . . ." This states the conclusion of law as applied to the facts as found by the court.
- Is there a dissenting or concurring opinion and how does it differ from the majority opinion?
- To what extent does the decision follow from the cited precedents? What guidance will the opinion offer future courts? Does this decision set a precedent?[15]

(b) Statutory Law

Statutory law encompasses those laws that are enacted by an elected legislative body, either at a federal or provincial level. Social workers may be familiar with statutes such as the *Child and Family Services Act*,[16] the *Youth Criminal Justice Act*,[17] and the *Family Law Act*.[18] As noted above, statutes and accompanying regulations may be enacted to replace the common law in a particular area, to correct a perceived deficiency in the common law, or to regulate activity that was previously unaddressed by law. If a statute applies (and this itself may be the subject of the disagreement between the parties in a lawsuit), the court must interperet and apply it, having regarding to any existing precedents regarding its interpretation and application.

There are three major rules for statutory interpretation, or how the statute is to be construed: the "literal rule;" the "golden rule;" and the "mischief rule." The literal rule speaks to the fact that words are to be understood in their literal or ordinary sense. The golden rule means that the courts must reach a conclusion in interpretation that will avoid an absurdity. The mischief rule requires the court to consider the evil or defect the law was meant to address and to see that the decision reached remediates, and does not compound, the mischief.[19]

(c) Subordinate Legislation

There is a distinction between primary legislation, which is enacted by Parliament and the Legislatures of the provinces, and subordinate legislation, which is enacted under the authority of a statute by a person, body, or tribunal that is subordinate to a sovereign legislative body. Examples of subordinate legislation include bylaws, regulations and rules, ordinances, statutory instruments, and orders-in-council.[20] All municipal enactments are subordinate legislation, made under the authority of a provincial statute. Municipalities and their councils are creatures of provincial legislation and their power to enact bylaws derives entirely from provincial enabling legislation. The Canadian territories, by contrast to the provinces, do not have constitutional standing as supreme parliamentary bodies, and therefore lack the constitutionally-based power to pass valid legislation. Rather, their laws are valid and have the force of law because they are authorized by the federal government.

Due to the proliferation of government regulation over the past several decades, both the federal and provincial governments have frequently delegated regulatory responsibility to bodies created by statute.[21] Governments often delegate to these bodies—be they boards, commissions, or tribunals—power to make regulations relating to the particular statutory regime each is responsible to administer. It has been argued that there are dangers inherent in this process because when passed, assuming they are within the limits of authority granted by the authorizing statute, these regulations have the force of the statute itself. Waddams points out that this practice makes it possible to withdraw difficult issues from public scrutiny by drafting universal rules (the statute) to which exceptions are then made through regulations (and are therefore not debated in the legislature).[22]

(i) How a Bill is Passed

A bill is passed into law once it has been approved by the provincial legislature or the federal Parliament. The government introduces a bill through a "First Reading" where it is passed without debate. It is then printed and released for public reaction. It may then be moved for a "Second Reading," followed by a full debate. If the bill passes the Second Reading, it is considered passed in principle. Next, the bill is usually referred to an appropriate committee for detailed study and amendment recommendations. It is at this phase that hearings may be held, at which time submissions on the bill from groups and individuals will often be received. It is then read a third time, amendments are debated and, if approved and passed, it goes to the Lieutenant Governor of the province or the Governor General of Canada for royal assent; in the case of federal bills, the process is repeated in the Senate. The bill then becomes law (a statute), unless there is a provision within the statute providing that it is to come into effect at a later date, or at a date to be proclaimed. Social workers anxious for legislative change need to be aware of the laborious process from idea to enactment.

(5) PROCEDURAL LAW

Procedural law refers to the processes to be followed in the resolution of legal disputes. These procedures determine what will happen, what steps must be included, and in what order and in what timeframe these steps must occur. The procedures for many decision-making bodies are expressly detailed in regulations; so, for example, the procedures governing cases in the courts are set out in detailed rules. This is also true for many administrative tribunals, while other tribunals are given the authority to determine their own procedures. Two centrally important ideas underpin procedure: that of "natural justice;" and that of the "adversary system."

(a) Natural Justice

At its simplest, "natural justice" refers to the notion that in all courts of law parties are entitled to an unbiased decision-maker and to to be heard. The latter right, "to be heard," is integral to the concept of a fair hearing, and includes the rights to receive notice, to call evidence, to make argument, to know the case against you, and to test the case against you through cross-examintion. The full content of "natural justice" or "fairness" will vary depending upon the nature of the matters in issue and the seriousness of the issues being determined.

The concept of "natural justice" is embodied in section 7 of the *Canadian Charter of Rights and Freedoms*, which guarantees to everyone the "right to life, liberty and security of the person" and the right not to be deprived thereof, "except in accordance with the principles of fundamental justice." These principles of fundamental justice include the procedural requirements of natural justice; thus, if one's life, liberty or security of the person is in issue, fair and adequate procedures are constitutionally mandated and cannot be revoked or diminished by statute (unless the Court were to find the departure from natural justice to be a reasonable limit within the meaning of section 1 of the *Charter*). Not only does section 7 protect the traditional realm of natural justice developed at common law, but moves beyond it. So, for example, in the case of *New Brunswick (Minister of Health & Community Services) v. G. (J.),*[23] the Supreme Court of Canada found that the principles of fundamental justice required not only entitlement to a fair hearing (as previously outlined) for a mother, but that given the serious nature and complexity of the matters in issue and the security of the person interests of both the mother and her children, state funded legal representation was also required. In other words, in this context, effective participation required state-funded legal representation.[24] Furthermore, as we describe below, the Court has also held that section 7 has both procedural and substantive dimensions.

(b) Adversary System

The second important concept in understanding procedural law is that of the "adversary system." The adversary system sets two opposing parties against one another to contend for a result favourable to one of them. The rationale behind this system is the belief that the rigour and zeal of each side to present the most compelling case in its favour, and the most damaging case against the opposition, ensures that the truth of any given situation will be revealed. In such a system, the judge is constrained to act passively; while the judge may ask questions for purposes of clarification, he or she is not to enter the fray, directing the questioning of witnesses nor determining the arguments to be made on the evidence. The theory of the adversary system is grounded in several assumptions, that are, problematically, often ill-founded in practice: that the parties are equally well resourced to participate; that the closest approximation of the truth arrives through conflict; and that the parties are necessarily self-interested, competitive, and seek to fully maximize their respective interests. It should be noted that in working with clients who come from countries where a different model of law is practised, or from cultures that are less competitive and individualistic (for example, Aboriginal cultures), the process can be profoundly alienating and confusing. So too, the process is often experienced, especially by victims of crime, as hostile, demeaning and unsatisfactory. Social workers frequently play an important role in describing the nature of the legal process and in some cases, aiding persons through legal processes.

Procedural rights only guarantee a fair hearing and not necessarily that the outcome will be just. For example, a person who appeals a decision of a court or tribunal may receive a full and fair hearing but the outcome allowed by the governing statute may be considered inadequate or unfair. Yet, procedural rights are integrally connected to substantive outcomes, since without the opportunity for full participation, there is little, if any, possibility to persuade the trier of fact.

(6) CONSTITUTIONAL ORDER AND JURISDICTIONAL POWERS

In a federal state, such as Canada, the power of government is distributed between a central or national authority and regional or provincial authority. The laws of the provincial legislature are considered "co-ordinate" in their relationship to Parliament. Co-ordination recognizes that there are two levels of government, each with respective powers, and neither being subordinate to the other. In contrast, local or municipal governments are subordinate to provincial authority. Although the balance of powers between the federal and provincial governments has shifted from time to time, the basis of this balancing act is the legal guarantee of co-ordinate power.[25] The topic of jurisdictional powers or federal-provincial relations is a highly complex issue that occupies a central position in Canadian political affairs. While the debate over federal-provincial power is beyond the scope of this book, a general understanding of the allocation of powers, as between the federal and provincial governments, is important for social workers.

Canada's Constitution is not expressed in a single document, nor entirely in written form. Rather, the Constitution is comprised of two main bodies of rules or priniciples:

1. legal rules in the formal Constitution as defined by the *Constitution Act, 1982* and in statutes, orders-in-council, and court decisions relating to the executive, judicial and legislative branches; and
2. informal rules, called conventions, that stem from political practices.[26]

The *Constitution Act, 1982*[27] defines the Constitution of Canada to include the *Canada Act, 1982*, the *Constitution Act, 1982* and several statutes referenced in a Schedule. Among these statutes is the *Constitution Act,*

1867, formerly called the *British North America Act,1867*. It is here that legislative power with respect to a variety of subject areas is allocated between the federal and provincial governments, respectively. The federal government is granted the broad residual power to make laws for the "peace, order and good government of Canada" in relation to all matters outside those exclusively assigned to the provincial legislatures, as well as exclusive jurisdiction in a number of areas, including:

1.   the regulation of trade and commerce;
2.   banking;
3.   marriage and divorce;
4.   criminal law and procedure;
5.   levy of indirect as well as direct taxes;
6.   "Indians, and Lands reserved for the Indians;" and
7.   immigration and naturalization.[28]

Among the powers of the provincial legislatures are the following:

1.   management of prisons in the province (sentences under two years);
2.   establishment, maintenance, and management of hospitals and charities in the province other than marine hospitals;
3.   solemnization of marriage in the province;
4.   property and civil rights in the province;
5.   maintenance of provincial courts of both criminal and civil jurisdiction;
6.   the administration of justice in the province, including the constitution, maintenance, and organization of provincial courts, both of civil and of criminal jurisdiction, and including procedure in civil matters in those courts; and
7.   education in the province.[29]

In some areas there is concurrent power; in other words, the areas of legislative competence of the federal and provincial governments overlap. So, for example, some driving offences fall under the provincial property and civil rights power, as well as the federal criminal law power. Where there exists concurrent legislative power and both the federal and provincial governments have legislated in respect of matters within that area, both will have the force of law, unless there is a conflict, in which case the federal law will govern. This is referred to as the doctrine of paramountcy.

Beyond issues of concurrency, sometimes a question arises as to whether legislation enacted by one level of government is, in fact, within its legislative powers as granted by the Constitution. If, for example, the federal government has enacted a statute that falls outside the powers conferred upon it by the Constitution, the statute is said to be *ultra vires* (beyond the power) and thus invalid. Courts are frequently called upon to determine whether a statute is *ultra vires*. In trying to answer this question it is often necessary for the Court to determine the legislation's "pith and substance," or real object and purpose. For instance, a province may claim that legislation to restrict solicitation by prostitutes constitutes, in pith and substance, the regulation of streets and sidewalks, and is thus within its legislative powers. By contrast, the federal government may dispute this characterization on the grounds that the province is attempting to create a criminal prohibition against solicitation. Since criminal law is exclusively vested in the federal government, it would likely argue that the province cannot exercise legislative power in the above situation.

The possibility of overlapping and contested jurisdictions is particularly relevant for social workers in the context of family law. As noted above, the provinces have jurisdiction in relation to the solemnization of marriage in the province, and in relation to property and civil rights. "Property and civil rights" is an expansive category encompassing property and contract law and other private relations including spousal support, child support, custody, guardianship and adoption.[30] Consequently, provincial legislatures have exercised their constitutional power to legislate in relation to custody, access, division of property, child and spousal support and child welfare, amongst other areas. It is important to observe that provincial legislatures have not, and cannot, legislate in relation to divorce, as it is a matter of exclusive federal jurisdiction.

The federal government has jurisdiction in relation to marriage and divorce, and has exercised that jurisdiction in relation to divorce through its enactment of the *Divorce Act*.[31] However, the *Divorce Act,* in addition to addressing divorce, contains provisions for maintenance and custody; matters often described as "corollory" to divorce. These forms of relief corollory to divorce were first introduced in 1968, and subsequently challenged as *ultra vires;* as beyond the power of the federal Parliament. Each of the challenges brought was unsuccessful, with the courts holding that because the matters of custody and support were intregally and rationally connected to the exercise of the federal divorce power and only available in connection with a divorce proceeding, the federal government's legislation was valid. Concurrent jurisdiction thus exists between the federal and provincial governments in relation to custody and support.[32] Peter Hogg, a leading constitutional expert, has suggested that while the federal government has not to date legislated with respect to matrimonial property as ancillary to divorce—property falling clearly within provincial competence—it is possible that were it to do so, the courts may apply a similar logic and find the exercise of such a power to be valid.[33] To complicate matters further, this allocation of legislative competence is interwoven with court jurisdiction, as we describe more fully in Chapter 4.

(7) THE *CANADIAN CHARTER OF RIGHTS AND FREEDOMS*

A fundamental change in our legal system was brought about by the proclamation of the *Constitution Act, 1982*. This Act not only terminated the authority of the United Kingdom Parliament over the Dominion of Canada, but it entrenched the *Canadian Charter of Rights and Freedoms* as part of Canada's Constitution and thus, as part of the "supreme law" of the land. While the courts have long played a role in adjudicating disputes regarding the allocation of legislative powers under the Constitution, the *Constitution Act, 1982* empowered the judiciary to determine whether laws enacted by government were consistent with the rights guaranteed to individuals by the *Canadian Charter of Rights and Freedoms* (the "*Charter*"). This power of courts to review whether government action complies with the Constitution is frequently referred to as "judicial review."[34] The Courts, however, do not always have the last say. Section 33 of the *Charter*, often referred to as the "opting out clause," allows either Parliament or the Provincial Legislatures to include, in a statute, a clause that allows a law to operate notwithstanding the violation of part or all of section 2 or 7-15 of the *Charter*.[35] Note that certain sections of the *Charter*—section 3 (democratic rights), section 6 (mobility rights) and sections 16-23 (minority language rights)—cannot be overridden by section 33. While some commentators have argued that the potential for a section 33 override furthers a constitutional dialogue between the courts and the government legislative bodies, others suggest that this dialogue is more theoretical than real, particularly given that section 33 has been rarely invoked.

The enhanced role of the courts in reviewing the constitutionality of government legislation and government action has promoted an ongoing debate regarding the legitimacy of judicial review, a debate that is rekindled by each controversial decision of the Supreme Court of Canada. For some, judicial review is profoundly anti-democratic; judges are not elected, are unrepresentative, and are appointed for life (subject to removal only on very limited grounds). When they embark on decision-making that overrules the will of an elected Parliament or provincial legislature they are regarded as having engaged in undemocratic law-making. Combined with concerns regarding the anti-democratic character of judicial review is the claim that the procedures and forums for dispute resolution before the Courts are ill-suited for the complex, polycentric forms of decision-making that are required to determine intricate issues of public policy. On the other hand, the very fact that judges are not elected helps to ensure judicial decision-making is not influenced by political allegiances nor a desire to cultivate popular support for decisions rendered. Judicial review is also seen to play a critical role in protecting the rights and interests of minorities from the tyranny of the will of the majority. Contrary to the view of those who see the procedures of the Courts as too limited, others suggest that judicial review opens up avenues of participation for many who are excluded from the political process.[36]

(a) Scope

The precise scope of the *Charter* is a matter of some debate. Clearly, the laws passed by Parliament and provincial legislatures are subject to the *Charter*. But the *Charter* also reaches beyond the legislation itself, and applies to a wide range of officials and agents (for example, police officers) who are charged with carrying out government laws and policies. On the other hand, the *Charter* does not apply as between private individuals; there must be some nexus to government, the precise strength of which is difficult to define. For example, the *Charter* has been found not to apply to mandatory retirement policies of universities and hospitals, although both receive sub-stantial government funding.[37] Yet, where a hospital is implementing a governmental program, the Courts have found that the *Charter* is engaged.[38] Thus, the nature of the entity and the entity's activity are both relevant to the inquiry.

While the common law is not directly subject to *Charter* challenge, the courts have held that it must be construed or interpreted in a manner that is consistent with *Charter* values.

(b) Whose Rights are Protected

Many of the provisions of the *Charter* provide that all "citizens" are entitled to the right in question, thus limiting their application to those with actual citizenship status. Other provisions, in contrast, refer to "everyone," which has been interpreted to include persons physically present in Canada—refugee claimants for example—and with respect to some provisions, as including corporations.

(c) Approach

In an early *Charter* decision, the Supreme Court of Canada enunciated a set of basic principles to guide *Charter* interpretation, distinguishing *Charter* interpretation from that of statutes without constitutional status. In

Hunter v. Southam Inc.,[39] Mr. Justice Dickson, identified the following interpretive guides:

1. the Living Tree Principle (capable of growth and expansion within its natural limits) applies to the *Charter* the same way as it does to other parts of the Constitution;
2. the *Charter* should be given a large and liberal interpretation; and
3. the *Charter* should be interpreted purposively ("its purpose is to guarantee and to protect, within the limits of reason, the enjoyment of the rights and freedoms it enshrines. It is intended to constrain governmental action inconsistent with those rights and freedoms. . .").[40]

Noting the difference between statutes and a constitution, Dickson J. writes:

> [A statute] is easily enacted and as easily repealed. . . A constitution, by contrast, is drafted with an eye to the future. Its function is to provide a continuing framework for the legitimate exercise of governmental power and, when joined by a Bill or Charter of Rights, for the unremitting protection of individual rights and liberties. Once enacted, its provisions cannot easily be repealed or amended. It must, therefore, be capable of growth and development over time to meet new social, political and historical realities often unimagined by its framers.[41]

(d) Structure

All sections of the *Charter* must be read in the context of section 1, which provides that all the rights and freedoms set out in it are guaranteed, "subject only to such reasonable limits prescribed by law as can be demonstrably justified in a free and democratic society." Therefore, the rights and freedoms set out are not absolute, but are subject to such reasonable limits as are justifiable in a "free and democratic society." Consequently, individual rights and freedoms must, in some instances, give way to a competing right of another individual or to the interests of the community as a whole. In terms of the structure of a court's reasoning, it will first entertain the question of whether a right has been violated, and if it has, will then go on to consider whether the violation is justified in a free and democratic society. So, for example, the Court has found that although the *Criminal Code* provision proscribing the willful promotion of hate against an identifiable group is a violation of the *Charter's* protected guarantee of freedom of expression, it is a reasonable limitation of that right under section 1.[42] By contrast, the Court held that federal tobacco legislation restricting advertising did not constitute a reasonable limit (although the Court was divided 5-4 on this question).[43]

Section 1 of the *Charter* encompasses two components: that the limits on the rights are "prescribed by law;" and that such limits be "reasonable" and demonstrably justifiable in a free and democratic society. Often referred to as the "Oakes' test," to establish that a limit is reasonable and demonstrably justified the government must satisfy two criteria:[44]

1. that the objective of the prescribed law relates to concerns that are pressing and substantial, which means that such concerns must be of sufficient importance to warrant the overriding of a constitutionally protected right; and
2. that the means chosen to meet that objective are reasonable and demonstrably justified, which entails three further thresholds: the measures adopted are rationally connected to the objective; the means minimally impair the right or freedom in question; and there exists proportionality between the effects of the measures and the objective (the benefits achieved outweigh the harms that would result from the rights violation).[45]

The precise role of section 1 changes from provision to provision. So, for example, a lot of balancing of interests occurs within section 15 (the equality rights provision) itself, and within section 7 (the right to life, liberty and security of the person and not to be deprived thereof except in accordance with the principles of fundamental justice).

(e) Remedies for *Charter* Breach

Section 24 creates a broad discretion for the courts to fashion a remedy for a *Charter* breach that it considers "appropriate and just in the circumstances." Subsection 24(2) provides for a more particular remedy; the exclusion of evidence obtained in a manner that infringed a *Charter* right if, having regard to all of the circumstances, its admission would bring the administration of justice into disrepute. Section 52 of the *Constitution Act, 1982* empowers the Court to declare a law to be of no force or effect to the extent that it is inconsistent with the Constitution, the supreme law of the land. This remedy is often referred to as "striking down" the legislation.

(f) *Charter* **Rights**

(i) *Fundamental Freedoms (Section 2)*

Under the category of "fundamental freedoms" within the *Charter* is freedom of conscience and religion, freedom of thought, belief and expression (which includes freedom of the press and the media), freedom of peaceful assembly and freedom of association.

Freedom of religion cases under the *Charter* have included a range of issues such as the right of businesses to operate on Sunday, the right of parents to refuse to consent to blood transfusions for a child, and the right of a child to wear a kirpan to school. In the latter case, *Multani c. Marguerite-Bourgeoys (Commission scolaire)*,[46] the Supreme Court of Canada held that the refusal by the respondent school to permit the wearing of a kirpan—a religious object resembling a dagger and worn at all times by orthodox Sikhs—infringed freedom of religion and could not be saved by section 1 since an absolute prohibition did not minimally impair the applicant's right.

In addition to the positive freedom to hold and manifest religious beliefs, freedom of religion also includes freedom from coerced conformity to religious doctrine and practice.

Freedom of expression has been given an expansive interpretation to include all manner of expression—political, artistic, and commercial—provided that expression occurs through an expressive form other than physical violence. As we have seen, limitations on freedom of expression have been upheld in some circumstances. Debates regarding limitations on expression have been especially pronounced in relation to limitations on sexual expression, particularly those within the obscenity provisions of the *Criminal Code*.[47]

(ii) *Democratic Rights (Sections 3-5)*

Democratic rights guaranteed to all citizens of Canada are the right to vote in federal and provincial elections, and the right to stand for office. Here, the *Charter* has resulted in the extension of the right to vote to inmates and in-patients of psychiatric hospitals. Both Parliament and the legislatures must sit at least once a year and must not continue for more than five years without a general election.

(iii) *Mobility Rights (Section 6)*

Mobility rights, under section 6, protect the right of every citizen to enter, remain in and leave Canada. Citizens and permanent residents are given the right to move and take up residence in any province and to pursue the gaining of livelihood in any province. Section 6 expressly contemplates that provinces may introduce reasonable residency requirements to qualify for the receipt of public benefits.

(iv) Legal Rights (Sections 7-14)

The legal rights entrenched in the *Charter* include section 7, which guarantees everyone the right not to be deprived of life, liberty and security of the person except in accordance with the principles of fundamental justice. Liberty has been interpreted to include not only freedom from physical constraint (such as imprisonment) but also freedom to make fundamental personal decisions.[48] "Security of the person" has been found to be engaged in a range of circumstances: the "security of the person" of children is adversely affected by the *Criminal Code* provision that creates a defence to a charge of assault against a teacher or parent who uses "reasonable" force "by way of correction";[49] the "security of the person" of parents is adversely affected by a warrantless apprehension of a child deemed to be in need of protection;[50] and "security of the person" is compromised where control over one's own body is diminished or denied.[51] Whether "security of the person" imposes a positive obligation upon governments to provide adequate welfare benefits is a matter of considerable controversy. To date, the view of most judges has been negative, although in *Gosselin c. Québec (Procureur général)*,[52] the majority did not close the door entirely to such an interpretation and one of the judges, in dissent, strongly supported this interpretation.

The right to life, liberty and security of the person can be limited by a law that conforms to the principles of fundamental justice. However, just what constitutes the "principles of fundamental justice" has been yet another matter of controversy. While it is virtually unanimously agreed that procedural fairness/natural justice is included, the controversy centers upon what exists beyond the procedural.[53] In *Reference re s. 94(2) of the Motor Vehicle Act (British Columbia)*,[54] the Court concluded that principles of fundamental justice include the "basic tenets of the legal system." Specifically, the court determined that an offence provision that carries the potential of imprisonment, but does not have the *mens rea* (guilty mind) element required to convict, runs afoul of a basic tenet of our legal system. However, over time it became increasingly clear that there was little agreement among judges as to what comprised the basic tenets of the legal system and that the "basic tenets of the legal system" test was unworkable as a proxy for the "principles of fundamental justice." In its latest attempt to define the "principles of fundamental justice," the court has established three criteria to be satisfied: it must be a legal principle; this principle must be one upon which there is significant societal consensus; and the principle must be capable of being identified with some precision.[55] This approach was applied in *Canadian Foundation for Children, Youth & the Law v. Canada (Attorney General)*,[56] where a challenge was made to the provisions of the *Criminal Code* that create a defence to assault for a parent or teacher who uses reasonable force to correct a child. While the court found that section 7 (security of the person) was engaged, it also concluded that there was no violation of the principles of fundamental justice. Specifically, the court maintained that, although a legal principle, the best interests of the child does not constitute a principle of fundamental justice because it is neither fundamental to the legal system nor is it capable of sufficiently precise identification.

The language of section 7 guaranteeing "everyone" the rights therein described has been interpreted to include all persons physically present in Canada. This has resulted in, for example, refugee claimants in Canada being able to assert a constitutional right to fair procedures in the determination of their refugee status.[57]

Section 8 guarantees the right to be secure against unreasonable search and seizure. A search occurs when the state violates that reasonable expectation of privacy, and a seizure, where there is some meaningful interference with a person's possessory interests in property. While there is no explicit provision in the *Charter* guaranteeing a right to privacy, the purpose of section 8 has been interpreted as that of securing each citizen's right to a reasonable expectation of privacy against governmental encroachments.[58] The Supreme Court of Canada has also interpreted section 8 in a manner that protects not only privacy interests in one's home and property, but also in controlling personal information about oneself.

Absent exigent circumstances, a search or seizure must be judicially authorized in advance. The authorization process entails the presentation of evidence before a judicial officer. For a warrant to be issued, the judicial officer must be satisfied that there are reasonable and probable grounds to believe an offence has been committed and that a search will afford evidence of that offence. A search may also be conducted absent a warrant if consent is given by the person whose privacy interests would be engaged by the search.[59]

Section 9 protects against arbitrary detention or imprisonment while section 10 provides for rights that arise upon arrest or detention, including the right to be informed promptly of the reasons thereof and the right to retain and instruct counsel without delay and to be informed of that right.

The rights under section 10 have been interpreted to require that the police not only inform a detainee of his or her rights, but also provide a detainee with a reasonable opportunity to exercise the right to retain and instruct counsel and to cease questioning or otherwise attempt to elicit information from the detainee until that opportunity has been provided.[60] The Court has expressly linked the right to counsel to the right against self-incrimination, noting that access to counsel enables the suspect to make an informed choice about whether or not she or he will speak to the police. Moreover, the police are under a positive duty to advise detainees of the existence and availability of legal duty counsel and Legal Aid plans and to explain how to access these available services.[61]

It is important to note that section 10 does not create a right to state-funded legal counsel. As discussed above, a right to state-funded counsel in some child welfare situations has been grounded in section 7 principles of fundamental justice. In the criminal context, a right to state-funded counsel has been grounded in the accused's right to a fair trial, and where the accused's fair trial rights will be infringed by the lack of representation, the state is obligated to provide representation. In considering whether the accused's fair trial rights would be infringed the court evaluates the complexity of the case, the seriousness of the charges, the financial circumstances of the accused, and the ability of the accused to self-represent.[62] The *Youth Criminal Justice Act* grants to young people charged with an offence statutory rights to legal representation at particular stages of the criminal process.[63]

Section 11 provides several rights to persons charged with an offence:

a) to be informed without unreasonable delay of the specific offence;
b) to be tried within a reasonable time;
c) not to be compelled to be a witness against him or herself in proceedings in respect of the offence;
d) to be presumed innocent until proven guilty according to law in a fair and public hearing by an independent and impartial tribunal;
e) not to be denied reasonable bail without just cause;
f) except in the case of an offence under military law tried before a military tribunal, to the benefit of trial by jury where the maximum punishment for the offence is imprisonment for five years or a more severe punishment;
g) not to be found guilty on account of any act or omission unless, at the time of the act or omission, it constituted an offence under Canadian or international law or was criminal according to the general principles of law recognized by the community of nations;
h) if finally acquitted of the offence, not to be tried for it again and, if finally found guilty and punished for the offence, not to be tried or punished for it again; and
i) if found guilty of the offence and if the punishment for the offence

has been varied between the time of commission and the time of sentencing, to the benefit of the lesser punishment.

An issue that has arisen under 11(d)—the accused's fair trial rights—that has particular relevance for social workers, is that of the accused's access to the therapeutic records of a complainant in a criminal law situation. This issue, which pits the accused's fair trial rights against the privacy and equality rights of complainants, is discussed fully in Chapter 8.

(v) Equality Rights (Section 15)

Section 15 of the *Charter*, which came into force three years after the other *Charter* provisions (thus in 1985), provides that:

> Every individual is equal before and under the law and has the right to the equal protection and equal benefit of the law without discrimination and, in particular, without discrimination based on race, national or ethnic origin, colour, religion, sex, age or mental or physical disability.[64]

In an early decision of the Supreme Court of Canada, *Andrews v. Law Society (British Columbia)*,[65] the "similarly situated" approach to equality, in which likes are to be treated alike, and those that are unalike differently in proportion to their unlikeness, was rejected. The court observed that differences in treatment do not necessarily amount to legal discrimination. Likewise, laws that treat everyone the same (and are therefore "facially neutral") can frequently produce situations of serious inequality through their impact. This is commonly referred to as "adverse effects discrimination." McIntyre J defined discrimination in the following manner:

> [D]iscrimination may be described as a distinction, whether intentional or not, based on grounds relating to personal characteristics of the individual or group which has the effect of imposing burdens, obligations, or disadvantages on such individual or group not imposed upon others, or which withholds or limits access to opportunities, benefits and advantages to other members of society. Distinctions based on personal characteristics attributed to an individual solely on the basis of association with a group will rarely escape the charge of discrimination, while those based on an individual's merits and capabilities will rarely be so classed.[66]

In determining whether discrimination has occurred, the Court in *Andrews* articulated a three-part test: 1) there be a distinction in treatment, either directly or in the law's effect; 2) that the distinction be based on an expressly prohibited ground, or on one analogous thereto; and 3) that the result of the distinction was an imposition of a burden or a denial of a benefit. In its later decision, *Law v. Canada (Minister of Employment &*

Immigration),[67] the Court added that difference in treatment on the basis of a prohibited or analogous ground would only amount to discrimination under section 15 if the distinction could reasonably be said to violate the human dignity of the claimant. However, since the *Law v. Canada (Minister of Employment & Immigration)* ruling, there has been a fair bit of controversy over the value added by the dignity portion of the test.[68]

The courts have recognized several "analogous grounds" of discrimination, including citizenship,[69] sexual orientation,[70] marital status[71] and receipt of social assistance.[72] Equality rights have been found to be infringed in a range of circumstances; examples include the refusal to fund interpretation services for the Deaf under provincial health insurance legislation,[73] and the failure to prohibit discrimination based on sexual orientation under provincial human rights law.[74]

Many equality-seeking groups have been disheartened by the limited reach of section 15 thus far, and by the lack of a demonstrable commitment by governments to the equality principles articulated in section 15. As the 20th Anniversary Committee of the Equality Clause notes:

> [t]he cutbacks to these [social] programmes and services disproportionately affect those most dependent upon them—women, immigrants and visible minorities, persons with disabilities, children and seniors, particularly older women, and the poor—precisely those whom section 15 is designed to protect. The disconnect between the *Charter*'s guarantee of equality and the daily lives of Canadians grows ever larger. These programmes and services must be restored and new pro-active, legislative remedies developed if section 15 is to live up to its promise.[75]

(8) ABORIGINAL RIGHTS UNDER THE CONSTITUTION

There are four main provisions in the Constitution dealing with Aboriginal peoples.[76] Subsection 91(24) of the *Constitution Act, 1967* assigns to Parliament exclusive legislative authority over "Indians and Lands reserved for the Indians;" section 25 of the *Charter* guarantees that other rights and freedoms shall not be interpreted "so as to abrogate or derogate from any aboriginal, treaty or other rights or freedoms that pertain to the aboriginal peoples of Canada;" section 35 of the *Constitution Act, 1982* recognizes and affirms "existing" aboriginal and treaty rights; and section 35.1 of the *Constitution Act, 1982,* commits Parliament to the principle that before any amendment is made to a part of the constitution dealing directly with Aboriginal peoples, it will convene a constitutional conference of first ministers of the provinces to which representatives of the Aboriginal peoples will be invited.

As Funston and Meehan note, while the treaty process was integral to the relationship between Aboriginal peoples and British and Canadian governments, until the passage of section 35 in 1982, the doctrine of Parliamentary supremacy "allowed the federal government to override, and even ignore, its treaty promises."[77] In interpreting section 35, the Supreme Court of Canada has taken the approach that so long as some vestige of Aboriginal and treaty rights remain, it is subject to constitutional protection as an "existing Aboriginal and treaty right."[78] Moreover, the intention of the Crown to extinguish an Aboriginal right must be "clear and plain."

SELECTED READINGS

Cameron, Jamie, "The Charter's Legislative Override: Feat or Figment of the Constitutional Imagination?" (2004) 23 Sup. Ct. L. Rev. 135.

Funston, Bernard & Eugene Meehan, *Canada's Constitutional Law in a Nutshell*, 2d ed. (Toronto: Thomson Canada Ltd., 1998).

Gall, Gerald, *The Canadian Legal System*, 4th ed. (Toronto: Thomson Canada Ltd., 1995).

Greschner, Donna, "Does *Law* Advance the Cause of Equality?" (2001) 27 Queen's L.J. 299.

Hogg, Peter, Allison Bushell Thornton & Wade K Wright, "Charter Dialogue Revisited—or 'Much Ado About Metaphors'" (2007) 45 Osgoode Hall L.J. 193.

Hogg, Peter, *Constitutional Law in Canada* (Toronto: Thomson Canada Ltd., 2005).

Hughes, Patricia, "Section 33 of the Charter: What's the Problem, Anyway? (Or, Why a Feminist Thinks Section 33 Does Matter)" (2000) 49 U.N.B.L.J. 169.

Manfredi, Christopher, "Judicial Power and the Charter: Reflections on the Activism Debate" (2004) 53 U.N.B.L.J. 185.

Russell, Peter, "Standing up for Notwithstanding" (1991) 29 Alta. L. Rev. 293.

Sharpe, Robert & Katherine Swinton, *The Charter of Rights and Freedoms* (Toronto: Irwin Law, 1998).

Waddams, S.M., *Introduction to the Study of Law,* 5th ed. (Toronto: Thomson Canada Ltd., 1997).

Whyte, John, "On Not Standing for Notwithstanding" (1989-1990) 28 Alta. L. Rev. 347.

ENDNOTES

1. Gerald Gall, *The Canadian Legal System*, 4th ed. (Toronto: Thomson Canada Ltd., 1995) at 385.
2. S.M.Waddams, *Introduction to the Study of Law*, 5th ed. (Toronto: Thomson Canada Ltd., 1997) at 2.
3. See *supra* note 1 at 1-2.
4. *Ibid.* at 3.
5. *Black's Law Dictionary*, 5th ed. (St. Paul, Minn.: West Publishing Co., 1979) at 795-6.
6. See *supra* note 1 at 10-11.
7. Frederick Morton, "The Rule of Law in the Canadian Constitution" in Frederick L. Morton, ed., *Law, Politics and the Judicial Process in Canada*, 3d ed. (Calgary: University of Calgary Press, 2002) at 5.
8. [1959] S.C.R. 121, 1959 CarswellQue 37, [1959] S.C.J. No. 1, 16 D.L.R. (2d) 689.
9. See *supra* note 7 at 1.
10. See *supra* note 2 at 71.
11. J. Burke, ed., *Jowitt's Dictionary of English Law*, 2d ed. (London: Sweet & Maxwell) Vol. 1 at 391.
12. Willard Estey, "Who Needs Courts?" (1981) 1 Windsor Y.B. Access Just. 264.
13. For a more detailed description on the application of a "trust," see Chapter 13.
14. See *supra* note 2 at Chapter 8.
15. Raymond Albert, *Law and Social Work Practice* (New York: Springer Publishing Co., 1986) at 19-20. Cited from *Black's Law Dictionary* (St. Paul, Minn.: West Publishing Co., 1968).
16. R.S.O. 1990, c. C.11.
17. S.C. 2002, c. 1.
18. R.S.O. 1990, c. F.3.
19. See E.A. Driedger, "Statutes: The Mischievous Literal Golden Rule" (1981) 59 Can. Bar Rev. 780; and Michael Zander, *The Law Making Process* (London: Butler & Tanner Ltd., 1980) at 38-39 and 57-58.
20. See *supra* note 1 at 38-39.
21. W.A. Bogart, *Courts and Country, The Limits of Litigation and the Social and Political Life of Canada* (Toronto: Oxford University Press, 1994).

22. See *supra* note 22 at 96-97.
23. *New Brunswick (Minister of Health and Community Services) v. G. (J.)*, [1999] 3 S.C.R. 46, 66 C.R.R. (2d) 267, 50 R.F.L. (4th) 63, 216 N.B.R. (2d) 25, 552 A.P.R. 25, 7 B.H.R.C. 615, REJB 1999-14250, 1999 CarswellNB 305, 1999 CarswellNB 306, 244 N.R. 276, 177 D.L.R. (4th) 124, [1999] S.C.J. No. 47, 26 C.R. (5th) 203.
24. *Ibid.*
25. Peter Hogg, *Constitutional Law of Canada*, student ed. (Toronto: Thomson Canada Ltd., 2005) at 105-108.
26. Bernard Funston & Eugene Meehan, *Canada's Constitutional Law in a Nutshell*, 2d ed. (Toronto: Thomson Canada Ltd., 1998) at 29.
27. Schedule B to the *Canada Act, 1982* (U.K.), S.C. 1982, c. 11.
28. *Constitution Act 1867,* (U.K.), 30 & 31 Victoria, c. 3, s. 91.
29. *Ibid.* at s. 92.
30. Peter Hogg, *Constitutional Law of Canada*, 5th ed. supp. (Toronto: Thomson Carswell, 2007) at Chapter 27.
31. R.S.C. 1985, c. 3 (2nd Supp.).
32. For a more detailed discussion see *supra* note 30.
33. *Ibid.*
34. Joel Bakan et al., eds., *Canadian Constitutional Law*, 3d ed. (Toronto: Emond Montgomery, 2003) at 29.
35. Note that legislation that expressly "opts out" remains in force for five years only, unless it is renewed by that government.
36. For a fuller sense of these debates see Peter Hogg & Allison Bushell, "The Charter Dialogue Between Courts and Legislatures" (1997) 35 Osgoode Hall L.J. 75; Frederick Morton, "Dialogue or Monologue? A Reply to Hogg and Thornton" in Frederick Morton, ed., *Law, Politics and the Judicial Process in Canada,* 3d ed. (Calgary: University of Calgary Press, 2002); and Peter Hogg, Allison Bushell Thornton & Wade Wright, "Charter Dialogue Revisited—or 'Much Ado About Metaphors'" (2007) 45 Osgoode Hall L.J. 193.
37. *McKinney v. University of Guelph*, [1990] 3 S.C.R. 229, 91 C.L.L.C. 17,004, 2 O.R. (3d) 319 (note), 13 C.H.R.R. D/171, 2 C.R.R. (2d) 1, 45 O.A.C. 1, 118 N.R. 1, 76 D.L.R. (4th) 545, [1990] S.C.J. No. 122, 1990 CarswellOnt 1019F, 1990 CarswellOnt 1019, EYB 1990-67618.
38. *Eldridge v. British Columbia (Attorney General)* (1997), 151 D.L.R. (4th) 577, 1997 CarswellBC 1939, 1997 CarswellBC 1940, [1998] 1 W.W.R. 50, 218 N.R. 161, 96 B.C.A.C. 81, 155 W.A.C. 81, [1997] S.C.J. No. 86, 46 C.R.R. (2d) 189, 3 B.H.R.C. 137, [1997] 3 S.C.R. 624, 38 B.C.L.R. (3d) 1 at para. 51.
39. [1984] 2 S.C.R. 145, (sub nom. *Canada (Director of Investigation & Research, Combines Investigation Branch) v. Southam Inc.*) 11 D.L.R.

(4th) 641, 33 Alta. L.R. (2d) 193, 55 A.R. 291, 27 B.L.R. 297, 41 C.R. (3d) 97, 84 D.T.C. 6467, 14 C.C.C. (3d) 97, (sub nom. *Director of Investigations & Research Combines Investigation Branch v. Southam Inc.*) [1984] 6 W.W.R. 577, 1984 CarswellAlta 121, 1984 CarswellAlta 415, 55 N.R. 241, 2 C.P.R. (3d) 1, 9 C.R.R. 355, [1984] S.C.J. No. 36.

40. *Ibid.* at para. 18-19; see also *R. v. Big M Drug Mart Ltd.*, [1985] 1 S.C.R. 295, 18 D.L.R. (4th) 321, 58 N.R. 81, [1985] 3 W.W.R. 481, 37 Alta. L.R. (2d) 97, 60 A.R. 161, 18 C.C.C. (3d) 385, 85 C.L.L.C. 14,023, 13 C.R.R. 64, 1985 CarswellAlta 316, 1985 CarswellAlta 609, [1985] S.C.J. No. 17.

41. *Ibid.* at para. 20.

42. *R. v. Keegstra*, [1990] 3 S.C.R. 697, 1990-66942, 1 C.R. (4th) 129, 77 Alta. L.R. (2d) 193, 117 N.R. 1, [1991] 2 W.W.R. 1, 114 A.R. 81, 61 C.C.C. (3d) 1, 3 C.R.R. (2d) 193, 1990 CarswellAlta 192, 1990 CarswellAlta 661, [1990] S.C.J. No. 131 at para. 13.

43. *RJR-MacDonald Inc. c. Canada (Procureur général)*, (sub nom. *RJR-MacDonald Inc. v. Canada (Attorney General)*) [1995] 3 S.C.R. 199, 127 D.L.R. (4th) 1, 1995 CarswellQue 119, EYB 1995-67815, 100 C.C.C. (3d) 449, 62 C.P.R. (3d) 417, 31 C.R.R. (2d) 189, 187 N.R. 1, [1995] S.C.J. No. 68, 1995 CarswellQue 119F at para. 176 and 190.

44. See *R. v. Oakes*, [1986] 1 S.C.R. 103, [1986] S.C.J. No. 7, EYB 1986-67556, 26 D.L.R. (4th) 200, 65 N.R. 87, 14 O.A.C. 335, 24 C.C.C. (3d) 321, 50 C.R. (3d) 1, 19 C.R.R. 308, 53 O.R. (2d) 719, 1986 CarswellOnt 95, 1986 CarswellOnt 1001.

45. Robert Sharpe & Katherine Swinton, *The Charter of Rights and Freedoms* (Toronto: Irwin Law, 1998) at 42-53.

46. [2006] 1 S.C.R. 256, 38 Admin. L.R. (4th) 159, (sub nom. *Multani v. Marguerite-Bourgeoys*) 55 C.H.R.R. D/463, 137 C.R.R. (2d) 326, 264 D.L.R. (4th) 577, 2006 SCC 6, 2006 CarswellQue 1368, 2006 CarswellQue 1369, [2006] S.C.J. No. 6, 345 N.R. 201.

47. See *Little Sisters Book & Art Emporium v. Canada (Minister of Justice)*, [2000] 2 S.C.R. 1120, 145 B.C.A.C. 1, 237 W.A.C. 1, 28 Admin. L.R. (3d) 1, 2000 SCC 69, 2000 CarswellBC 2442, [1998] S.C.C.A. No. 448, 2000 CarswellBC 2452, 79 C.R.R. (2d) 189, REJB 2000-21529, 38 C.R. (5th) 209, 83 B.C.L.R. (3d) 1, [2001] 2 W.W.R. 1, [2000] S.C.J. No. 66, 263 N.R. 203, 150 C.C.C. (3d) 1, 193 D.L.R. (4th) 193.

48. *Blencoe v. British Columbia (Human Rights Commission)*, [2000] 2 S.C.R. 307, 2000 SCC 44, 2000 CarswellBC 1860, 2000 CarswellBC 1861, 3 C.C.E.L. (3d) 165, (sub nom. *British Columbia (Human Rights Commission) v. Blencoe*) 38 C.H.R.R. D/153, 81 B.C.L.R. (3d) 1, 190 D.L.R. (4th) 513, [2000] 10 W.W.R. 567, [2000] S.C.J. No. 43, 23 Admin. L.R. (3d) 175, 2000 C.L.L.C. 230-040, 260 N.R. 1, REJB 2000-

20288, 77 C.R.R. (2d) 189, 141 B.C.A.C. 161, 231 W.A.C. 161 at para. 49-50.

49. *Canadian Foundation for Children, Youth & the Law v. Canada (Attorney General)*, (sub nom. *Canadian Foundation for Children v. Canada*) [2004] 1 S.C.R. 76, 2004 SCC 4, 2004 CarswellOnt 252, 2004 CarswellOnt 253, 315 N.R. 201, 183 O.A.C. 1, [2004] S.C.J. No. 6, 70 O.R. (3d) 94 (note), 115 C.R.R. (2d) 88, REJB 2004-53164, 16 C.R. (6th) 203, 46 R.F.L. (5th) 1, 234 D.L.R. (4th) 257, 180 C.C.C. (3d) 353 at 132 [S.C.R.] but upheld on the ground that there was no breach of the principles of fundamental justice.

50. *Winnipeg Child & Family Services (Central Area) v. W. (K.L.)*, [2000] 2 S.C.R. 519, 2000 SCC 48, 2000 CarswellMan 469, 2000 CarswellMan 470, 260 N.R. 203, 191 D.L.R. (4th) 1, 10 R.F.L. (5th) 122, [2001] 1 W.W.R. 1, REJB 2000-20378, [2000] S.C.J. No. 48, 78 C.R.R. (2d) 1, 150 Man. R. (2d) 161, 230 W.A.C. 161 at para. 85-86. While a warrantless apprehension of a child deemed to be "in need of protection" was a breach of the parents' security of the person, the majority held that there was no violation of the principles of fundamental justice.

51. *Rodriguez v. British Columbia (Attorney General)*, [1993] 3 S.C.R. 519, 1993 CarswellBC 1267, EYB 1993-67109, [1993] S.C.J. No. 94, 82 B.C.L.R. (2d) 273, 85 C.C.C. (3d) 15, 107 D.L.R. (4th) 342, 17 C.R.R. (2d) 193, 24 C.R. (4th) 281, 158 N.R. 1, 34 B.C.A.C. 1, 56 W.A.C. 1, [1993] 7 W.W.R. 641, 1993 CarswellBC 228 at para. 9. Rodriguez, who was terminally ill, challenged the provisions of the *Criminal Code* making it an offence to assist a person to commit suicide. Five of nine judges concluded that the impugned provision did not offend the principles of fundamental justice.

52. [2002] 4 S.C.R. 429, (sub nom. *Gosselin v. Quebec (Attorney General)*) 221 D.L.R. (4th) 257, 100 C.R.R. (2d) 1, 44 C.H.R.R. D/363, 2002 SCC 84, 2002 CarswellQue 2706, 2002 CarswellQue 2707, [2002] S.C.J. No. 85, 298 N.R. 1, REJB 2002-36302. Excellent bibliographic references on the justifiability of social and economic rights can be found at http://www.socialrights.ca/publications.html.

53. Early on, the Supreme Court rejected the view that the principles of fundamental justice were simply synonymous with natural justice. Fundamental justice includes procedural fairness/natural justice; *Reference re s. 94(2) of the Motor Vehicle Act (British Columbia)* (1985), [1985] 2 S.C.R. 486, 1985 CarswellBC 398, [1986] D.L.Q. 90, 1985 CarswellBC 816, [1985] S.C.J. No. 73, 24 D.L.R. (4th) 536, 63 N.R. 266, 69 B.C.L.R. 145, 23 C.C.C. (3d) 289, 18 C.R.R. 30, 36 M.V.R. 240, [1986] 1 W.W.R. 481, 48 C.R. (3d) 289 (Lamer J.).

54. (1985), [1985] 2 S.C.R. 486, 1985 CarswellBC 398, [1986] D.L.Q. 90,

1985 CarswellBC 816, [1985] S.C.J. No. 73, 24 D.L.R. (4th) 536, 63
N.R. 266, 69 B.C.L.R. 145, 23 C.C.C. (3d) 289, 18 C.R.R. 30, 36
M.V.R. 240, [1986] 1 W.W.R. 481, 48 C.R. (3d) 289.
55. *R. v. Malmo-Levine* (2003), 233 D.L.R. (4th) 415, [2003] S.C.J. No.
79, [2004] 4 W.W.R. 407, 191 B.C.A.C. 1, 314 W.A.C. 1, 16 C.R. (6th)
1, [2003] 3 S.C.R. 571, 114 C.R.R. (2d) 189, REJB 2003-51751, 2003
CarswellBC 3133, 2003 CarswellBC 3134, 2003 SCC 74, 179 C.C.C.
(3d) 417, 314 N.R. 1, 23 B.C.L.R. (4th) 1 at para. 113; Malmo-Levine
challenged the criminalization of the possession of marihuana. The
Court rejected the accused's argument that the "harm principle" (only
truly harmful conduct should be subject to criminal prohibition) constituted a principle of fundamental justice. In the subsequent case of *R.
v. Parker* (2000), 49 O.R. (3d) 481, 188 D.L.R. (4th) 385, 146 C.C.C.
(3d) 193, 75 C.R.R. (2d) 233, 37 C.R. (5th) 97, 135 O.A.C. 1, 2000
CarswellOnt 2627, [2000] O.J. No. 2787 (C.A.), the Ontario Court of
Appeal did however find that the lack of a health exemption for the
medical use of marihuana (an absolute prohibition on possession that
threatened health) was a breach of fundamental justice. Parliament
subsequently enacted the Marihuana Medical Access Regulations,
which were challenged, and found unconstitutional in *Hitzig v. R.*
(2003), (sub nom. *Hitzig v. Canada*) 231 D.L.R. (4th) 104, 177 O.A.C.
321, 111 C.R.R. (2d) 201, 2003 CarswellOnt 3795, [2003] O.J. No.
3873, 14 C.R. (6th) 1, 177 C.C.C. (3d) 449 (Ont. C.A.), leave to appeal
refused (2004), 2004 CarswellOnt 1830, 2004 CarswellOnt 1831, 112
C.R.R. (2d) 376n, 197 O.A.C. 400 (note), [2004] S.C.C.A. No. 5, 331
N.R. 394 (note) (S.C.C.).
56. 234 D.L.R. (4th) 257, 2004 SCC 4, 2004 CarswellOnt 252, 2004
CarswellOnt 253, 315 N.R. 201, 183 O.A.C. 1, [2004] S.C.J. No. 6, 70
O.R. (3d) 94 (note), (sub nom. *Canadian Foundation for Children v.
Canada*) [2004] 1 S.C.R. 76, 115 C.R.R. (2d) 88, REJB 2004-53164,
16 C.R. (6th) 203, 46 R.F.L. (5th) 1, 180 C.C.C. (3d) 353.
57. *Singh v.Canada (Minister of Employment & Immigration)*, [1985] 1
S.C.R. 177, 1985 CarswellNat 663, 17 D.L.R. (4th) 422, 58 N.R. 1, 12
Admin. L.R. 137, 14 C.R.R. 13, 1985 CarswellNat 152, [1985] S.C.J.
No. 11.
58. *Hunter v. Southam Inc.*, [1984] 2 S.C.R. 145 (sub nom. *Canada (Director of Investigation & Research, Combines Investigation Branch) v.
Southam Inc.*) 11 D.L.R. (4th) 641, 33 Alta. L.R. (2d) 193, 55 A.R.
291, 27 B.L.R. 297, 41 C.R. (3d) 97, 84 D.T.C. 6467, 14 C.C.C. (3d)
97, (sub nom. *Director of Investigations & Research Combines Investigation Branch v. Southam Inc.*) [1984] 6 W.W.R. 577, 1984
CarswellAlta 121, 1984 CarswellAlta 415, 55 N.R. 241, 2 C.P.R. (3d)

1, 9 C.R.R. 355, [1984] S.C.J. No. 36; *R. v. Edwards*, [1996] 1 S.C.R. 128, 45 C.R. (4th) 307, 192 N.R. 81, 26 O.R. (3d) 736 (note), 104 C.C.C. (3d) 136, 132 D.L.R. (4th) 31, 33 C.R.R. (2d) 226, 88 O.A.C. 321, 1996 CarswellOnt 2126, [1996] S.C.J. No. 11, EYB 1996-67692, 1996 CarswellOnt 1916.

59. Alan Gold, "Search and Seizure Evidence," prepared for the Program on Criminal Evidence, Federation of Law Societies, Halifax, Nova Scotia, July 14-18, 1997, Alan D. Gold Collection of Criminal Law Articles.

60. *R. v. Manninen*, [1987] 1 S.C.R. 1233, EYB 1987-67474, 76 N.R. 198, 1987 CarswellOnt 967, 1987 CarswellOnt 99, [1987] S.C.J. No. 41, 38 C.R.R. 37, 58 C.R. (3d) 97, 21 O.A.C. 192, 34 C.C.C. (3d) 385, 41 D.L.R. (4th) 301, 61 O.R. (2d) 736 (note); *R. v. Hebert*, [1990] 2 S.C.R. 151, EYB 1990-67969, 47 B.C.L.R. (2d) 1, 1990 CarswellYukon 4, 1990 CarswellYukon 7, 77 C.R. (3d) 145, [1990] 5 W.W.R. 1, 57 C.C.C. (3d) 1, 110 N.R. 1, 49 C.R.R. 114, [1990] S.C.J. No. 64.

61. *R. v. Brydges*, [1990] 1 S.C.R. 190, [1990] 2 W.W.R. 220, 46 C.R.R. 236, 103 N.R. 282, 71 Alta. L.R. (2d) 145, 104 A.R. 124, 53 C.C.C. (3d) 330, 74 C.R. (3d) 129, [1990] S.C.J. No. 8, EYB 1990-66929, 1990 CarswellAlta 3, 1990 CarswellAlta 648; *R. v. Bartle*, [1994] 3 S.C.R. 173, 33 C.R. (4th) 1, 23 C.R.R. (2d) 193, 172 N.R. 1, 92 C.C.C. (3d) 289, 74 O.A.C. 161, 118 D.L.R. (4th) 83, EYB 1994-67664, 6 M.V.R. (3d) 1, 19 O.R. (3d) 802 (note), 1994 CarswellOnt 1164, 1994 CarswellOnt 100, [1994] S.C.J. No. 74. The availability of legal aid is discussed in Chapter 7.

62. The leading case is *R. v. Rowbotham* (1988), 63 C.R. (3d) 113, [1988] O.J. No. 271, 25 O.A.C. 321, 35 C.R.R. 207, 1988 CarswellOnt 58, 41 C.C.C. (3d) 1 at para. 169.

63. For a fuller discussion of these provisions, see Chapter 21, *Youth Criminal Justice Act,* S.C. 2002, c. 1.

64. For an excellent review of equality rights see William Black & Lynn Smith, "The Equality Rights" in Gerald Beaudoin and Errol Mendes, eds., *The Canadian Charter of Rights and Freedoms*, 4th ed. (Markham, Ontario: LexisNexis Butterworths, 2005) at 927-963 and 1018-1024.

65. [1989] 2 W.W.R. 289, EYB 1989-66977, 10 C.H.R.R. D/5719, 56 D.L.R. (4th) 1, 91 N.R. 255, 34 B.C.L.R. (2d) 273, 25 C.C.E.L. 255, 36 C.R.R. 193, [1989] 1 S.C.R. 143, 1989 CarswellBC 16, 1989 CarswellBC 701, [1989] S.C.J. No. 6.

66. *Ibid.* at para. 19.

67. [1999] 1 S.C.R. 497, 170 D.L.R. (4th) 1, 1999 CarswellNat 359, 1999 CarswellNat 360, (sub nom. *Law v. Canada (Minister of Human Re-*

sources Development)) 60 C.R.R. (2d) 1, 236 N.R. 1, [1999] S.C.J. No. 12, 43 C.C.E.L. (2d) 49, 1999 C.E.B. & P.G.R. 8350 (headnote only).

68. See for example Donna Greschner, "Does *Law* Advance the Cause of Equality?" (2001) 27 Queen's L.J. 299.

69. See *supra* note 57 at 51.

70. *Vriend v. Alberta*, [1998] 1 S.C.R. 493, 50 C.R.R. (2d) 1, 224 N.R. 1, 212 A.R. 237, 168 W.A.C. 237, 31 C.H.R.R. D/1, [1999] 5 W.W.R. 451, 67 Alta. L.R. (3d) 1, 98 C.L.L.C. 230-021, 4 B.H.R.C. 140, 1998 CarswellAlta 210, 1998 CarswellAlta 211, 156 D.L.R. (4th) 385, [1998] S.C.J. No. 29; *Egan v. Canada*, [1995] 2 S.C.R. 513, 95 C.L.L.C. 210-025, 12 R.F.L. (4th) 201, 1995 C.E.B. & P.G.R. 8216, 124 D.L.R. (4th) 609, 182 N.R. 161, 29 C.R.R. (2d) 79, 96 F.T.R. 80 (note), 1995 CarswellNat 6, 1995 CarswellNat 703; *M v. H*, [1999] S.C.R. 3, 171 D.L.R. (4th) 577, 121 O.A.C. 1, 238 N.R. 179, 1999 CarswellOnt 1348, 1999 CarswellOnt 1349, 43 O.R. (3d) 254 (headnote only), 46 R.F.L. (4th) 32, 62 C.R.R. (2d) 1, 7 B.H.R.C. 489, [1999] S.C.J. No. 23, (sub nom. *Attorney General for Ontario v. M. & H.*) 1999 C.E.B. & P.G.R. 8354 (headnote only).

71. *Miron v. Trudel*, [1995] 2 S.C.R. 418, 10 M.V.R. (3d) 151, 23 O.R. (3d) 160 (note), [1995] I.L.R. 1-3185, 13 R.F.L. (4th) 1, 1995 C.E.B. & P.G.R. 8217, 181 N.R. 253, 124 D.L.R. (4th) 693, 81 O.A.C. 253, 29 C.R.R. (2d) 189, 1995 CarswellOnt 93, 1995 CarswellOnt 526, EYB 1995-67430, [1995] S.C.J. No. 44; *Nova Scotia (Attorney General) v. Walsh*, (sub nom. *Nova Scotia (Attorney General) v. Walsh*) [2002] 4 S.C.R. 325, 211 N.S.R. (2d) 273, 659 A.P.R. 273, 2002 SCC 83, 2002 CarswellNS 511, 2002 CarswellNS 512, 102 C.R.R. (2d) 1, [2002] S.C.J. No. 84, 32 R.F.L. (5th) 81, 221 D.L.R. (4th) 1, 297 N.R. 203, REJB 2002-36303.

72. *Falkiner v. Ontario (Director of Income Maintenance, Ministry of Community & Social Services)* (2002), 212 D.L.R. (4th) 633, [2002] O.J. No. 1771, 1 Admin. L.R. (4th) 235, 59 O.R. (3d) 481, 159 O.A.C. 135, 101 C.R.R. (2d) 188 (note), 2002 CarswellOnt 1558, 94 C.R.R. (2d) 22 (Ont. C.A.), leave to appeal allowed (2003), 2003 CarswellOnt 1025, 2003 CarswellOnt 1026, 312 N.R. 200 (note), [2002] S.C.C.A. No. 297, 181 O.A.C. 197 (note) (S.C.C.).

73. *Eldridge v. British Columbia (Attorney General)* (1997), 151 D.L.R. (4th) 577, 1997 CarswellBC 1939, 1997 CarswellBC 1940, [1998] 1 W.W.R. 50, 218 N.R. 161, 96 B.C.A.C. 81, 155 W.A.C. 81, [1997] S.C.J. No. 86, 46 C.R.R. (2d) 189, 3 B.H.R.C. 137, [1997] 3 S.C.R. 624, 38 B.C.L.R. (3d) 1.

74. *Vriend v. Alberta* (1998), [1998] 1 S.C.R. 493, 50 C.R.R. (2d) 1, 224 N.R. 1, 212 A.R. 237, 168 W.A.C. 237, 31 C.H.R.R. D/1, [1999] 5

W.W.R. 451, 67 Alta. L.R. (3d) 1, 98 C.L.L.C. 230-021, 4 B.H.R.C. 140, 1998 CarswellAlta 210, 1998 CarswellAlta 211, 156 D.L.R. (4th) 385, [1998] S.C.J. No. 29; *Egan v. Canada*, [1995] 2 S.C.R. 513, 95 C.L.L.C. 210-025, 12 R.F.L. (4th) 201, 1995 C.E.B. & P.G.R. 8216, 124 D.L.R. (4th) 609, 182 N.R. 161, 29 C.R.R. (2d) 79, 96 F.T.R. 80 (note), 1995 CarswellNat 6, 1995 CarswellNat 703.

75. *Promises to Keep: Section 15 of the Canadian Charter of Rights and Freedoms*, online: Twentieth Anniversary Committee of the Equality Clause <http://www.20years.ca/promises_to_keep.pdf>.

76. Bernard Funston & Eugene Meehan, *Canada's Constitutional Law in a Nutshell*, 2d ed. (Toronto: Thomson Canada Ltd., 1998) at 29 at Chapter 8.

77. *Ibid.* at 148.

78. See *R. v. Sparrow*, [1990] 1 S.C.R. 1075, EYB 1990-68598, 1990 CarswellBC 105, 1990 CarswellBC 756, 70 D.L.R. (4th) 385, 111 N.R. 241, [1990] 3 C.N.L.R. 160, 46 B.C.L.R. (2d) 1, 56 C.C.C. (3d) 263, [1990] 4 W.W.R. 410, [1990] S.C.J. No. 49 at para. 1.

3

Human Rights

(1) THE EVOLUTION OF HUMAN RIGHTS LEGISLATION

Under the *Constitution Act, 1867*,[1] responsibility for civil rights and property falls under provincial jurisdiction. Consequently, the regulation of discriminatory practices is predominantly a matter within provincial responsibility. Each province has enacted anti-discrimination legislation that prohibits discrimination based upon listed grounds and creates processes and remedies for those experiencing discrimination. Such legislation often includes a broad educational mandate to prevent discrimination and to promote human rights, as well as vehicles that seek to combat systemic forms of discrimination.

At the federal level, Parliament has enacted anti-discrimination legislation, the *Canadian Human Rights Act*,[2] which applies to federal public services, federal government departments, Crown corporations, and federally regulated industries, such as airlines, railways, and inter-provincial trucking companies.

Anti-discrimination legislation first emerged in Canada following World War II, a time when the horrific consequences of state-sanctioned racism from abroad and at home were vividly clear. At the international level, the United Nations was established as a direct response to the calamities witnessed in WW II, and Canada became a participant in that institution as well as a signatory to the Universal Declaration of Human Rights.[3] These events combined to create a climate ripe for the development of Canadian legislation to address concerns of discrimination.

The first anti-discrimination legislation in Ontario, the *Racial Discrimination Act*, enacted in 1944, was intended to target a "single, narrowly defined problem: the phenomenon of shopkeepers and other service providers announcing their unwillingness to deal with non-white members of the public by displaying "Whites Only" signs."[4] Other legislation addressing specific forms of discrimination followed. The first comprehensive anti-discrimination legislation emerged in Saskatchewan with its *Bill of Rights*.[5] Ontario followed suit, consolidating various anti-discrimination statutes into the *Ontario Code of 1962*.[6] The Preamble to the *Code* expressly references the importance of the Universal Declaration of Human Rights,

> Whereas recognition of the inherent dignity and the equal and inalienable rights of all members of the human family is the foundation of freedom, justice and peace in the world and is in accord with the Universal Declaration of Human Rights as proclaimed by the United Nations;
>
> And Whereas it is public policy in Ontario to recognize the dignity and worth of every person and to provide for equal rights and opportunities without discrimination that is contrary to law, and having as its aim the creation of a climate of understanding and mutual respect for the dignity and worth of each person so that each person feels a part of the community and able to contribute fully to the development and well-being of the community and the Province. . .[7]

Over time the scope of anti-discrimination legislation has expanded through the recognition of additional grounds of discrimination, as well as a broadening of the concept of discrimination itself.

(2) RELATIONSHIP TO THE *CHARTER*

As discussed in Chapter 2, the *Charter* only applies to state action. The *Charter's* status is that of the supreme law of the land, and all legislation—whether provincially or federally enacted—must comport with it. The reach of anti-discrimination statutes is both broader and simultaneously more circumscribed than the *Charter*. The reach is broader in that unlike the *Charter*, anti-discrimination statutes reach beyond state action to include the relationships between individuals and between individuals and private entities. However, the reach of human rights legislation is simultaneously more circumscribed; while accorded a special status (as discussed below), human rights legislation does not comprise part of the supreme law of the land and thus provincial legislatures, or Parliament, may expressly choose to enact legislation that is contrary to the human rights protections created through anti-discrimination legislation.

(3) STATUS OF HUMAN RIGHTS LEGISLATION

While not enjoying constitutional status equivalent to the *Charter*, human rights legislation has been recognized as having "quasi-constitutional" status. This enhanced status has three important features: as with the interpretation of constitutional documents, human rights legislation must be interpreted liberally and purposively; absent a clear legislative expression to the contrary, it has primacy over other legislation; and the protections granted may not be overridden by private contract.[8] Ontario's *Code* expressly provides that where a provision in another statute or regulation conflicts with the *Code*, the *Code* prevails unless the provision in question specially provides that it is to apply notwithstanding the *Code*.[9]

An important recent decision of the Supreme Court of Canada is that of *Werbeski v. Ontario (Director of Disability Support Program, Ministry of Community & Social Services)*.[10] Both the applicants, Mr. Tranchemontagne and Mr. Werbeski, had applied for Ontario Disability Support Program benefits and both were denied on the basis of subsection 5(2) of the *Ontario Disability Support Program Act (ODSPA)*, which renders applicants ineligible if their disability derives from an addiction. On the facts of the case, both applicants were found to suffer from alcoholism. On appeal to the Social Benefits Tribunal, the applicants argued that subsection 5(2) contravened the *Human Rights Code* as it discriminated against them on the basis of their disability and as such, should be given no effect. The Tribunal concluded that it did not have the jurisdiction to do so. When ultimately decided by the Supreme Court of Canada, the Court divided 5/4. The majority found that the Tribunal did have the jurisdiction to consider the *Human Rights Code*, including the jurisdiction to render inoperable a provision of its own enabling statute (here subsection 5(2) of the *ODSPA*) if in conflict with the *Code*. The Court relied in part upon subsection 47(2) of the *Code,* which, as noted above, gives the *Code* primacy over other legislation. The majority was particularly concerned about access to justice and troubled that were it to decide differently, persons in the position of the applicants—low-income and disabled—would be required to proceed both under the *Human Rights Code* (to determine if the provision contravened the *Code*) *and* under the *ODSPA* (in order to apply for a determination of eligibility for benefits) before a final and binding determination could be rendered. While the judges writing the minority decision were clearly of the view that the Social Benefits Tribunal can and must take into account the principles and values underlying the *Code* in its interpretation of its enabling statute, they concluded that the Tribunal could not go so far as to render a provision of its enabling statute inapplicable.

(4) DISCRIMINATION

(a) The Concept

The concept of discrimination has evolved significantly over the past half century. Earlier understandings of discrimination were limited to "intentional acts of unjustified differential conduct carried out by individuals motivated by prejudice."[11] This approach was consistent with the concept of formal equality, or treating everyone in the same way. Beginning in the 1970s, the concept of discrimination began to broaden by moving away from the necessity of establishing intention to consider discriminatory results or adverse effects. Importantly, this expanded conceptualization recognized that a law could be neutral on its face yet disproportionately and negatively impact upon a particular group.

In the case of *Bhinder v. Canadian National Railway*,[12] for example, the Supreme Court found that an employment rule which required all employees to wear hard hats at a particular work site for safety reasons discriminated against the claimant *Bhinder* (an employee of CN), whose religion forbade the wearing of any head-covering aside from a turban. The rule, while neutral on its face, adversely affected a particular group, and as such constituted a practice that was *prima facie* discriminatory.[13] The Court then went on to consider whether the wearing of a hard hat was a *bona fide* occupational requirement, which could constitute a defence to the finding of *prima facie* discrimination. On the facts, the Court concluded that the wearing of hard hats was indeed a *bona fide* occupational requirement. The approach in *Bhinder* was a two-step one: *prima facie* discrimination was met by the complainant demonstrating differential treatment connected with a prohibited ground; and the onus then shifted to the respondent to justify the practice by establishing it as a *bona fide* occupational requirement.

Over time the Court has melded the two-step approach, as outlined in *Bhinder,* into a single step in determining whether a policy or practice that has discriminatory effects is justified.[14] The Court has also further developed the concept of a *bona fide* occupational requirement. The employer must show it adopted the standard for a purpose rationally connected to the performance of the job, in an honest and good faith belief that it was necessary for a legitimate work-related purpose, and that the standard is reasonably necessary to accomplish that purpose.[15] Significantly, to show that the standard is reasonably necessary, the employer must demonstrate that it is impossible to accommodate individual employees sharing characteristics of the claimant without imposing undue hardship upon the employer.[16]

A further development is reflected in the concept of "systemic" discrimination. In *Canadian National Railway v. Canada (Canadian Human*

Rights Commission)[17] the Action Travail des Femmes alleged that the Canadian National Railway had pursued policies and/or practices that deprived women of employment opportunities. The evidence led by the claimants revealed several discriminatory stereotypes at play; that women could not do physically demanding work; that women lacked drive or ambition; and that women could not handle pressure. There was also evidence of discriminatory practices, including the requirement for women to undertake tests that men were not required to take and the hiring of women into only traditional female job categories. The Supreme Court of Canada found there to be "systemic discrimination," which in the employment context is defined as "discrimination that results from the simple operation of established procedures of recruitment, hiring and promotion, none of which is necessarily designed to promote discrimination. The discrimination is then reinforced by the very exclusion of the disadvantaged group because the exclusion fosters the belief, both within and outside the group, that the exclusion is the result of 'natural' forces, for example, that women 'just can't do the job.'"[18]

As the Canadian Human Rights Review Panel noted in its report,

> Looking at discrimination in this way recognizes that human activities, such as employment and the provision of services, proceed on the basis of assumptions and value judgments about the needs and capabilities of individuals. These assumptions often reflect ideas about the place in society of particular individuals because of their personal characteristics. This in turn may be reflected in the way the workplace is ordered, in the terms and conditions of employment, and in decisions about who should be hired and promoted. While some of these assumptions may be accurate, others are harmful, in that they create barriers to the full participation of individuals in the workplace or in access to services.[19]

The Court not only found there to be systemic discrimination, but also stressed the importance of a systemic remedy; "to combat systemic discrimination, it is essential to create a climate in which both negative practices and negative attitudes can be challenged and discouraged."[20] Here the Tribunal had ordered an employment equity plan, requiring the CN to hire one woman for every four blue-collar positions to be filled. The Court upheld this remedy, noting that the remedy served both to correct past wrongs and to prevent future discrimination by destroying discriminatory stereotypes and creating a critical mass of female employees that would encourage more women to apply.

(b) The Grounds

The grounds, or bases, upon which discrimination is prohibited are listed in each of the provincial and the federal human rights statutes. While there is considerable overlap across jurisdictions, there are also some significant differences. Several general observations about these grounds are in order. First, unlike section 15 of the *Charter*, which provides a non-exhaustive list of grounds, human rights legislation works from defined or closed lists. Thus, unlike the *Charter*, it is not possible to make an argument for the recognition of an analogous ground under human rights legislation.

While human rights legislation has traditionally protected against discrimination based upon grounds such as race, country of origin, sex, age, citizenship, and disability, other grounds—such as sexual orientation and family or marital status—have come to be recognized only more recently. One ground that continues to be controversial and inadequately protected is that of "social condition." While some provinces recognize limited forms of protection based on, for example, receipt of social assistance or source of income, Quebec is the only province to fully recognize social condition as a protected ground. The Canadian Human Rights Act Review Panel, in its report, strongly recommends the inclusion of social condition in the *Canadian Human Rights Act*. The review panel noted that it had heard more about poverty than any other issue, and documented the stereotypes and consequent discrimination routinely experienced by those living in conditions of poverty.[21] In seeking to elucidate the concept of social condition, the review panel identified both objective and subjective components. The objective component includes such factors as standing in society, occupation, income, and education (the social and economic indicators of disadvantage), while the subjective component encompasses how those occupying such social positions are regarded by others. As the Review Panel notes, "the idea that a group can suffer because of the perceptions of others and can be defined by those perceptions is contrary to the concept of equality. This is how stereotypes work."[22]

Two further observations regarding prohibited grounds are in order. First, each statute will set out prohibited grounds in relation to particular matters, such as the provision of services, employment, or accommodation. The prohibited grounds may vary depending upon the matter in issue. So, for example, in Ontario receipt of social assistance is a prohibited ground of discrimination in relation to the provision of accommodation, but not in relation to the provision of services, goods, and facilities.

The final observation is that the approach to human rights protection of creating a closed list of prohibited grounds has been widely criticized. In this pigeonhole approach, a recognition of the violation of one's right or dignity turns upon whether the affront can be neatly packaged within the pre-existing category. Many indignities cannot be boxed in this way. A related concern is that a person experiencing discrimination must choose a particular box when in reality, the experience often arises as a result of multiple and overlapping forms of discrimination.[23]

(c) The Procedures

As noted at the outset, human rights regimes are often designed both to create procedures that redress individual complaints regarding discrimination and to more systemically promote human rights and prevent discrimination. As one can readily imagine, in the context of limited and inadequate funding for human rights regimes, these goals compete with, rather than complement, one another. As discussed in Chapter 5, there has long been a concern in Ontario that in fact neither goal has been adequately pursued. Many hope that the new procedures described in Chapter 5—procedures that will shift more of the responsibility for individual complaints onto individual complainants—will free up the Commission to more vigorously pursue its role in preventing discrimination and promoting and advancing human rights.

(5) ENSURING ACCESSIBILITY

In Ontario the *Accessibility for Ontarians with Disabilities Act, 2005*[24] seeks to identify, remove and prevent barriers experienced by persons with disabilities in fully participating in the life of Ontario, with a goal of creating a barrier-free Ontario by 2025.[25] The *Act* applies to all individuals and entities, in both the public and private sectors, that provide goods and services, offer employment or accommodation, or own or occupy premises open to the public. The *Act* provides for the creation of standards development committees, each of which must include in its membership persons with disabilities, to develop standards in five areas: customer support; transportation; information; communication; built environment; and employment. Once developed and approved, individuals and organizations covered by the *Act* must comply with these standards and must report annually on their performance in relation to the standards. An earlier statute, the *Ontarians with Disabilities Act, 2001*, which applied only to the provincial and municipal governments, is to be repealed on a date to be named by proclamation.[26]

SELECTED READINGS

Anderson, Gavin, "Filling the "Charter Gap?": Human Rights Codes in the Private Sector" (1995) 33 Osgoode Hall L.J. 749.

Grant, Isbabel & Judith Mossof, "Disability and Performance Standards Under the Ontario Human Rights Code" (2002) 1 J.L. & Equality 205.

Howe, Robert Brian & David Johnson, *Restraining Equality: Human Rights Commissions in Canada* (Toronto, Ont.: University of Toronto Press, 2000).

Keene, Judith, "The Ontario Human Rights Code and the Right to Accommodation in the Workplace for Employees with Disabilities" (2001) 16 J.L. & Soc. Pol'y 185.

Ontario Human Rights Commission, "An Intersectional Approach to Discrimination: Addressing Multiple Grounds in Human Rights Claims" (Discussion Paper, October 9, 2001).

Ontario Human Rights Commission, Policy Guidelines on Disability and the Duty to Accommodate (November, 2000), available at www.ohrc.on.ca/en/issues/disability.

Pothier, Dianne, "Connecting Grounds of Discrimination to Real People's Real Experiences" (2001) 13 C.J.W.L.

Reaume, Denise, "Of Pigeonholes and Principles: A Reconsideration of Discrimination Law" (2002) 40 Osgoode Hall L.J. 113.

Report of the Canadian Human Rights Act Review Panel, chaired by former Justice Gerard V. LaForest, *Promoting Equality: A New Vision* (Ottawa: Department of Justice, June, 2000).

ENDNOTES

1. (U.K.), 30 & 31 Victoria, c. 3, at s. 92(13).
2. R.S.C. 1985, c. H-6.
3. Robert Brian Howe & David Johnson, *Restraining Equality: Human Rights Commissions in Canada* (Toronto, Ont.: University of Toronto Press, 2000) at 6.
4. Denise Reaume, "Of Pigeonholes and Principles: A Reconsideration of Discrimination Law" (2002) 40 Osgoode Hall L.J. 113 at 125-126.
5. S.S. 1947, c. 35.
6. See *supra* note 4 at 126.

7. R.S.O. 1990, c. H.19.
8. *Insurance Corp. of British Columbia v. Heerspink* (1982), [1982] 2 S.C.R. 145, 1982 CarswellBC 224, [1983] 1 W.W.R. 137, 39 B.C.L.R. 145, 137 D.L.R. (3d) 219, 82 C.L.L.C. 17,014, [1982] I.L.R. 1-1555, 3 C.H.R.R. D/1163, 43 N.R. 168, 1982 CarswellBC 742, [1982] S.C.J. No. 65 at para. 25; *O'Malley v. Simpson-Sears*, (sub nom. *Ontario Human Rights Commission v. Simpsons-Sears Ltd.*) [1985] 2 S.C.R. 536, [1985] S.C.J. No. 74, [1986] D.L.Q. 89 (note), 23 D.L.R. (4th) 321, 64 N.R. 161, 12 O.A.C. 241, 17 Admin. L.R. 89, 9 C.C.E.L. 185, 86 C.L.L.C. 17,002, 7 C.H.R.R. D/3102, 52 O.R. (2d) 799 (note), 1985 CarswellOnt 887, 1985 CarswellOnt 946; *A. v. B.* (2002), (sub nom. *B v. Ontario (Human Rights Commission)*) [2002] 3 S.C.R. 403, 2002 C.L.L.C. 230-037, (sub nom. *Human Rights Commission (Ont.) v. A*) 166 O.A.C. 1, 22 C.C.E.L. (3d) 153, 44 C.H.R.R. D/1, [2001] C.S.C.R. No. 29, [2002] S.C.J. No. 67, 2002 SCC 66, 2002 CarswellOnt 3554, 2002 CarswellOnt 3555, 219 D.L.R. (4th) 701, 294 N.R. 140, 99 C.R.R. (2d) 65, REJB 2002-35060 at para. 44.
9. See *supra* note 7 at s. 47(2).
10. (sub nom. *Tranchemontagne v. Ontario (Director, Disability Support Program)*) [2006] 1 S.C.R. 513, 42 Admin. L.R. (4th) 104, (sub nom. *Tranchemontagne v. Disability Support Program (Ont.)*) 210 O.A.C. 267, 2006 SCC 14, 2006 CarswellOnt 2350, 2006 CarswellOnt 2351, [2006] S.C.J. No. 14, 56 C.H.R.R. D/1, 347 N.R. 144, 266 D.L.R. (4th) 287.
11. See *supra* note 3 at 23.
12. (1985), [1985] 2 S.C.R. 561, 7 C.H.R.R. D/3093, [1986] D.L.Q. 88, 1985 CarswellNat 670, 23 D.L.R. (4th) 481, 63 N.R. 185, 17 Admin. L.R. 111, 9 C.C.E.L. 135, 86 C.L.L.C. 17,003, 1985 CarswellNat 144, [1985] S.C.J. No. 75.
13. *Ibid.*
14. *British Columbia (Public Service Employee Relations Commission) v. B.C.G.E.U.*, [1999] 3 S.C.R. 3, (sub nom. *Public Service Employee Relations Commission (B.C.) v. British Columbia Government & Service Employees' Union*) 127 B.C.A.C. 161, 207 W.A.C. 161, 35 C.H.R.R. D/257, 46 C.C.E.L. (2d) 206, 68 C.R.R. (2d) 1, 7 B.H.R.C. 437, 244 N.R. 145, 99 C.L.L.C. 230-028, [1999] 10 W.W.R. 1, 66 B.C.L.R. (3d) 253, (sub nom. *British Columbia (Public Service Employee Relations Commission) v. B.C.G.S.E.U.*) 176 D.L.R. (4th) 1, [1999] S.C.J. No. 46, 1999 CarswellBC 1907, 1999 CarswellBC 1908 at para. 50 (also referred to as "Meiorin").
15. *Ibid.* at para. 54.
16. *Ibid.* at para. 52.

17. 40 D.L.R. (4th) 193, 27 Admin. L.R. 172, [1987] 1 S.C.R. 1114, (sub nom. *Action Travail des Femmes v. Canadian National Railway*) 76 N.R. 161, 87 C.L.L.C. 17,022, 8 C.H.R.R. D/4210, 1987 CarswellNat 831, 1987 CarswellNat 905, [1987] S.C.J. No. 42.

18. *Ibid.* at para. 36. For an account of the implementation of the order and subsequent developments see: *The Human Rights Tribunal Order*, online: Department of Justice Canada <http://www.justice.gc.ca/char/en/action1.html>.

19. *Report of the Canadian Human Rights Act Review Panel, Promoting Equality: A New Vision*, online: Department of Justice <http://www.canadajustice.ca/char/en/chrareview_report_2000.pdf>.

20. 40 D.L.R. (4th) 193, 27 Admin. L.R. 172, [1987] 1 S.C.R. 1114, (sub nom. *Action Travail des Femmes v. Canadian National Railway*) 76 N.R. 161, 87 C.L.L.C. 17,022, 8 C.H.R.R. D/4210, 1987 CarswellNat 831, 1987 CarswellNat 905, [1987] S.C.J. No. 42 at para. 36.

21. *Supra* note 19 at 106.

22. *Ibid.* at 107.

23. See *supra* note 4, for usage of "pigeonholes" as a metaphor; see also Nitya Duclos, "Disappearing Women: Racial Minority Women in Human Rights Cases" (1993) 6 C.J.W.L. 25.

24. S.O. 2005, c. 11.

25. *Ibid.* at para. 9(3)(b).

26. S.O. 2001, c. 32; at the time of writing the proclamation date had not been announced.

4

Confronting the Courts

(1) THE COURT SYSTEM

"All rise."

"Oyez! Oyez! All persons having business before this Honourable Court draw near and you shall be heard. God save the Queen."

"Be seated please."[1]

The black-robed crier shuffles papers on a raised dais. Behind him or her, above everyone else sits a solemn faced person in silken robes, dwarfed by an enormous Coat of Arms. Beside the crier sits yet another person, not robed, fidgeting with a flat grey box—a recording machine! Two black-robed people stand at either end of a long table at the foot of the dais, respectfully facing the silken robe.

In a typical courtroom, civility, ceremony and solemnity prevail. The judge is always addressed by a standing, bowing participant and is referred to as "Your Honour."[2] Lawyers at the long counsel table are referred to as "counsel" in court, opposing lawyers refer to one another as "my friend." The clerk of the court opens the court, calls cases and records decisions on court documents while the court reporter records all the evidence in trial—every word! Symbols of solemnity proclaims that this is where JUSTICE is done.

Every person appearing before a court must enter into a predetermined role. In effect, before any matter is tried, both the person and the issue are re-defined in legal terms. The contrast with social work practice and training is marked. All social work training is directed at making people comfortable in an atmosphere of informality. The entire court process, by contrast, demands formality and assigns prescribed roles to all participants. The effect on clients is to increase, not lessen, their anxiety.

On many occasions, social workers are called upon to appear in court to give evidence in connection with their professional employment, or to assist clients who are summoned to appear as witnesses, or are themselves the subject of a court proceeding. On other occasions, clients are required to appear before a board or tribunal to have a dispute settled. For most citizens outside the legal profession the experience is intimidating and confusing, affecting client and social worker alike.

The courts are society's formal means of dispute resolution. They are divided into courts of civil and criminal jurisdiction. Criminal law matters are always determined in the courts, while civil matters are determined both in courts and in decision-making boards and tribunals. Both criminal and civil courts are further divided into courts of superior and inferior jurisdiction. Tribunals are special bodies set up to decide many specific matters, including immigration, labour, and income maintenance disputes such as social assistance benefits and unemployment insurance. The function of all courts is to decide disputes rationally and fairly according to established rules of procedure and evidence. Many boards and tribunals also have a decision-making function similar to that of the courts, but their powers are much narrower in scope since their authority is entirely statutory.

(2) A FIELD GUIDE TO THE PROPER COURT

Why a particular matter must be heard in a particular court is a mystery to the non-lawyer. Why can custody and access be decided either in a provincial family court or a superior court (in Ontario the Ontario Court of Justice and the Family Court branch of the Superior Court of Justice respectively), whereas family property matters must always be decided at the superior court level? In determining the appropriate court, it is not sufficient to be aware of the difference between civil and criminals matters. The issues to be addressed, the quantum or amount of money involved, the parties to the dispute, federal and provincial powers, and rules of procedure all combine to determine under what circumstance and in which court a case will be heard.[3]

To confound the confusion, the Province of Ontario, and other jurisdictions across Canada, have been engaged in major revisions and consolidations. For example, there has been considerable progress in combining all family matters in unified family courts which have authority to deal with all matters arising from family relationships, including all custody, support, property and child protection disputes. The monetary jurisdiction of provincial Small Claims Court continues to expand, and in Ontario, it is now a part of the Superior Court of Justice. Rules of the Court, which set out court procedure and the documents required to bring a claim before a judge, are also being subjected to major revisions.

Further initiatives have introduced various processes to reduce the number of cases going to trial and more efficiently deal with those that do. In order to encourage settlement in Ontario, a mandatory mediation program for all civil matters, except those dealing with family law, was introduced in January, 1999 in both Toronto and Ottawa and expanded to Windsor in December, 2002. Through this program litigants are required to participate in mediation in the early phases of the litigation process. A system of "case management" seeks to reduce delay and costs, encourage settlement, and narrow the issues for trial through the active participation of the court and the creation of timeframes for completion of steps in the litigation. These changes are designed to avoid costly and lengthy court proceedings where possible, which would likely be advantageous to all potential litigants. Non-adversarial methods of resolution are being encouraged in some instances, and mandated in others, but formal court proceedings are available if necessary, or if other approaches fail (see also Chapter 6).

(a) Superior Courts

The provinces, under subsection 92(14) of the *Constitution Act, 1867,* are given the power to make laws in relation to the administration of justice in the province, including the constitution, maintenance and organization of the provincial courts (both of civil and criminal jurisdiction), and the determination of procedure in civil matters. On the other hand, the federal government is granted power with respect to criminal procedure. The federal government is also granted the authority, under section 96, to appoint judges to the superior, district and county courts of each province (note that the district and county courts have more recently been merged with the superior courts). Thus, the superior courts, although established and administered by the provinces, are staffed by judges appointed and paid for by the federal government. The superior courts have jurisdiction over federal law (unless expressly taken away by an applicable federal statute), provincial law, and constitutional law.[4] Moreover the superior courts, or "section 96 courts," exercise all the adjudicative and remedial powers that were historically exercised by the courts of common law and equity.

In Ontario, the superior court is called the Superior Court of Justice, and has both trial and appellate divisions (the latter called the Court of Appeal). The Superior Court of Justice is further delineated by three branches: the Divisional Court (which exercises some appellate jurisdiction, as well as hearing appeals from decisions of administrative tribunals, applications for judicial review of tribunal decisions, and exercising a judicial supervisory role over them), the Family Court and the Small Claims Court. The Family Court of the Superior Court of Justice (often referred to as the Unified Family Court) is staffed by section 96 judges and where it sits in the province, exercises comprehensive family law jurisdiction. The Small Claims Court, with monetary jurisdiction up to $10,000 is somewhat of an anomaly; while all judges of the Superior Court of Justice are judges of the Small Claims Court, in practice the Small Claims Court is staffed primarily by provincially appointed judges and deputy judges (lawyers appointed by the Attorney General to act as deputy judges for a three-year term).

In civil matters, the superior courts have power to hear all monetary claims, have concurrent jurisdiction with the inferior (provincial) courts in many family law matters, and have exclusive jurisdiction to hear divorce petitions and family property claims. Jury trials are available with some exceptions, but are infrequently selected by the parties in civil matters. In criminal proceedings, the federal government has assigned substantial jurisdiction to the provincial inferior courts and consequently, the provincial courts hear the vast majority of criminal matters. However, trials by jury must be heard in a superior court. In many instances, the accused may elect to be tried by judge and jury or judge alone, and if the latter, the accused may choose between a superior or inferior court judge.

(b) Inferior Courts

While the inferior courts (so termed because of their location in the hierarchy of courts) are also maintained and administered by the provinces, the crucial feature that distinguishes them from the superior courts is the level of government responsible for the appointment, salary and tenure of their judges. Unlike the superior courts, the judges of the inferior courts (often referred to as "provincial" courts) are appointed and paid by the provinces. While the subject of the jurisdiction of the inferior courts is a complex one, it is important to appreciate that the jurisdiction of the inferior courts is more limited than that of the superior courts. Although it is certainly less than an exacting test, the approach of the Supreme Court of Canada in relation to the jurisdiction of the inferior courts has been to ask whether the province has attempted to bestow a jurisdiction which has historically been exercised by section 96 or superior courts. If answered affirmatively—that is, if the jurisdiction is characterized as one exercised historically by superior courts, or as an analogous jurisdiction—the province is precluded from vesting this jurisdiction in an inferior court. For example, in the 1938 *Adoption Reference*[5] the Supreme Court of Canada was asked to determine the validity of four Ontario statutes dealing with adoption, neglected children, "illegitimate" children and deserted wives, where the statutes conferred jurisdiction in relation to these matters upon inferior courts. The Supreme Court ruled that the powers exercised pursuant to these four statutes were more closely analogous to those historically exercised by the summary conviction (or inferior) courts, rather than section 96 courts, and therefore validated the conferral of jurisdiction. By contrast, in a later case, the Supreme Court ruled that jurisdiction over occupancy of the family residence, as it involved proprietary rights and a form of injunctive relief, was more closely analogous to the jurisdiction exercised by section 96 courts and therefore could not be conferred upon an inferior (provincial) court.[6]

It is also important to observe that the federal government, in relation to matters over which it has legislative competence, may expressly confer jurisdiction to adjudicate such matters upon an inferior court or tribunal. Significantly, it has done so in relation to many criminal law matters. Virtually all summary conviction (less serious) offences, all preliminary hearings of indictable offences and many indictable (more serious) offences are heard by the provincial courts.

In Ontario the inferior court is called the Ontario Court of Justice (formerly called the Ontario Court (provincial division)). In addition to jurisdiction in relation to many criminal law matters as described above, the Ontario Court of Justice exercises important jurisdiction in relation to the *Family Law Act*[7] (but not property), the *Children's Law Reform Act*,[8] and the *Child and Family Services Act*.[9] Moreover, the Ontario Court of Justice has been designated by Ontario as its youth court for the purposes of the *Youth Criminal Justice Act*,[10] giving it expansive jurisdiction over youth criminal justice matters (but note, some youth justice proceedings—such as a trial by jury—must be heard by a superior court judge).[11] It is also the Ontario Court of Justice that hears matters arising under the *Provincial Offences Act of Ontario*,[12] which applies to all provincial legislation that creates a penalty upon violation. Provincial legislation includes a broad range of violations such as environmental offences, violations of municipal bylaws, and highway traffic and liquor offences.

(c) Supreme Court of Canada

Established by the federal government, the Supreme Court of Canada is a general court of appeal for Canada, with power to hear appeals from the highest level of court from each province. Appeals may be taken on matters of law either with leave (permission) of the court or as a matter of right (in a limited range of cases), depending on the decision being appealed. The Court also hears reference cases, where particular questions posed by the federal government, often constitutional in nature, are referred to the

Court by the federal government in order to receive the Court's opinion (each province also has legislation enabling the provincial government to direct a reference to the provincial court of appeal). While in theory the opinion of the court is advisory only, in practice the rulings are followed by the parties and followed by subsequent courts.[13] A recent example where the federal government directed a reference to the Supreme Court of Canada was in relation to same-sex marriage. The government asked the Court to provide its opinion on the following questions:

1. Is the annexed *Proposal for an Act respecting certain aspects of legal capacity for marriage for civil purposes* within the exclusive legislative authority of the Parliament of Canada? If not, in what particular or particulars, and to what extent?

2. If the answer to question 1 is yes, is section 1 of the proposal, which extends capacity to marry to persons of the same sex, consistent with the *Canadian Charter of Rights and Freedoms*? If not, in what particular or particulars, and to what extent?

3. Does the freedom of religion guaranteed by paragraph 2(*a*) of the *Canadian Charter of Rights and Freedoms* protect religious officials from being compelled to perform a marriage between two persons of the same sex that is contrary to their religious beliefs?

4. Is the opposite-sex requirement for marriage for civil purposes, as established by the common law and set out for Quebec in section 5 of the *Federal Law—Civil Law Harmonization Act, No. 1*, consistent with the *Canadian Charter of Rights and Freedoms*? If not, in what particular or particulars and to what extent?[14]

One further important feature of the Supreme Court of Canada lies in the fact that its decisions are binding on all other courts and must be followed by them.

(d) Federal Court

While as a general matter the provincially constituted superior courts hear and adjudicate matters of federal law, the *Constitution Act, 1867* does authorize the federal Parliament to establish federal courts for the purpose of administering federal laws. The Federal Court of Canada, first constituted in 1875 as the Exchequer Court, presently exercises jurisdiction over particular areas of federal law; for example, trademarks, immigration, and admiralty. The Federal Court also hears appeals from, and applications for judicial review of, decisions of federal administrative tribunals. Appeals from the Federal Court, Trial Division, are heard by the Appeal Division and further appeals may be heard by the Supreme Court of Canada.

(e) Boards, Commissions and Tribunals

In addition to the civil and criminal court systems, a number of special-purpose commissions, boards, and tribunals have been established under both federal and provincial legislation. Examples of federally established tribunals include the Immigration and Refugee Appeal Board and the Canada Employment Insurance Commission Board of Referees. Provincially constituted boards include the Social Benefits Tribunal, the Workplace Safety and Insurance Board, and the Criminal Injuries Compensation Board. A board's purpose is to provide a simplified means of dispute resolution outside of the court system. Generally speaking, hearings before tribunals are usually less formal than proceedings before the courts to provide a quicker and less expensive determination of the issues. However, many tribunals have built up their own precedents and procedures over the years, often as a result of arguments raised by participating parties about the requirements of "natural justice" or "fairness" (see Chapter 2), with the result that hearings before some tribunals have become increasingly complex and protracted, often requiring legal representation to protect the interests of the parties. In many instances, statutory boards and tribunals may permit parties to be represented by agents, including social workers. In such cases, representation by an agent is at the discretion of the chair of the hearing and is not necessarily a right.[15]

All tribunals have a number of common characteristics. Principally, they are entirely creatures of the statutes which create them; they possess only those powers granted in the governing Acts. The tribunal members may be drawn from members of the public at large or from those with special expertise, such as labour and management representatives on labour boards, or from lawyers who may comprise a majority or minority.

(f) The *Statutory Powers Procedures Act*[16]

The legal concepts of "natural justice" and "fairness" discussed in Chapter 2 apply specifically to the manner in which tribunals conduct their hearings and arrive at their decisions. Where a tribunal, by statute, is granted a power of decision in relation to particular matters, the *Statutory Powers Procedure Act* ("SPPA") will apply, unless the statute that creates the tribunal specially exempts it from all or some of the provisions of the *SPPA*. At a broad and general level, the *SPPA* requires tribunals, in exercising their statutory powers of decision, to comport with the requirements of natural justice and fairness, including the right of those affected to adequate notice of a hearing, the right to call and examine evidence and to present evidence and submissions, the right to cross-examine, and the right to reasons for a decision. In addition to the general procedural requirements of the *SPPA,* the *SPPA* authorizes tribunals to create their own detailed procedures (which must conform with the *SPPA* and with their respective enabling statutes). Hence, in dealing with any particular tribunal—and the clients of social workers are far more likely to have matters before tribunals than before a court—it is imperative to discern its unique procedural, requirements.

SELECTED READINGS

Gall, Gerald, *The Canadian Legal System* 4th ed. (Toronto: Thomson Canada Ltd., 1995).

Ontario Civil Justice Review, *First Report* and *Supplemental and Final Report* (Ontario: Ministry of the Attorney General, March, 1995 and November, 1996, respectively).

Report of the Ontario Courts Inquiry, *The Zuber Commission Report* (Ontario: Ministry of the Attorney General, 1987).

Hogg, Peter, *Constitutional Law of Canada*, Student ed. (Toronto: Thomson Canada Ltd., 2005).

WEBSITES

Canadian Forum on Civil Justice, www.cfcj-fcjc.org

ENDNOTES

1. The cry which opens every sitting of the General Sessions of the Peace in the Ontario Superior Court of Justice sitting in criminal matters.
2. Report of the Ontario Courts Inquiry, *The Zuber Commission Report* (Ontario: Ministry of the Attorney General, 1987).
3. See Gerald Gall, *The Canadian Legal System*, 4th ed. (Toronto: Thomson Canada Ltd., 1995) at Chapter 7.
4. Peter Hogg, *Constitutional Law of Canada*, Student ed. (Toronto: Thomson Canada Ltd., 2005) at 179.
5. *Reference re Adoption Act (Ontario)*, [1938] S.C.R. 398, 71 C.C.C. 110, [1938] 3 D.L.R. 497, 1938 CarswellNat 49.
6. See *supra* note 4 at 209-213.
7. R.S.O. 1990, c. F.3.
8. R.S.O. 1990, c. C.12.
9. R.S.O. 1990, c. C.11.

10. S.C. 2002, c. 1.
11. *Courts of Justice Act*, R.S.O. 1990, c. C.43, s. 38(3); *Youth Criminal Justice Act*, S.C. 2002, c. 1, s. 13.
12. R.S.O. 1990, c. P.33.
13. See *supra* note 4 at 243-48.
14. *Same-Sex Marriage, Re* (2004), [2004] 3 S.C.R. 698, 246 D.L.R. (4th) 193, 2004 CarswellNat 4422, 2004 CarswellNat 4423, 2004 SCC 79, [2003] S.C.C.A. No. 325, 12 R.F.L. (6th) 153, 328 N.R. 1, 125 C.R.R. (2d) 122, REJB 2004-81254, [2004] S.C.J. No. 75 at paras. 2-3.
15. See Chapter 5 for a discussion of the regulatory regime for paralegals.
16. R.S.O. 1990, c. S.22.

5

The Litigation Process

(1) ADVERSARIAL ADJUDICATION

In Canada, the dominant method of dispute resolution, both in the civil and criminal context, has long been that of adversarial adjudication. Adjudication, in essence, captures the idea of an impartial, third-party decision-maker who renders a binding decision based upon the evidence adduced and arguments advanced by the parties to the dispute. The "adversarial" nature of the process, as noted in Chapter 2, denotes the assignment of responsibility to each party to fully advance his or her respective case and to fully challenge the case of his or her opponent. The theory behind adversarial adjudication is that the truth will most likely emerge when opposing parties to a dispute engage in a battle fuelled by self-interest and competitive motivation. Indeed, war metaphors are commonly invoked to describe the adversarial process. The *Rules of Professional Conduct* that govern lawyers' conduct make clear that in the role of advocate, the lawyer's duty is openly and zealously partisan.

> The lawyer has a duty to the client to raise fearlessly every issue, advance every argument, and ask every question, no matter how distasteful, which the lawyer thinks will help the client's case. The lawyer must also endeavour to obtain for the client the benefit of every remedy and defence authorized by law.

> In adversary proceedings the lawyer's function as advocate is openly and necessarily partisan. Accordingly, the lawyer is not obliged (save as required by law or under these rules and subject to the duties of a prosecutor set out below) to assist an adversary or advance matters derogatory to the client's case.[1]

(a) Party Autonomy

Adversarial adjudication is characterized by two central features: party autonomy and party prosecution.[2] The principle of party autonomy provides that the decision of whether a legal complaint or proceeding will be initiated belongs to the person or entity that has been aggrieved. In other words, the justice system does not proactively respond to legal wrongs in the world, but rather responds only when called upon to do so by a party asserting a legal wrong. While in the view of many commentators this approach respects the autonomy of individuals, critics have argued that such an approach obscures the reality that the vast majority of people who experience legal wrongs either do not know a legal wrong has been committed or are unable (due to lack of resources, vulnerability to retaliation, etc.) to proceed with a legal complaint. Others question why autonomy should be the governing value. In one famous American case for example, a man on death row chose not to engage the available legal processes to contest his sentence. His mother, however, sought to do so. The principle of party autonomy was invoked to deny his mother "standing" to challenge his sentence.

(b) Party Prosecution

The second principle, party prosecution, dictates that it is the parties, rather than the judge, who have responsibility for the development of the case; what evidence to call, what arguments to make, etc. are all decisions that rest with the parties. In other words, the parties have ultimate responsibility for how the case will be presented. By contrast, the judge (or other decision-maker) is to remain largely passive, intervening only for the purposes of clarification. Indeed, if a judge actively participates in the examination or cross-examination of a witness, for example, his or her decision will likely be set aside on appeal on the grounds that the judge improperly "descended into the forum." The rationale for this approach lies in the concern that the impartiality of judges would be compromised if they were to take an active role at trial.

(2) INQUISITIONAL ADJUDICATION

Adversarial adjudication may be contrasted with inquisitorial adjudication. Unlike its adversarial counterpart, inquisitorial adjudication places responsibility for the development of the case upon (or primarily upon) an institution or person other than the actual parties to the lawsuit.[3] Similar to the adversarial approach, however, a binding decision is rendered by an impartial third-party at the end of the inquisitorial process.[4] Inquisitorial legal processes are common in much of Europe and are often found in the context of administrative regimes within Canada.

(a) Ontario's Human Rights Regime

In Ontario, a substantial controversy recently erupted over proposed changes to Ontario's *Human Rights Code*. For many years the Ontario Human Rights Commission functioned through a largely—although not entirely—inquisitorial system. Persons who believed their human rights had been violated filed a complaint with the Commission, and the Commission, rather than the claimant and respondent (the person or entity against whom the complaint is made), was responsible for the investigation of the complaint. If the complaint was well-founded and the matter not settled between the parties, the complaint could be referred by the Commission to the Human Rights Tribunal for adjudication. While parties could, if they chose, retain their own lawyer to provide representation, the Commission had responsibility to carry the case forward, presenting the evidence and arguments to the Tribunal. In a review of these procedures undertaken in 1992, a pervasive concern expressed by both claimants and respondents was the lack of control they had over the development of their cases. While they valued and appreciated that the Commission provided the funding and expertise for investigations and case development, they expressed the desire for greater involvement and control with regard to how the case was shaped.[5]

In 2006, the passage of Bill 107, *An Act to Reform the Ontario Human Rights Act*, shifted the model from one that was primarily inquisitorial to one more closely approximating the adversarial approach. Rather than the Commission being charged with investigation and carriage of cases, complainants will, when the new system is fully implemented, have direct access to the tribunal and responsibility for investigating and presenting their own cases.[6] While human rights advocates and equality seeking communities were in agreement that many problems existed with the operation of the human rights regime, they were—and continue to be—divided over whether the reforms will enhance the protection and promotion of human rights in Ontario. While the new legislation includes the creation of the Human Rights Legal Support Centre, which would provide legal support to individuals throughout the province, many worry that claimants will not be able to access the legal advice, information, and representation that is needed to successfully bring their claims. This is especially of concern for those who experience multiple and intersecting forms of discrimination and consequent vulnerability, such as those who are consumers of mental health services. On the other hand, proponents of the reforms applaud the control that parties have over their own cases as well as their ability to access the tribunal directly for authoritative decision-making.

While this shift moves the human rights regime in Ontario much closer to a pure adversarial adjudication model, interestingly, the legislation does contemplate that the tribunal, in crafting its procedural rules, may adopt inquisitorial elements. So, for example, the legislation authorizes the tribunal to include among its procedural rules the ability of the tribunal to conduct examinations-in-chief or cross-examinations of witnesses itself, a practice unheard of in a purely adversarial process.

(3) ALTERNATIVE DISPUTE RESOLUTION

In addition to the departures from adversarialism, there has been an increasing shift away from adjudication toward what is often characterized as "alternative dispute resolution," a topic that we canvass in Chapter 6. However, it is adversarial adjudication that continues to dominate the pre-trial and trial phases of both civil and criminal proceedings. Before turning to a fuller description of both the criminal and civil litigation processes, a brief description of the distinction between civil and criminal law is essential.

(4) CIVIL AND CRIMINAL LAW

Civil law deals with private matters such as property, contracts, financial matters, matrimonial disputes, custody of children, private wrongs, civil rights, and some regulatory matters. Civil law is largely, although by no means exclusively, a provincial responsibility. Some civil matters which affect the whole nation, such as immigration and telecommunications, are federal.

On the other hand, criminal law deals with prohibited acts that are "crimes" or offences against society at large and are punished by the state on behalf of all of society. Criminal law and criminal procedure are exclusively within federal jurisdiction. There are also large numbers of provincial statutes that are regulatory in nature, create penalties, and are dealt with as "quasi-criminal" offences. The same conduct may sometimes incur both civil damages and criminal penalties. For example, a person who is criminally convicted of wilfully damaging property may also be required to pay civil damages for the same act.

(a) Civil Actions

In Ontario civil actions before the Superior Court of Justice are commenced by the issuance of either a statement of claim or notice of application.[7] The statement of claim commences a proceeding, known as an action, where particular pre-trial steps are taken followed by a trial if the dispute is not resolved. The notice of application, by contrast, commences a proceeding known as an application where different pre-trial steps take place. For instance, unlike an action where the evidence is tendered at trial through the calling of witnesses, the evidence on an application is gathered through affidavits (written documents sworn as to their truth by the "deponent;" the person whose statements are contained in the affidavit) and cross-examinations on those affidavits outside of court. Applications are usually appropriate for cases where there are no serious issues regarding the credibility of witnesses; that is, where it will not be necessary for a judge to observe a witness giving evidence in court in order to assess his or her demeanour. For example, applications are used where a document, such as a will, must be interpreted or where there are no material facts in dispute. Both the action and the application entail numerous steps designed to put the other party on full notice of the case they are up against.

In an action, the originating document, known as the statement of claim, determines the parameters of the case. It contains a succinct statement of the material facts upon which the claim is based, and those facts must give rise to a cause of action known in law. For example, in a well-known case, *Jane Doe v. Metropolitan Toronto (Municipality) Commissioners of Police*,[8] Jane Doe alleged that the police had been negligent by failing to warn women—including herself—that a serial rapist was targeting particular women in her neighbourhood.[9] The defendants challenged her claim arguing that even if all the facts alleged in her statement of claim were true, they did not amount to a cause of action recognized at law. The defendants were unsuccessful in this argument and ultimately Jane Doe won not only on this procedural challenge, but also on the substantive argument, with the court holding that the police had a duty to warn, had failed to do so, and were liable in damages to her.

The statement of claim must be served personally on all those named as defendants; that is, upon all those who the plaintiff asserts are liable. The defendants must then prepare, serve, and file a Statement of Defence or risk being noted into default. A default judgment occurs when, in the defendant's absence, the plaintiff is granted an order from the court. Together the statement of claim, the statement of defence and any counter-claims that may arise are known as the "pleadings."[10]

Each of the parties to the action is required to prepare an Affidavit of Documents, which lists all documents in their possession that are relevant to the matters at issue, and must provide this to the opposing side. Each party is also entitled to copies of the other side's documents. In some respects, this requirement represents a departure from a pure adversarial model in that a party is required to provide documents to the other side whether they advance or hinder his or her case. This is in stark contrast to oral testimony, where a party has no obligation to advance "matters derogatory" to his or her own case. The theory of adversarialism maintains that one has no duty to assist one's opponent; if there are weaknesses in one's case, it is up to the other side to discover them. That said, often lawyers will want to strategically advance evidence that is harmful to a client's case, rather than risk having it adduced as part of the opponent's case, where it may do even greater harm.

The other major pre-trial step is that of examination for discovery. This is a process whereby each party is entitled to examine all parties named in the proceeding who are "adverse in interest." The examination, conducted under oath, does not take place in court but rather before an "official examiner," often in the offices of one of the lawyers representing a party to the dispute. The official examiner prepares a *verbatim* transcript of the questions asked and answers given. Examinations for discovery serve an important notice giving function, enabling parties to know more fully the strength and weaknesses of their respective positions.

A system of active case management by a judge or case management master applies in some parts of Ontario. As discussed in Chapter 6, the case management system is intended to move matters more expeditiously through the pre-trial process and to facilitate the early resolution of disputes.

The vast majority of civil trials are heard by a judge alone rather than by a jury. The basic contours of the trial entail first the presentation by the plaintiff of all of his or her evidence (witnesses and documents), followed by evidence proffered by the defendant, and then closing arguments by both plaintiff and defendant. The evidence of witnesses proceeds with the party calling the witness conducting a direct examination, otherwise known as an examination-in-chief, in which leading questions (a question which implies an answer) are prohibited.[11] Following the examination-in-chief, the opposing party is given the opportunity to cross-examine the same witness. During the cross-examination, leading questions are permitted and therefore, tend to be the most common method of framing questions. Once the cross-examination is complete, the party who originally called the witness may then undertake a "re-direct" examination, which is limited to new matters raised in the cross-examination.

(b) Criminal Cases

Both criminal law and criminal procedure are matters that fall under federal jurisdiction. The most important statutes creating criminal offences are the *Criminal Code*[12] and the *Controlled Drugs and Substances Act*.[13] However, full criminal offences can also be created by other federal statutes (for example, offence provisions in the *Income Tax Act* have been interpreted as full criminal offences). In addition to the federal criminal law power, provinces may create offence provisions in relation to matters that fall within provincial jurisdiction. As discussed in Chapter 19, these sorts of offences are often referred to as "quasi-criminal" or "provincial offences." In Ontario, the procedure governing the prosecution of these "quasi-criminal" offences is governed by the *Provincial Offences Act*.[14] Below, we focus on the procedures contained in the *Criminal Code*.

There are three types of criminal offences under the *Criminal Code*: indictable, summary conviction, and hybrid or "Crown election." Indictable offences are generally the more serious, such as murder, sexual assault with a weapon, and robbery. Due to the serious nature of an indictable offence, the trial process for these cases is more formal and complex. The person charged, who is referred to as the "accused," or "defendant," is usually entitled to a preliminary hearing before a provincial court judge to determine whether there is sufficient evidence to commit the accused to stand trial. The test applied, by a judge, in making this decision is whether a cautious jury, properly instructed, could convict based on the evidence presented at the preliminary hearing.

If the accused is committed for trial, in most cases he or she is entitled to elect to be tried by a judge of the provincial court, a judge of the superior court, or by a judge and jury in the superior court. Depending upon the circumstances of each case and whether or not a mandatory minimum sentence is imposed by the *Criminal Code* or another statute, penalties upon conviction range from a discharge to life imprisonment. The sentencing hearing is far less formal than the trial, and a much greater range of information is admissible.[15]

Summary conviction offences, as the name suggests, are prosecuted by a simpler and more expeditious procedure. They are initiated by the laying of an information—the document which details the charge—and are tried by a provincial court judge without a jury. Summary offences are generally less serious in nature, such as causing a disturbance, trespass at night and committing an indecent act. The maximum penalty to be imposed upon conviction is a fine of no more than two thousand dollars or six months imprisonment, or both.

Crown election means that the prosecutor has the right to proceed either summarily or by indictment. If the Crown elects to proceed by indictment, it will proceed as other indictable offences do. Similarly, if the Crown elects to proceed summarily, the less formal procedure for summary conviction offences will apply. So too, the penalty framework will be determined based upon the Crown's election. Examples of hybrid offences are assault, assault with a weapon and sexual assault (sexual assault with a weapon and aggravated sexual assault are indictable offences). Hybrid offences are discussed in more detail in Chapter 19.

As with civil proceedings, criminal proceedings are held in open court. However, there are certain exceptions where the public will be excluded. Amendments to the *Criminal Code* in 2005, for example, expanded the circumstances in which the public will be excluded where the matter being tried involves a young person. Subsection 486(1) of the *Code* authorizes a judge to exclude all or a portion of the public from all or some of a proceeding, in the interest of public morals, the maintenance of order or the proper administration of justice. Ensuring that the interests of witnesses under 18 years of age are safeguarded in all proceedings is then expressly enumerated as a feature of the proper administration of justice.

It is also important to note that every accused person has the constitutional right to a fair trial, and the right to be tried within reasonable time.[16] If not tried within a reasonable time, the charges against the accused may be stayed.[17]

While it may seem axiomatic that full pre-trial disclosure is essential to the accused's right to a fair trial, and to his or her ability to make full answer and defence in particular, pre-trial disclosure practices in the criminal context are far less developed than in the civil context. A 1991 decision of the Supreme Court of Canada, in *R. v. Stinchcombe*,[18] established the right of accused persons to full disclosure by the Crown of all relevant information, whether inculpatory or exculpatory. There is no corresponding obligation on the defence (the accused) to provide disclosure to the Crown; the accused has a constitutional right to silence while it is the Crown who bears the onus of establishing the accused's guilt beyond a reasonable doubt. Mr. Justice Sopinka, writing for the majority in *Stinchcombe*, places disclosure in the context of the historical unfolding of the adversary system, as quoted below. Note as well, the emphasis placed on the role of the Crown in criminal proceedings to ensure that justice is done, not that a conviction is secured.

> Production and discovery were foreign to the adversary process of adjudication in its earlier history when the element of surprise was one of the accepted weapons in the arsenal of the adversaries. This applied to both

criminal and civil proceedings. Significantly, in civil proceedings this aspect of the adversary process has long since disappeared, and full discovery of documents and oral examination of parties and even witnesses are familiar features of the practice. This change resulted from acceptance of the principle that justice was better served when the element of surprise was eliminated from the trial and the parties were prepared to address issues on the basis of complete information of the case to be met. Surprisingly, in criminal cases in which the liberty of the subject is usually at stake, this aspect of the adversary system has lingered on. While the prosecution bar has generally co-operated in making disclosure on a voluntary basis, there has been considerable resistance to the enactment of comprehensive rules which would make the practice mandatory. This may be attributed to the fact that proposals for reform in this regard do not provide for reciprocal disclosure by the defence (see 1974 Working Paper at pp. 29-31; 1984 Report at pp. 13-15; Marshall Commission Report, *infra*, Vol. 1, at pp. 242-44).

It is difficult to justify the position which clings to the notion that the Crown has no legal duty to disclose all relevant information. The arguments against the existence of such a duty are groundless while those in favour, are, in my view, overwhelming. The suggestion that the duty should be reciprocal may deserve consideration by this Court in the future but is not a valid reason for absolving the Crown of its duty. The contrary contention fails to take account of the fundamental difference in the respective roles of the prosecution and the defence. In *R. v. Boucher* (1954), (sub nom. *Boucher v. R.*) [1955] S.C.R. 16, 110 C.C.C. 263, 1954 CarswellQue 14, 20 C.R. 1, Rand J. states, at pp. 23-24 [S.C.R.]:

> It cannot be over-emphasized that the purpose of a criminal prosecution is not to obtain a conviction, it is to lay before a jury what the Crown considers to be credible evidence relevant to what is alleged to be a crime. Counsel have a duty to see that all available legal proof of the facts is presented: it should be done firmly and pressed to its legitimate strength but it must also be done fairly. The role of prosecutor excludes any notion of winning or losing; his function is a matter of public duty than which in civil life there can be none charged with greater personal responsibility. It is to be efficiently performed with an ingrained sense of the dignity, the seriousness and the justness of judicial proceedings.

I would add that the fruits of the investigation which are in the possession of counsel for the Crown are not the property of the Crown for use in securing a conviction but the property of the public to be used to ensure that justice is done. In contrast, the defence has no obligation to assist the prosecution and is entitled to assume a purely adversarial role toward the prosecution. The absence of a duty to disclose can, therefore, be justified as being consistent with this role.[19]

Subsequent to *Stinchcombe*, a major review of disclosure was undertaken by an advisory committee to the Attorney General and new disclosure rules were implemented.[20]

(c) Appeals

As a safeguard, the decisions of trial judges, justices, and chairs of tribunals are subject to appeal or to judicial review where an error is alleged, unless specifically exempt by statute. Reasons for appeal or judicial review are classified as "errors in fact," "errors in law," "procedural errors," and "jurisdictional errors." Errors in fact are said to occur when it is alleged that the facts presented in evidence at the trial or hearing have been improperly interpreted by the judge or chairperson. Errors in law are said to occur where it is believed that the relevant law has been misapplied. When a procedural right has been denied or omitted, a procedural error can be alleged, and where the decision-maker's power to hear a matter is challenged, it is then described as a jurisdictional error.

If an appeal is contemplated, it is always advisable to consult a lawyer without delay or the opportunity may be lost. There are strict time limitations governing appeals in both civil and criminal matters.

(5) DRAMATIS PERSONAE

(a) Judges

The function of all judges is to decide the matters brought before them in an impartial and fair manner. In the course of a trial, the judge makes rulings on trial procedure and on the admissibility of evidence but, as noted, generally takes no initiative in the presentation of evidence. One exception may occur in family law matters, where a judge will sometimes play an active role, since a fully adversarial proceeding is not necessarily the appropriate means of resolving a family dispute.

Not all judges have equal decision-making powers. As discussed in Chapters 2 and 4, the *Constitution Act, 1867* gives both the federal government and the provincial governments certain powers. All superior court judges of a province are appointed by the federal government, as are Federal Court judges and judges of the Supreme Court of Canada. Superior court judges sit in the superior court as well as the Court of Appeal for the province. In contrast to the superior court, provincial court judges are appointed by the province. The source of a judicial appointment and the court to which judges are appointed determines their jurisdiction to hear and adjudicate particular matters. Judges of the superior courts have the broadest power, as they are able to hear most matters. Matters which they are excluded from hearing are set out in statutes. For example, the *Youth Criminal Justice Act* confers upon a "youth court," which is a provincial court designated by the province, jurisdiction to hear and determine most matters related to criminal offences committed by young persons.

Impartiality of judges is preserved by their security of tenure, except in the most extreme circumstances. Judges are therefore independent of the government that appoints them, or any other government body for that matter.

(b) Masters

Masters are judicial officers of the Superior Court of Justice in Ontario, and are appointed by the province. Masters hear and decide the vast majority of "motions" (hearings to resolve disputes that may arise over the application of the procedural rules). For example, if in the course of an examination for discovery a party refuses to answer a question posed by the other side on the basis that the question is irrelevant, the party who asked the question may bring the matter before a Master, who would render a binding decision as to whether the question must be answered.

(c) Justices of the Peace

Justices of the Peace, commonly referred to as "JPs," may have a significant impact on the lives of social work clients since they have decision-making powers in criminal and "quasi-criminal" matters, albeit in limited circumstances.[21] Their jurisdiction is conferred primarily by the *Criminal Code* and *Provincial Offences Act*, but other statutes also confer jurisdiction. "JPs" are the persons who issue summonses to appear in court and warrants to apprehend upon failure to appear. They also preside over most bail (judicial interim release) hearings. "JPs" also have the power to conduct trials for most provincial offences, including highway traffic offences, bylaw infractions, and liquor law violations. Justices of the Peace are appointed by the province, and legal training is not a pre-requisite to appointment.

(d) Parties

Persons appearing before the court who are named in the initiating document are referred to as "parties." In civil actions in the superior courts they are called "plaintiff" and "defendant", and in applications, "applicant" and "respondent." Similary, in Ontario family law proceedings, the parties are referred to as "applicant" and "respondent."

In criminal matters the parties are always the Crown, who represents the state, and the accused person. The Crown is represented by a "Crown prosecutor" or Crown attorney. The accused person is referred to as the "defendant" or the "accused."

On appeal, the party initiating the appeal is called the "appellant" and the other party, the "respondent."

(e) Lawyers

In serious civil actions or criminal proceedings, parties are often represented by lawyers, who are referred to as "counsel" in the court. All lawyers practising in Canada are members of their provincial Law Society, which controls admission to the profession in the province, establishes rules of conduct, and is responsible for the enforcement of the rules. In order to appear as counsel in superior court matters, whether civil or criminal, the lawyer must have been admitted to the Bar of the province. In all indictable criminal proceedings, both the Crown prosecutor and defence counsel must be members of the Bar. Only in certain provincial court matters may the party be represented by someone other than a lawyer, although a party is always able to speak on his or her own behalf. Increasingly, parties appearing in court, on family law matters in particular, are without legal counsel, and representing themselves.

Lawyers are officers of the court in which they appear, and are therefore obligated to assist the court. At the same time, they are retained by one of the parties and have a duty to zealously advance and defend the interests of that client. As a result, actions which are seen as harsh or unreasonable from a social work perspective may be considered appropriate and necessary to the lawyer who is trying to protect his or her own client's interests in an adversarial system.

(f) Crown Attorneys

In criminal matters, the Attorney General or Solicitor General of a province or the Attorney General of Canada, as representative of the Crown, has responsibility for the prosecution of criminal offences. The duty is delegated to assistant Crown attorneys, who are agents of the Attorney General and conduct criminal prosecutions at all court levels. As part of the prosecutorial function, Crown attorneys advise the police with respect to the evidence required to sustain a criminal charge, decide whether a charge which has been laid should proceed, and make submissions to the court with respect to bail pending trial and to sentencing upon conviction. As noted above, the duty of the Crown is not to secure a conviction, but to ensure that justice is done. The Rules of Professional Conduct provide that, "[w]hen engaged as a prosecutor, the lawyer's prime duty is not to seek to convict but to see that justice is done through a fair trial on the merits. The prosecutor exercises a public function involving much discretion and power and must act fairly and dispassionately."[22]

(g) Agents/Paralegals

Non-lawyers who provide forms of legal advice and assistance without the supervision of a lawyer are frequently referred to as "paralegals." In Ontario, as in other jurisdictions, there has been a long debate regarding the appropriate role and regulatory framework for paralegals. On the one hand, the work of paralegals may enhance access to justice, especially for those with limited financial resources. Not only are the services of paralegals generally less expensive than lawyers, but in some areas of law, particular paralegals have developed substantial expertise that enables them to provide high quality legal advice and representation. On the other hand, an ongoing issue of concern has been that until recently, paralegals were unregulated; anyone could offer particular legal services (although always limited by provincial legislation regulating the legal profession[23]), no training thresholds were in place, and no system of insurance protected clients in the event of negligence. After many reports and protracted negotiations, the Law Society of Upper Canada now regulates paralegals in Ontario. The regime, which came into place as of May, 2007, prohibits anyone other than a person licensed under the *Act* from practicing law or offering legal services.[24] The *Act* contemplates various gradations of licenses in relation to the provision of legal services.[25] One category of license authorizes licensed paralegals to provide advice, representation and to negotiate on a client's behalf in relation to specific matters: Small Claims Court cases; summary conviction criminal cases that fall under the *Provincial Offences Act* and are tried in the Ontario Court of Justice; and cases heard before tribunals created by either the provincial or federal government. While a transitional provision will enable some of those with existing paralegal practices to be licensed, on a going-forward basis paralegals will be required to complete an accredited educational program in order to obtain a license. Of particular mention, in Ontario paralegals cannot be licensed to provide legal services in relation to family law. The regulation of paralegals is a matter of provincial jurisdiction; therefore, the particulars of each provincial regulatory framework should be consulted.

Bylaw 4 of the Law Society of Upper Canada provides some exceptions to the general prohibition on providing legal services without a license, some of which are relevant to social work practice.[26] It is important for social workers in particular practice contexts to ascertain whether their work is caught by the definition of "legal services" and if so, whether it falls within an exemption, under Bylaw 4. Discussions are presently under way between the Ontario College of Social Workers and Social Service Workers and the Law Society of Upper Canada to try to provide greater clarity.

(i) Immigration Consultants

It is also important to note that a separate and newly created regime governs the regulation of immigration paralegals or consultants. The Canadian Society of Immigration Consultants sets out educational requirements and standards of practices for immigration consultants. At present, Immigration and Citizenship Canada will only deal with those client representatives who are either a member of a provincial law society (a lawyer in good standing) or a member of the Canadian Society of Immigration Consultants. An appreciation of the background to this new regulatory framework is important, since while the risks to clients have been diminished they have certainly not been extinguished; concerns about some consultants continuing to exploit vulnerable newcomers to Canada continue to exist. The Report of the Advisory Committee on Regulating Immigration Consultants describes the nature of the risks.

> For many years, there have been many concerns voiced about the conduct of immigration consultants both inside and outside of Canada. Although there are many consultants who conduct their work in an ethical manner, there are many who do not. These unethical consultants and their behaviour—often criminal—have been the subject of many media reports over the past years. This behaviour harms Canada's reputation abroad. It harms Canada's national security. It harms vulnerable applicants and it causes serious problems for Canada's economic self-interest. We know that some consultants are involved in people smuggling. We know that some immigration consultants use, or fabricate, fraudulent documents for aliens to enter this country. We know that some immigration consultants abuse their client's trust by promising the impossible and failing to deliver. We know that some immigration consultants charge exorbitant fees for their services.

> And we know that some immigration consultants have little or no training, education or experience in immigration law, policies or procedures and yet hold themselves out to the unwitting applicant as immigration authorities.[27]

(h) Witnesses

All persons who appear before the court to give testimony under oath in a proceeding are referred to as witnesses for one of the parties. Generally, the witness is a person who has personal knowledge of the matter, or has specialized knowledge that will assist the court.

(i) Juries

A jury is a group of citizens who are eligible for jury duty under the provincial *Juries Act*,[28] are selected at random, and are summoned to attend superior court for a specified period.[29] From the persons summoned, called the jury panel, the jury is selected in open court and is sworn to be impartial between the parties. A civil jury has six members; a criminal jury has twelve.

Although the task of the jury is to assist the judge in decision-making, it holds a separate function from that of the judge. The judge is the arbiter of the law, instructs the jury on the relevant law, and rules on the admissibility of evidence in the trial. The jury decides on the facts in dispute, applying the law as given by the judge to the facts in reaching its decision. The ultimate decision in both civil and criminal cases heard by judge and jury is determined by the jury. In civil cases, judgment for the plaintiff or defendant is "found" by the jury, including the amount of monetary damages awarded. A verdict of "conviction" or "acquittal" is reached in criminal cases, but where the jury convicts, the sentence imposed is at the discretion of the trial judge. Only where the conviction is for murder does the jury participate in sentencing, by recommending the minimum period of imprisonment before parole eligibility. Members of a jury in Canada, in contrast to those in the United States, are precluded from discussing with others the deliberations of the jury. Indeed, the *Criminal Code* makes it a summary conviction offence to do so.[30]

SELECTED READINGS

Advisory Committee on Regulating Immigration Consultants, *Report of the Advisory Committee on Regulating Immigration Consultants* (Ottawa: Citizenship and Immigration Canada, May, 2003).

Attorney General's Advisory Committee, *Report of the Attorney General's Advisory Committee, Charge Screening, Disclosure, and Resolution Discussions* (Ontario: Ministry of the Attorney General, 1993).

Brooks, Neil, "The Judge and the Adversary System" in Allen Linden, ed., *The Canadian Judiciary*.

Langbein, John, "The German Advantage in Civil Procedure" (1985) 52 U. Chicago L. Rev. 823.

Ontario Human Rights Review Task Force, *Achieving Equality: A Report on Human Rights Reform* (Ontario: Ministry of Citizenship, June 26, 1992).

Paralegal Task Force, *Report of the Task Force on Paralegal Regulation 2204* (Law Society of Upper Canada: March, 2000).

ENDNOTES

1. Rules of Professional Conduct, Law Society of Upper Canada, commentary to Rule 4.01(1). Note that the rules do contemplate a limited departure from strict adversarialism in proceedings involving a child: "In adversary proceedings that will likely affect the health, welfare, or security of a child, a lawyer should advise the client to take into account the best interests of the child, where this can be done without prejudicing the legitimate interests of the client." The rules are available at <http://www.lsuc.on.ca/regulations/a/profconduct/>.
2. Neil Brooks, "The Judge and the Adversary System" in Allen Linden ed., *The Canadian Judiciary* (Toronto: Osgoode Hall Law School, York University, 1976) at 93.
3. John Langbein, "The German Advantage in Civil Procedure" (1985) 52 U. Chicago L. Rev. 823.
4. *Ibid.*
5. Ontario Human Rights Review Task Force, *Achieving Equality: A Report on Human Rights Reform* (Ontario: Ministry of Citizenship, June 26, 1992). The report also identifies several other concerns, including delay, lack of attention to systemic discrimination, and lack of access to a hearing.
6. At the time of writing, the proposed date for the launch of the new regime was June 30, 2008.
7. R.R.O. 1990, Reg. 194. Different procedures, which are less complex and demanding, apply to Small Claims Court actions (see O. Reg. 258/98). Also family law matters are guided by a discrete set of family law rules (see O. Reg. 114/99).
8. (1990), (sub nom. *Doe v. Metropolitan Toronto (Municipality) Commissioners of Police*) 74 O.R. (2d) 225, 1 C.R.R. (2d) 211, 72 D.L.R. (4th) 580, 1990 CarswellOnt 442, (sub nom. *Jane Doe v. Board of Police Commissioners of Metropolitan Toronto*) 40 O.A.C. 161, 5 C.C.L.T. (2d) 77, 50 C.P.C. (2d) 92, [1990] O.J. No. 1584 (Div. Ct.),

leave to appeal refused (1991), 1991 CarswellOnt 1009, 1 O.R. (3d) 416 (note) (C.A.).

9. *Ibid.* at para. 29; on the question of whether her claim disclosed a reasonable cause of action.

10. Other pleadings are possible too, including a cross-claim (where, for example, one named defendant claims against another named defendant) and a third-party claim (where, for example, a defendant makes a claim against a new party not originally named by the plaintiff, but arising out of the same or a related matter).

11. An example to distinguish a leading from a non-leading question would be, "What colour is your shirt?" (non-leading) in contrast to, "You were wearing a blue shirt, weren't you?" See also Chapter 8.

12. R.S.C. 1985, c. C-46.

13. S.C. 1996, c. 19.

14. R.S.O. 1990, c. P.33.

15. For a fuller discussion of sentencing, see Chapter 20.

16. Sections 7 and 11(b) of the *Canadian Charter of Rights and Freedoms;* see also Chapter 2.

17. In *R. v. Askov,* [1990] S.C.R. 1199, 79 C.R. (3d) 273, 59 C.C.C. (3d) 449, 49 C.R.R. 1, 74 D.L.R. (4th) 355, 75 O.R. (2d) 673, 113 N.R. 241, 42 O.A.C. 81, [1990] S.C.J. No. 106, 1990 CarswellOnt 111, 1990 CarswellOnt 1005, the Supreme Court of Canada found that the accused had not been tried within a reasonable time and stayed the proceedings. Subsequently, thousands of cases were dismissed for delay.

18. (1991), [1991] 3 S.C.R. 326, 18 C.R.R. (2d) 210, 68 C.C.C. (3d) 1, 8 W.A.C. 161, EYB 1991-66887, 1991 CarswellAlta 559, 1991 CarswellAlta 192, [1992] 1 W.W.R. 97, 130 N.R. 277, 83 Alta. L.R. (2d) 193, 120 A.R. 161, 8 C.R. (4th) 277, [1991] S.C.J. No. 83.

19. *Ibid* at paras.10-12.

20. Attorney General's Advisory Committee, *Charge Screening, Disclosure, and Resolution Discussions* (Ontario: Ministry of the Attorney General, 1993).

21. *Justices of the Peace Act,* R.S.O. 1990, c. J.4.

22. *Commentary to Rule 4.01(3), Rules of Professional Conduct,* online: Law Society of Upper Canada <http://www.lsuc.on.ca/regulations/a/profconduct/>.

23. In Ontario the legislation is the *Law Society Act,* R.S.O. 1990, c. L.8.

24. *Ibid.* s. 26.1.

25. *Ibid.* s. 27(1)

26. *Bylaw 4,* online: Law Society of Upper Canada <http://www.lsuc.on.ca/media/bylaw4.pdf>.

27. Advisory Committee on Regulating Immigration Consultants, *Report*

of the Advisory Committee on Regulating Immigration Consultants (Ottawa: Citizenship and Immigration Canada, May, 2003).

28. R.S.O. 1990, c. J.3.
29. *Ibid.* at s. 6(2) and s. 13, respectively.
30. See *supra* note 12 at s. 649.

6

Alternative Dispute Resolution

(1) INTRODUCTION

Disputes, unlike wine, do not improve with aging. Many things happen to a cause and to parties in a dispute by the simple passage of time, and none of them are good.[1]

Increasing costs and delays associated with court-based adjudication together with concerns regarding the limitations, if not harms, of adversarial adjudication in some contexts, have resulted in a proliferation of "alternative dispute resolution" processes. While the concept of alternative dispute resolution (ADR) has no fixed meaning, it is frequently used to capture a broad array of dispute resolution processes that all share one thing in common; the absence of institutionally-based adversarial adjudication (discussed in Chapter 5). A definition of some of the terms associated with ADR may help to identify the different processes. To some extent, these distinctions depend on the level of activity of the neutral third-party. They include, but are not limted to:

1. **Negotiation**—two or more parties enter into discussions between themselves with the intention of resolving the issues in dispute without the assistance of an outside party. This process can also involve lawyers. Negotiation is certainly not a new process on the legal front; indeed the overwhelming majority of civil cases have long been settled through negotiations (only 3-5% of cases proceed to trial). Moreover, negotiations—in the form of the plea bargain—have long existed in the criminal context.

2. **Parenting Coordination**—a mental health professional provides

assistance with implementing, monitoring, and modifying a parenting plan.

3. **Mediation**—a process of dispute resolution, faciliated by a neutral third party, to help the parties achieve a mutual agreeement to resolve their dispute on their own terms (although they are not bound to follow the substantive law, knowledge of legal rights and entitlements is crucial). While this neutral third-party may recommend ways to resolve the dispute, he or she has no power to decide for the parties or bind them to any particular solution.

4. **Co-Mediation**—two outside parties provide a structured process to assist in dispute resolution; this generally occurs where there are many disputants or extremely complex issues to be resolved.

5. **Collaborative Law**—a cooperative form of negotiation between lawyers and their clients in the family law context where they all work together to resolve problems arising from the breakdown of the relationship. In this process both the lawyers and clients undertake a commitment to avoid the traditional adversarial approach by signing an agreement towards that end. They agree to full financial disclosure and to act with respect and in good faith.

6. **Arbitration**—an outside party, chosen by the disputants, hears and assesses the opposing sides to a dispute and makes a decision as to how it is to be resolved. Depending on what the parties have agreed to in advance, the decision may be advisory only or may be binding on the disputing parties. The parties often determine the procedures and in some areas of law may determine what norms (those of the law of Canada or of another jurisdiction, or the rules of a voluntary organization for instance) are to be applied. Arbitrations often take the form of adversarial adjudication, but are heard and determined by a person other than a judge.

7. **Early Neutral Evaluation**—an early assessment by an outside expert of the strengths and weaknesses of the case.

The potential advantages of these different processes of course varies depending upon the particular process and the context in which it is employed. However, the advantages claimed for most of these processes generally fall along two axes, one quantitative and the other qualitative.[2] The quantitive axis emphasizes the potential savings in both cost and time; put simply, ADR processes are claimed to be more efficient. Reviews undertaken of civil justice systems across the country and subsequent reforms have virtually all embraced ADR as a means of reducing the twin trojan horses—costs and delay—of the civil justice system.[3] The qualitative axis emphasizes the potential process benefits of ADR, including direct participation (as in mediation), the ability to put all interests on the table (not only those recognized by law), the ability to structure future relationships, and the potential for creative resolutions and remedies (again, not boxed by the formal law and not reduced to zero-sum, win-lose outcomes). These process benefits may also lead to other desirable results, including the reduction of hostility, improved communication, and greater respect for, and hence compliance with, the outcome. But as we discuss more fully below, while all or many of these advantages may be realized in particular contexts and cases, this is not universally so.

(2) ADR AND THE COURTS

In Ontario, ADR has not only provided an alternative to the formal civil justice system, it has altered the civil justice system itself. The rules of procedure governing proceedings in the Superior Court of Justice were amended in 1999 to provide for mandatory mediation of most case-managed, non-family civil cases (initially in Toronto and Ottawa, and since 2002 in Windsor). Parties—and if represented, their lawyers—are required to participate in a minimum of three hours of mediation.[4] The rules governing mediation expressly articulate its goals: reducing cost and delay; and facilitating early and fair dispute settlement. Case management, another tool introduced in the late 1990s, was implemented with these same express goals.

(a) Case Management

In Ontario, many civil cases are assigned to case management schemes, where proceedings are more actively managed by a judge or case management master. Case conferences are structured into the case mangement system to create a timetable for steps in the proceeding and to explore methods of resolving the contested issues. At the case conference, parties may be encouraged to explore alternative dispute methods. In addition, after the completion of the pre-trial "discovery" process (the exchange of documents and the examinations for discovery discussed in Chapter 5), the parties must participate in a settlement conference, where again, a judge will explore with the parties the possibilities for settlement. A third form of conference, the pre-trial conference, creates yet a further opportunity for a judge to explore the potential for settlement with the parties.

During the various pre-trial conferences, the judge will often make comments, ask questions, and do whatever else seems necessary to focus the discussion, clarify issues and search for resolution. The discussions during settlement conferences are confidential and the parties and their respective lawyers are ensured that the proceedings are conducted "without prejudice," meaning that the pre-trial proceedings cannot be referred to at trial. Moreover, the judge at a settlement or pre-trial conference cannot preside at trial regarding the same issue. Agreements that are reached on any of the issues in dispute are recorded by the respective lawyers as Minutes of Settlement, signed by the parties, and usually converted into court orders that may form part of the judgment of the court.

Pre-trial, settlement, and case conferences encompass aspects of both mediation and neutral evaluation by the judge of the likely outcome if the issues were tried in court. No resolution can be imposed on the parties, so the judge must use his or her skills as a mediator to focus and isolate the areas of common agreement that do exist. However, the authority that resides in a judge and the weight of his or her experience are powerful influences on the willingness of the parties to resolve issues in dispute. The judge's comments can also help the parties to assess their alternatives, which may promote settlement without trial.

(b) ADR and Lawyers

Additionally, the Rules of Professional Conduct governing members of the Law Society of Upper Canada provide that a "lawyer should consider the appropriateness of ADR to the resolution of issues in every case and if appropriate, the lawyer should inform the client of the ADR options and, if so instructed, take steps to pursue those options."[5] A more far-reaching proposal that would have imposed a mandatory duty on lawyers to inform clients of ADR options was rejected.

(c) ADR's Reach

The proliferation of ADR has by no means been confined to non-family civil proceedings. As we canvass in some detail below, ADR has had an enormous impact in the area of family law dispute resolution. A large number of administrative tribunals now employ ADR processes, and mediation in particular. Even within the criminal justice system, alternative processes, such as restorative justice and the conference in dealing with young persons in conflict with the law (See Chapter 21), have found a place.

(3) ADR AND FAMILY LAW DISPUTES

There has been a growing recognition that the traditional adversarial system often does not serve well the complex emotional and social aspects of family disputes. Moreover, social science research has demonstrated that separation and divorce carry significant long-lasting private and public costs for children and their families.[6] In recognition of the inadequacy of the judicial process, there has been embracement of alternate forms of dispute resolution within the family law context, and more recently, in the context of child welfare disputes.[7]

Judges, lawyers, and social workers are showing increased interest in resolving conflicts at the point where a marriage or relationship has broken down. By appointing a neutral third-party skilled in dispute resolution, or choosing a collaborative law approach, a lengthy court battle may be averted. Custody and access matters concerning children are particularly well-suited to social work mediation. Parents are often in a better position to know what is best for their children than any third party, whether it be a judge, lawyer, or social worker. ADR processes enable some parents to work constructively to fashion not only a resolution of their existing disputes but a forward-looking plan built upon the base of knowledge that they possess regarding their children's interests and needs.

Voluntary settlements, which are worked out by both spouses (or sometimes with the help of professionals) are often, on an emotional level as well as an intellectual one, not only more humane than those forced by litigation, but also more practical. If genuine mutual agreement exists, neither party is the "loser" nor feels taken advantage of, so there is less likelihood of acrimony erupting later, leading to new and prolonged legal battles. More importantly, a mediated agreement between parties tends to be more long lasting as each party has more ownership of the result than they would have if imposed from the outside (*e.g.* by a judge).

Below we outline in more detail three prominent forms of alternative dispute resolution in the family law context: mediation; collaborative lawyering; and arbitration.

(a) Mediation

The purpose of mediation is not reconciliation of the couple. Rather, mediation provides an informal process outside the court system, and its adversarial atmosphere, for couples to work out arrangements for custody, access, support, and/or property through faciliated negotiation. The purpose is to move on from the fact of marriage breakdown and instead assist couples to arrive at decisions through mutual agreement. Unlike the adversarial approach, no blame is attached to either party in an attempt to bring forth realistic options so that the parties can examine their choices and potential compromises. Some characteristics of effective mediation services are crisis-oriented, short-term, available when needed, and voluntary. Often mediation agreements are turned into court orders after the parties have mutually agreed on a parenting plan.

Mediation services have been developed in many jurisdictions throughout the United States and Canada.[8] In Ontario, mediation is still voluntary in family law matters, while in Quebec it is mandatory. The reader should consult each individual province to more fully understand the procedures. In Ontario, family court mediation services are attached to all Family Courts of the Superior Court of Justice (or Unified Family Courts). These services are provided by skilled mediators and frequently divert the parties from custody and access motions or trials which can be devastating to both parents and their children.[9]

While mediation will often be the preferred process for many separating couples, it is not ideal in all situations. Substantial concerns exist about the use of mediation processes where there has been a history of domestic violence and most programs, including Ontario's, attempt to screen out such cases at the point of intake.[10] The underlying concern relates to inequalities of bargaining power, where the parties may not be equally able to articulate and secure their respective interests. This unease arises not only in the family context but in a host of other contexts where mediation is now practiced; landlord tenant disputes and human rights complaints are but two further examples. Important American research also suggests that individuals who experience social marginalization and disadvantage fair less well in informal settings. The work of Richard Delgado indicates, for example, that persons who are racialized fair better in formal proceedings, such as adversarial court-based adjudication, while the informality of mediation can work in favour of more powerful parties.[11]

(i) The Mediator

The role of the mediator, as the word suggests, is to come between the disputing parties, identify issues, and look for areas of agreement as well as possible resolutions. The objective is to assist the parties to reach agreement on outstanding issues. The function of the mediator is to facilitate communication between the parties to help them work out their own solutions. However, in mediation, the two parties may be so antagonistic that the mediator may need to go back and forth between the parties in an attempt to find potential areas of agreement upon which to build decisions. This process may reduce the number of issues to come before the court and may be the most appropriate approach for parties who are unable to communicate with one another.

In Ontario, the *Children's Law Reform Act*[12] specifically provides for mediation as does the *Divorce Act.* [13] Once an application for custody and/ or access is made, at the request of both parties, the court may appoint a person to mediate any matter specified in the order. The mediator must consent to act in this capacity and agree to file a report with the court, within the specified time, about the matters in issue.

As already discussed, mediators, unlike arbitratrators, do not make binding decisions or awards. Instead, mediation provides the parties with a neutral third-party to help them isolate those issues on which they can agree so that few, if any, issues need to come to court. If no agreement can be reached at mediation, the court route is available to the parties. The mediation process can be either open or closed, as the parties select. [14]

There has been an increase in recourse to mediation to resolve all aspects of family disputes. Across Canada and internationally, there has been a thrust toward the establishment of organizations directed at encouraging a more extensive use of mediation services. In Ontario, as in other provinces, there are provincial organizations such as the Ontario Association of Family Mediation. On the national front, Family Mediation, Canada provides and updates a national directory of mediators and mediation services. Internationally, the Association of Family and Conciliation Courts and the Academy of Family Mediators actively promote the mediation of family disputes outside the normal litigation process. However, there continues to be no uniformly recognized standards for mediators, although development is currently underway.

(b) Collaborative Law

As with many of the alternative dispute resolution approaches in family law, collaborative law arose not only as a means to facilitate the early resolution of family disputes, but as a response to the harm of family law litigation on children and families.[15] In collaborative law, the parties sign an agreement to participate as a "team" to seek mutual cooperative strategies to resolve their dispute. They also agree to make full financial disclosure and to speak to one another with respect. This process is another method used to address the marriage breakup and the proceedings are kept confidential. Collaborative law is not mediation; the lawyers are not neutral and are there to specifically guide their clients through the process by offering their legal expertise. During this process, neither the parties nor their lawyers engage in any litigation so that the focus can be on promoting awareness and creativity during negotiations. However, if an impasse is reached, the parties must retain new lawyers to proceed to litigation. Some have suggested that the process is transformative for both parties and their lawyers as its strength rests on the healing effects that distinguish it from the adversarial approach.[16]

(c) Arbitration

Arbitration, wherein the decision-making power is vested in the arbitrator agreed upon by the parties, offers another form of dispute resolution in the family law context and beyond (arbitrations are, for example, very common in resolving commercial disputes and labour disputes).[17] The arbitrator sits as an adjudicator, who must make a decision about the issues and is empowered to do so by the parties. He or she must therefore remain impartial between the parties.[18]

In Ontario, recent amendments to the *Arbitration Act, 1991*[19] and the *Family Law Act*[20] deal specifically with family law arbitrations. The impetus for these reforms was an announcement by the Islamic Institute of Civil Justice that it would conduct arbitrations of family disputes according to Islamic personal law. This announcement prompted concern regarding the impact, upon women in particular, of the application of Islamic personal law. A review conducted by Marion Boyd, at the request of the Attorney General of Ontario, made clear that family matters have long been arbitrated based on religious teachings in Jewish, Muslim and Christian settings.[21] The structure of the then existing *Arbitrations Act*[22] enabled parties to an arbitration to choose the law—secular or religious—to govern the resolution of their dispute, and provided the mechanism for the enforcement of arbitration awards. While a range of competing positions were advanced during the review—from the elimination of arbitration in family matters to the continued use of religious law in family arbitrations—the government ultimately chose to retain arbitrations in the family context, but to require that they be decided in accordance with the laws of Canada. Amendments to both the *Arbitrations Act* and the *Family Law Act* in force as of May, 2007 require that:

1. to be enforceable, family arbitrations in Ontario must be conducted in exclusive reliance upon the law of Ontario (or other named Canadian jurisidiction) and the law of Canada as it applies in Ontario;
2. the parties entering arbitration obtain independent legal advice about their specific legal rights and responsibilities;
3. family law arbitrators be required to undertake training, including how to screen for family violence and power imbalances (and must screen parties separately in practice);

4.   arbitrations be monitored through mandatory record keeping and reporting to the Attorney General; and
5.   arbitrations be included in the definition of "domestic contracts."[23]

Arbitration hearings are arranged by the parties rather than imposed by the court system. The parties select their own procedure; for example, they can choose whether there will be oral or written evidence, what documentary evidence will be introduced, and whether witnesses, including experts, will be called. Issues which are in dispute between the parties may include property, the amount and form of equalization payments, spousal and child support, as well as custody and access concerning children. Issues arising from the terms of contracts or the rights and obligations deriving from common-law relationships may also be presented for consideration and resolution.

When custody and access issues are in dispute and the parents appear to be using the child (ren) against one another, the arbitrator may need to call for an independent child custody and access assessment which will provide assistance in making recommendations in the best interest of the child. It may also be appropriate to retain other experts in complex financial and business matters.

Whenever a domestic contract such as a marriage contract or a separation agreement is contemplated, a clause requiring future contractual disputes to be settled by mediation or arbitration is often included. Such a provision can deflect future litigation.

(4) SOCIAL WORKERS AS MEDIATORS OR ARBITRATORS

As in many cases dealing with children and families, the social worker must have requisite training and skill to perform mediation and arbitration. Social work expertise is especially valuable because social workers are aware of the many contradictions and balances to be considered when determining which parenting arrangement would best meet the interests of children to the family dispute. In family matters, the needs of the family, both economic and psychological, are interdependent and must therefore be addressed in mediation. However, social workers who practice in family law should seek advice on issues concerning property matters given its tax implications for families.

Many schools of social work across the country now include courses in family dispute resolution and divorce mediation in their curriculum courses.[24] Practice and academic texts written by both social workers and lawyers have provided a forum for public consumption and understanding of the complicated language and practice of family law as well as all the various forms of alternative dispute resolution techniques. In addition, faculties of law have also introduced courses in alternate dispute resolution.[25]

Those interested in training programmes have recognized the need for standards in determining the qualifications for those who would provide mediation services. Presently, there does exist a *caveat emptor* (buyer beware) market in the private sector, but codes of ethics have now been developed by professional mediation organizations.[26] Training programmes focus on communication skills and recognition of the unique needs and interests of the parties as the basis for a mutually acceptable resolution. As noted above, minimum training and qualifications must be satisfied in order to act as a family law arbitrator.[27]

(5) CONCLUSION

A growing body of social science and empirical literature and an expanding experience in other forms of dispute resolution confirm the utility of alternative dispute resolution processes in conjunction with, or in place of, court-based adjudication. Programs and services designed to provide for mediation, mediation/arbitration, parenting coordination, and collaborative law have expanded in many communities, both in Canada and the United States, and some multi-service neighbourhood centres. As court systems become clogged with cases delayed or postponed for long periods of time and as the cost of legal services increases, those involved in disputes with family members, neighbours, other persons in the community, or with consumer complaints have begun to utilize ADR services. ADR focuses on facilitating negotiation so that a voluntary resolution, one which is acceptable to both disputing parties, is produced. These alternative forms are often more expeditious than the adversarial process, less expensive, and consequently, far less draining from an emotional and psychological perspective. Yet, as with any dispute resolution process, theory often departs from practices on the ground. In some contexts, disputants are compelled to mediate (mandatory mediation) or feel coerced to do so. Inequalities of bargaining power may be exacerbated and/or exploited in informal settings. In some instances, ADR adds to the costs of litigation, particularly where participation is mandatory as a pre-condition to proceeding. ADR processes often occur in private, where neither the process nor the results are open to public scrutiny, and some worry about the implications of this for justice. And finally, the question must be asked of whether justice requires, at least in particular contexts, an authoritative determination of right and wrong; should not a person who has experienced racial or sexual discrimination, for example, be entitled to an authoritive pronoucement that his or her rights have been violated?

SELECTED READINGS

Barsky, Allan E., *Conflict Resolution for the Helping Professions* (Pacific Grove, Calif.: Wadsworth Brooks/Cole, 2000).

Boyd, Marion, "Dispute Resolution in Family Law: Protecting Choice, Promoting Inclusion" prepared for the Attorney General of Ontario (20 December, 2004), online: Ministry of the Attorney General <http:// www.attorneygeneral.jus.gov.on.ca/English/about/pubs/boyd>.

Crush, Linda, "When Mediation Fails Child Protection: Lessons for the Future" (2007) 23(1) Can. J. Fam. Law.

Ellis, Desmond & Noreen Stuckless, *Mediating and Negotiating Marital Conflicts* (Thousand Oaks, Calif.: Sage Publications, 1996).

Fisher, Roger & William Ury, *Getting to Yes: Negotiating Agreement Without Giving In* (New York: Penguin Books, 1983).

Hart, Barbara, "Gentle Jeopardy: The Further Endangerment of Battered Women and Children in Custody Mediation" (1990: Summer) 7(4) Mediation Quarterly 28.

Himel, Andrea, "Mediation/arbitration: The binding comes undone" (2002) 20 Can. Fam. L.Q. 55.

Imbrogno, Andre & Salvatore Imbrogno, "Mediation in court cases of domestic violence" (2000) 81(4) Families in Society 392.

Irving, Howard & Michael Benjamin, *Family Mediation: Contemporary Issues* (Thousand Oaks: Sage Publications, 1995).

Johnson, Holly, *Dangerous Domains, Violence Against Women in Canada* (Scarborough, Ont.: Nelson Canada, 1996).

Madden, Robert, "Legal content in social work education: Preparing students for interprofessional practice" in Raymond Albert, ed., *Law and Social Work Practice: A Legal Systems Approach*, 2d ed., (New York: Springer Publishing Company, 2000) at 333.

Macfarlane, Julie, "Experiences of Collaborative Law: Preliminary results from the collaborative lawyering research project" (2004) 1 J. Disp. Resol. 179.

Macfarlane, Julie, *The New Lawyer: How Settlement is Transforming the Practice of Law* (Vancouver: University of British Columbia Press, 2007).

Menkel-Meadow, Carrie, "For and Against Settlement: Uses and Abuses of the Mandatory Settlement Conference" (1985) 33(1) U.C.L.A. Law Rev. 485.

Morrison, Ian & Janet Mosher, "Barriers to Access to Civil Justice for Disadvantaged Groups" in Ontario Law Reform Commission, *Rethinking Civil Justice: Research Studies for The Civil Justice Review Vol. 2* (Ontario: Ontario Law Reform Commission, 1996).

Preston-Shoot, M., G. Roberts, & S.Vernon, "Developing a conceptual framework for teaching and assessing law within training for professional practice: Lessons from social work" (1998) 1(1) Journal of Practice Teaching in Social Work 41.

Saposnek, Donald T., "The art of family mediation" (1993) 11 Mediation Quarterly 5.

Sheehy, Elizabeth, "Legal responses to violence against women in Canada" (1999) 19 (1&2) Canadian Women's Studies: Special Issue on Women and Justice 19.

Shields, Richard, Julie Ryan, & Victoria Smith, *Collaborative family law: Another way to resolve family disputes* (Toronto: Thomson Canada Ltd., 2003).

Tessler, Pauline, "Collaborative law: A new paradigm for divorce lawyers" (1999) 5(4) Psychol. Pub. Pol'y & L. 967.

WEBSITES

Academy of Family Mediators, www.mediators.org

Association for Conflict Resolution, www.acresolution.org

Family Mediation Canada, www.fmc.ca

The Society for Professionals in Dispute Resolution, www.spidr.org

---

ENDNOTES

1.   Willard Estey, as quoted in Ministry of the Attorney General, *Civil Justice Review, First Report*, (Toronto: Civil Justice Review, 1995) at 2.
2.   Carrie Menkel-Meadow, "For and Against Settlement: Uses and Abuses

of the Mandatory Settlement Conference" (1985) 33(1) U.C.L.A. Law Rev. 485.

3. See for example, *supra* note 1; Roderick Macdonald, "Study Paper on Prospects for Civil Justice" (Ontario: Ontario Law Reform Commission, 1995).

4. See Rule 24.01, Rules of Civil Procedure, R.R.O. 1990, Reg. 194; the Ministry of the Attorney General also has helpful information about the Mandatory Mediation Program on its website, online: <http://www.attorneygeneral.jus.gov.on.ca/english/courts/manmed>.

5. *Rules of Professional Conduct*, online: Law Society of Upper Canada <http://www.lsuc.on.ca/regulations/a/profconduct/>.

6. Paul Amato, "Reconciling divergent perspectives: Judith Wallerstein, quantitative family research, and children of divorce" (2003) 52(4) Family Relations 332; William Fabricus, "Listening to Children of Divorce: New findings that diverge from Wallerstein, Lewis, and Blakeslee" (2003) 52(4) Family Relations 385; Janet Johnston & Vivienne Roseby, *In the Name of the Child. A Developmental Approach to Understanding and Helping Children of Conflicted and Violent Divorce* (New York: The Free Press, 1997).

7. In Ontario, Bill 210 amendment to the *Child and Family Services Act* proclaimed in November, 2006 allows for mediation to take place in child protection matters.

8. *Divorce Act*, R.S.C. 1985, c. C.3, s. 9(2) has one reference to mediation which requires lawyers to advise their clients of the availability of mediation services.

9. Mediators are required to have qualifications comparable to those practicing family mediation as set by the Ontario Association of Family Mediation (OAFM). See also *Policies for Government Funded Mediation Services*, online: Ministry of the Attorney General <http://www.attorneygeneral.jus.gov.on.ca/English/family/policies.asp>. Mediation services can be on-site in the court or off-site in the mediator's offices.

10. There is a substantial body of literature on the issue of domestic violence and mediation; see for example, Nancy Johnson, Dennis Saccuzzo & Wendy Koen, "Child Custody Mediation in Cases of Domestic Violence; Empirical Evidence of a Failure to Protect" (2005) 11(6) Violence Against Women 1022; and Barbara Hart, "Gentle Jeopardy: The Further Endangerment of Battered Women and Children in Custody Mediation" (1990: Summer) 7(4) Mediation Quarterly 28. On domestic violence and restorative justice processes in the criminal context see Alan Edwards & Jennifer Haslett, "Domestic Violence and Restorative Justice: Advancing the Dialogue" online: Simon Fraser University Cen-

tre for Restorative Justice <http://www.sfu.ca/cfrj/fulltext/has-lett.pdf>.

11. Ian Morrison & Janet Mosher, "Barriers to Access to Civil Justice for Disadvantaged Groups" in Ontario Law Reform Commission, *Rethinking Civil Justice: Research Studies for The Civil Justice Review Vol. 2* (Ontario: Ontario Law Reform Commission, 1996) at 671.

12. R.S.O. 1990, c. C.12.

13. *Divorce Act, supra* note 8.

14. In open mediation, the mediator writes a report that includes everything relevant to the dispute. The information provided by the parties to the mediator is not confidential. In closed mediation, the mediator writes a report that includes what the parties have and have not agreed to. The information provided by the parties to the mediator is confidential except with the consent of both parties.

15. Julie Macfarlane, "Experiences of Collaborative Law: Preliminary results from the collaborative lawyering research project" (2004) 1 J. Disp. Resol. 179; Richard Shields, Julie Ryan, & Victoria Smith, *Collaborative Family Law: Another Way to Resolve Family Disputes* (Toronto: Thomson Canada Ltd., 2003); Pauline Tessler, "Collaborative law: A new paradigm for divorce lawyers" (1999) 5(4) Psych. Pub. Pol'y & L. 967.

16. Tessler, *ibid.*

17. *Family Arbitration*, O. Reg. 134/07.

18. *Kainz* v. *Potter* (2006), 2006 CarswellOnt 3703, 33 R.F.L. (6th) 62 (Ont. S.C.J.); *Acimovic* v. *Acimovic* (2006), 2006 CarswellOnt 6228, 33 R.F.L. (6th) 158 (Ont. S.C.J.); *Shoval* v. *Shoval* (2005), 2005 CarswellOnt 2383 (Ont. S.C.J.); *Duguay* v. *Thompson-Duguay*, 7 R.F.L. (5th) 301, 2000 CarswellOnt 1462, [2000] O.J. No. 1541, [2000] O.T.C. 299 (S.C.J.). All involve cases where the court had to review and set aside arbitration awards to ensure parties were treated equally and fairly and where it was found that the arbitrator had not exercised procedural fairness.

19. S.O. 1991, c. 17, as amended.

20. R.S.O. 1990, c. F.3, as amended

21. Marion Boyd, "Dispute Resolution in Family Law: Protecting Choice, Promoting Inclusion" prepared for the Attorney General of Ontario (20 December, 2004), online: Ministry of the Attorney General <http://www.attorneygeneral.jus.gov.on.ca/English/about/pubs/boyd>.

22. R.S.O. 1990, c. M.48.

23. See ss. 51 and 59.2 of the *Family Law Act, supra* note 20 and ss. 2.2(1), 32(4), 58 and 59.6 of the *Arbitrations Act, supra.*

24. Collaborative Law courses are now being offered at several law schools.

25. In the United States, the Family Law Education Reform Project (FLER) has been systematically addressing the gap between teaching and the practice of family law. FLER is the first interdisciplinary approach taken to combine social sciences with law. See Andrew Schepard & Peter Salem, "Forward to the Special Issue on the Family Law Education Reform Project" (2006) 44(4) Fam. Ct. Rev. 513 and the subsequent articles in this special issue for the pros and cons of this approach.

26. See, for example, Family Mediation Canada—Members Code of Professional Conduct, The Society for Professionals in Dispute Resolution, and the Arbitration and Mediation Institute (Canada).

27. *Training required to be a family arbitrator*, online: Ministry of the Attorney General <http://www.attorneygeneral.jus.gov.on.ca/English/family/arbitration/training.asp>.

7

Finding and Using Legal Services

(1) INTRODUCTION

While we tend to associate "legal services" with retaining a lawyer in relation to a specific legal dispute or problem, a more expansive interpretation invites us to consider access to legal information to assist in preventing disputes. Analogous to the concept of preventative medicine, "preventative law" directs attention to the importance of equipping people with the information and resources they need to avoid significant legal problems down the road.

Additionally, the focus commonly placed upon retaining a lawyer in relation to a particular dispute presupposes that those affected have not only identified a problem, but have characterized the problem as potentially "legal" in nature, are prepared to blame someone else for it and to make a claim against that person or entity.[1] These presuppositions obscure the reality that people do not have access to the information that they need to name a wrong or to characterize it as potentially "legal." Access to relevant and timely legal information is thus critically important to even the naming of a legal dispute. Lack of access to information is but one of the obstacles to the naming, blaming and claiming process. A range of other obstacles, from financial, to vulnerability to retaliation, to lack of trust in the legal system, operate to keep particular claims and particular people largely out of the formal legal system.[2]

It is also important to recognize that while lawyers play a vital role in the provision of legal services, others play a role as well. Although legislation in each province restricts the practice of law to members of the provincial law society who are in good standing—and making it an offence to engage in the unauthorized practice of law—there are a variety of mechanisms through which others can play a legitimate and authorized role. While the approach varies between provinces, some specifically authorize limited forms of legal practice undertaken by paralegals. New legislation in Ontario, for example, creates a separate licensing regime authorizing paralegals to practice in particular areas.[3] Community-based organizations play a critical role in providing general legal information (not legal advice or representation); indeed for many Canadians these organizations are their primary source of information about the law.

(2) ACCESSING LEGAL INFORMATION

Not surprisingly, the internet is a source of a tremendous amount of information about law. While one should always be attentive to issues of timeliness and accuracy, many websites provide excellent public legal education materials. Community Legal Education Ontario (CLEO), for example, is a community legal clinic "dedicated to providing low-income and disadvantaged people in Ontario with the legal information they need to understand and exercise their legal rights."[4] CLEO's materials cover a range of legal areas that impact upon low-income people, including social assistance, tenants' rights, immigration and refugee law, workers' rights, family law, elder abuse and youth justice.

(3) FINDING A LAWYER

Most lawyers specialize in one or two fields of law which means it is important to find a lawyer who specializes in the area or areas of law that relate to the particular situation. For many persons seeking lawyers, they are also anxious to find a lawyer with whom they can communicate in their first language and who will understand the cultural context in which the legal issues are embedded.

How then does a person set about finding an appropriate lawyer? Word of mouth and a recommendation from friends and neighbours both provide good starting-points in many instances. Other lawyers who do not practice in the relevant field can also provide a referral to an appropriate lawyer. The Law Society of each province (which has responsibility for regulating lawyers practicing within the province) will assist in locating a lawyer, often by providing the names of several lawyers in the area. This referral will not guarantee that the lawyer will act, but only that the person is qualified to practice law. The Law Society of Upper Canada, for example, has a lawyer referral service. For a small fee, the service will provide a person with the phone number of a lawyer in the person's geographic area who practices in the area of law related to that person's situation. This lawyer will provide a free consultation of up to thirty minutes. The lawyer referral service also offers a free service for people in crisis situations, including those in a shelter, in police custody, or with no fixed address. Community based organizations, such as settlement organizations and women's shelters, are often a good source for appropriate referrals.

(a) Costs

Legal fees vary widely between cities and rural areas and from one part of Canada to another. Most lawyers charge an hourly rate depending upon the locality and the lawyer's level of expertise or years of practice. For certain matters, such as wills, contracts or home sales, lawyers usually charge a "block" or set fee. In addition to the lawyers' fees, clients are also required to pay the costs of disbursements, which are the expenses incurred such as photocopying, filing fees, and postage. Legal services are indisputably costly; indeed for most Canadians, prohibitively so.

(b) Working with a Lawyer

In general, the following are some useful guides to selecting and making the best use of a lawyer.

1. Know your area of concern and try to find a lawyer who possesses some special expertise in that area. Family law, immigration, landlord and tenant, criminal law, or real estate are some areas of specialization. Lawyers in rural areas are more likely to be generalists and may need to consult with or refer you to a specialist after discussing your problem.
2. Write down your concerns and questions in advance.
3. Collect any relevant papers and documents that relate to your concern.
4. Discuss fees and expenses. Do not be afraid to ask about fees and about the amount of time that may be required to prepare and present your case. Most legal matters are brief but situations such as a full blown lawsuit may extend over several years.
5. Do not hesitate to shop for a lawyer if the first person you see does not give you a sense of confidence. You are purchasing knowledge and expertise as well as a sense of security and trust in that person.
6. Communication and mutual understanding are essential. Do not hesitate to say you do not understand and to ask for further explanation or elaboration.

(4) LEGAL NEEDS

Statistics demonstrating unmet legal needs in Chapter 1 bear repeating here. In a survey of 4500 low and middle-income Canadians conducted in March, 2004, 47.7% reported experiencing one or more legal problems that were difficult to resolve in a three year period, while 14% experienced three or more such problems.[5] Just over one third (33.9%) reported that a problem had remained unresolved during the study period.[6] Of those who had "resolved" a legal problem, 29.5 % perceived the resolution to have been unfair.[7] The survey also revealed that the distribution of legal problems is anything but equitable. Rather, single parents, persons with disabilities, persons between the ages of 18–29, those who were unemployed and those in receipt of social assistance benefits showed the greatest likelihood of experiencing one or more legal problems. Aboriginal people and members of visible minority groups were slightly more likely than others to report at least one problem.[8]

As Stephen Wexler so astutely observed more than thirty years ago, "[p]oor people are not just like rich people without money."[9] Rather, their relationship to the law is both qualitatively and quantitatively different.

> If you are poor, you depend on the law, regulations, and bureaucracies for the necessities of life. Chances are great that you will have problems at some point, and more likely at many points, requiring knowledge of laws and regulations concerning your main source of income, such as social assistance, unemployment insurance, workers' compensation, disability benefits or pension programs for the elderly poor.[10]

Yet problematically, low and moderate income Canadians have little, if any, access to formal legal advice and representation to assist in the resolution of the ubiquitous legal problems in their lives. Many Canadians simply cannot afford to assert the rights granted to them by law. While one is always entitled to "represent" oneself, this rarely leads to a satisfactory outcome, especially if the opposing party is represented by counsel. As the National Council of Welfare has observed,

> For people who have no money to pay court fees or hire a legal expert to advise and represent them, the right to subsidized legal services is the most fundamental of all rights. What use is a Charter of Rights and Freedoms guaranteeing your right to life and liberty, freedom of speech or equality before the law, if you cannot defend yourself against unjust accusations or discriminatory treatment? What is the point of laws entitling citizens to benefits, such as unemployment insurance or support payments from an ex-spouse, if program administrators or your ex-husband know you cannot afford the appeal or lawsuit required to get your rights enforced?[11]

(a) Legal Aid

While every province in Canada has some form of legal aid plan, what is actually available varies dramatically depending upon where one resides. Even in those provinces with the most generous legal aid plans, large numbers of people are still unable to access legal advice and representation, either because their income is above low-income qualifying thresholds or because the substantive area of law pertaining to their matter is not covered. While the most expansive coverage is in the criminal law area, those seeking help are still required to meet very low income thresholds and other criteria.

Coverage across the country is greatly limited in the civil arena, including both family law and poverty law.[12] British Columbia, for example, largely eviscerated its civil legal services in 2002. Ontario and Quebec are the only two provinces that offer relatively significant poverty law services, and even in those jurisdictions, demand far outstrips available resources.[13]

Melina Buckley, in research undertaken for the Canadian Bar Association, describes the legal aid crisis in Canada as having three dimensions: under-funding; disparities in coverage across jurisdictions (resulting in, for example, a matter being funded in one province but not in another); and fragmentation of coverage within each legal aid program.[14] Indeed, the sorry state of civil legal aid services in Canada as a whole, and especially in British Columbia, prompted the Canadian Bar Association to commence a legal proceeding in British Columbia in which it asserted a constitutional right to civil legal aid.[15] The claim was denied on the basis of a finding by the Supreme Court of British Columbia that the Canadian Bar Association lacked "standing" to bring such a claim and that the claim failed to disclose a cause of action.[16]

While the broad right to civil legal aid argued for by the Canadian Bar Association has yet to be recognized by the courts, the Supreme Court of Canada has found a constitutional guarantee of a right to state-funded counsel in particular circumstances. As discussed in Chapter 2, a right to state-funded counsel has been recognized in some child welfare matters. Recall that in the case of *G. (J.)*,[17] the Supreme Court of Canada found that given the security of the person interests at stake, the capacity of the mother to self-represent, and the complexities of the particular case, the principles of fundamental justice within section 7 of the *Charter of Rights and Freedoms*[18] required that state-funded legal representation be provided to the mother. In the criminal context, a right to state-funded counsel for particular cases has been grounded in the accused's right to a fair trial. The courts have held that where the accused's fair trial rights will be infringed due to a lack of representation, the state is obligated to fund representation. In considering whether the accused's fair trial rights would be infringed the court evaluates the complexity of the case, the seriousness of the charges, the financial circumstances of the accused, and the ability of the accused to self-represent.[19]

Thus far, the effect of the constitutional right to legal aid has been quite limited. The level of legal aid provided above the constitutional threshold varies, as noted, across jurisdictions. In the end, this means that very significant numbers of Canadians simply cannot afford to retain legal counsel. Absent legal aid, those without the economic resources to retain counsel have little chance of protecting themselves against exploitation in both civil and criminal matters. Police and courts are intimidating to most people, and the justice system can be especially difficult to navigate for those with limited education or who are from other countries with different systems of law, or who experience a disability. In the end, the fundamental assumption of the adversary system as discussed earlier—equality of resources as between parties—is frequently not borne out in reality.

(b) Legal Aid Service Delivery Models

Each province has its own unique blend of service delivery models. Below we describe the four common models: judicare; staff offices; community clinics; and duty counsel. A judicare model is one that depends upon private lawyers for the delivery of legal services. Individuals in need of legal services apply for what is known as a "certificate" and their applications are assessed both on the basis of financial and substantive criteria. While many people seem to believe that both the wealthy and the poor have access to legal representation—the former as fee paying clients and the latter as legal aid recipients—this is not the reality. While some low-income individuals may qualify for assistance in certain matters, qualification in most provinces requires one to be below or near the poverty line, and at the same time the range of substantive law matters covered is quite limited. In Ontario, for example, certificates for criminal law matters are available only if there is a probability that as a result of a guilty plea or a finding of guilt, one will be sentenced to jail. Certificates are also issued in some family law matters, where priority is given to cases involving the safety of a child or a spouse and to child protection cases.

While in theory the certificate enables its holder to retain the lawyer of his or her choice, in practice some lawyers refuse to accept certificates. This is so largely because the amount paid by legal aid for services rendered under the certificate is well below that which would be charged to a fee paying client.

Staff offices, by contrast, are offices in which the legal aid plan employs salaried staff lawyers to deliver legal aid services. There is an extensive debate as to the benefits and disadvantages of staff offices in comparison to a judicare model, much of which is rather inconclusive.[20] Ontario is now experimenting with staff models in criminal, family and immigration offices and conducting evaluation studies for each.

Community clinics, by contrast to staff offices, are governed by community-based boards of directors. Ontario has a relatively extensive system of community legal clinics, having just recently added the 80th clinic. While many of these clinics provide "clinic law services"—defined by the legislation as the areas of law which particularly affect low-income individuals or disadvantaged communities—to geographically defined areas of the province, others provide legal services to particular communities of interest.[21] This latter form of clinic is often referred to as a "specialty" clinic; examples include the African Canadian Legal Clinic, Justice for Children and Youth, Aboriginal Legal Services, South Asian Legal Clinic and Advocacy Centre for the Elderly. In addition, two clinics are specifically set up to address systemic issues: the Income Security Advocacy Clinic and the Advocacy Centre for Tenants of Ontario. Most of the clinics provide summary advice and/or representation in areas of law that significantly impact the lives of low income people, while others concentrate on areas of law that impact their respective communities of interest. Most clinics also engage in broader change-oriented activities that seek to improve the laws that regulate their clients' lives. This form of work can include law reform activities, community organizing and development and test cases. Clinics are staffed by both lawyers and community legal workers.

(c) Duty Counsel

Duty counsel are lawyers located within the courts, available on site to provide limited forms of legal advice and representation to those who appear in court without counsel. Again, the structure will vary from province-to-province, but often there will be duty counsel in criminal courts, and in family court and youth court in some provinces. Ontario also has duty counsel at the Ontario Rental Housing Tribunal to provide information and limited legal assistance to eligible tenants. Duty counsel will generally assist in such matters as providing information about what will happen in court, seeking an adjournment, assisting in the completion of forms, and in criminal court, explaining the criminal charge, its consequences and possible sentencing outcomes should the accused choose to plead guilty.

SELECTED READINGS

Buckley, Melina, for the Canadian Bar Association, *The Legal Aid Crisis: Time for Action* (Ottawa: Canadian Bar Association, June, 2000).

Curry, Ab, *A National Survey of the Civil Justice Problems of Low and Moderate Income Canadians: Incidence and Patterns* (Ottawa: Research and Statistics Division, Department of Justice, December, 2005).

Curry, Ab, *Legal Aid Delivery Models in Canada: Past Experience and Future Directions* (Ottawa: Research and Statistics Division, Department of Justice, April, 1999).

Galanter, Marc, "Access to Justice as a Moving Frontier" in Julia Bass, W.A. Bogart & Frederick H. Zemans, eds., *Access to Justice for a New Century The Way Forward* (Toronto: The Law Society of Upper Canada, 2005) at 147.

Long, Andrea & Anne Beveridge, *Delivering Poverty Law Services: Lessons from BC and Abroad* (British Columbia: Social Planning and Research Council, August 30, 2004).

Ontario Legal Aid Review, *Report of the Ontario Legal Aid Review: A Blueprint for Publicly Funded Legal Services* (Ontario: Ministry of the Attorney General, 1997).

National Council of Welfare, *Legal Aid and the Poor* (Ottawa: National Council of Welfare, 1995).

Social Planning and Research Council of B.C., *An Analysis of Poverty Law Services in Canada* (Ottawa: Research and Statistics Division, Department of Justice Canada, July 29, 2002).

ENDNOTES

1. See William L.F. Felstiner, Richard L. Abel & Austin Sarat, "The Emergence and Transformation of Disputes: Naming, Blaming, Claiming," (1980-81) 15 Law & Soc'y Rev. 631 and Marc Galanter, "Access to Justice as a Moving Frontier" in Julia Bass, W.A. Bogart & Frederick H. Zemans, *Access to Justice for a New Century the Way Forward* (Toronto: The Law Society of Upper Canada, 2005) at 147.
2. Ian Morrison & Janet Mosher, "Barriers to Access to Civil Justice for Disadvantaged Groups" in Ontario Law Reform Commission, *Rethinking Civil Justice: Research Studies for the Civil Justice Review* (Toronto: Ontario Law Reform Commission, 1996) at 637.

3. *Law Society Act*, R.S.O. 1990, c. L.8; for a fuller discussion of the regulation of paralegals see Chapter 5.

4. CLEO's website is www.cleo.on.ca.

5. Ab Currie, *A National Survey of the Civil Justice Problems of Low and Moderate Income Canadians: Incidence and Patterns* (Ottawa: Research and Statistics Division, Department of Justice, December, 2005).

6. *Ibid.* at 11.

7. *Ibid.* at 13.

8. *Ibid.* at 6.

9. Stephen Wexler, "Practicing Law for Poor People" (1970) 79(5) Yale L.J. 1049.

10. National Council of Welfare, *Legal Aid and the Poor* (Ottawa: National Council of Welfare, 1995).

11. *Ibid.*

12. See Social Planning and Research Council of B.C., *An Analysis of Poverty Law Services in Canada* (Ottawa: Research and Statistics Division, Department of Justice Canada, July 29, 2002) which provides a profile of poverty law legal aid services offered in each Canadian province and the Northwest Territories as well as detailing the poverty law legal services delivered by community organizations.

13. For extensive documentation of, and discussion regarding, Ontario's legal aid system see, Ontario Legal Aid Review, *Report of the Ontario Legal Aid Review: A Blueprint for Publicly Funded Legal Services ("McCamus Report")* (Ontario: Ministry of the Attorney General, 1997). Volume 1 contains the analysis and recommendations of Review Panel and Volumes 2 and 3 provide several background research papers commissioned by the Panel. Volume 1 is available at http://www.attorneygeneral.jus.gov.on.ca/english/about/pubs/olar/toc.asp.

14. Melina Buckley, *The Legal Aid Crisis: Time for Action* (Ottawa: Canadian Bar Association, June, 2000) at 33.

15. *Canadian Bar Assn. v. British Columbia* (2006), [2007] 1 W.W.R. 331, 59 B.C.L.R. (4th) 38, 144 C.R.R. (2d) 291, 2006 CarswellBC 2193, 2006 BCSC 1342 (S.C.), additional reasons at 64 B.C.L.R. (4th) 394, 2007 BCSC 182, 2007 CarswellBC 361, [2007] 5 W.W.R. 381 (S.C. [In Chambers]).

16. Standing to bring a legal case is usually reserved for those who are directly affected by a law, but in some instances will be granted if it is the "public interest." A "cause of action" refers to a type of claim that the courts have traditionally recognized. The decision in this case is under appeal.

17. *New Brunswick (Minister of Health & Community Services) v. G. (J.)*, [1999] 3 S.C.R.46, 66 C.R.R. (2d) 267, 50 R.F.L. (4th) 63, 216 N.B.R.

(2d) 25, 552 A.P.R. 25, 7 B.H.R.C. 615, REJB 1999-14250, 1999 CarswellNB 305, 1999 CarswellNB 306, 244 N.R. 276, 177 D.L.R. (4th) 124, [1999] S.C.J. No. 47, 26 C.R. (5th) 203.

18. *Canadian Charter of Rights and Freedoms, The Constitution Act, 1982,* being Schedule B to the *Canada Act 1982* (U.K.), 1982, c. 11.

19. The leading case is *R. v. Rowbotham* (1988), 41 C.C.C. (3d) 1, [1988] O.J. No. 271, 25 O.A.C. 321, 35 C.R.R. 207, 1988 CarswellOnt 58, 63 C.R. (3d) 113 (C.A.).

20. Andrea Long & Anne Beveridge, *Delivering Poverty Law Services: Lessons from BC and Abroad* (British Columbia: Social Planning and Research Council, August 30, 2004); and Ab Currie, *Legal Aid Delivery Models in Canada: Past Experience and Future Directions* (Ottawa: Research and Statistics Division, Department of Justice, April, 1999).

21. Examples of such legal matters given in the legislation include housing and shelter, income maintenance, social assistance and other similar government programs, human rights, health, employment and education; *Legal Aid Services Act, 1998*, S.O. 1998, c. 26.

8

The Social Worker and the Court:
Evidentiary Issues

(1) INTRODUCTION

It is possible for social workers to practice for many years without ever being called to appear in court in a professional capacity. Most, however, have had at least one experience as a participant in a court hearing. Workers in agencies with a legal obligation to protect the welfare of children and those workers directly involved with correctional services are most likely to encounter the experience, but private practitioners, those in medical and mental health settings, and workers engaged as client advocates may also be required to appear and give evidence. The process is one that many clients will also encounter. Apprehension and intimidation are felt by both workers and clients as they anticipate their day in court. The uninformed worker can offer little assurance to the client. For this reason, social workers need information on the rules of evidence, guidelines for presenting evidence, withstanding cross-examination, and surviving the entire ordeal.

(2) NATURE OF EVIDENCE

Before courts or tribunals can apply the substantive law, they must first resolve contested issues of fact.[1] Indeed, in reading judicial decisions you will notice that the judge often refers to his or her "findings of fact." In most trials, the real dispute is focused upon what happened—that is, upon the "facts"—rather than upon the substantive law. The law of evidence determines what information the "trier of fact"—the judge in a bench trial, the jurors in a jury trial or an adjudicator in an administrative hearing—will be allowed to consider in deciding on the facts of the case, who may supply that information or "evidence," and how evidence received is to be used.

> Evidence of a fact is that which tends to prove it—something which may satisfy an enquirer of the fact's existence. Courts of law usually have to find that certain facts exist before pronouncing on the rights, duties and liabilities of the parties, and such evidence as they will receive in furtherance of the task is described as "judicial evidence."[2]

While the law of evidence seeks to advance the truth-seeking function of the adversarial trial, truth-seeking is not the only value or principle recognized within the legal system. In some instances, when principles conflict, truth-seeking takes second place. So, for example, evidence obtained in violation of the accused's *Charter* rights will be excluded under section 24 of the *Charter of Rights and Freedoms*,[3] if its admission would bring the administration of justice into disrepute. Such disrepute may occur if, for example, the admission of the evidence could be interpreted as rewarding the police for unconstitutional behaviour and consequently, encourage further breaches. Thus, while the admission of illegally obtained evidence may further the search for the truth in the particular case, it may be excluded because of its systemic implications for the proper administration of justice. Another example of competing principles may be found in the common law rule which provides that a spouse is not a competent witness for the Crown in criminal proceedings when the other spouse is an accused, except where the charge involves the person, liberty or health of the witness spouse.[4] Again, the truth-seeking function must take a back seat to a competing policy goal, that of preserving matrimonial harmony and of avoiding the "natural repugnance" of compelling one spouse to testify against the other.

The law of evidence has multiple sources, among them the common law, the *Canada Evidence Act*,[5] provincial evidence legislation, the *Criminal Code*,[6] and other specific statutes, such as the *Youth Criminal Justice Act*.[7] It is also important to note that the rules of evidence do not apply uniformly to all decision-making bodies, nor all decision-making processes. For example, evidence that is inadmissible in a criminal trial may be admissible in a child welfare proceeding. Generally speaking, the rules of evidence are more stringent in criminal matters than in civil, and in civil matters, more stringent in the Superior Courts than in the Small Claims Courts. In the criminal context, the rules of evidence are more lax in the context of sentencing than at trial. Many administrative tribunals are subject to section 15 of the *Statutory Powers Procedures Act*,[8] which creates a broad discretion to admit evidence. Subject to a few named exceptions, a tribunal may admit as evidence at a hearing, whether or not given or proven under oath or affirmation or admissible as evidence in a court,

(a) any oral testimony; and

(b) any document or other thing,

relevant to the subject-matter of the proceeding and may act on such evidence, but the tribunal may exclude anything unduly repetitious.[9]

Similarly, in child protection proceedings, the *Child and Family Services Act*[10] provides an expansive discretion to admit relevant evidence. Subsection 50(1) provides that,

despite anything in the *Evidence Act*, in any proceeding under this Part,

(a) the court may consider the past conduct of a person toward any child if that person is caring for or has access to or may care for or have access to a child who is the subject of the proceeding; and

(b) any oral or written statement or report that the court considers relevant to the proceeding, including a transcript, exhibit or finding or the reasons for a decision in an earlier civil or criminal proceeding, is admissible into evidence.[11]

(a) Types of Evidence

There are a number of ways of classifying evidence, but evidence essentially falls into four major groupings: testimonial; real; direct; and circumstantial, with considerable overlap among them.[12]

Testimonial evidence is spoken evidence, which includes statements and assertions by a witness. Real evidence is an object, thing, or location which speaks for itself. The physical appearance of a person, his or her demeanour, an object, a view of the scene of a crime, tape-recordings, photographs, documents, papers, and agency records, are all real evidence.

Direct evidence is evidence that, if believed, establishes a material fact in issue without the need for any inferences to be drawn.[13] So, for example, if a witness testifies that he or she saw the person who stole his or her laptop and that the accused is that person, this would be direct evidence. In the process, the witness will also be giving testimonial evidence.

Circumstantial evidence is the statement of a fact from which the existence of another fact may be inferred. It requires an inference to be drawn before it is of use in resolving material isues.[14] For example, where money is missing and only one person had access to the place it was kept, access to the money is circumstantial evidence from which theft by that person may be inferred. Circumstantial evidence may be presented in testimonial, real or direct form.

(b) Admissibility

Evidence is said to be "admissible" when it can be properly considered by the trier of fact (judge or jury). The admissibility of evidence is determined through a three-step process. In the first step—the most basic rule of admissibility—the evidence offered must be evaluated to determine whether it is relevant. For one fact to be relevant to another there must be a connection or nexus between the two which makes it possible to infer the existence of one from the existence of the other. Framed differently, before admitting proof of some fact the trier of fact must be satisfied that the evidence offered tends to make the proposition for which it is tendered slightly more probable. Whether this connection or nexus exists is said to be "a matter of human experience, common sense and logic."[15] In one of the leading cases on the question of relevance, the evidence in dispute was paraphernalia associated with the use of marijuana (tweezers, pipes, a scale, and a pot containing a marijuana plant) found in the accused's home and certificates of analysis establishing that the pipes, tweezers and scale had traces of marijuana, and that the plant was indeed marijuana. The accused, Cloutier, had been charged with unlawfully importing a narcotic, after marijuana was found hidden in furniture shipped to him by friends. Cloutier claimed to have no knowledge of the marijuana hidden in the furniture that he acknowledged he had agreed to store for his friends. Is any of the contested evidence relevant? Does it make more likely either the proposition that the accused knew of the marijuana hidden in the furniture or that he had a motive to import?[16]

For decades evidence of the sexual reputation of a complainant in sexual assault cases was regarded as relevant to her credibility, as a matter of common sense and logic.[17] What formed the bridge between the information (sexual reputation) and the proposition (not a credible witness)? Is the bridge a premise or generalization that those who are unchaste were not credible? Only more recently was this "common sense and logic" challenged as a deeply problematic stereotype and the rules of evidence changed.

If evidence is found not to be relevant in the first step, it is excluded. If relevant, the second step requires the trier of fact to consider whether the evidence is subject to an exclusionary rule. Not only are there numerous exclusionary rules, but many of these rules are themselves subject to exceptions, hence, even if subject to an exclusionary rule, one then has to consider if the evidence falls within an exception.

In the third step, the trier of fact exercises a judicial discretion to exclude evidence which is otherwise admissible if its prejudicial effect outweighs its probative value. This last step reflects a current trend in the law of evidence away from what has been described as a categorical approach (or a rigid application of the rules of evidence) to a more broadly principled approach. In considering the prejudicial effects the trier of fact will consider a range of factors including whether the evidence is likely to be given more weight than it deserves (this is particularly relevant in jury trials), whether its presentation will consume an inordinate amount of time, whether it will appeal to the emotions, and whether it will unduly distract the jury.

(c) Hearsay

Certainly one of the most widely known exclusionary rules is that of the hearsay rule. "Hearsay" refers to statements made out of court which a party seeks to tender at trial for the truth of the content of the statement. Second-hand testimony is not good enough for the courtroom. What a witness "heard" someone who is not present "say" is not admissible in evidence, except in special circumstances. Instead, evidence must be given by the person who heard, saw, or sensed the event. The reason for the hearsay rule is rather sensible. Events become distorted and diluted in the retelling and are therefore less reliable. Moreover, usually the person who made the statement was not under oath (sworn to tell the truth) at the time the statement was made, and is not presently in the court where his or her evidence and credibility can be tested through cross-examination.

(i) Exceptions

The hearsay rule is itself subject to several exceptions and as with the law of evidence more generally, there has been a shift toward a more principled approach. Essentially the courts will consider whether the hearsay evidence is necessary and whether it is sufficiently reliable to be admitted. The many exceptions to the hearsay rule developed at common law continue to play a role, in that they are considered instances where the evidence is likely to satisfy the twin criteria of necessity and reliability. However, they operate in a less categorical manner than in the past, so that even if evidence fits into a categorical exception it may still be excluded if it is not sufficiently reliable or necessary.[18]

An important hearsay exception is that of the admission, defined as the "acts or words of a party offered as evidence against that party."[19] As noted by the Supreme Court of Canada, "its admissibility rests on the theory of the adversary system that what a party has previously stated can be admitted against that party in whose mouth it does not lie to complain of the unreliability of his or her own statements."[20]

Another important exception is that for business records, an exception that arises commonly in the context of civil cases. In order to be admissible under this exception the party seeking to introduce the records must prove that the record was made in the usual and ordinary course of business, was made contemporanesouly with the event recorded, records "facts" and not expert opinion, and the person making the record was acting under a business duty when the record was made.[21]

While the rules of hearsay operate in a strict fashion in the criminal context, the same cannot be said for the family law or child welfare contexts. In the family law and child welfare contexts, many judges apply the necessity and reliability criteria less rigourously and allow for the admissibility of evidence. However, some judges do take a rigourous approach. As such, the treatment of hearsay in the family and child welfare contexts tends to be varied and uneven.[22]

(d) Lay and Expert Opinion Evidence

A witness is normally restricted to testifying about what he or she experienced first hand; that is, what the witness saw, heard, or did. Generally, a witness is not allowed to give his or her opinion about an event. This is known as the opinion evidence rule. For example, a witness at a child abuse hearing can testify to hearing a child cry and parents shouting, but cannot offer the opinion that the parents were abusing the child unless he or she actually witnessed the abuse. The rationale for this rule is that the drawing of inferences or conclusions is solely within the province of the trier of fact, be it judge or jury.

There are, however, two exceptions to the opinion rule.

(i) Exceptions

First, there is the lay opinion exception. A witness is entitled to give an opinion with respect to matters that are within common knowledge and which are based on multiple perceptions that are more easily summed up by way of an opinion. So, for example, a witness may offer an opinion about matters such as age, speed, identity of person, handwriting, the condition of things, or the physical and emotional state of a person (for example, intoxication).

The second exception relates to expert witnesses. In a legal proceeding, a properly qualified expert witnesses may be permitted to assist "the trier of fact in drawing inferences about facts in issue by testifying as to their opinion."[23] The evidence must be more than merely helpful in assisting the judge to draw the necessary inferences from the facts presented; it must be necessary in the sense that it "is likely to be outside the experience and knowledge of a judge or jury" such that an ordinary person is unlikely to form a correct judgment without such assistance. In *Mayfield v. Mayfield*[24] for example, a social worker's testimony critiquing another social worker's assessment report in a custody case was excluded on the basis that it was unnecessary.[25] Justice Wein concluded,

> While I would not go so far as to say that a critique of an assessment report could never meet the test for admissibility in a custody case, I am confident in ruling that in this case the necesssity aspect of the test is not met. I would go so far as to say that in most cases, it is simply not necessary or appropriate to have the parties bring forward the evidence of a collateral critique. . .[26]

In one of the leading decisions of the Supreme Court of Canada, *R. v. Mohan*,[27] the court expressed reservation and caution regarding the use of experts.[28] In particular, the court identified a host of concerns regarding the use of expert evidence, including: it consumes an inordinate amount of time; it may be misleading in that the weight assigned to it may be out of proportion to its reliability; and it may overwhelm the trier of fact and distort the fact-finding processs. These concerns must be carefully weighed in a cost-benefit analysis to determine whether the assistance potentially offered by the expert is worth the costs. The Court also cautioned against the reception of "junk science," holding that heightened scrutiny must be brought to bear on novel theories and techniques that are not widely accepted within the relevant scientifc community.[29]

While *Mohan* was a criminal case it has been widely applied in general civil cases, but only sporadically in family law proceedings.[30] Some courts have concluded that the cost benefit analysis will differ depending upon the nature of the proceeding, and there are both judicial decisions and academic commentators who support the view that the criteria established in *Mohan*, while providing guideposts, should not be slavishly followed in child welfare or family law matters.[31] By contrast, others express concern that the rules regarding expert evidence are too relaxed in the context of family law proceedings and inadequate attention is paid to the reliability of expert evidence offered and to its prejudicial impact, including increased cost and delay.[32] In the decision of *Mayfield* discussed above, Justice Wein, applying the decision of *Mohan*, cautions that "the practice of calling unnecessary evidence of experts which does not meet the test of necessity should be discouraged for the benefit of the parties to litigation."[33]

(ii) Who May Qualify as an Expert Witness

The expert must be properly qualified, having gained special or peculiar knowledge through study, experience or observation in respect of matters on which he or she undertakes to testify.There is no specific formula to determine who is an expert. Neither practical experience nor academic training is the sole criterion. Rather, the court must be satisfied that the witness is skilled, but how the skill was acquired is immaterial. The test of expertness is skill alone, in the field in which the witness's opinion is sought.[34] A working definition of a skilled person is one who has, by dint of training and practice, acquired a good knowledge of the science or art concerning which his or her opinion is sought and the practical ability to use his or her judgment in that science.[35] Nevertheless, the way the expertise was acquired may affect the importance or weight given to the evidence by the trial judge. For example, a judge may give greater weight to the evidence of an experienced social worker than to that of a newly-graduated social worker.With increasing frequency, social workers are being called as expert witnesses, especially in cases involving child protection, custody, access, adoptions, and in criminal behaviour such as domestic violence and abuse. The expert witness is primarily called to give evidence on matters which he or she has investigated in his or her professional capacity and about the conclusions drawn as a result of this professional inquiry. The distinction which permits the expert in a field to be qualified is his or her personal knowledge in a field and the expected application of a more precise and careful method of applying the observed or perceived data to his or her expert personal knowledge and experience.[36] It therefore follows that an expert may be qualified to give expert opinion evidence only in his or her field of expertise. Outside this field, the expert is treated like any other witness and opinion evidence outside the specific field of expertise is excluded.[37]

(iii) Guidelines for an Expert Witness

The person seeking to be qualified as an expert witness should first prepare a current *curriculum vitae*. A written *curriculum vitae* is a great help to the judge or lawyer in qualifying a person to give expert testimony. Expert qualifications should include as many of the following as are pertinent:

1. employment history and relevant experience in the field;
2. relevant education;
3. special courses and training in the field;
4. supervisory experience;
5. special awards or citations;
6. speeches, articles, lectures, workshops in the relevant field, including groups to which they were addressed;
7. membership in professional associations;
8. previous court experience whether qualified or not, including the level of court (provincial or superior); and
9. work and training under recognized experts in the field.

(iv) Preparing to be an Expert

1. First present the *curriculum vitae* as the basis for qualification.
2. Settle precisely what area of expertise is expected and why counsel requires expert opinions. If possible, get this information in a written request from counsel. It will help in preparation and can minimize the risk of misunderstanding what is being asked of you.
3. Ascertain whether a written report of your investigation or assessment is required. Try to get as clear an understanding as possible of what questions to address in your report and respond to these succinctly and in clear language. Be certain to obtain consent and authorization for any interviews you conduct or any relevant material you may request.
4. Determine whether you will be required to be involved in any pre-trial meetings.
5. Find out if other experts are testifying and try to anticipate questions or challenges to your testimony.
6. Ascertain how much time will be required and whether you may specify times convenient to you.
7. Some persons may prefer to be formally ordered by the court to testify rather than appearing at the request of a party to the proceedings because it may minimize the appearance of bias and so raise the perception of objectivity which is expected of an expert witness.
8. Take with you to court only what has been required, including any files, documents, records, or notes that have been specified.
9. Review your file and be familiar with your information, facts, and relevant issues so that you can respond without undue hesitation.
10. Use plain language, avoid jargon and explain technical terms that

you cannot avoid. Respond to questions asked but offer no gratuitous information. If necessary, acknowledge the fact that a second interpretation may be a possibility where appropriate. Do not attempt to answer questions about which you have no knowledge or that are beyond your scope of expertise and do not guess.

11. The main objections raised by counsel to expert testimony arise because of hearsay questions (the validity of what someone else told you) and whether there is a proper basis for the opinions you expressed. After an objection is raised, the court rules on the objection and instructs counsel or the witness on how to proceed. Do not engage in this exchange.

12. After you have testified, find out whether you are excused and can leave or whether you are asked to remain or return. You may try to negotiate times favourable to you which the court may or may not accommodate.[38]

The process of qualifying a person as an expert witness is as follows. The party or his or her lawyer informs the court of his or her wish to have the person qualified as an expert witness and leads the witness through his or her qualifications and experience. The opposing party may then cross-examine to challenge whether the expertise is relevant to the particular issue. Only the judge has the authority to qualify or disqualify a person as an expert. Only after qualification may a witness give expert evidence, but it does not necessarily follow that the testimony will be accepted by the judge.

(v) What Disqualifies Expert Testimony

Expert testimony may be rejected where the judge finds that:

1. the testimony is not relevant to the issue before the court; or
2. the expert witness is indeed expert, but not in the relevant field; or
3. the theory or technique is novel and not widely recognized in the relevant scientific field; or
4. the value of the evidence does not exceed its costs; or
5. the evidence is not necessary to assist the trier of fact.[39]

(e) Privileged Communications

The ethical principle of confidentiality is a familiar one to all social workers. However the concept of "privilege" and its relationship to confidentiality can be confusing. If a privilege attaches to a communication it means that a court cannot compel its disclosure, even though it may be highly relevant. This is in contrast to a confidential communication to which no privilege attaches where courts may—and do—compel disclosure. There is a further distinction between a categorical privilege and a case-by-case privilege. Categorical privilege refers to a category or class of communications where apart from very narrow exceptions, all communications in that category are privileged. For example, confidential communications between a client and his or her lawyer for the purposes of obtaining legal advice are not only confidential but also privileged. The privilege is that of the client, and he or she may waive it, but the lawyer cannot, nor can the court compel it. No categorical privilege attaches to communications made by a client to a social worker. Nor does a categorical privilege attach to a host of other confidential relationships including doctor-patient, therapist-client, and religious advisor-advisee. One of the few other relationships to which a categorical privilege attaches is that between spouses. Subsection 4(3) of the *Canada Evidence Act* and a similar provision (section 11) of the *Ontario Evidence Act*,[40] provide that no husband may be compelled to disclose any communciaton made to him by his wife during their marriage and similarly, no wife may be compelled to disclose any communication made to her by her husband during their marriage. Another important categorial privilege is that which attaches to communications made in the context of a litigious dispute for the purpose of effectuating settlement and with the express or implied intention that they would not be disclosed to the court.

In some instances, social workers and other professionals retained by counsel to assist in the preparation of a legal proceeding may fall under the cloak of the lawyer-client privilege. In *Smith v. Jones*[41] the accused was charged with aggravated assault. His defence counsel retained a psychiatrist to prepare a forensic assessment to assist counsel in preparing a defence for the accused.[42] The accused, in the course of conversations with the psychiatrist, revealed an elaborate plan to abduct and murder prostitutes.[43] At issue in the case was whether the psychiatrist could disclose this information other than to defence counsel. It was acknowledged by Crown counsel and accepted by the Court that the communications made by the accused to the psychiatrist were covered by the solicitor-client privilege. The Court then considered whether there were any circumstances in which the recipient of a privileged communication could disclose the communication. The Court recognized a narrow public safety exception, justifying disclosure only where there was an imminent risk of serious bodily harm or death to an identifiable person or group.[44] It is important to appreciate that the Court expressly noted that it was not deciding the extent of liability in tort for the failure to make a disclosure to protect a person from harm (or the duty to warn or protect), but rather only deciding on the question of the limits of privilege (see Chapter 26).

As noted, the courts have also distinguished categorical privilege from case-by-case privilege. In recent decisions, the courts have quite clearly rejected the finding of new categorial privileges, preferring instead to address on a case-by-case basis whether the communications (oral or written) should be protected by a privilege. There is a four part test applied to determine whether such a privilege will be found: the communication must originate in a confidence; confidentiality must be esssential to the full and satisfactory maintenance of the relation between the parties; the relationship must be one which, in the opinion of the community, ought to be sedulously fostered; and the injury that the relationship would endure by the disclosure of the communciation must be greater than the benefit thereby gained for the correct disposal of the litigation.[45]

In the past decade much of the litigation surrounding privilege has focused on the therapeutic records maintained by service providers—including social workers—who counsel survivors of sexual assault. Two of these cases, *R. v. O'Connor*[46] and *A. (L.L.) v. B. (A.)*,[47] made their way to the Supreme Court of Canada in 1995 and the judgments were released simultaneously. Both were cases where defence counsel sought disclosure of therapeutic counselling records that were not in the hands of the Crown, but rather with the agencies that had created the records. Importantly, the Court recognized that both the holder of the record (the agency) and the person to whom the record related (the "complainant" in the context of the sexual assault trial) had standing in motions (interim hearings) brought to obtain access. In *A.(L.L.)* the Court embarked on an analysis of privilege, answering each of the first three questions in the privilege analysis affirmatively. However, the Court concluded that because the final step of the privilege analysis did not enable sufficient consideration of the constitutional interests an alternate conceptual approach, as set out in *O'Connor*, was to be preferred.

In *O'Connor* the Court found several constitutional rights to be engaged: the accused's right to make full answer and defence under the section 7 principles of fundamental justice; the complainant's section 8 privacy interests; and the section 15 equality interests of complainants. In addition the Court recognized several public interests in issue: preventing a miscarriage of justice; ensuring victims have access to treatment; avoiding the perpetuation of myths and stereotypes about sexual assault complainants; and facilitating the reporting of crimes of sexual assault. *O'Connor* set out a procedure and thresholds for disclosure that were quickly altered by changes to the *Criminal Code*. A constitutional challenge to these reforms in *R. v. Mills*[48] was ultimately unsuccessful, thus leaving the *Code* reforms in place.[49]

While over-simplifying the procedure, the basic process is that an application is made to the trial judge by the accused, who must establish that the record likely is relevant and that production of the record is necessary in the interests of justice. In making this determination the judge is to consider a number of factors, including the constitutional rights and societal interests recognized in *O'Connor*. The record is given to the trial judge to be reviewed, and then the same considerations are applied to determine whether it should be released to the accused.

Finally, it is important to pay attention to the outcome in *R. v. Carosella*,[50] as it has important implications for record keeping in social work practice. In that case the court, by a bare majority, stayed proceedings against a school teacher charged with sexual assault because a counselor's notes, made in an interview with the complainant at a rape crisis centre, had been destroyed in accordance with the centre's policy.

Confidential records of third parties may also be sought in civil cases. In *M. (A.) v. Ryan*,[51] the plaintiff sued her previous psychiatrist, alleging that she had been harmed as a result of sexual relations with him.[52] The defendant sought disclosure of the records of another psychiatrist, who the plaintiff had subsequently seen for treatment. As in the criminal context, the Court applied the four-part test described earlier. The Court found that while each of the first three conditions had been satisfied, the interests of the court in ascertaining the truth and avoiding an unjust result outweighed the plaintiff's privacy interest. The Court introduced the concept of a partial privilege, which it suggested was particularly relevant in the civil context. "Partial privilege" refers to circumscribed protection of the records: the records should be reviewed by the trial judge before disclosure is ordered; only that information necessary to get at the truth and prevent unjust results should be disclosed; and conditions may be attached to the disclosure limiting who may have access to the records (for example, only the lawyer representing the defendant and not the defendant himself).

In sum, conversations with a social worker in a confidential client-worker relationship are not likely protected by a privilege and may be ordered to be divulged in court, unless a successful claim to a case-by-case or partial privilege can be made.[53] Similarly, records relating to worker-client interviews and involvement are subject to subpoena and must be produced if required by the court. Similarly, if it is a criminal matter for any listed offence, production must be in accordance with the procedures now set out in the *Criminal Code*. Where some possibility of an eventual court appearance exists, clients should be informed that the worker may be required to divulge the content of their interviews as well as their records to the court; otherwise the client may feel that confidentiality has been betrayed.

(3) TESTIFYING IN A COURT OR PROCEEDING

When a person is sworn in as a witness, he or she is required to promise to tell the truth, usually by placing a hand on the Bible. If a person chooses, he or she has the right to state that he or she wishes "to affirm" that he or she will tell the truth, and the Bible is omitted.[54] The significance of the oath, which is rooted in religious and social morality, lies in the solemn public declaration by the witness of his or her intention to tell the truth, because he or she is aware of the moral and criminal consequences should he or she lie.[55]

(a) Examination-in-Chief

"Examination-in-chief" refers to the initial statements made by a witness in support of facts as he or she knows them. Once a person is sworn and identified for the record, that person will be asked a series of non-leading questions by the lawyer who has requested his or her testimony. A non-leading question is one which does not suggest an answer. Answers should be in response to the questions. They may be either brief or lengthy, as the question requires, but they *must* be on topic. The witness should not ramble and should not volunteer information or opinions without being asked. If the answer is unknown or uncertain, the witness should say so and not guess. Even where a lawyer is present, the judge may intervene for clarification.[56]

Where a social worker has been qualified as an expert witness, the lawyer will ask a series of questions about the worker's contact with the person or circumstances about which the expert evidence is being sought. The facts on which the opinion is based will be elicited. On the basis of these facts, the social worker will be asked his or her opinion about the issue in question. It is therefore particularly important that the social worker and lawyer review both the worker's qualifications and the nature of his or her evidence. This will increase the likelihood that the social worker's expert opinion will be accepted by the court.

(b) Cross-Examination

The purpose of cross-examination is to test the reliability of a witness's testimony and to elicit further information which the opposing lawyer hopes will be favourable to his or her client. Cross-examination may challenge the witness' perception, memory, sincerity, expertise and ability to answer questions directly. The cross-examiner is allowed to lead the witness. It is not a personal attack upon the witness, even if that is the way it feels to the person being cross-examined. Instead, it is an attack on the evidence which has been presented and is very much a part of the adversarial process. Nevertheless, it is a very stressful experience, even for the most seasoned witness.

(c) Guidelines for Giving Testimony

The need to be concrete and specific when giving testimony is a point worth repeating and reinforcing. It is almost always preferable for a witness to describe what he or she saw, heard, or did. Although the lay opinion exception allows a witness to testify in the form of an opinion about matters such as a person's mental or physical condition, or the appearance of a condition or a thing, such evidence is usually more useful when the witness actually explains what they observed. If a witness finds it difficult to find words to describe his or her observations, then he or she should probably reconsider whether his or her generalized judgment has a basis in fact or is only an impression which cannot be defended.

When testifying in court, the witness is bound by legal rules and must give evidence within these boundaries. The following guidelines should help:

(i) Examination-in-Chief

1. Keep in mind the purpose of the hearing, for example, custody of a child, a criminal charge against an adult or against a young person, or a landlord and tenant dispute.
2. Refresh your memory from the case file and your case notes but be prepared to produce the relevant parts of the file and your notes.
3. You must produce the file for the court if it is subpoenaed.
4. Be guided by the lawyer representing your client as to the type of questions he or she will ask, and the way you should answer them.
5. Listen carefully and answer the question asked, as concisely as possible. Do not ramble and do not guess. If you do not understand the question, ask for clarification.
6. When giving expert testimony, state the relevant facts first, then your opinion based on those facts.
7. If you are giving testimony without a lawyer representing your client, or as an officer of the court (perhaps as a probation officer), state the facts as you know them, and then your conclusion based

on the facts. Make a recommendation to the court only when you are asked to do so.[57]

(ii) Cross-Examination

1. Listen carefully and answer *only* the question that is asked. Do not ramble or volunteer information.
2. Do not guess. If you do not know the answer, say so. Avoid comments such as "I don't remember." Either you know the answer or you do not.
3. Watch for catch questions, such as, "Did you discuss this case with anyone?" Of course you did, with the lawyer, your supervisor, and probably others, which is of course allowed. Always answer honestly.
4. It may feel like a battle and your impulse may be to resist or disagree when a suggestion is put to you in cross-examination, but listen carefully and agree or admit where and as appropriate.
5. If you contradict an earlier statement, do not get flustered. For example, you may have testified that a person was calm at a given time and later in your testimony say that this same person appeared upset. When challenged, simply state which statement is correct.
6. Answer every question put to you, unless the lawyer for your client objects.
7. Keep calm. Remember it is your evidence which is being tested, not you as a person. Do not cut off the lawyer posing the questions or engage in argument. Such behaviour suggests a lack of objectivity. If you disagree with a suggestion, say so clearly but politely.
8. Admit your beliefs honestly if asked. For example:
   Q: Do you have a preference about what you would like to happen in this case?
   A: Yes, I do.
   Q: You want the Society to get custody of Mary so that she will not be living with her mother?
   A: Yes. I do think that would be best for Mary.
9. If you are being paid, remember that it is acceptable that experts be paid and that other witnesses receive a per diem allowance to appear in court.[58]

(d) Preparing Clients for Court

Explanations to clients about the court process usually help them to deal with their anxiety and to give their evidence with greater clarity. It is usually helpful to explain what a courtroom looks like (and indeed to physically visit the court facility if possible), where the judge, court reporter, parties, and lawyers sit, and where the witness box is located. It also helps to describe how a trial is conducted, and what issue is to be tried.

It may be helpful to impress upon the client that the lawyer and presiding judge will only want to hear that part of the story which is relevant to the issue before the court. The client is not likely to have the opportunity to tell his or her whole story, which may be frustrating to him or her. It is usually reassuring to a potential witness to know that judges hear many cases, understand the law, and are trying to ensure everyone has a fair hearing.

(i) Guidelines for Clients

In addition to the guidelines listed above, the following matters should also be impressed on the client.

1. If summoned or subpoenaed, the client must attend. There can be serious consequences for failing to do so, including the issuance of a warrant for his or her arrest and the possibility of being held in custody.
2. He or she must tell the truth, even if it is painful. Lying under oath, called perjury, is a serious matter—in fact a criminal offence—which can hurt both the witness and others.
3. A witness must always be respectful to the judge and cannot dispute what the judge says or argue in any way.
4. Neat and clean dress and appropriate behaviour always operates in a client's favour and makes it possible for his or her evidence to be considered on its own merits.
5. Once an order is made, it is binding on the persons involved unless it is appealed successfully or expires according to its terms.

(4) REPORTS TO THE COURT

Social workers are often required to provide reports to the court in both civil and criminal proceedings. These reports call upon the worker's expertise to provide information that may not otherwise be available to the court. The civil proceedings which most frequently accept such reports into evidence are those dealing with custody and adoption. In criminal proceedings, reports are usually ordered after a finding of guilt to assist the judge in making an appropriate disposition that is "fit" in all the circumstances.

In preparing these reports, the factors to be considered are relevance to the matter before the court, intelligibility to the judge and the parties, and accuracy. Sources of information must be correctly acknowledged and opinions must have a basis in fact or observation.

Most reports and assessments which are to be presented to the court or to the lawyer will be divided into specific sub-headings. The most important part of the report, however, will be the summary statement since frequently, this statement is all a busy judge or lawyer will read. The summary must therefore convey a succinct and accurate response to the question that the social worker was asked to address in his or her investigation. The summary statement is more than a restatement of what was said previously; it is an integration of the information that reflects the worker's thinking about the matter.

Where a court has ordered an assessment there will invariably be a statutory basis for such an order. It is critical that the relevant statute be consulted and the spirit and purpose of the *Act* be considered in undertaking the assessment and preparing a report. For example, the *Children's Law Reform Act* authorizes the court, in determining matters of custody and access, to "appoint a person who has technical or professional skill to assess and report to the court on the needs of the child and the ability and willingness of the parties or any of them to satisfy the needs of the child."[59] The *Act* also authorizes the court to compel the parties the child and any other person to attend for the assessment. The report prepared by the assessor is admissible as evidence in the proceeding. The *Child and Family Services Act* also provides for court-appointed assessments, as does the *Youth Criminal Justice Act*.[60] Chapter 15 provides more detailed information about the preparation of court-ordered assessments in the family law context.

(5) SPECIAL RULES GOVERNING TESTIMONY OF CHILDREN

(a) The Criminal Context

The evidence that children may provide, particularly in the criminal context, has long been a matter of contention. Historically, problematic assumptions about their testimentary capacity, their inability to distinguish fact from fantasy, their propensity to fabricate, and their under-developed faith in divine retribution should they fail to tell the truth have greatly limited the ability of children to testify in court. Not surprisingly, securing convictions against those accused of crimes against children was tremendously difficult if there were no adult witnesses to the crime. In the past two decades, substantial reforms, both statutory and common law, have markedly changed the laws of evidence governing children's testimony. In the criminal context, as a result of the most recent reforms to the *Criminal Code* and the *Canada Evidence Act*, the evidence of children is now much easier to adduce, and the trial process made less intimidating for children. While many of the predecessors to these reforms have been subjected to constitutional challenge on the basis that they infringe the accused's right to a fair trial, to date such reforms have withstood constitutional challenge. [61]

In the criminal context, youths and children under fourteen years of age are now, as a result of these reforms, presumed to have the capacity to testify. Previously, a judge was required to conduct an inquiry into each proposed child witness' capacity to do so. Inquiries into capacity are now limited to circumstances where the party challenging the witness's capacity first satisfies a judge that there is a genuine issue as to capacity. A child's evidence is to be received if the child is able to understand and respond to questions. No longer is the child required to take an oath or make a solemn declaration; rather, a child under fourteen is required to promise to tell the truth. Again, no inquiry is permitted into a child's understanding of the nature of such a promise, and the evidence given by the child has the same effect as if it were taken under oath.[62]

A number of reforms also seek to facilitate the testimony of young witnesses in criminal matters, whether or not they are themselves victims of crime. There are six broad areas of reform designed with this end in mind.

1. A judge may order the public be excluded for all or a portion of any hearing where necessary in the proper administration of justice, expressly defined to include safeguarding the interests of witnesses under eighteen years of age.

2. A witness under eighteen years of age may be accompanied by a support person while testifying in any proceeding.

3. A witness under eighteen years of age may testify from outside the courtroom or behind a screen.[63]

4. The accused may not personally cross-examine a witness under eighteen years of age in any proceeding unless the proper administration of justice requires the accused to do so.

5. The publication of identifying information of a witness or complainant in a list of mostly sexual offences is prohibited.

6. A witness under eighteen years of age may be permitted to give evidence by way of video recording in particular circumstances.[64]

A common feature of many of these reforms is that their applicability has been broadened from being available in only a limited number of primarily sexual offences to include all proceedings. A second common feature is that, presumptively, accommodation is provided by legislation unless to do so would interfere with the proper administration of justice.

Social workers often play a key role in notifying prosecutors that one or more of these accommodations are required and in testifying to this effect in court.

(b) The Civil Context

In the civil context children's evidence is governed by both the common law and provincial evidence statutes. In Ontario, reforms to the *Evidence Act* have been similar to those at the federal level. For example, provisions exist for support persons, screens, and videotapes where a witness is less than eighteen years of age. In addition, a party adverse in interest may be prohibited from personally cross-examining a witness under the age of eighteen. The rules regarding testimentary capacity differ slightly from those in the criminal context. In Ontario all witnesses are presumed to be competent, but this is subject to challenge by a party adverse in interest. If the competency of a witness under fourteen years of age is challenged, the judge must undertake an inquiry into the child's capacity. Moreover, the evidence of witnesses under fourteen years of age is to be given under oath or solemn affirmation. Significantly, if the child does not understand the nature of an oath or solemn affirmation, the judge has discretion to receive the evidence if the child understands what it means to tell the truth and promises to do so. Even if the child does not demonstrate an understanding of what it means to tell the truth, the judge also has discretion to admit the evidence if satisfied that the child's testimony is sufficiently reliable.[65]

(c) Preparing Children to Give Evidence

Children, not surprisingly, are often frightened about testifying in court. As noted by the Centre for Children and Families in the Justice System,

> Testifying in court can be a difficult or even traumatic experience for child witnesses. Describing what happened in an open courtroom, trying to remember and recount upsetting events or giving evidence against a family member or a person who is feared can be overwhelming. Coping with the verdict, whether it is a finding of guilt or an acquittal, is a difficult process.[66]

Children may fear the accused, that they will not be believed by the judge, or the courtroom of strangers. They may also feel shame and embarassment. In tandem with the many evidentiary reforms outlined above, several child witness programs have been developed across the country. Such programs endeavour to facilitate conditions so that child witnesses are able to give a full and candid account of what has occurred and to ensure that the child is not re-traumatized by the legal process itself.[67] While these specialized programs are not accessible in all jurisdictions, many excellent resources accessible to social workers and other service providers who are working with child witnesses outside of such programs have been developed. Where programs do exist, it is important to refer a child witness to a local victim witness assistance program or child witness project as soon as it is identified that the child's evidence will be necessary.

SELECTED READINGS

Anderson, Glenn, *Expert Evidence* (Markham, Ontario: LexisNexis Butterworths, 2005).

Bala, Nicholas, "Mohan, Assessments & Expert Evidence: Understanding the Family Law Context" in *Experts in Family Law Proceedings: Effective Strategies and Best Practices for Family Law Practitioners* (Toronto, Ont.: Osgoode Hall Law School, York University, Osgoode Professional Development, 2007).

Child Witness Project: Helping Courts Hear the Evidence of Children, available at http://www.lfcc.on.ca/cwp.htm.

Hurley, Pam, Dawn Lashbrook, Alison Cunningham & Lynda Stevens, *My Day in Court* (Child Witness Project, Centre for Children and Families in the Justice System, 2007).

Paciocco, David and Lee Stuesser, *The Law of Evidence*, 4th ed. (Toronto: Ont.: Irwin Law, 2005).

Palys, Ted and John Lowman, "Anticipating Research Methods, Ethics and the Law of Privilege" (2001) 32 Sociological Methodology 1.

Sopinka, John, Sidney Lederman & Alan Bryant, *The Law of Evidence in Canada* (Markham, Ontario: LexisNexis Butterworths, 2004).

Thompson, Rollie, "Are There *Any* Rules of Evidence in Family Law?" 21 Can. Fam. L.Q. 245.

Thompson, Rollie, "The Cheshire Cat, or Just his Smile? Evidence Law in Child Protection" 21 Can. Fam. L.Q. 319.

Vogl, Robin and Nicholas Bala. *Testifying on Behalf of Children: A Handbook for Children* (Toronto: Thompson Educational Publishing, 2001).

ENDNOTES

1. David Paciocco and Lee Stuesser, *The Law of Evidence*, 4th ed. (Toronto, Ontario: Irwin Law, 2005) at 1. In some legal proceedings, the parties proceed by way of an agreed statement of fact, that is, where they have agreed in advance upon the "facts" to be presented. This is common, for example, in criminal proceedings where the accused enters a plea of guilt.
2. *Cross on Evidence*, 4th ed. (London: Butterworths, 1974) at 9.
3. *The Constitution Act, 1982* being Schedule B to the *Canada Act, 1982* (U.K.), 1982, c. 11 at Part I.
4. *R. v. Couture*, [2007] S.C.R. 28. In addition to the common law, section 4 of the *Canada Evidence Act*, R.S.C. 1985, c. C-5 provides that a spouse is a competent witness for the defence (whether also compellable is a matter of debate) and that neither husband nor wife can be compelled to disclose any communication made to other during the marriage. An important exception is that either a husband or wife is both competent and compellable if his or her spouse has been charged with particular offences against a child under fourteen years of age. As the Court discusses in *Couture*, while there is general agreement that the current treatment of spouses and testimony is problematic, there is much disagreement regarding how the law ought to be reformed.
5. R.S.C. 1985, c. C-5.
6. R.S.C. 1985, c. C-46.
7. S.C. 2002, c. 1.
8. R.S.O. 1990, c. S.22.
9. *Ibid.* at s. 15.
10. R.S.O. 1990, c. C.11.
11. For an excellent and detailed discussion of the evidence properly admissible under this and similar provisions in other provinces see Rollie Thompson, "The Cheshire Cat, or Just his Smile? Evidence Law in Child Protection" (2003) 21 Can. Fam. L.Q. 319.
12. H.J. Glasbeek, *Evidence: Cases and Materials* (Toronto: Butterworths, 1977) at 28.
13. See *supra* note 1 at 21.
14. *Ibid.*
15. *R. v. Cloutier*, [1979] 2 S.C.R. 709, 1979 CarswellQue 15, 1979 CarswellQue 164, 12 C.R. (3d) 10, 28 N.R. 1, 48 C.C.C. (2d) 1, 99 D.L.R. (3d) 577.
16. *Ibid.*, the court itself divided on this question.
17. We intentionally use the female pronoun here as the victims of sexual

assault are overwhelming women, and the particular stereotypes described attached to female complainants.

18. *R. v. Starr* (2000), [2000] 2 S.C.R. 144, 2000 CarswellMan 449, 2000 CarswellMan 450, [2000] S.C.J. No. 40, 36 C.R. (5th) 1, 2000 SCC 40, 190 D.L.R. (4th) 591, [2000] 11 W.W.R. 1, 147 C.C.C. (3d) 449, 148 Man. R. (2d) 161, 224 W.A.C. 161, 258 N.R. 250, [1998] S.C.C.A. No. 141, REJB 2000-20233; *R. v. Khelawon*, [2006] 2 S.C.R. 787, 355 N.R. 267, 274 D.L.R. (4th) 385, 220 O.A.C. 338, [2006] 2 S.C.R. 787, 42 C.R. (6th) 1, 2006 CarswellOnt 7825, 2006 CarswellOnt 7826, 2006 SCC 57, 215 C.C.C. (3d) 161, [2006] S.C.J. No. 57.

19. See *supra* note 1 at 96.

20. *R. v. Evans*, [1993] 3 S.C.R. 653, EYB 1993-66901, [1993] S.C.J. No. 115, 13 Alta. L.R. (3d) 1, 145 A.R. 81, 158 N.R. 278, 25 C.R. (4th) 46, 55 W.A.C. 81, 85 C.C.C. (3d) 97, 108 D.L.R. (4th) 32, 1993 CarswellAlta 111, 1993 CarswellAlta 567.

21. Rollie Thompson, "Are There *Any* Rules of Evidence in Family Law?" (2003) 21 Can. Fam. L.Q. 245 at 299 and in particular, his discussion on the role of this exception in family law proceedings.

22. *Ibid.*

23. Glenn Anderson, *Expert Evidence* (Markham, Ont.: LexisNexis Butterworths, 2005) at 15.

24. 18 R.F.L. (5th) 328, [2001] O.J. No. 2212, [2001] O.T.C. 429, 2001 CarswellOnt 2036 (S.C.J.).

25. *Ibid.* at para. 38.

26. *Ibid.* at para. 44.

27. [1994] 2 S.C.R. 9, 18 O.R. (3d) 160 (note), EYB 1994-67655, 29 C.R. (4th) 243, 71 O.A.C. 241, 166 N.R. 245, 89 C.C.C. (3d) 402, 114 D.L.R. (4th) 419, 1994 CarswellOnt 1155, 1994 CarswellOnt 66, [1994] S.C.J. No. 36.

28. *Ibid.* at para. 49.

29. *R. v. J. (J.-L.)* (2000), 192 D.L.R. (4th) 416, 2000 SCC 51, 2000 CarswellQue 2310, 2000 CarswellQue 2311, [2000] S.C.J. No. 52, 261 N.R. 111, 37 C.R. (5th) 203, 148 C.C.C. (3d) 487, REJB 2000-20861, [2000] 2 S.C.R. 600 at para. 25.

30. See *supra* note 21.

31. Nicholas Bala, "Mohan, Assessments & Expert Evidence: Understanding the Family Law Context" in *Experts in Family Law Proceedings*: *Effective Strategies and Best Practices for Family Law Practitioners* (Toronto, Ont.: Osgoode Hall Law School, York University, Osgoode Professional Development, 2007) at 8.

32. See *supra* note 21 at 274-281.

33. See *supra* note 24 at para. 38.

34. *R. v. Silverlock*, 18 Cox C.C. 104, [1894] 2 Q.B. 766 (Eng. Q.B.).
35. *R. v. Bunniss* (1964), [1965] 3 C.C.C. 236, 44 C.R. 262, 1964 CarswellBC 184, 50 W.W.R. 422 (B.C. Co. Ct.).
36. *Brownlee v. Hand Firework Co.*, [1931] 1 D.L.R. 127, 65 O.L.R. 646 (C.A.).
37. See *supra* note 12 at 352-8.
38. See Robin Vogl & Nick Bala, *Testifying on Behalf of Children: A Handbook for Children* (Toronto: Thompson Educational Publishing, 2001) at 109-113 and Timothy T. Daley, "Guidelines for the Expert Witness," (1996) 65 The Social Worker 3-5.
39. See *supra* note 27.
40. R.S.O. 1990, c. E.23.
41. [1999] 169 D.L.R. (4th) 385, 132 C.C.C. (3d) 225, 22 C.R. (5th) 203, [1999] S.C.J. No. 15, (sub nom. *Jones v. Smith*) 60 C.R.R. (2d) 46, 236 N.R. 201, 1999 CarswellBC 590, 1999 CarswellBC 591, [1999] 1 S.C.R. 455, 120 B.C.A.C. 161, 196 W.A.C. 161, 62 B.C.L.R. (3d) 209, [1999] 8 W.W.R. 364, 1999 SCC 16.
42. *Ibid.* at para. 9.
43. *Ibid.* at para. 37.
44. *Ibid.* at paras. 19 and 28.
45. *R. v. Fosty*, [1991] 3 S.C.R. 263, [1991] S.C.J. No. 80, EYB 1991-67160, [1991] 6 W.W.R. 673, (sub nom. *R. v. Gruenke*) 67 C.C.C. (3d) 289, 130 N.R. 161, 8 C.R. (4th) 368, 75 Man. R. (2d) 112, 6 W.A.C. 112, 7 C.R.R. (2d) 108, 1991 CarswellMan 206, 1991 CarswellMan 285 at para. 25.
46. (1995), [1995] 4 S.C.R. 411, [1996] 2 W.W.R. 153, 1995 CarswellBC 1098, 1995 CarswellBC 1151, EYB 1995-67073, 44 C.R. (4th) 1, 103 C.C.C. (3d) 1, 130 D.L.R. (4th) 235, 191 N.R. 1, 68 B.C.A.C. 1, 112 W.A.C. 1, 33 C.R.R. (2d) 1, [1995] S.C.J. No. 98.
47. (1995), 130 D.L.R. (4th) 422, 1995 CarswellOnt 955, 1995 CarswellOnt 1188, [1995] S.C.J. No. 102, EYB 1995-67686, 103 C.C.C. (3d) 92, 44 C.R. (4th) 91, 190 N.R. 329, 33 C.R.R. (2d) 87, [1995] 4 S.C.R. 536, 88 O.A.C. 241.
48. (1999), [1999] 3 S.C.R. 668, 180 D.L.R. (4th) 1, 1999 CarswellAlta 1055, 1999 CarswellAlta 1056, [1999] S.C.J. No. 68, 139 C.C.C. (3d) 321, 248 N.R. 101, 28 C.R. (5th) 207, 75 Alta. L.R. (3d) 1, 69 C.R.R. (2d) 1, [2000] 2 W.W.R. 180, 244 A.R. 201, 209 W.A.C. 201.
49. See *Criminal Code* ss. 278.1 to 278.91.
50. [1997] 1 S.C.R. 80, 1997 CarswellOnt 85, 1997 CarswellOnt 86, 2 B.H.R.C. 23, 112 C.C.C. (3d) 289, [1997] S.C.J. No. 12, 98 O.A.C. 81, 4 C.R. (5th) 139, 31 O.R. (3d) 575 (headnote only), 142 D.L.R. (4th) 595, 207 N.R. 321, 41 C.R.R. (2d) 189.

51. [1997] 1 S.C.R. 157, [1997] S.C.J. No. 13, 143 D.L.R. (4th) 1, 34 C.C.L.T. (2d) 1, 1997 CarswellBC 99, 1997 CarswellBC 100, 85 B.C.A.C. 81, 138 W.A.C. 81, 207 N.R. 81, 4 C.R. (5th) 220, 29 B.C.L.R. (3d) 133, [1997] 4 W.W.R. 1, 8 C.P.C. (4th) 1, 42 C.R.R. (2d) 37.

52. *Ibid.* at para 2.

53. Similar issues also arise in the context of research. Russel Ogden, a graduate student at Simon Fraser University, successfully argued for a case-by-case privilege to protect the confidentiality of his research participants in a study on AIDS and euthanasia. See also a critical comment on the role of universities in failing to adequately support their researchers in protecting confidentiality of research participants, Ted Palys & John Lowman, "Anticipating Research Methods, Ethics and the Law of Privilege" (2001) 32 Sociological Methodology 1.

54. See *supra* note 5 at s. 14.

55. For tips on preparing in advance, see Vogl and Bala, *supra* note 38 at 98.

56. *Ibid.* at 104-106 for tips on coming to court and examination-in-chief.

57. *Ibid.*

58. *Ibid at* 106-09 and see R. Albert, *Law and Social Work Practice* (New York: Springer Co., 1986) at 180.

59. *Children's Law Reform Act*, R.S.O. 1990, c. C.12 at s. 30(1).

60. *Youth Criminal Justice Act*, *supra* note 7, and *Child and Family Services Act*, *supra* note 10.

61. See for example *R. v. Levogiannis*, [1993] 4 S.C.R. 475, 1993 CarswellOnt 131, EYB 1993-67541, 25 C.R. (4th) 325, 160 N.R. 371, 85 C.C.C. (3d) 327, 67 O.A.C. 321, 18 C.R.R. (2d) 242, 16 O.R. (3d) 384 (note), 1993 CarswellOnt 996.

62. *Canada Evidence Act*, R.S.C. 1985, c. C-5 at s. 16.1.

63. Testifying in the presence of the accused person has been recognized as the most significant stressor for child witnesses; see the Child Witness Project, Centre for Children and Families in the Justice System, London, Ontario. See also their report, Pam Hurley, Dawn Lashbrook, Alison Cunningham & Lynda Stevens, "My Day in Court," *Child Witness Project, Helping Courts Hear the Evidence of Children* (2007), online: Centre for Children and Families in the Justice System <http://www.lfcc.on.ca/cwp.htm>.

64. R.S.C. 1985, c. C-46 at ss. 486, 715.1, 715.2.

65. See *supra* note 40 at s. 18.

66. *Supra* note 63 at 4.

67. Pam Hurley, Dawn Lashbrook, Alison Cunningham & Lynda Stevens, "My Day in Court," *Child Witness Project, Helping Courts Hear the*

Evidence of Children (2007), online: Centre for Children and Families in the Justice System <http://www.lfcc.on.ca/cwp.htm>.

PART II

CHILDREN, FAMILIES AND LAW

9

The Social and Legal Dynamics of Families

(1) WHO AND WHAT IS THE FAMILY?

. . . . . . .the essence of family is:

who it is,
how it feels, and
what it does.[1]

Defining what a family is today and what benefits and obligations (social, legal and economic) accrue to it continues to remain fluid and controversial. Janz,[2] Stacey,[3] and Cossman & Ryder[4] suggest that defining the family has not only become an important social policy matter over the past several years, but more importantly, defines who is and who is not included in society. They argue that historically, legislation has been based on conjugal versus non-conjugal rights and suggest that a different legal approach, one that is focused on supporting and promoting relationships of caring and commitment, would be more useful.

Historically, the family was defined as:

> characterized by common residence, economic cooperation, and reproduction. It includes adults of both sexes, at least two of whom maintain a socially approved sexual relationship, and one or more children, [their] own or adopted, of the sexually cohabiting adults.[5]

In other words, the family was focused exclusively on a conjugal union between members of the opposite sex and served a basic function of procreation. In Canada, the historical definition of marriage has been based on the classic 1866 English formulation of Lord Penzance from *Hyde v. Hyde*[6] in which he stated:

> I conceive that marriage, as understood in Christendom, may for this purpose be defined as the voluntary union for life of one man and one woman, to the exclusion of all others.

More recently, the Vanier Institute of the Family has defined family as:

> . . . any combination of two or more persons who are bound together over time by mutual consent, birth, and/or adoption or placement and who, together, assume responsibilities for variant combinations of some of the following: (i) physical maintenance and care of group members; (ii) addition of new members through procreation and or adoption; (iii) socialization of children; (iv) social control of members; (v) production, consumption, distribution of goods and services, and (vi) affective nurturance-love.[7]

This definition of the family broadens the lens to include diversity in relationships. Policies and laws for the family of today need to be based on the social reality of Canada's diverse family forms. That is, the contemporary family is viewed as more of a partnership (economic, social, sexual) of equals and can be composed of heterosexual and/or lesbian/gay partners, single parents and children.[8]

In 2003, the Ontario Court of Appeal reformulated the definition of marriage in Ontario as, "the voluntary union for life of two persons to the exclusion of all others."[9] This was later enshrined in federal legislation when the *Civil Marriage Act*[10] was passed by Parliament on July 20, 2005 in order to include same-sex couples in civil marriages. However, this has not been without controversy.[11]

With the ever changing social, economic, religious perspectives, and issues of *Charter* rights, provinces have re-examined the definitions of family and marriage along with the legal regulation of the family.[12] Both provincial and federal courts are attempting to redress discrimination based on gender, marital status, and sexual orientation as well as provide the subsequent financial benefits that flow from these changes,[13] such as the status of unmarried opposite-sex and same-sex partners and economic benefits solely contemplated for a partner of the opposite sex.[14] Other examples include laws affecting adoption, spousal support obligations in same-sex relationships,[15] social welfare benefits, and establishing parentage for the purposes of registration on birth certificates.[16] Disputes of custody and access to children by non-biological parents[17] are among the challenges being faced by the courts.[18]

Recognizing diversity in relationship patterns not only raises significant legal issues and social policy implications, it forces society to examine its collective values, beliefs, and customs about what constitutes the family. As a result, the law, the courts, and society are under increasing pressure to find solutions that no longer conform to a one-size-fits-all approach. Like the outdated notion of eighteenth-century legal commentator Sir William Blackstone, who stated: "[b]y marriage the husband and wife are one person in law,"[19] the historical definition of family based on a man, woman and child no longer exists across Canada.[20]

Both legal and social work interventions with families have been made more complex not only by this growing recognition of diversity in family form, but also a growing recognition of the extent of violence in families. The ideology of the family as a loving, nurturing respite from the harsh world of work, together with the legal construct of "privacy" in the home, long operated to keep hidden the violence occurring within families.

The General Social Survey conducted in 2004 found that roughly 7% of women and 6% of men reported experiencing spousal violence in the previous five years.[21] These findings, which some interpret as revealing similar patterns of violence among men and women, need to be put into context. Importantly, the General Social Survey found that women were significantly more likely to report serious types of violence (23% versus 15%), more like to report repeated incidents of violence (44% versus 18%) and three times more likely to report fear for their life.

Moreover, one needs to carefully evaluate the survey instruments used in generating data about domestic violence. For example, many instruments do not distinguish between aggressive violence and the defensive use of violence to protect oneself; they frequently simply ask whether you have ever been hit, slapped, punched, etc. Some research suggests that women's use of violence is far more likely to be defensive than offensive, and also that women are more likely to be candid about their use of violence than are men. While some men are indeed assaulted by their intimate female partners, it is clear that women experience more violence (including a much higher risk of lethal violence) and more serious harm as a result (American research for example indicates that domestic violence is the leading cause of injury to women of reproductive age).

Children are all too often the direct targets of violence or abuse (an issue that we address more fully in Chapters 16 and 17). Moreover, there is now a substantial and growing body of research that documents the harms to many children of witnessing domestic violence. Mental health professional and researchers have consistently demonstrated the array of difficulties children face emotionally, academically, physically and behaviourally as a result of being exposed to domestic violence.[22] Moreover, these children are equally psychologically damaged in similar ways to children subjected to child maltreatment.[23] In a review of more than 30 studies regarding the link between domestic violence and child maltreatment, Appel & Holden found that there was a 40% co-occurrence between the two.[24]

Yet despite all of the negative consequences found for children who witness domestic violence, the state of knowledge is still quite limited as a result of methodological limitations, reliance on untested theories and a lack of reliable measures to assess child exposure to domestic violence.[25] Important questions remain, for example, as to which risk and resiliency factors influence children's adjustment both in the short and long term. That is, not all children experience domestic violence in the same manner. [26] How well a child copes with witnessing and being exposed to domestic violence is dependent on their individual risk factors (presence of parental mental health problems, alcohol/substance abuse problem, lack of access to resources, family vulnerability issues) and resiliency factors or protective factors (supportive parental relationships, supportive relationships with a caregiver outside the immediate family, academic success, and access to resources to support the child and family).[27]

Elderly members of families are also vulnerable to abuse and are frequently in a position, given their dependence upon other family members, where it can be extremely difficult to reach out for help. Elder abuse often takes the form of neglect by family or caregivers who are themselves physically and economically over-extended. Add to this fact their concern that good care of the elder family member will deplete assets. The result may be neglect in the form of malnutrition, poor hygiene and lack of physical and mental attention, or physical violence.

While resort to the criminal justice system, in particular to address domestic violence, has been a vigorously pursued strategy in the past two decades, family law has also been pressed to respond. Domestic violence will, as we review later, have implications for custody and access orders. Additionally, family law legislation frequently provides other forms of specific remedies. In Ontario, for example, the *Family Law Act* requires consideration of any violence committed by one spouse against the other, or against the children, in determining whether an order for exclusive possession of the matrimonial home should be issued.[28] The *Act* also provides for the issuance of civil restraining order (sometimes referred to as a non-molestation order). Such orders direct the offending spouse/parent to restrain from molesting, annoying or harassing the applicant or children in the applicant's lawful custody or from communicating with the applicant or children. The police may arrest without warrant, if they have reasonable and probable grounds to believe that the person subject to the order is in violation of it, and a violation can lead to a fine of $5000 or to three months' imprisonment or both.[29]

Not surprisingly then, those who practice family law today find that the diversity of the family and the difficulties that can occur during or that may have precipitated family breakdown (*i.e.*, domestic violence, physical, sexual, emotional, and verbal abuse) defies a purely legalistic approach to problem-solving. In other words, the law has to play catch up to the changing nature of the family and the consequences that result upon family breakdown. More significantly, social workers involved with children and families during marriage breakdown need to understand that family law carries significant legal, as well as social and economic, implications and consequences.

Family law is different from many branches of law because the very nature of the legal conflict arises from the intimate relationships within a family. Family law matters are future oriented; for instance, the courts must decide the best interests of a child if the matter concerns child protection and/or custody and access.[30] Therefore, decision-making is commonly prospective: that is, what will be the best parenting arrangement (custody and access) for a child based on the best interests of the child? By contrast, in criminal law there is an accused person (the "defendant") and the goal is to establish guilt or innocence with respect to actions that have already taken place; decision-making is, for the most part, retrospective.

How does the court, with its emphasis on rules, statutes, and case law, interact with children and families and their social and emotional needs? Historically, there exists a dynamic tension amongst competing social, political, and cultural realities of the family. The courts attempt to balance in their judicial decision-making the need to protect the most vulnerable in society with families' rights to autonomy, privacy, and respect. For example, in family law cases judges make decisions about child custody and access and child protection matters knowing that their decisions carry significant weight and responsibility; they apply the principles of the law fairly and equally to all. However, despite judges' efforts towards impartiality, questions sometimes remain about how to translate the social and emotional needs of the family through the rule of law. For example, how does caring and commitment in a social relationship translate into rights and obligations in a legal sense? The latter is typically rigid in orientation and often times conflicts with human behaviour and its variable strengths and limitations. Legal academics and social scientists have long argued that the family law system, and particularly family law reform, may not bring about the required solutions to family problems as the law by itself cannot regulate human relationships.[31]

The purpose of the following chapters is to facilitate an understanding of Canada's family law system and what the law says about divorce, property, child custody and access, child support, spousal support, and child welfare matters. In doing so, it will become apparent what impact law has on individual members of society facing the above noted situations—who is included and who is not. Equally important is an understanding of how social workers, in particular, interpret family law and interact with the family.

SELECTED READINGS

Ambert, Anne-Marie, "Divorce: Facts, Causes, and Consequences," *Contemporary Family Trends Paper* (2005), online: The Vanier Institute of the Family <http://www.vifamily.ca/library/cft/divorce_05.pdf>.

Bailey, Martha, "Regulation of Cohabitation and Marriage in Canada" (2004) 26(1) Law & Pol'y 153.

Bala, Nicholas, "Mental Health Professionals in Child-Related Proceedings: Understanding the Ambivalence of the Judiciary" (1996) 13 Can. Fam. L.Q. 261.

Bala, Nicholas, "The History & Future of Marriage in Canada" (2006) 4 J.L. & Equality 20.

Bala, Nicholas, "The Evolving Canadian Definition of the Family: Towards A Pluralistic and Functional Approach" (1994) 8(3) Int'l J.L. Pol'y & Fam. 293.

Bala, Nicholas & Rebecca Bromwich, "Context and Inclusivity in Canada's Evolving Definition of the Family" (2002) 16 Int'l J.Law. Pol'y & Fam. 145.

Cheal, David, "Unity and Difference in Postmodern Families" (1993),14 Journal of Family Issues 5.

Cossman, Brenda & Bruce Ryder, "What is Marriage-like Like: The Irrelevance of Conjugality" (2001), 18(2) Can. J. Fam. L. 269.

Eichler, Margrit, *Family Shifts: Families, Policies, and Gender Equality* (Don Mills, Ont.: Oxford University Press, 1997).

Emery, Robert E., "Postdivorce Family Life for Children: An Overview of Research and Some Implications for Policy" in Ross Thompson & Paul Amato, eds., *The Postdivorce Family* (Thousand Oaks, Calif.: Sage, 1999) 3.

Holstein, James & Jay Gubrium, "What is family? Further Thoughts on a Social Constructionist Approach" (1999) 28(3/4) Marriage and Family Review 3.

McCarthy, Martha & Joanna Radbord, "Family Law for Same Sex Couples: Chart(er)ing the Course" (1998) 15(2) Can. J. Fam. L. 101.

Mossman, Mary Jane, *Families and the Law in Canada: Cases and Commentary* (Toronto: Emond Montgomery Publications Limited, 2004).

Teachman, Joanna, "Childhood Living Arrangements and the Intergenerational Transmission of Divorce" (2002) 64 Journal of Marriage and the Family 717.

ENDNOTES

1. Letty C. Pogrebin, *Family Politics: Love and Power on an Intimate Frontier* (Toronto: McGraw-Hill Ryerson, 1983) at 26.
2. Teresa Janz, *The Evolution and Diversity of Relationships in Canadian Families* (Ottawa: Law Commission of Canada, 2000).
3. Judith Stacey, *Brave New Families* (New York: Basic Books, 1990).
4. Brenda Cossman & Bruce Ryder, *The Legal Regulation of Adult Personal Relationships: Evaluating Policy Objectives and Legal Options in Federal Legislation* (Ottawa: Law Commission of Canada, 2000).
5. George Peter Murdoch, *Social Structure* (Glencoe, IL: The Free Press, 1949) at 1.
6. (1866), L.R. 1 P.D. 130 at 130, 35 L.J. P. & M. 57 (Eng. P.D.A.).
7. *The Vanier Institute of the Family: A Short History, How the Vanier Institute of the Family Began*, online: <http://www.vifamily.ca/about/vif.html>.
8. *M v. H*, [1999] 2 S.C.R. 3, 171 D.L.R. (4th) 577, 121 O.A.C. 1, 238 N.R. 179, 1999 CarswellOnt 1348, 1999 CarswellOnt 1349, 43 O.R. (3d) 254 (headnote only), 46 R.F.L. (4th) 32, 62 C.R.R. (2d) 1, 7 B.H.R.C. 489, [1999] S.C.J. No. 23, (sub nom. *Attorney General for Ontario v. M. & H.*) 1999 C.E.B. & P.G.R. 8354 (headnote only), reconsideration refused (2000), 2000 CarswellOnt 1913, 2000 CarswellOnt 1914 (S.C.C.); *Moge v. Moge* (1992), [1992] 3 S.C.R. 813, [1993] R.D.F. 168, [1992] S.C.J. No. 107, EYB 1992-67141, [1993] 1 W.W.R. 481, 99 D.L.R. (4th) 456, 81 Man. R. (2d) 161, 30 W.A.C. 161, 43 R.F.L. (3d) 345, 145 N.R. 1, 1992 CarswellMan 143, 1992 CarswellMan 222; and *Tremblay c. Daigle*, [1989] 2 S.C.R. 530, 62

D.L.R. (4th) 634, 102 N.R. 81, (sub nom. *Daigle v. Tremblay*) 11 C.H.R.R. D/165, 27 Q.A.C. 81, EYB 1989-67833, 1989 CarswellQue 124F, 1989 CarswellQue 124, [1989] S.C.J. No. 79.

9. *Halpern v. Toronto (City)* (2003), 225 D.L.R. (4th) 529, 2003 CarswellOnt 2159, (sub nom. *Halpern v. Canada (Attorney General)*) [2003] O.J. No. 2268, 172 O.A.C. 276, 65 O.R. (3d) 161, 65 O.R. (3d) 201, 36 R.F.L. (5th) 127, 106 C.R.R. (2d) 329 (C.A.) led the way to significant changes in inclusionary rights for same-sex couples as well as the definition of marriage at para. 148.

10. R.S.C. 2005, c. 33.

11. For a review of the controversy see: W. Bradford Wilcox, "Reconcilable Differences, What Social Sciences Show About the Complementarity of the Sexes & Parenting" (2005), online: Touchstone <http://www.touchstonemag.com/archives/print.php?id=18-09-032-f> and Margaret Somerville, "Same-sex marriage and ethics: Harper is right to say the issue of gay unions has raised special issues among Canada's cultural communities," *The [Montreal]Gazette* (20 February 2005) IN8.

12. The Court of Appeal in British Columbia effectively changed the province's legislation on July 8, 2003, followed by the Quebec Court of Appeal on March 19, 2004, the Supreme Court of the Yukon Territory on July 14, 2004, the Manitoba Court of Queen's Bench on September 16, 2004, the Supreme Court of Nova Scotia on September 24, 2004, the Saskatchewan Court of Queen's Bench on November 5, 2004, the Supreme Court of Newfoundland and Labrador on December 21, 2004, and the Court of Queen's Bench of New Brunswick on June 23, 2005.

13. Irwin Cotler, "Marriage in Canada: Evolution or revolution?" 44(1) Fam. Ct. Rev. 60, for an examination by the former Attorney General of Canada of how the *Civil Marriage Act* became law. For example, in Ontario, Bill 171 was introduced in 2005 to amend or repeal all statutes to reflect the changes in the term "spouse" and the rights of same-sex couples to marry in Ontario.

14. *Egan v. Canada*, [1995] 2 S.C.R. 513, 1995 CarswellNat 6, 1995 CarswellNat 703, 95 C.L.L.C. 210-025, 12 R.F.L. (4th) 201, 1995 C.E.B. & P.G.R. 8216, 124 D.L.R. (4th) 609, 182 N.R. 161, 29 C.R.R. (2d) 79, 96 F.T.R. 80 (note). The Supreme Court considered a constitutionally based claim by long-term same-sex partners to spousal benefits under the *Old Age Security Act*. While the majority of the Court did not accept the claim of a same-sex partner to the status of a spouse, sexual orientation was considered a ground of discrimination. However, a subsequent court decision concerning spousal benefits for same-sex partners was successful in, *Vriend v. Alberta*, [1998] 1 S.C.R. 493, 1998

CarswellAlta 210, 1998 CarswellAlta 211, [1998] S.C.J. No. 29, 50 C.R.R. (2d) 1, 224 N.R. 1, 212 A.R. 237, 168 W.A.C. 237, 31 C.H.R.R. D/1, [1999] 5 W.W.R. 451, 67 Alta. L.R. (3d) 1, 98 C.L.L.C. 230-021, 4 B.H.R.C. 140, 156 D.L.R. (4th) 385. More and more cases are now being successfully challenged based on *Charter* arguments of unconstitutionality.

15. *Supra* note 8. In Ontario, the Conservative government at the time added the term "same-sex partner" to the *Family Law Act*, preserving the term "spouse" for married heterosexuals or those in long-term relationships.

16. See *Rutherford v. Ontario (Deputy Registrar General)* (2006), 270 D.L.R. (4th) 90, 2006 CarswellOnt 3463, (sub nom. *M.D.R. v. Ontario (Deputy Registrar General)*) [2006] O.J. No. 2268, 81 O.R. (3d) 81, 141 C.R.R. (2d) 292, 30 R.F.L. (6th) 25 (S.C.J.), and more recently the case of *A. (A.) v. B. (B.)*, 278 D.L.R. (4th) 519, EYB 2007-112046, 2007 CarswellOnt 2, 150 C.R.R. (2d) 110, 220 O.A.C. 115, 35 R.F.L. (6th) 1, 83 O.R. (3d) 561, [2007] O.J. No. 2, 2007 ONCA 2 (C.A.), as an example of the changes sweeping family law today.

17. *Sharman v. C. (D.L.)* (2004), [2006] 1 W.W.R. 186, 2004 SKQB 189, 2004 CarswellSask 291, 5 R.F.L. (6th) 196 (Q.B.). This is a case where a man paid for his friend's in-vitro fertilization. After they were no longer friends, the man asked the court for access to his twin children, as he had already established a relationship with them.

18. *Cobb v. Wardrop* (1995), 1995 CarswellOnt 623, [1995] O.J. No. 4110 (Ont. Prov. Div.); *B. (B.) v. D. (L.)*, [2002] A.J. No. 550, 2002 CarswellAlta 531, 3 Alta. L.R. (4th) 317, [2002] 8 W.W.R. 178, 2002 ABQB 429, 313 A.R. 291 (Q.B.); *P. (M.) v. A. (E.)*, [2004] A.J. No. 249, 2004 CarswellAlta 288, 356 A.R. 82, 35 Alta. L.R. (4th) 151, 2004 ABPC 42 (Prov. Ct.).

19. Sir William Blackstone, "Commentaries on the Laws of England. In Four Books" (Oxford: Clarendon Press, 1765-1769) at 442.

20. See Statistics Canada, 2001 census report on how descriptions and demographics of families across Canada delineate this particular issue.

21. Statistics Canada, *Family Violence in Canada: A Statistical Profile 2005* (Ottawa: Canadian Centre for Justice Statistics, 2006).

22. See Lundy Bancroft & Jay G. Silverman, "Assessing abusers' risks to children" in Peter G. Jaffe, Linda L. Baker & Allison Cunningham (eds.), *Protecting children from domestic violence: Strategies for community intervention* (New York: Guilford Press, 2004) at 101 and Janet Johnston, "A child-centered approach to high conflict and domestic violence families: Differential assessment and interventions" (2006) 12(1) Journal of Family Issues 15.

23. Peter G. Jaffe, Nancy K.D. Lemon & Samantha E. Poisson, *Child Custody and Domestic Violence* (Thousand Oaks, Calif.: Sage, 2003).

24. Anne E. Appel & George W. Holden, "The co-occurrence of spouse and physical child abuse: A review and appraisal" (1998) 12(4) Journal of Family Psychology 578. Straus and Gelles also found that the presence of adult domestic violence correlates with an increased risk of physical abuse of children. See Murray A. Straus & Richard J. Gelles, *Physical Violence in American Families: Risk Factors and Adaptations to Family Violence in 8,145 Families.* (New Brunswick, NJ: Transaction Publishers, 1990).

25. See Jerome R. Kolbo, Eleanor H. Blakely & David Engleman, "Children who witness violence: A review of the empirical literature" (1996) 11(2) Journal of Interpersonal Violence 281; John W. Fantuzzo & Wanda K. Mohr, "Prevalence and Effects of Child Exposure to Domestic Violence" (Winter 1999), online: The Future of Children <http://www.futureofchildren.org/usr_doc/vol9no3Art2.pdf>; and Jennifer McIntosh, "Thought in the face of violence: A child's need" (2002), 26 Child Abuse and Neglect 229. Also see Jennifer McIntosh, "Children living with domestic violence: Research foundations for early intervention" (2003) 9(2) Journal of Family Studies 219.

26. See *supra* note 23.

27. See *supra* note 23, Ann S. Masten & J. Douglas Coatsworth, "The development of competence in favorable and unfavorable environments: Lessons from research on successful children" (1998) 53(2) American Psychologist 205.

28. *Family Law Act*, R.S.O. 1990, c. F.3, s. 24(3).

29. *Ibid.*, s. 46. Note that in Ontario, these provisions in the *Family Law Act* will be replaced by the *Domestic Violence Protection Act, 2000*, S.O. 2000, c. C.33 when it is proclaimed. Although passed in 2000, the *Act* has yet to be proclaimed in force.

30. *Children's Law Reform Act*, R.S.O. 1990, c. C.12.

31. Andrew Bainham, "Changing Families and Changing Concepts. Reforming the Language of Family Law" 10 Child and Family Law Quarterly 1; Kristen Douglas, Parliamentary Research Branch, *Child Custody and Access* (Ottawa: Government of Canada, 1997); and Gregory Firestone & Jennifer Weinstein, "In the Best Interests of Children: A proposal to transform the adversarial system" 42(2) Fam. Ct. Rev. 203.

10

Structure of the Court System in Family Law

(1) INTRODUCTION

*Pooh was puzzled. Actually, he wasn't so much puzzled as he was **confuzzled**. Confuzzled was almost the longest word that Pooh knew, and he hadn't known that until Christopher Robin had explained that it **meant sort of mixed up and baffled**.*[1] (emphasis added)

In Canada, family law matters may fall within federal or provincial jurisdiction, or concurrent federal-provincial jurisdiction, depending upon the nature of the matter. The *Constitution Act, 1867*[2] establishes divorce as exclusively a federal matter, and divorce matters must be heard before a federally appointed (or section 96, superior court) judge. Family property matters are entirely within provincial legislative power but, as noted in Chapter 4, because jurisdiction over property matters has historically been one exercised by the superior courts, property matters must be heard by federally appointed judges in the superior court. On the other hand, matters dealing with children, such as child welfare and adoption, fall within provincial legislative competence, and each province may determine whether such matters are to be heard by a federally appointed judge in superior court and/or by a provincially appointed judge in an "inferior" or provincial court. The only federal legislative competence in relation to children occurs as corollary relief in a divorce action in the form of support, custody and access orders (for a fuller discussion of this see Chapter 2).

Although the court system has already been discussed in Chapter 4, this chapter will identify those courts which deal with family law matters.

The reader should be aware that each province has a slightly different designation of its family courts in both provincial and superior courts.[3]

(2) FAMILY COURT BRANCH OF THE SUPERIOR COURT OF JUSTICE

Some provinces have established a family court branch of their superior courts, often referred to as Unified Family Courts, so that all matters pertaining to the family could be conducted in "one step."[4] In Ontario the Family Court branch of the Superior Court of Justice has jurisdiction over all legal matters pertaining to the family: divorce; custody; access; equalization of net family property; support of dependents; trusts claims; child protection; and adoption. In addition to the adjudicative function of the court, the Family Court branch also provides services under its "social arm," that we describe later in the chapter.

(3) DIVIDED JURISDICTION

In Ontario, there are presently seventeen Family Courts of the Superior Court of Justice, yet this still leaves parts of the province without access to a Family Court. Where there is no Family Court of the Superior Court of Justice jurisdiction continues to be divided between the Ontario Court of Justice and the Superior Court of Justice. In these parts of the province, property and divorce matters must be commenced in the Superior Court of Justice; child protection and adoption in the Ontario Court of Justice. Child custody and both child and spousal support may be commenced in either, provided that if proceeding in the Superior Court of Justice they are claimed as corollary relief in an application for a divorce.

The passage of the *Family Law Act*[5] and supporting legislation, such as the *Family Responsibility and Support Arrears Enforcement Act*[6] and the *Child and Family Services Act,*[7] in Ontario and similar legislation in other provinces had the effect of broadening the jurisdiction of the provincial courts (the Ontario Court of Justice). While the provincial courts have long had jurisdiction in relation to support and custody, they are now empowered to enforce support of dependants by garnishing wages and pensions and to issue judgment summons with the power to imprison for default.[8]

(4) FAMILY LAW RULES

A distinct set of procedural rules govern practice before both the Ontario Court of Justice and the Family Court Branch of the Ontario Court of Justice.[9] As with the rules governing other civil matters, case management occupies a central place in the rules governing family law proceedings. Case conferences, settlement conferences and trial management conferences all seek to narrow the issues for trial and to promote the early and fair resolution of disputes.[10] The vast majority of cases, over 80 per cent, settle at the conference stage, either in whole or in part. There are, in fact, relatively few trials in family law matters.

(5) INTERIM MATTERS

While the parties and their lawyers are working to resolve the family dispute, interim proceedings may be commenced to determine such necessary and urgent matters as interim custody and access, support of children and residence in the matrimonial home until trial or final resolution of the family breakdown.

(6) THE SOCIAL ARM OF THE FAMILY COURT

The evolution of unified family courts has derived not only from the desire to unit the fragmented jurisdiction of the courts in relation to family law matters, but also to address the reality that the legal issues are embedded in a complex array of social, psychological and emotional needs. In Ontario, the Family Courts of the Superior Court of Justice offer a range of services in addition to court-based adjudication, services which the Ministry of the Attorney General on its website identifies as forming the "social arm" of the court.

(a) Information Booths

Information booths at each of the Family Court sites in Ontario provide to parents information dealing with all aspects of legal, financial, and custody and access issues related to separation and divorce and information about community resources.[11] These Family Law Information Centers, also known as FLICs, provide free written information in different languages on all of these topics. The FLICs are staffed by three different types of personnel: court staff to provide procedural information and court forms; social work staff through the mediation service to assist in assessing the needs of the parties and referring them to services; and advice duty counsel to provide basic legal advice.

(b) Mediation

Fee-for-service mediation is offered off-sight on a sliding scale basis and limited forms of mediation are available on site.[12]

(c) Legal Support

Legal support is provided by duty counsel, available to provide short term and limited legal assistance.

(d) Family Law Information Meetings

These sessions, provided by the mediation office, provide information to parents about the impacts of separation and divorce upon children.

(e) Supervised Access and Exchange Centres

These are now 54 supervised access centres funded by the Ministry of the Attorney General throughout Ontario. Each province maintains some form of private and public services regarding supervised access. The reader can obtain the locations in each provice through their Ministry websites.

ENDNOTES

1   Robert Edward Allen, *Winnie-the-pooh on management: In which a very important bear and his friends are introduced to a very important subject* (New York: E.P. Dutton & Co., Inc., 1994) at 21.
2. Schedule B of the *Canada Act, 1982* (U.K.), 1982, c. 11.
3. See Cheryl Regehr and Karima Kanani, *Essential Law for Social Work Practice in Canada* (Toronto: Oxford University Press, 2006) for a detailed description of family law legislation by jurisdiction across Canada.
4. The Family Court Branch is governed by s. 21.1 of the *Courts of Justice Act.*
5. R.S.O. 1990, c. F.3.
6. S.O. 1996, c. 31.
7. R.S.O. 1990, c. C.11.
8. The Supreme Court of Canada has confirmed the ability of lower courts to imprison debtors for default of child and spousal support payments. See *Dickie v. Dickie*, [2007] 1 S.C.R. 346, 221 O.A.C. 394, 43 C.P.C. (6th) 1, 2007 CarswellOnt 606, 2007 CarswellOnt 607, [2007] S.C.J.

No. 8, 84 O.R. (3d) 799 (note), 2007 SCC 8, 357 N.R. 196, 279 D.L.R. (4th) 625, 39 R.F.L. (6th) 30.

9. O. Reg. 114/99.

10. Chapter 5 contains a more detailed discussion of case management and conferences.

11. In the Superior Court of Justice, Toronto, Ontario, every party must attend a mandatory information session that provides information on legal procedures and resources in their community, separation and divorce issues, alternative dispute resolution, and the effects of separation and divorce on them and their children before they can proceed to the next stage. The Ontario Court of Justice, Toronto, Ontario runs a similar program but it is voluntary. This particular program also provides additional sessions on how separated partners can work together for the sake of their children. Manitoba has been a leader in this field with respect to providing information services to families. Many provinces have since followed in the footsteps of Manitoba's program, For the Sake of the Child. Readers should consult their own individual provinces for further information on these valuable information services.

12. For a detailed discussion of mediation, see Chapter 6.

11

Marriage and Divorce

(1) MARRIAGE DEFINED

> I will be the master of what is my own. She is my goods, my chattels, she is
> my house, my household stuff, my field, my barn, my horse, my ox, my ass,
> my anything.[1]

The most commonly referred to judicial definition of marriage is
". . .the voluntary union for life of one man and one woman to the exclusion
of all others."[2] The passage by Parliament on July 20, 2005 of the *Civil
Marriage Act*[3] included the recognition of same-sex couples in civil marriages, changing the earlier definition to include, "the lawful union of two
persons to the exclusion of all others."[4]

While the definition of a valid marriage is equivocal, there are certain
criteria that are not disputed. For instance, both parties must consent to the
marriage, which ultimately entails the mental capacity of both parties to
understand the marriage contract and the responsibilities and duties that
follow. If consent is given by one spouse under duress, the marriage could
be found anulling due to the lack of one party's true consent. Another criteria
is that there be no prior subsisting marriage; if one of the parties has a prior
valid marriage still in effect at the time of the marriage, then he or she lacks
the legal capacity to marry. In other words, if one's divorce to a former
spouse is not legally recognized, his or her second marriage will be found
invalid.[5] Provincial statutes also provide certain age requirements. For example, under the Ontario *Marriage Act*,[6] the issuance of a licence to marry
is restricted to persons who are at least 18 years of age or 16 years of age
with parental consent.[7] Since the federal government has not legislated with
respect to age requirements, it is the common law that defines one's capacity
with respect to age; under common law, boys must be at least 14

years of age while girls must be at least 12.[8] There are also certain prohibitions against marriage between those who are lineally related. However, marriage to first cousins, a deceased spouse's brother, sister, niece or nephew is permitted.[9]

All of the above examples illustrate that mental and physical capacity to understand marriage in addition to the consent of both parties are fundamental prerequisites to a legally valid marriage in Canada.[10] It is evident that one's ability to freely consent involves the issue of mental capacity to understand the commitment and its consequences; it is therefore imperative that a marriage does not occur under duress and is not entered into for fraudulent purposes.

(2) DIVORCE

The *Divorce Act* of 1986 replaced the earlier 1968 *Act* that had been law in Canada. As a federal *Act*, it applies to all parts of Canada, and the legal rules for obtaining a divorce are the same in all provinces and territories across the country. With the passage of the *Civil Marriage Ac* to include same sex couples, the *Divorce Act* was also amended to apply to same-sex, married couples. It is important to note that an order under federal jurisdiction will trump a prior order under provincial jurisdiction.[11] For example, if a mother is granted an interim custody order under Ontario's *Family Law Act* but her husband later applies for a divorce and makes an application under the *Divorce Act* for, and is granted, custody, the federal order will be paramount. Additionally, where an action for divorce is commenced under the *Divorce Act*, any application under the *Children's Law Reform Act* (or any other similar provincial legislation) for custody of or access to a child that has not been determined is stayed except by leave of the court.[12]

(a) Three Main Types of Proceedings under the *Divorce Act*

The main relief provided by the *Divorce Act* is the granting of a judgment dissolving the marriage. A second type of proceeding involves requesting corollary relief, which provides for orders of child support, custody of children, and spousal support. Either party can request a divorce and deal with corollary issues at another time. A third type of proceeding is for a variation of a previous order for corollary relief. In order to request a variation of an order, there must be one in place. The court can vary, rescind, or suspend an order for child support, spousal support, custody or any other provision contained in such orders.

Since divorce is a federal matter, proceedings for divorce, with or without relief (spousal support/child support/custody), are heard only in the Superior Courts.

(b) Divorce Judgments

A divorce is not effective until 31 days after a judgment has been rendered unless the parties, by written consent, agree to abridge the waiting period and undertake in writing not to appeal the judgment.[13] In any event, the court can grant the divorce effective the day judgment is rendered, or when the judge decides it is appropriate. Once a divorce is granted, it is enforceable throughout Canada.

(c) Residency Requirement

In order to have an application under the *Divorce Act* heard, at least one of the parties, to the proceeding must have been ordinarily resident in the province for at least one year immediately preceding the application.[14] A court can hear and determine corollary relief or a variation application if either former spouse is ordinarily a resident of the province at the commencement of the proceeding[15] or, alternatively, that both spouses accept the court's jurisdication.[16]

(d) Central Divorce Registry

Before an application can be considered, it is necessary to establish that no other applications for divorce have been filed in the matter. A Central Divorce Registry has been established to digitally record all applications, and a routine process has been set up to check for duplicated applications.[17] Where there is a prior application concerning the same parties, that application takes precedence over all others, unless it has been discontinued.

(e) Grounds for Divorce

In Canada the only ground for divorce under the *Divorce Act* is the "breakdown of their marriage."[18] Although it is the only ground for divorce, the "breakdown of their marriage" is established on the basis of the following factors. First, the divorcing couple must have lived separate and apart for at least one year prior to the date the divorce is granted.[19] They must also be living separate and apart when the divorce application is commenced.[20] The effect of this provision is that a divorce application can be commenced at any time after separation, but the divorce judgment cannot be granted until one year after the date of separation (living separate and apart). The secondary effect of this provision is that an application for corollary relief, such as custody or support, can be brought immediately as part of the divorce, instead of having to bring a separate action during the waiting period.

During separation, the spouses can attempt one or more reconciliations for a period not exceeding 90 days without interrupting the one year requirement.[21] The provision essentially promotes marriage by giving spouses the opportunity to reconcile without interrupting the accumulation of time that has lapsed,[22] in fulfilling the one year separation requirement, in the event that the attempt to reconcile fails. Therefore, the continuing policy in favour of reconciliation is preserved. For the purpose of determining the starting point of a separation, only one of the spouses must have the intention to live separate and apart.[23] Thus, it does not matter if one of the spouses is opposed to the separation; separation begins once either of the two spouses has formed the intent to do so.

Secondly, marriage breakdown will also be established if one spouse has committed adultery.[24] Where fault such as adultery is cited, the third party does not have to be named. However, if the person is named, he or she will be served with the divorce application and is allowed all the rights of a respondent in the action.[25]

The last accepted way to establish marriage breakdown is where one spouse has treated the other with physical or mental cruelty to the extent that continued cohabitation is rendered intolerable.[26]

(f) Barriers to Divorce: Duty of the Court

Under the *Divorce Act*, the court has the obligation to delay a divorce judgment or deny it altogether in certain circumstances. First, if the court is not satisfied that reasonable arrangements have been made for support of the children of the marriage, the court must stay the granting of the divorce until satisfied that such arrangements have been made.[27] Secondly, if the court believes that there has been collusion, it can also delay or deny a judgment.[28] Collusion has been interpreted by the courts to include marriages to obtain immigration status that brings the administration of justice into disrepute. These situations occur when a Canadian citizen enters into a marriage for the sole purpose of enabling his or her partner to obtain residency in Canada. Thirdly, the court can deny a divorce where it has reason to believe that the parties to the divorce have connived in creating evidence of adultery or cruelty to facillitate the granting of a divorce. Similarly, if the faulty conduct has previously been condoned or approved of by the applicant, he or she cannot later rely on that ground to obtain a divorce.

(g) Provision for Reconciliation

The *Divorce Act* specifies that every lawyer acting on behalf of a spouse in a divorce proceeding, except in those circumstances where it would be clearly inappropriate, must: inform her or his client of those provisions in the *Divorce Act* that have as their object the reconciliation of the spouses; inform his or her client of appropriate resources providing marriage counselling and guidance that might assist reconciliation; and present to the court a certificate attesting to the fact that these conditions have been met.[29]

The main provisions of the *Act* that encourage reconciliation include:

1. allowance for a 90 day trial period of cohabitation without interrupting the required period of separation and without appearing to condone conduct by the respondent that has been presented as grounds for the application to divorce;[30]

2. empowering the court to adjourn the hearing to provide the opportunity for reconciliation;[31] and

3. the power to appoint a qualified person to assist the parties in reconciliation.[32]

Such persons cannot be compelled in any legal proceeding to disclose admissions or communications made to them in their capacity as a court-appointed experts in reconciliation. Discussions between spouses that relate to their possible reconciliation during such sessions are protected from disclosure.

As previously mentioned, the intention of the law is to promote reconciliation and the means to accomplish that intention are specified; however, attempts at reconciliation during a divorce action are often futile or observed in form only because the problems with the marriage seem unsolvable during the time. By that time, it is most likely a case of too little, too late. Nevertheless, it is a time during which co-operation between the professions of social work and law might make reconciliation a better prospect. It is important to note that a social worker employed by a family law practice cannot serve as a marriage counsellor since a firm can act for only one of the parties in a dispute.

SELECTED READINGS

Barrett, Michele and Mary McIntosh. *The Anti-Social Family,* 2d ed. (London: Verso, 1991).

Cochrane, Michael, G. "Surviving Your Parents' Divorce": A Guide for Young Canadians (1999).

Cossman, Brenda. "Lesbians, Gay Men, and the Canadian Charter of Rights and Freedoms" (2002) 40 Osgoode Hall L.J. 223.

Mossman, Mary Jane. Families and The Law in Canada: Case Commentary, Edmond Montgomery Publications, (2004).

ENDNOTES

1. William Shakespeare, *The Taming of the Shrew* (1596), Act 3, Scene 2, as spoken by Petrucchio.
2. *Hyde v. Hyde* (1866), L.R. 1 P.D. 130 at 133, 35 L.J. P. & M. 57 (Eng. P.D.A.).
3. S.C. 2005, c. 33.
4. *Ibid.*, s. 2.
5. *Knight v. Knight* (1995), 16 R.F.L. (4th) 48, 1995 CarswellOnt 886, [1995] O.J. No. 3242 (Ont. Gen. Div.).
6. R.S.O. 1990, c. M.3
7. *Ibid.* at s. 5(2).
8. See <http://www.parouise.com/marriage/marriage_in_canada.htm>.
9. *Marriage (Prohibited Degrees) Act,* S.C. 1990, c. 46, s. 2.
10. See *supra* note 6 at s. 7—This appears to turn on the issue of mental capacity to understand the commitment and consequences, whether or not it occurred under duress or was entered into for fraudulent purposes.
11. *Divorce Act*, R.S.C. 1985, c. 3 (2nd Supp.), s. 3(3).
12. *Children's Law Reform Act*, R.S.O. 1990 c. C.12, s. 27.
13. *Supra* note 11 at s. 12(1).
14. *Ibid.* at s. 3(1).
15. *Ibid.* at s. 4(1).
16. *Ibid.* at s. 5(1)(b) and 5(1)(a).
17. *Central Registry of Divorce Proceedings Regulations*, SOR/86-600.
18. See *supra* note 11 at s. 8(1).
19. *Ibid.* at s. 8(2)(a).
20. *Ibid.*
21. *Ibid.* at s. 8(3)(b)(ii).
22. *Ibid.* at s. 10(2).
23. *Ibid.* at s. 8(3)(a).
24. *Ibid.* at s. 8(2)(b)(i).

25. *Rekhovskyy v. Ilina* (2001), [2001] O.J. No. 1067, 2001 CarswellOnt 914 (Ont. S.C.J.) at para. 6.
26. See *supra* note 11 at s. 8(2)(b)(ii).
27. *Ibid.* at s. 11(1)(b).
28. *Ibid.* at s. 11(1)(a).
29. *Ibid.* at s. 9.
30. *Ibid.* at s. 8(3)(b)(ii).
31. *Ibid.* at s. 10(1).
32. *Ibid.* at s. 10(2).

12

Spousal and Child Support

(1) INTRODUCTION

Child and spousal support is a matter of provincial jurisdiction and every province has its own specific legislation that governs these areas. However, as we discussed in Chapter 2, the courts have upheld as a valid exercise of federal power the regulation of child and spousal support when claimed as corollary relief in a divorce proceeding, divorce being a matter of federal jurisdiction. Consequently, the federal *Divorce Act*[1] regulates not only divorce, but also child and spousal support. This means that the provincial and federal governments exercise concurrent jurisdiction in relation to child and spousal support. It is important to note, however, that spousal or child support under the *Divorce Act* can only be claimed in tandem with an application for divorce or as a corollary relief proceeding to a divorce. Moreover, as we discuss more fully below, should there be a conflict between orders issued pursuant to provincial and federal legislation, the order issued under the *Divorce Act* (federal) will prevail.

While support regimes vary across provinces and as between the provinces and the federal *Divorce Act*, it is possible to identify several broad principles governing support. Below we focus primarily upon support under the *Divorce Act*, drawing out some of these broad principles. For child and spousal support claimed under provincial legislation, in Ontario the *Family Law Act*[2] is the specific legislation that should be consulted.

Since the *Divorce Act* makes provision for custody and access of children, as well as support of both spouses and children, either may be claimed as relief in the divorce application and granted as relief in the divorce order.

(2) SPOUSAL SUPPORT

Historically, the law of spousal support rested on the assumption that a wife was entitled to support upon breakdown of a marriage. Spousal support was viewed as an expectation resulting from damages (*i.e.* the breakdown of the marriage). The actual amount of support involved 'needs' and 'means.' That is, the wife (typically) had to be provided for, financially, based on her standard of living during the marriage.

With the introduction in Canada of a no-fault divorce regime in 1986, the rationale for fault and expectation was supposedly eliminated. Section 15.2(5) of the *Divorce Act* excludes fault or misconduct as considerations in determining a spousal support application. Yet, spousal support remains and continues to be a difficult policy issue given the nature of marriage and the kinds of obligations that marriage generates.[3]

The *Divorce Act* sets out the circumstances under which interim or permanent support is payable to a (married) spouse or former spouse. Some of the factors the court must consider are the length of the marriage and cohabitation, the roles adopted by the parties during the marriage, the economic advantages or disadvantages arising from the marriage and its breakdown, and any economic hardship resulting from the marriage breakdown.[4] The expectation of self-sufficiency on the part of either spouse within a reasonable period of time after the breakdown of the relationship has been interpreted by the Supreme Court of Canada to be tempered by the other considerations. It may now be reasonable for a long-term stay at home spouse to receive permanent spousal support upon marriage breakdown, if his or her income earning capacity is permanently reduced.[5]

Historically, in order to justify the variation of an existing order or separation agreement dealing with spousal support, a causal connection between the changed circumstances that precipitated the application for support and the marriage itself was required.[6] In other words, the changed circumstances were to be rooted in a pattern of economic dependency created by the marriage. Otherwise, the applicant spouse, usually the wife, was not entitled to support or to an increase in established support unless it could be established that the material change in circumstance was connected to the marriage.

The law governing spousal support, where no pre-existing separation agreement or order existed, was less clear. The applicant's need for support was to be established together with the payer's ability to pay. There was considerable variation in judicial interpretation about the need to establish a causal connection between the marriage and the present need as a precondition to an award of spousal support.

Social workers who are working with clients, particularly women, should be aware that spousal support is not automatic. The role a social worker could provide is to make sure that his or her client receives assistance from a lawyer as soon as possible upon the breakdown of a relationship.

(3) WHO IS A SPOUSE?

As defined by the *Divorce* Act, a spouse means either of two persons who are maried to each other. In the *Family Law Act*, a spouse means, " either of two persons who, "(a) are married to each other, or (b) have together entered into a marriage that is voidable or void, in good faith on the part of the person relying on this clause to assert any right."[7] For purposes of support obligations, a spouse is defined as above but includes either of two persons who are not married to each other and have cohabitated,

(a) continuously for a period of not less than three years, or
(b) in a relationship of some permanence, if they are the natural or adoptive parents of a child."[8]

When two parties cohabit in circumstances where they do not become spouses, there is no legal obligation to provide support. If an application is made, the court will base the decision as to whether they are spouses on the specific facts of each situation. For example, in Ontario, if cohabitation existed for less than three years and no child was born, or adopted, no support obligation would arise. Even if there was intimacy from time to time, it may not be enough to establish cohabitation. Where a child is born, it must be proven that it is the natural or adoptive child of the couple in question for the man or woman to incur support obligations as a spouse.

(4) CRITERIA IN DETERMINING THE NEED FOR SUPPORT

In determining the degree of need, the court will consider a number of variables. For instance, the needs and capacities of both the parties to support the other will be considered with particular attention given to age and health, length of cohabitation, customary standard of living, ability of the dependent spouse to become self-supporting, and the desirability of one spouse to remain in the home to care for the children and provide for their support. For this last point, care and educational needs include continuing care for an ill or disabled child over the age of 18. Consideration is also given to the period of time contributed by the non-working spouse in household and child care responsibilities.[9]

(5) POWERS OF THE COURT IN MAKING SUPPORT ORDERS

The court has wide reaching powers. Under Ontario's *Family Law Act*,[10] the court has a variety of options to choose from, as outlined below:

   (a) requiring that an amount be paid periodically, whether annually or otherwise and whether for an indefinite or limited period, or until the happening of a specified event;
   (b) requiring a lump sum be paid or held in trust;
   (c) requiring that property be transferred to or in trust for or vested in the dependant, whether absolutely, for life or for a term of years;
   (d) respecting any matter authorized to be ordered under clause 24 (1) (a), (b), (c), (d), or (e) (matrimonial home);
   (e) requiring that some or all of the money payable under the order be paid into court or to another appropriate person or agency for the dependant's benefit;
   (f) requiring that support be paid in respect of any period before the date of the order;
   (g) requiring payment to an agency referred to in subsection 33(3) of an amount in reimbursement for a benefit or assistance referred to in that subsection, including a benefit or assistance provided before the date of that order;
   (h) requiring payment of expenses in respect of a child's prenatal care and birth;
   (i) requiring that a spouse who has a policy of life insurance as defined in the *Insurance Act* designate the other spouse or a child as the beneficiary irrevocably;
   (j) requiring that a spouse who has an interest in a pension plan or other benefit plan designate the other spouse or a child as beneficiary under the plan and not change that designation, and
   (k) requiring the securing of payment under the order, by a charge on property or otherwise.[11]

However, it should be noted that there are limitations on the jurisdiction of the provincial family court to order lump sum payments, property transfers or charges upon property. Generally, this type of relief must be sought in the Superior Court of Justice.

(6) OBLIGATION OF PARENTS TO SUPPORT CHILDREN

Every parent has an obligation to provide support of his or her unmarried child who is a minor or is enrolled in a full-time program of education, to the extent that the parent is capable of doing so.[12] The obligation to provide support does not extend to a child 16 years of age or older who has withdrawn from parental control.

In *Haskell v. Letourneau*[13] the appeal judge held that the continued obligation of child support means that a child must leave parental control voluntarily.[14] In this case, it was determined that the son could not remain with the mother because it would jeopardize her mental well-being; since he did not leave her home voluntarily, he could not be denied support. In *Jamieson v. Bolton,*[15] the court upheld the 19 year old son's application for support. The court found that the young man did not voluntarily withdraw from his parents care as there was an intolerable sitiuation that was created for him to leave their care.[16] Consequently, the parents were obligated to pay support.[17]

Ontario's *Family Law Act* is at times difficult to understand if you are not a lawyer. For example, the *Act* uses the term "control,"[18] which does not distinguish between attending school while being under parents "control" and the age of the children. As a result, many parents who pay child support are left to argue the ambiguous nature of the *Act,* which only adds fuel to an already exacerbated family situation. Moreover, the *Act* does not take into account the possible split in custodial arrangements (shared/joint), discretion regarding high-income earners (those over $150,000.00), hardship (unemployed or laid off), and add-ons/extraordinary benefits (special classes or costs of competitive sport-related activities). However, the *Child Support Guidelines,* which are mandatory across Canada, do provide some degree of consistency and predictability which was lacking for some time.[19]

(7) VARIATION OF ORDERS

In the normal course of human affairs, circumstances never remain static. Where an order has been made, for example, for custody, support, access or exclusive possession, any person named in that order can bring an application to vary. There must be evidence of material change in circumstances, or new evidence in support of a variation, for a variation to be granted. In order to prevent frivolous applications, an application to vary cannot be brought within six months of the original order except with leave of the court.

(8) VARIATION OF SPOUSAL SUPPORT

The court retains jurisdiction to vary a support provision under both the *Divorce Act*[20] and, in Ontario, the *Family Law Act.*[21] The reader is advised to consult individual provincial legislation regarding this issue. Typically, the conditions under which a court can vary support are: (1) a change in economic conditions; (2) a loss of employment; (3) unanticipated income or assets; (4) receiving a promotion with a higher income; (5) serious inflation; (6) a change in health; and (7) unforseen significant expenses.[22] This is only a partial listing of conditions; there are others.

In 2001, the Federal Department of Justice set out to develop *Spousal Support Guidelines* to assist in determining the amount and duration of spousal support under the *Divorce Act*. The court continues to determine whether in fact there is a case for spousal support in the first instance. To date, every court in every province has a different method of determining the amount and duration of spousal support. The *Guidelines* were designed as a way of providing predictability to lawyers advising their clients and to judges who make these decisions.[23] It is important to note, however, that judges are not obligated to use the guidelines; they can use it at their discretion.

(9) CHILD SUPPORT GUIDELINES

Amendments to the *Divorce Act* have ushered in a new era concerning child support, the result of which at present apply to all child support orders made under the *Act*.[24] After many years of concern that child support orders did not provide adequately for children, the federal government took action in the form of the *Child Support Guidelines*, which came into effect on May 1, 1997.[25] Each of the provinces has adopted the guidelines so that they apply to provincial child support legislation as well.

Prior to enactment of the *Child Support Guidelines*, child support payments were treated under the *Income Tax Act* as income in the hands of the recipient (usually the wife) and as a deduction from income for the husband. The usual result was that the custodial parent received less than the face amount of the support order, which was very often inadequate. Under the *Guidelines*, support amounts geared to the income of the payor spouse are set out in Schedules for each province. In fact, the name "*Guidelines*" is a misnomer for all practical purposes, since the amounts to be paid under the *Guidelines* are mandatory, except in very limited circumstances. The only exception at present occurs *if* the payor can demonstrate a lower standard of living than the recipient, based on a mandatory formula. What's more, the payor must establish financial hardship—not just a lower standard of living.

Another significant feature of support paid under the *Guidelines* is that it is no longer taxable as income to the recipient, and is not a deduction to the payor. All orders for child support made under the *Divorce Act* after May 1, 1997 are caught by this provision. However, child support orders made before that date are still taxable and deductible under the prior rules.

In its attempt to increase child support payments across the nation, Parliament provided that support orders for less than the applicable *Child Support Guideline* amount could be varied by applying to the court for the *Guideline* amount.

(10) ENFORCEMENT MEASURES FOR CHILD SUPPORT

Each province in Canada has specific enforcement provisions in its legislation. The reader is again reminded to turn to the specific provisions of each jurisdiction.

In Ontario, the *Family Responsibility and Support Arrears Enforcement Act, 1996*[26] has a range of powers to obtain child and spousal support from a parent. For example, the payor's drivers licence, passport, and other professional licences (such as a pilot's licence) can be suspended. Other remedies include: issuing a writ of seizure and sale against a payor's property or assets; registering the support order as security under the *Personal Property Security Act*[27] (*i.e.* registering a lien or charge on any interest in all property in Ontario that the payor might own or hold at the time of registration); intercepting lottery winnings; and reporting the payor who is in arrears to a credit bureau.

All Canadian jurisdictions have created reciprocal support enforcement arrangements with one another. This enables, for example, a spouse who has a support order in one province, but whose ex-spouse (against whom the order was made) resides in another, to have the order enforced in the province where the payor spouse resides.[28] Agreements also exeist with many other jurisdictions around the world.

The underlying policy reason behind enforcement measures is to place greater responsibility on parents in financially providing for their child/ren.

(11) OBLIGATION OF CHILDREN TO SUPPORT PARENTS

A child who is not a minor is obligated to provide for a parent who has cared or provided support for him or her.[29] However, it does not impose an obligation upon children to pay debts incurred by their parents. The support provisions set up a mutual support obligation.

(12) DEATH OF A SPOUSE

The *Family Law Act* expressly requires the continuation of support obligations after the death of the payor spouse. If the deceased person's will does not make provision for pre-existing support obligations, a court may impose them as a charge against the deceased person's estate. The intent is clear: support obligations cannot be avoided, even on death. Imagine the following circumstance. A man dies leaving a support obligation, which was not insured at his death, to his two teenaged children and his first wife. In his will he leaves everything, comprising his home and a small pension, to his second wife. Are his first wife and children entitled to anything?

On application by the first wife, a court awarded her and the children the continuing support to which they were entitled as a first charge against the estate. As a result, the second wife was to share her inheritance with those to whom her husband had an obligation to support.

Death of a spouse also triggers division and equalization of the property of the parties. There will be more on this matter in Chapter 13.

SELECTED READINGS

Canadian Centre for Justice Statistics: *Child and Spousal Support: Introduction to the Maintenance Enforcement Survey* (Ottawa: Statistics, Canada, 2002).

Rogerson, Carol, "The Canadian Law of Spousal Support" (2004–2005) 38 Fam. L.Q. 69.

Thompson, Rollie, "The Chemistry of Support: The Interaction of Child and Spousal Support"(2006) 25 Can. Fam. L.Q. 251.

ENDNOTES

1. R.S.C. 1985, c. 3 (2nd Supp.).
2. R.S.O. 1990, c. F.3.
3. For an excellent analysis on both the historical and current understanding of spousal support across Canada, see Carol Rogerson, "The Canadian Law of Spousal Support" (2004), 38 Fam. L.Q. 69. See also Prof. Rogerson's webpage on the spousal support guidelines at <http://www.law.utoronto.ca>.
4. See *supra* note 1 at s. 15.2(4) and (6).
5. *Moge v. Moge* (1992), [1992] 3 S.C.R. 813, [1993] R.D.F. 168, [1992] S.C.J. No. 107, EYB 1992-67141, [1993] 1 W.W.R. 481, 99 D.L.R. (4th) 456, 81 Man. R. (2d) 161, 30 W.A.C. 161, 43 R.F.L. (3d) 345, 145 N.R. 1, 1992 CarswellMan 143, 1992 CarswellMan 222; and *Bracklow v. Bracklow*, [1999] 1 S.C.R. 420, 1999 CarswellBC 532, 1999 CarswellBC 533, [1999] S.C.J. No. 14, 169 D.L.R. (4th) 577, 236 N.R. 79, 44 R.F.L. (4th) 1, 120 B.C.A.C. 211, 196 W.A.C. 211, [1999] 8 W.W.R. 740, 63 B.C.L.R. (3d) 77. Both cases dealt with compensatory support. In *Bracklow v. Bracklow*, Justice McLachlin for the Su-

preme Court of Canada stated: "it is now well-settled law that spouses must compensate each other for foregone careers and missed opportunities during the marriage upon the breakdown of their union" at para. 1.

6. *Pelech v. Pelech*, [1987] 1 S.C.R. 801, EYB 1987-80055, [1987] 4 W.W.R. 481, 38 D.L.R. (4th) 641, 76 N.R. 81, 14 B.C.L.R. (2d) 145, 17 C.P.C. (2d) 1, 7 R.F.L. (3d) 225, [1987] S.C.J. No. 31, 1987 CarswellBC 147, 1987 CarswellBC 703; *Richardson v. Richardson*, [1987] 1 S.C.R. 857, [1987] S.C.J. No. 30, EYB 1987-67464, 1987 CarswellOnt 315, 1987 CarswellOnt 963, 17 C.P.C. (2d) 104, 38 D.L.R. (4th) 699, 77 N.R. 1, 22 O.A.C. 1, 7 R.F.L. (3d) 304; *Caron v. Caron*, [1987] 1 S.C.R. 892, EYB 1987-67973, 1987 CarswellYukon 8, 1987 CarswellYukon 43, [1987] S.C.J. No. 32, 38 D.L.R. (4th) 735, 75 N.R. 36, [1987] 4 W.W.R. 522, 14 B.C.L.R. (2d) 186, 2 Y.R. 246, 7 R.F.L. (3d) 274.

7. See *supra* note 2 at s. 1.
8. *Ibid.* at s. 29.
9. *Ibid.* at s. 33(9) for the factors listed under Ontario's *Family Law Act*.
10. *Ibid.* at ss. 33 and 34.
11. *Ibid.* at s. 34(1).
12. *Ibid.* at s. 31(1).
13. (1979), 25 O.R. (2d) 139, 1 F.L.R.A.C. 306, 1979 CarswellOnt 101, 100 D.L.R. (3d) 329 (Co. Ct.).
14. *Ibid.* at para. 74.
15. (1994), 1994 CarswellOnt 2081, [1994] O.J. No. 3228 (Ont. Prov. Div.).
16. *Ibid.* at para. 38.
17. *Ibid.* at paras. 54-56.
18. See *supra* note 2 at s. 31(1) and (2).
19. The reader can access their government website for the specific amounts a parent would pay for child support based on their income and number of children.
20. See *supra* note 1 at s. 17.
21. See *supra* note 2.
22. *Ibid.* at s. 37.
23. Professors Carol Rogerson of the Faculty of Law, University of Toronto and Rollie Thompson of Dalhousie Law School, Nova Scotia were retained by Justice Canada to develop spousal support guidelines. See Carol Rogerson & Rollie Thompson, *Spousal Support Advisory Guidelines: A Draft Proposal* (Department of Justice Canada, 2005) which details the draft proposals.
24. See *supra* note 1 at s. 15.1. Under the *Divorce Act* there are different guidelines. The federal *Child Support Guidelines* created a different set

of guidelines for each province and territory. Each province and territory adopted the federal guidelines irrespective of court jurisdiction.

25. For a historical analysis of the politics of change in spousal support, see Nicholas Bala, "A report from Canada's 'Gender War Zone': Reforming the child-related provisions of the *Divorce Act*" (1999) 16(2) Can. J. Fam. L. 163.

26. S.O. 1996, c. 31.

27. R.S.O. 1990, c. P.10.

28. For an overview and details regarding each province see "Overview of the Canadian System of Support Enforcement" online: <http://www.justice.gc.ca/en/ps/sup/enforcement/enforcement_overview.html>.

29. See *supra* note 2 at s. 32.

13

Family Property

(1) FAMILY PROPERTY: DIVISION OF PROPERTY

Property law in Canada is a provincial matter under the *Constitution Act, 1867.*[1] Property matters are always brought in the Superior Court of the province in which the parties are resident.

All provinces have community of property rules that require division of property upon marriage breakdown, although the definitions of property may vary from province to province. In Ontario, the definition of property is extremely broad and all-encompassing, including real property, money, shares, R.R.S.P.s, pensions, life insurance, retirement benefits, and more—virtually everything acquired by the parties during marriage. Property that is not equalized includes the value of property owned by a spouse before marriage (except a matrimonial home) on the date of marriage and property received by inheritance or gift from third parties during marriage.

In Ontario, the matrimonial home is treated differently from other property. Regardless of registered ownership, a spouse is entitled to share in the value of a matrimonial home upon marriage breakdown, even if it was owned by the other spouse before marriage. The definition of "matrimonial home" is as broad as the definition of property, and includes every residential property in which a spouse has an interest and which was ordinarily occupied by the spouses or children at the time of separation as their family residence. There can be more than one matrimonial home. For example, the courts have found the following to qualify as matrimonial homes where the above requirements were met: boat with sleeping accommodation; ski chalet; cottage; Florida condominium; trailer; camper; apartment; and residence above a restaurant and the part of the restaurant where the family ate their meals.

It should be noted that in Ontario, statutory property rights only apply to *married* spouses on a marriage breakdown. Unmarried spouses have no property rights under statute. However, the law of trusts at common law may give some of the same rights to a common law spouse in similar circumstances. The unmarried spouse must show actual contribution to the acquisition, preservation, or maintenance of the property in order to creat a trust interest in the property. In one case, heard by the Supreme Court of Canada, a long-term unmarried spouse who had cared for and worked with her common law husband and contributed to his welfare for many years, while raising her own children, was given title to the husband's house, even though he had always been the registered owner.[2] This case attempted to redress and recognize the woman's contribution to the family by equitable distribution of the family resources.

Family law and family property law are exceedingly complex areas that require expert legal advice in order to protect the rights of the spouses and children upon separation or divorce. Without such advice, separated spouses may unwittingly give up important and valuable custodial and property rights. Social workers working with these families are strongly advised to urge their clients to obtain independent legal advice about their custodial and property rights in the event of a significant change in their status, such as at cohabitation, marriage, separation, divorce or death.

In the past three decades, most provincial legislatures across Canada have devised statutory schemes that have brought family law into line with contemporary modes of family interaction.[3] Before this period there was a half-century of benign parliamentary neglect that permitted courts to sanction notions of matrimonial misconduct and to render decisions based on prevailing assumptions as they saw fit.[4] Since then, notions of morality have evolved in favour of principles of equity in property and support matters and in regard to the best interests and needs of children. Prevailing provincial concepts of spousal or parental relationships and parent-child responsibilities are built on principles of equality and demonstrated need as is the present federal legislation.

The Supreme Court of Canada case of *Murdoch v. Murdoch,*[5] seemed to shock the provinces into moving toward reform and therefore was, in many respects, the watershed case that led to a new era in family law. The facts of this case are these:

> The plaintiff wife sought a beneficial interest in certain properties and assets vested in the name of her defendant husband. These properties were ranch properties acquired over a period of 18 years, and upon which the plaintiff carried out her duties as ranch wife. It was found as a fact by a majority of the court that "what the appellant had done, while living with the respondent, was the work done by any ranch wife." Although the plaintiff had from time

to time advanced money to the defendant for the purpose of acquiring lands and chattels, these were recorded as loans and paid back. The plaintiff founded her claim on the basis of a trust.[6]

It was held by the court that the plaintiff's claim must fail. A dissenting opinion was filed by Mr. Justice Laskin, the late Chief Justice of the Supreme Court of Canada, who wrote that the plaintiff should be entitled to a proprietary interest in the properties.[7] Such share was to be determined upon a proper inquiry and report. The plaintiff, in fact, had acquired substantial household furnishings for the matrimonial home, advanced money towards the acquisition of properties and assets, and contributed labour far in excess of ordinary housekeeping duties. This was a case where the spouses over a period of some 15 years improved their lot in life through progressively larger acquisitions of ranch property to which the plaintiff contributed the necessary labour in seeing that the ranches were productive. There was no reason to treat this contribution as any less significant than a direct financial contribution, which to a lesser degree she also made. The relations of husband and wife in such circumstances should not be allowed to rest on the mere obligation of support and shelter that arose from the fact of marriage where the husband was able to provide for an impecunious wife nor be allowed to rest on her statutory dower rights under the law of Alberta. The dowery rights represented a minimum amount and reflected the law's protection for a dependent wife. However, the right to dower should not be regarded as exhausting a wife's claim upon her husband where she had, as in the instant case, been anything but dependent. In Justice Laskin's view, the appropriate mechanism to give relief to a spouse who is unable to prove a common intention for interest in property, or to a spouse whose contribution to the acquisition of property is physical labour rather than financial contribution, is the constructive trust,[8] which does not depend on evidence of intention. The basis of the constructive trust is the unjust enrichment that would result if the person having the property were permitted to retain it.

In *Rathwell v. Rathwell*,[9] Mr. Justice Dickson following the dissent in *Murdoch* stated:

> Many factors, legal and non-legal, have emerged to modify the position of earlier days. Among these factors are a more enlightened attitude toward the status of women, altered life-styles, dynamic socio-economic changes. Increasingly, the work of a woman in the management of the home and rearing of the children, as wife and mother, is recognized as an economic contribution to the family unit.[10]

The pressure for reform gained momentum; in Ontario the *Family Law Reform Act*,[11] was proclaimed in 1978. The Preamble of the *Family Law Reform Act* stated:

Whereas . . . it is necessary to recognize the equal position of spouses as individuals within marriage and to recognize marriage as a form of partnership;

And whereas in support of such recognition it is necessary to provide in law for the orderly and equitable settlement of the affairs of the spouses upon the breakdown of the partnership; and to provide for other mutual obligations in family relationships, including the equitable sharing by parents of responsibility for their children.[12]

The *Family Law Act*[13] preamble today states:

Whereas it is desirable to encourage and strengthen the role of the family; and whereas for that purpose it is necessary to recognize the equal position of spouses as individuals within marriage and to recognize as a form of partnership;

And whereas in support of such recognition it is necessary to provide in law for the orderly and equitable settlement of the affairs of the spouses upon the breakdown of the partnership, and to provide for other mutual obligations in family relationships, including the equitable sharing by parents of responsibility for their children.[14]

From 1986 until today, the *Act* has also provided for division (or equalization) of all property acquired by the parties during marriage and cohabitation, regardless of the registered ownership. Upon separation, divorce or death, a married spouse is legally entitled to claim equalization of all such property.

In effect, many of the old common law inequities concerning the status of women and children have been swept away as courts came to recognize that each spouse has the right to support from the other when need is demonstrated, that there exists an expectation that each will become self-supporting to the extent of his or her ability, and that there will be a fair sharing of assets.[15] The old common law rules were disadvantageous to women by presuming that the spouse who holds title, usually the husband, had a primary right to property of a marriage unless the other spouse could produce evidence of legal title or direct financial contribution. Men were disadvantaged with respect to custody of the children of a marriage because of a presumption that children of "tender years" should remain with their mother. It was also presumed that a father had continuing support obligations toward his wife and children. In addition, children born outside of marriage had no right to inherit property and fathers of such children had no right to custody.

The enactment of the *Family Law Act* in Ontario, and similar legislation in other provinces, meant that married women would have equal entitlement to a division of property at the point of marriage breakdown. It also created new responsibilities for support for both spouses and their children. These egalitarian concepts have been entrenched by such *Acts*, moving from partial division of property on marriage breakdown to a full equalization of the value of property acquired during the course of the marriage upon breakdown, divorce, or death. With few exceptions, the value of all property acquired during the marriage must be divided equally.

(2) *FAMILY LAW ACT*, ONTARIO

Ontario's *Family Law Act* is divided into six parts, each dealing with one of the following: property division, special rules respecting the matrimonial home, child and spousal support obligations, domestic contracts, dependants' claims for damages in the event of accident, injury or death, and amendments to the common law. The whole *Act* is preceded by a definition section.

The *Act* defines a "child" as one born within or outside marriage and includes a person to whom the parent has demonstrated a settled intention to treat as a child of his or her family. This includes both adopted or biological children and step-children, but does not include a child placed in a foster home by a person having lawful custody.[16] To cohabit is to live together in a conjugal relationship, whether inside or outside marriage.[17] "Spouse" for purposes of property is defined as two persons who are married to each other. For the purposes of support, "spouse" is defined more broadly to include two persons who are married or who have cohabited continuously for a period of not less than three years or are in a relationship of some permanence, if they are the natural or adoptive parents of a child.

"Property" for purposes of the *Act* has a very broad definition and includes virtually everything—the home, pensions, money in bank accounts, and property over which a person may exercise some control now or in the future, regardless of ownership, and whether or not a third party has an ownership interest.[18] The value of property is determined at the date of marriage and on the date of separation, divorce, and/or death. Gifts or inheritances from third parties during marriage are excluded, with a few exceptions, as are other enumerated assets or sources of income. The effect of the property provisions is that it requires spouses to value all of their property at marriage and at marriage breakdown, deduct the value of debts and liabilities, and arrive at the net family property for each of them. The spouse with the smaller total is entitled to one-half the difference between their net family properties. In order to enforce property entitlement, a person may have to apply to a superior court to have his or her property rights determined by the court.[19]

Formal recognition is given to the concept of marriage as a partnership, obliterating the traditional assumptions of sex-linked roles and tasks. Child care, household management, and financial provision are the joint responsibilities of the spouses. Inherent to the marital relationship is joint contribution, whether financial or otherwise, in assuming these responsibilities, entitling each spouse to share equally in the value of property.

It is on the dissolution of a marriage (or a common law relationship) that the law is strained. For example, it is presumed that partners begin their relationship as equals in their capacity to earn. However, there continues to be a gendered difference in rates of pay and the physical care of children is still largely the principal responsibility of women. Moreover, separation and divorce agreements leave many women and children economically disadvantaged.

Social workers may wish to use the statutory concept of shared responsibilities as a model of community standards in working with couples experiencing difficulties in their family relationships. Indeed, children become part of the family unit as their capacity to make a contribution to its everyday function develops and they are included in family counselling sessions. The *Act* has included the essential components of a marital partnership; that is, child care, household management, and financial maintenance. It has not indicated which partner shall perform these tasks nor in what spirit they shall be performed. A discussion centred on how these tasks are to be divided and the feelings surrounding the division may uncover discrepancies in each family member's concept of appropriate roles and functions, and this can open new channels of communication and new models for family roles.

(3) COMMON LAW RELATIONSHIPS AND PROPERTY MATTERS

The *Family Law Act*, when dealing with property rights, defines spouse narrowly as it only recognizes a spouse by marriage. In other words, couples who are not or have never been married have no claim under the legislation to a share of property owned in the name of the other. For example:

> Carol and Bob lived together for nine years but were never married. Both worked but Carol, having been brought up to believe that the man was the head of the household, always let Bob look after their finances. Everything was in his name. In the fullness of time they separated. Carol wanted to claim her share of the marriage property, but discovered she had no claim under the *Family Law Act* to any part of the furniture, bank account or car.

If a remedy were to be sought, one may be available in common law through a claim under the doctrine of constructive trust.[20] However, establishing a constructive trust may be a long and costly procedure. Clients should be advised to make sure that joint assets are always in the name of both partners to a common law relationship or that they enter into a cohabitation agreement that includes division of property upon separation.

An important case testing the scope of family law legislation is found in the following story:

> · A man and woman lived together as man and wife for approximately 20 years. The woman supported the couple during the first five years while the man saved so as to be able to acquire a farm. The woman aided the man in obtaining and maintaining his bee-keeping business and helped with the farm labours. The man subsequently purchased additional land on which a home was built. The farm was then sold and the proceeds deposited into the man's bank account. The woman maintained that she was entitled to one-half interest in the property and business. The trial judge dismissed her claim. She appealed and was awarded her share based on the principle of constructive trust. The man appealed to the Supreme Court of Canada but the appeal was dismissed and the principle upheld.[21]

(4) POSSESSION OF THE MATRIMONIAL HOME

Married spouses are equally entitled to possession of the matrimonial home, including rental accommodation. In Ontario, common law spouses are not eligible since they are excluded by the definition of "spouse." In the event of emergency need, the court is empowered to make orders for temporary possession of the home. This decision is usually based on protecting the best interests of the children or to prevent the eviction of a parent and children.

(5) DOMESTIC CONTRACTS

The *Family Law Act* (Ontario) provides that parties may enter into various domestic contracts, establishes rules that determine the validity and enforceability of the terms of the contract, and in some cases gives the court jurisdiction to override the terms of the contract to promote a social value seen to be compelling.[22]

Family law legislation regulates domestic contracts in the form of marriage contracts, cohabitation agreements and separation agreements.[23] The distinction is based on the status of the parties at the time the contract is made. A marriage contract, for example, is valid only so long as the parties remain married unless the contract states otherwise. Parties to an agreement, which must be in writing and signed by the parties, are free to make any arrangements they consider suitable to regulate their own relationships, lives, and property, including the right to direct the education and moral training of their children. Separation agreements may also include the right to decide custody and access to children. The court is authorized to disregard any agreement concerning support, education, 'moral' training, or custody and access to children where it considers the contractual provisions not to be in the child's best interests. The *Family Law Act* also requires full financial disclosure between spouses before a domestic contract is signed, otherwise the contract is at risk of being set aside for material non-disclosure of financial assets.[24] Moreover, full disclosure must be provided as a matter of course even if no disclosure is ever requested from either party.[25]

In Ontario, property rights falling within the scope of the contract are seen as valid and enforceable. Courts cannot override property contracts in the province as they can support contracts with a few exceptions. A marriage or contract purporting to limit a spouse's interest in matrimonial property will be unenforceable. Moreover, subsection 56(1) of the *Family Law Act* provides that, "in the determination of a matter respecting the education, moral training or custody of or access to a child, the court may disregard any provision of a domestic contract pertaining to the matter where, in the opinion of the court, to do so is in the best interests of the child." Moreover, in subsection 56(1.1) of the *Act* it is stated that, "in the determination of a matter respecting the support of a child, the court may disregard any provision of a domestic contract pertaining to the matter where the provision is unreasonable having regard to the child support guidelines, as well as to any other provision relating to support of the child in the contract."

Despite the subsection 33(11) requirement that child support guidelines are to be followed, subsection 33(12) says that a court may award an amount that is different from the amount that would be determined in accordance with the child support guidelines if the court is satisfied,

(a) that special provisions in an order or a written agreement respecting the financial obligations of the parents, or the division or transfer of their property, directly or indirectly benefit a child, or that special provisions have otherwise been made for the benefit of a child; and

(b) that the application of the child support guidelines would result in an amount of child support that is inequitable given those special provisions.

In *Deiter v. Sampson*[26] the court stated that it is entitled to review the agreement to ensure it meets the child's best interests.[27] In another case, *Reinhardt v. Reinhardt,*[28] the court refused to accept a separation agreement whose provisions regarding child support were inadequate.[29]

SELECTED READINGS

Benson, Marjorie Lynne & Marie-Ann Bowden, *Understanding Property: A Guide to Canada's Property Law* (Toronto: Carswell, 1997).

Hovius, Berend & Timothy G. Youdan, *The Law of Family Property* (Toronto, Carswell: 1991).

Wu, Zheng, *Cohabitation: An Alternative Form of Family Living* (Don Mills: Oxford University Press, 2000).

ENDNOTES

1. (U.K.), 30 & 31 Victoria, c. 3, s. 92.
2. *Peter v. Beblow*, [1993] 1 S.C.R. 980, EYB 1993-67100, [1993] 3 W.W.R. 337, 23 B.C.A.C. 81, 39 W.A.C. 81, 101 D.L.R. (4th) 621, 150 N.R. 1, 48 E.T.R. 1, 77 B.C.L.R. (2d) 1, 44 R.F.L. (3d) 329, [1993] R.D.F. 369, [1993] S.C.J. No. 36, 1993 CarswellBC 44, 1993 CarswellBC 1258. This case was confirmed as the leading authority in *Wylie v. LeClair* (2003), 38 R.F.L. (5th) 227, [2003] O.J. No. 1938, 2003 CarswellOnt 1966, 172 O.A.C. 187, 226 D.L.R. (4th) 439, 64 O.R. (3d) 782 (C.A.).
3. See the Tables of Concordance.
4. Judge Rosalie Abella, "Family Law in Ontario: Changing Assumption" (1981) 13 Ottawa L. Rev. 1.
5. (1973), [1975] 1 S.C.R. 423, [1974] 1 W.W.R. 361, 1973 CarswellAlta 119, 13 R.F.L. 185, 41 D.L.R. (3d) 367, 1973 CarswellAlta 156.
6. *Ibid.*
7. *Ibid.* at para. 75.
8. A trust is created when money or property is held by one person for the benefit of another. When there is no express intention to create a trust, but in fairness or equity a trust should exist, the court may construe (construct) a trust. See *Becker v. Pettkus*, [1980] 2 S.C.R. 834, 1980 CarswellOnt 299, 1980 CarswellOnt 644, [1980] S.C.J. No. 103, 117 D.L.R. (3d) 257, 34 N.R. 384, 8 E.T.R. 143, 19 R.F.L. (2d) 165 and *Arndt v. Arndt* (1993), 48 R.F.L. (3d) 353, 1993 CarswellOnt 351, [1993] O.J. No. 2350, 107 D.L.R. (4th) 1, 66 O.A.C. 4, 15 O.R. (3d) 389 (C.A.), leave to appeal refused (1994), 109 D.L.R. (4th) vii (note), 17 O.R. (3d) xvi (note), 71 O.A.C. 72 (note), 170 N.R. 160 (note), 1 R.F.L. (4th) 63n (S.C.C.).
9. [1978] 2 S.C.R. 436, 1978 CarswellSask 36, 1978 CarswellSask 129,

[1978] 2 W.W.R. 101, 83 D.L.R. (3d) 289, 19 N.R. 91, 1 E.T.R. 307, 1 R.F.L. (2d) 1.

10. *Ibid.* at para. 3.

11. R.S.O. 1980, c. 152.

12. *Ibid.* at Preamble.

13. R.S.O. 1990, c. F.3.

14. *Ibid.* at Preamble.

15. However, there have been more recent cases that while acknowledging that the *Divorce Act* preceeds consideration of misconduct in assessing support, have held that the emotional devastation caused by that misconduct may be considered as relevant to the spouse's capacity to be self-sufficient. See *Leskun v. Leskun*, [2006] 1 S.C.R. 920, 2006 SCC 25, 2006 CarswellBC 1492, 2006 CarswellBC 1493, [2006] S.C.J. No. 25, 349 N.R. 158, 34 R.F.L. (6th) 1, [2006] 1 S.C.R. 25, 226 B.C.A.C. 1, 268 D.L.R. (4th) 577, 373 W.A.C. 1, 62 B.C.L.R. (4th) 197.

16. See *supra* note 14 at s. 1(1).

17. *Ibid.*

18. *Ibid.* at s. 4(1).

19. *Ibid.*, s. 4. In discussing this *Act*, we have selected those provisions of particular interest to social workers and their clients. It is strongly recommended that the *Act* be read in its entirety.

20. See the definition of constructive trust at *supra* note 9.

21. This case was previously mentioned (*Becker v. Pettkus*) at *supra* note 9. For additional cases dealing with common law relationships and death, see *Stephen v. Stawecki* (2006), 32 R.F.L. (6th) 282, 2006 CarswellOnt 3653, 213 O.A.C. 199, 24 E.T.R. (3d) 186 (C.A.) where the common law partner of the deceased qualified as a "spouse" under the *Family Law Act*. The fact that one party maintained a separate residence did not preclude the finding that the parties were living together in a conjugal relationship. Also see *Taylor v. Rossu* (1998), 161 D.L.R. (4th) 266, 216 A.R. 348, 175 W.A.C. 348, [1998] A.J. No. 648, 1998 ABCA 193, 1998 CarswellAlta 523, 39 R.F.L. (4th) 242, 68 Alta. L.R. (3d) 213, [1999] 1 W.W.R. 85, (sub nom. *Rossu v. Taylor*) 53 C.R.R. (2d) 219 (C.A.); in this case, the trial judge read in "common law spouse" into legislation so as to allow unmarried parties to apply for spousal support where limited spousal support would violate *Charter* rights.

22. See *supra* note 14 at Part IV.

23. *Ibid.* at ss. 51-60.

24. *Ibid.* at s. 56; *Le Van v. Le Van* (2006), 2006 CarswellOnt 5393, [2006] O.J. No. 3584, 82 O.R. (3d) 1, 32 R.F.L. (6th) 291 (S.C.J.), additional reasons at (2006), 2006 CarswellOnt 7334, 82 O.R. (3d) 1 at 76, 32

R.F.L. (6th) 359 (S.C.J.) is a case where a domestic contract was set aside based on the husband not disclosing the existence and value of assets and liabilities when a domestic contract was being negotiated.

25. *Underwood v. Underwood* (1995), 11 R.F.L. (4th) 361, 1995 CarswellOnt 88, [1995] O.J. No. 4335 (Ont. Div. Ct.); and *Dubin v. Dubin* (2003), 34 R.F.L. (5th) 227, [2003] O.J. No. 547, 2003 CarswellOnt 534 (Ont. S.C.J.).

26. *Deiter v. Sampson* (2002), 31 R.F.L. (5th) 296, 2002 CarswellOnt 3603 (Ont. S.C.J.), affirmed (2004), 184 O.A.C. 198, 2004 CarswellOnt 934, 50 R.F.L. (5th) 338 (C.A.).

27. *Ibid.* at para. 8.

28. *Reinhardt v. Reinhardt* (2004), 8 R.F.L. (6th) 340, [2004] O.J. No. 3318, 2004 CarswellOnt 3275 (Ont. S.C.J.), additional reasons at (2004), 2004 CarswellOnt 4374 (Ont. S.C.J.).

29. *Ibid.* at para. 59 and para. 83.

14

Enforcement of Family Court Orders

(1) INTRODUCTION

Orders for custody, access and support under the *Divorce Act*[1] are enforceable across Canada. By the simple process of registering an order obtained under the *Divorce Act* in the province where a party to the divorce is resident, the order is enforceable in that province. Orders made under provincial statutes and in particular under the *Children's Law Reform Act*[2] are also enforceable across Canada through the operation of reciprocal legislation. However, the actual process of enforcement can be time-consuming, frustrating, costly and ineffective.

In many ways the enforcement of access is the most troublesome aspect of an order and is frequently used as leverage by one spouse against the other in a continuing post-separation battle. The only loser in many instances is the child.

While the court may cancel or restrict access as a result of the access parent's action, it is usually not realistic to change custody because of the importance of the child's attachment to the custodial parent and the familiar environment. If the parents' relationship deteriorates to the extent that they cannot work cooperatively, a court may cancel access arrangements.[3] In *Eid v. Eid*, where the parents were arguing over custody and access of the children, the court found,

> that Mr. Eid has demonstrated in his relationship with Ms. Eid a pattern of controlling, argumentative, self centred and emotionally abusive conduct. . . . however, abusive husbands do not necessarily make abusive parents. . . I conclude that it would be in the best interests of the children to try to provide a framework of access that would at least give the development of their relationship with their father a chance.[4]

However, the court always reserves the right to vary custody in order to enforce access in an extreme case.

(2) REMOVAL OF A CHILD TO ANOTHER COUNTRY

If a child has been removed to a foreign country, recourse may be had to *The Hague Convention on the Civil Aspects of International Child Abduction,*[5] if that country is a signatory to the *Convention.* Many countries, including Canada, are signatories to this *Convention.*[6] Enforcement provisions of the *Criminal Code*[7] of Canada may also be helpful. With these provisions, the client's chances to regain the child are improved but by no means can success be assured. In any event, retrieval is a complex and costly process when the non-custodial parent is determined to have the child. Expert legal advice is always needed.

Changes to the *Children's Law Reform Act* in Ontario and in some other provinces give both the provincial and superior courts the power to take preventative measures against the possibility of kidnapping a child or contempt of a custody order. For example, it is now possible for the court, upon the application of the aggrieved party, to require a person to surrender his or her passport and that of the child, to post a bonder to transfer specific property to a named trustee.[8] Because most of the evidence regarding a child's best interest is available in the country of habitual residence, it is held that custody and access matters are best determined in that jurisdiction, which is the basis of any request to return a child.[9]

The parent who is concerned about a child not being returned to the appropriate jurisdiction must prove that there is a risk of harm that would come to the child under Article 13(b) of the *Hague Convention.*[10]

(3) *EXTRADITION ACT*[11]

The *Extradition Act* is another method by which a parent can secure the return of a child who has been wrongfully removed. Child abduction is a serious offense and is punishable by a prison term of greater than one year under this *Act.* The *Fugitive Offenders Act*[12] also provides for extradiction between Commonwealth countries for a child who has been abducted. However, the abduction must be a crime in the requesting country and in the country where the parent is making the request.[13] For example, in *Urbanczyk v. Urbanczyk,*[14] a case that began in Florida and ended in British Columbia where the father refused to return the child to the mother in Florida. The court declared that the child had been wrongfully removed from Florida and the lawful custody of her mother. The father had to return the child to her mother and pay all the legal costs.

SELECTED READINGS

Brodkin, Phyllis, "The Application of the *Convention*-From the Practitioner's Perspective" (2005) 23(3) Can. Fam. L.Q. 219.

Carson, Georgina & Ian Vallance, *Custody and Access* (Bar Admission materials: Law Society of Upper Canada, 2004).

Himel, Andrea, "Parents Stealing Kids (Part 1): A Canadian Perspective on the Legal and Social Problem of Parental Abduction" (2000) 18 Can. Fam. L.Q. 225.

Himel, Andrea, "Parents Stealing Kids (Part 2): Profiling the Parental Abductor" (2000) 18 Can. Fam. L.Q. 247.

Himel, Andrea, "Parents Stealing Kids (Part 3): Protecting Canadian Children from Parental Abduction through Effective Prevention and Response Techniques" (2000) 18 Can. Fam. L.Q. 269.

Johnstone, Bruce, "Parental Child Abduction under the Criminal Code" (1987) 6 Can. J. of Fam. L. 271.

MacPhail, Julie, "Responses to Inter-Jurisdictional Custody and Access Breaches" (2005) 23(2) Can. Fam. L.Q. 123.

Niman, Harold, "Custody, Access and Parental Mobility Rights (Ont.)" (1988/89) 11 Advocates' Q. 117.

ENDNOTES

1. *Divorce Act*, R.S.C. 1985, c. 3 (2nd Supp.).
2. *Children's Law Reform Act*, R.S.O. 1990, c. C.12.
3. See *M. (B.P.) v. M. (B.L.D.E.)* (1992), 42 R.F.L. (3d) 349, 59 O.A.C. 19, 97 D.L.R. (4th) 437, 1992 CarswellOnt 295, [1992] O.J. No. 2299 (C.A.), leave to appeal refused 48 R.F.L. (3d) 232 (note), 65 O.A.C. 290 (note), 157 N.R. 348 (note), 106 D.L.R. (4th) vii (note), [1993] S.C.R. vii; *Abdo v. Abdo* (1993), 50 R.F.L. (3d) 171, 126 N.S.R. (2d) 1, 352 A.P.R. 1, 109 D.L.R. (4th) 78, 1993 CarswellNS 52, [1993] N.S.J. No. 445 (C.A.); *Pollon v. Pollon* (1993), 1993 CarswellBC 2981 (B.C. S.C.).
4. *Eid v. Eid*, 220 N.S.R. (2d) 81, 2003 NSSF 54, 2003 CarswellNS 472, 694 A.P.R. 81 (S.C.) at paras. 15 and 42.
5. *The Hague Convention on the Civil Aspects of International Child Abduction* (October 25, 1980), Hague Conference on Private International Law, 14th session, No. 28 *(Hague Convention)*.

6. See *List of Hague Convention Signatory Countries,* online: U.S. Department of State <http://travel.state.gov/family/adoption/convention/convention_461.html> which identifies the countries that are part of the *Convention* (accessed on February 13, 2007).

7. *Criminal Code,* R.S.C. 1985, c. C-46; see *R. v. Gettliffe-Grant,* 217 C.C.C. (3d) 474, 2006 BCSC 1943, 2006 CarswellBC 3232 (S.C.). This was a case where the parents had joint custody and the mother applied to the court to move with the child to France. Her application was dismissed. Shortly thereafter, she took the child to France without the court's permission. After five years she returned to British Columbia and was incarcerated.

8. See *supra* note 2 at ss. 18 and 37.

9. See *Thomson v. Thomson,* [1994] 3 S.C.R. 551, [1994] S.C.J. No. 6, EYB 1994-67190, 1994 CarswellMan 91, 1994 CarswellMan 382, [1994] 10 W.W.R. 513, 173 N.R. 83, 6 R.F.L. (4th) 290, 97 Man. R. (2d) 81, 79 W.A.C. 81, 119 D.L.R. (4th) 253 where the parents were living in Scotland and the Scottish court prohibited the mother from moving away. The mother came to Canada with the child and the Manitoba court ordered the child return to Scotland. The Supreme Court held that the *Hague Convention* must be respected.

10. See *supra* note 5. Also see *Pollastro v. Pollastro* (1999), 1999 CarswellOnt 848, [1999] O.J. No. 911, 171 D.L.R. (4th) 32, 45 R.F.L. (4th) 404, (sub nom. *J.A.P. v. R.S.P.*) 118 O.A.C. 169, 43 O.R. (3d) 485, 43 O.R. (3d) 497 (Fr.) (C.A.).

11. S.C. 1999, c.18.

12. S.C. 1999, c. 3.

13. *Gribben v. Gribben* (1972), 9 R.F.L. 114, 1972 CarswellBC 41, [1972] B.C.J. No. 550 (B.C. S.C.).

14. *Urbanczyk v. Urbanczyk,* 2005 BCSC 1242, 2005 CarswellBC 2061 (S.C.).

15

Child Custody and Access in Separation and Divorce: In Whose Best Interest?

(1) BACKGROUND: CHILD CUSTODY AND ACCESS

In 1997, the Parliamentary Special Joint Committee on Child Custody and Access held hearings across Canada regarding children's interests following separation and/or divorce. The focus of the hearings was to determine whether maximum contact between children and both parents should prevail following divorce. In 1998, the Committee released its report, *For the Sake of the Children,* recommending reforms to the current legislation.

In May, 1999, the Government of Canada released its response, *Strategy for Reform,* acknowledging that there was a need for reform.[1] In December of the same year the federal government directed the Family Law Committee (representatives from each of the provinces and territories) to report on a comprehensive plan for changes to custody and access of children. Their mandate was to:

> Identify and make recommendations respecting custody and access issues that arise before, during, and after family disputes. This will involve developing a strategy to deal with legislative and service delivery issues requiring immediate priority for action, also identifying an integrated, multi-sectoral process to respond to the longer term legal, environmental and service needs of children and families, for the purposes of: 1) responding nationally to the public concerns which continue to be raised concerning current practice, law and services, available in the custody and access area; 2) promoting the development of a public consensus or dialogue on appropriate types and levels of response; and 3) developing integrated and diversity sensitive approaches to services that better serve the client and the public interest.[2]

In addition, over the next several years, the Federal Department of Justice commissioned a variety of reports on custody and access issues. Ron Stewart[3] examined the early identification and streamlining of high conflict families[4] during separation and divorce. Brenda Cossman[5] provided a critical analysis of different custodial and access arrangements for children and families with respect to proposed changes in child custody and access laws. Rhonda Bessner[6] authored a background paper on the voice of the child in divorce, custody, and access proceedings. Pauline O'Connor[7] wrote about child access in Canada and models of legislative approaches to the issue. Dominque Goubau[8] provided a background paper describing the civil law notion of the joint exercise of parental authority and how it is applied in the province of Quebec.

Following these reports, in early December, 2002, the Minister of Justice and Attorney General of Canada introduced Bill C-22, a comprehensive document about custody and access of children, in the House of Commons. The most significant change focused on eliminating the words "custody" and "access" from the *Divorce Act*,[9] and replacing both words with a model referred to as "parental responsibilities." The amendments would mean that both parents would be responsible for the well-being of their children after separation and divorce. Furthermore, both parents would decide on parenting arrangements and how they would carry out their respective obligations to their children following the dissolution of their relationship. The change in terminology was premised on three underlying principles for a child-centered family justice system. The underlying principles are: 1) to minimize the negative impact of separation and divorce on children; 2) to provide parents with the tools they need to reach appropriate parenting arrangements; and 3) to ensure that the legal process is less adversarial. The federal government focused on alternative dispute processes, as described in the Chapter 6 (parent education programs, mediation services, and other early dispute resolution processes).

Although Bill C-22 did not come to fruition due to changes in government, other changes, such as alternative dispute resolution, have taken place across Canada to reduce conflict for children and families undergoing separation and divorce.[10]

(2) LEGISLATION: CUSTODY AND ACCESS

In Canada there is a shared responsibility between the federal government and the provinces and territories with respect to family law matters. As indicated previously, the federal government is responsible for divorce, and may regulate child and spousal support, and the resolution of child related issues (custody and access) as corollary relief when married couples apply for a divorce.[11] The provincial and territorial governments have jurisdiction over child custody and access issues, property matters, and all matters between both married and unmarried parents. In addition, the provinces and territories have responsibility for the enforcement of child and spousal support. There is considerable overlap in jurisdictions between governments and how they intervene in the lives of children and families with respect to children's interests post separation and/or divorce.

It is important to note that the *Divorce Act* does not clearly define custody and access. The *Divorce Act* defines custody as including the, "care, upbringing and any other incidents of custody."[12] Access is not defined at all in the *Act*. However, subsection 16(5) of the *Divorce Act* states that the spouse who is granted access to their child/ren, "has the right to make inquiries, and to be given information, as to health, education and welfare of the child" unless the court orders otherwise.

(3) LEGISLATION: BEST INTEREST TEST

The current standard for matters concerning custody of and access to children is the "best interests of the child." The *Divorce Act* states that in making an order for custody or access "the court shall take into consideration only the best interests of the child of the marriage as determined by reference to the condition, means, needs and other circumstances of the child."[13] The best interests test can be defined as a myriad of factors relating to the interests of the child (parents' conduct, maximum contact with each parent, statutory factors).

It has often been argued that the best interest is a legal question with insufficient social science outcome data (*i.e.* as to the benefits of one parenting arrangement over another).[14] Moreover, assessing the best interests of the child can be highly subjective and difficult, if not impossible, to evaluate. In *MacGyver v. Richards*,[15] Justice Abella stated:

> Clearly, there is an inherent indeterminacy and elasticity to the "best interests" test which makes it more useful as legal aspiration than as legal analysis. It can be no more than an informed opinion made at a moment in the life of a child about what seems likely to prove to be in that child's best interests. Deciding what is in a child's best interests means deciding what, objectively appears most likely in the circumstances to be conducive to the kind of environment in which a particular child has the best opportunity for receiving the needed care and attention. Because there are stages to childhood, what is in a child's best interest may vary from child to child, from year to year, and possibly from month to month. This unavoidable fluidity makes it important to attempt to minimize the prospects for stress and instability.[16]

The *Divorce Act* also provides that, "the court shall not take into consideration the past conduct of any person unless the conduct is relevant to the ability of that person to act as a parent of a child."[17] At present, there is no uniformity in provincial legislation across Canada that contains a specific reference to spousal violence (emotional, physical, sexual and/or verbal) as a factor to be considered during custody and access determinations. However, Ontario's *Children's Law Reform Act*,[18] in sections 24(3) and (4), specifically refers the court to examine the person's past conduct and assess violence and abuse in relation to a person's ability to act as a parent when determining an order for custody and/or access to the child. Most provinces now have specific statutes that refer to domestic violence.[19] Critics have pointed out that references to violence do not clearly address how violence should be taken into account and thus, judicial approaches with respect to domestic violence continue to be inconsistent throughout the country.[20]

Under the federal *Divorce Act* there are also provisions that require the court, when making an order for custody or access, to "give effect to the principle that a child of the marriage should have as much contact with each spouse as is consistent with the best interests of the child, and for that purpose, shall take into consideration the willingness of the person for whom custody is sought to facilitate such contact."[21] There is a presumption that access between a child and his or her non-custodial parent is an important factor, amongst many others, that also needs to be considered when judges make child custody and access determinations.

Where no divorce is claimed, or the parents have never been married, provincial legislation will govern custody and access issues. However, once a matter is commenced under the *Divorce Act,* then all matters relating to the regime of custody and access will supercede any order made under provincial legislation. In Ontario, the governing statute is the *Children's Law Reform Act.* Similar legislation has been enacted in every other province.

Regardless of whether custody and access is being requested under the *Divorce Act* or the *Children's Law Reform Act,* there is no area of law that creates as much confusion, challenge, controversy, and more often than not, unnecessary litigation as found in custody and access disputes. The late law professor of the University of Western Ontario, James McLeod, once stated, "many parents do not understand the meaning of 'custody' or 'access', or 'joint custody' so that their insistence on, or opposition to, a particular form of order is often more emotional than rational."[22]

(4) CUSTODY AND ACCESS DECISION-MAKING

When child custody disputes enter the legal system, mental health professionals (social workers, psychologists and psychiatrists) who have expertise in understanding children's development and family dynamics are often called upon to assist the court in its decision- making by conducting child custody and access assessments.[23] These assessments are carried out by mental health professionals in both private and publicly funded sectors. Each province has a provincially designated department that carries out child custody and access assessments. Ontario is the only province that has both legal and clinical investigators (The Office of the Children's Lawyer[24]) that focus exclusively on children's interests before the court.

In Ontario there are two pieces of legislation that guide the determination of who should conduct the child custody and access assessments, and when. These two pieces of legislation are Section 30 of the *Children's Law Reform Act*[25] and Section 112 of the *Courts of Justice Act*.[26] While each piece of legislation is different in its scope and mandate, the mental health professional produces a written report that outlines the custodial and access responsibilities of each parent after thorough interviews are conducted with those involved in the child/ren's lives.

Decision-making about children's best interests is intended to provide a parenting plan upon the breakdown of the relationship that will best meet the emotional and physical needs of the child. By definition, decision-making is future oriented.[27] Notwithstanding the controversy that exists regarding the recommendations made by assessors for the court on behalf of children, these can carry significant weight in the court's final decision.[28]

There are numerous textbooks written by mental health professionals to guide the custody and access assessor in the process and methodology of conducting a custody and access assessment.[29] Birnbaum, McCarty, and McTavish[30] argue that there are in fact multiple guidelines[31] and few, if any, mandatory standards for the child custody evaluators across Canada to follow.[32] At present, the only online course that exists to provide education to mental health professionals on how to conduct child custody and access assessments is through the Justice Institute of British Columbia (Corrections and Community Justice Division, JIBC). This is the only online course that offers a hands-on approach to educate mental health professionals about the process and functions of conducting these assessments.[33]

In one highly regarded textbook on all aspects of forensic evaluations, there is an absence of discussion about domestic violence.[34] Additionally, there also appears to be a lack of consistent training across disciplines to guide assessors in their work, particularly when dealing with domestic violence or any other significant practice issue that is raised in custody and access disputes.[35]

Given the types of practice issues that can and often do arise during child custody disputes (*e.g.* a child being alienated from one parent,[36] gay and lesbian child custody disputes,[37] issues of race and culture,[38] children being raised in different religious faiths,[39] and where there are concerns about domestic violence and the effects on children[40]) it is imperative that comprehensive education and training takes place for social workers who practice in this area of family law.[41]

(5) CHILD LEGAL REPRESENTATION

Child legal representation in custody and access matters is an evolving concept. Historically, children had few rights and it is only recently that children have begun to be perceived as persons with independent rights and interests. The United Nations adopted the *Convention on the Rights of the Child* in 1989.[42]

Child legal representation was one of 48 recommendations made by the Special Joint Committee of the Senate and the House of Commons (*Committee*). As previously stated, Ontario is the only province in Canada that has a formalized child legal representation program (Office of the Children's Lawyer: OCL).[43] Each province offers different models. These include but are not limited to:

1. the traditional lawyer advocate for the child;
2. a *guardian ad litem* (this person may be a lawyer, a volunteer lay person, or a mental health professional) who may or may not have legal and/or mental health training in the area of child custody. The *guardian ad litem* acts as the child's counsel and guardian of his or her best interests; or
3. an *amicus curiae* (a neutral person who is appointed by the court to advise and inform both the child and the court about the facts of the case). This person is responsible to the court and not the child.[44]

In Ontario, the lawyer for the child provides for a combination of all three models and represents the child's interest. The role of the lawyer is defined by a solicitor-client relationship between the lawyer and the child, but at the same time the lawyer assists the adult parties in resolving the dispute before the court. The lawyer acts as a broker for the child and advocates the child's interests so that the child may be understood by not only to the parents, but to the court as well. Children do not "instruct" their lawyer. Rather, the lawyer conveys the child's wishes and views by providing context to those wishes and views to the family and the court. The lawyer is able to gather information about the family situation through interviews with parents, significant caregivers, relatives, and other professional sources, as well as the child's views and wishes. The child's lawyer then presents this information to the court.

(6) TYPES OF CUSTODIAL ARRANGEMENTS

The court may grant custody of a child to one or more persons pursuant to either the *Children's Law Reform Act* or the *Divorce Act*.[45] When both parents are granted the ability to make decisions about their child/ren together, this is referred to as joint custody. However, Parliament stopped short of enacting a presumption of joint custody. Such a presumption would assume that joint custody would endure unless one of the parties satisfied an onus that he or she should be awarded sole custody. The decision not to enact presumptive joint custody preserves the primacy of the "best interests" doctrine.

Much has been written and debated upon regarding joint custody,[46] also called shared parenting. Some have argued that for an order for joint custody to be successful, it is essential that both parents be able to work together in a co-operative manner in matters concerning the child; this would entail putting aside differences and hostility toward one another where the children are involved. However, conflict is not a unidimensional concept and not all conflict is bad. There is often conflict in households where parents have not separated, particlarly when it comes to child-rearing.

Joint custody does not always require a 50-50 split residence for the child; one parent may provide a permanent address and have care and control, subject to generous visits to the other parent. Nevertheless, both parents retain the right to participate in the upbringing of the child through consultation over major decisions affecting the child. Another model of shared parenting is one where parents alternate designated periods of care and control, which may be a few days at a time, every other week or month, or in accordance with school terms or vacations. Both parents, again, retain the right to participate in the upbringing of the child through consultation over major decisions affecting the child, including education, health factors, and religious training. Shared custody goes further by including not only joint decision-making, but also a sharing of physical custody.[47]

Joint custody is not an appropriate order when there is a history of domestic violence between parties or where communication is largely governed by verbal and physical hostility and poor communication. However, it has been found that where parents, in spite of personal differences, can demonstrate an ability to cooperate to meet the children's needs, joint custody may be awarded; alternatively, a parallel parenting arrangement can be worked out between the parents.[48]

(7) PARENTING SCHEDULES

When custody is granted to one parent, the order usually provides for "reasonable access" or "liberal access" to the other parent. If the parents cannot agree on the specific terms, the court will specify the times. The order might call for access on particular weekends, such as alternating weekends, and specify the division of holiday time. The parent who has access must not change the child's basic mode of life or conduct during the period of access. That parent may only exercise control which is necessary to safeguard the child while they are together. For example, the access parent cannot unilaterally determine or alter the arrangements made for the child's schooling, medical treatment, or religious training. Religious differences between spouses are not necessarily bars to access orders. The court may make access orders for a definite or indefinite period, or until the occurrence of a specified event, and may impose terms and conditions at its discretion. For example, the court may require the non-custodial parent to have day access only until suitable accommodation is obtained.

Parenting schedules are hard on the spontaneity of relationships but worth the time to work out through guidance to both parents. Children's self-esteem is connected to a continuity of relationship with both parents, including the non-custodial parent.[49]

(8) INTERFERENCE WITH ACCESS

There are times when one parent may interfere with the other parent's time with the child for a host of reasons. Under the *Divorce Act* maximum contact between a child and his or her parent is a mandatory condition providing it is in the best interests of the child.[50] However, the maximum contact principle has created a double-edged sword. For example, the principle can be used against some women who do not want to facilitate contact to avoid further abuse.

Specifically, the abusive partner may use the maximum contact principle against his partner as a means of gaining sole or joint custody, which can also amount to a continuation of abuse against the woman. There have been cases, such as *South v. Tichelaar*,[51] where a court has ordered joint custody to facilitate a mother's relationship with her children. For the most part, though, courts are reluctant to change custody orders because the need for stability and continuity in children's lives is imperative, as can be seen in *Broz v. Broz.*[52] One exception is if a parent continually demonstrates contempt against a court order for access, the court can proceed with a contempt application or impose conditions against that parent.[53]

For example, in the case of *Einstoss v. Starkman*[54] custody and access orders were in place for many years following the parents' divorce. The father was to exercise his access by picking up the child at the wife's home. The wife attempted to change the pick-up at her home and denied the father access to her home. In addition, she continuously ignored court orders regarding access. The father brought an application to court to find her in contempt of the order and he was successful in doing so.[55] In another case, *Starzycka v. Wronski,*[56] the mother denied access of their son to the father for two years. She also ignored orders directing her to pay court costs and fines. While there was legal representation for the son, the mother refused to cooperate with anyone. Custody of the son was transferred to the father after the court heard evidence from both parents and a social worker.[57]

(9) WHEN ONE PARENT WISHES TO MOVE (MOBILITY ISSUES)

Relocation, or moving away, is becoming a reality for more and more families. Parents relocate for many reasons, such as better employment opportunities, better housing, to be closer to social supports, and/or to be with a new partner. Even though these changes may improve the parent's quality of life, they can affect children differently. When parents cannot agree on the move or there is a court order that restricts children from moving away from their non-custodial parent, many of these parents turn to the court for permission to move.

In *Gordon v. Goertz,* an estranged Saskatchewan couple were disputing the right of the custodial parent, Ms. Gordon, to take their daughter to Australia. This case became a landmark Supreme Court of Canada decision in May, 1996.[58] The mother and daughter had resided in Australia since early 1995 as a result of lower court rulings which granted the mother a variance in the access agreement. In a 7-2 decision, the court said that "the child's best interests are not merely paramount, they are the only consideration", and that "the rights and interests of the parents, except as they impact on the best interests of the child, are irrelevant."[59] In this case, the child was permitted to remain with her mother because the father had the means to maintain his access visits.

The above decision reaffirms the principle of the best interests of the child as the overriding test in any custody and access dispute, which means that a custodial parent wishing to move for any reason (ie. job relocation, education, or new relationship) could run the risk of losing custody if the court decides that such a move would create serious disruption in the life of the child. On the other hand, the two dissenting justices in *Gordon* argued that more weight should be given to the custodial parent's rights, based on the principle that the original decision to award custody is a major one from which subsequent decisions flow. The key to the majority decision lies in the finding that a geographical move constitutes a "material change in circumstances," which according to existing law can automatically result in a court evaluation of custody and access in light of the new circumstances.

Since the best interests of the child is recognized as the only consideration when it comes to custody, it implies that the courts have greater decision-making power over the freedom of custodial parents; if the custodial parent makes life decisions without the access parent's approval, this may result in costly litigation. The courts have been directed to consider *only* the best interests of the child and not the merits of the custodial parent's plan.[60]

Gordon v. Goertz[61] effectively overruled an earlier Ontario Court of Appeal decision which held that where the custodial parent, usually the mother, has good reason to move to a new location, such a move will be considered consistent with the best interests of the child. Madam Justice Abella wrote in her *MacGyver* decision,

> We must . . . forcefully acknowledge that the custodial parent's best interests are inexplicably tied to those of the child. The non-custodial father lost his petition at the appeal court to keep his wife and daughter from moving to the U.S. where the mother planned to remarry. The ruling, said the court, applies not only to decisions about family moves, but to other decisions from "the trivia; to the dramatic" and includes whether to change neighbourhoods, or provinces, or partners, or jobs, or friends, or schools, or religions.[62]

Mobility cases are fact driven and different decisions have been made regarding this matter across Canada since *Gordon v. Goertz*. For example, the court in British Columbia, in *Creighton v. Creighton*,[63] allowed the move. Both parents were equally involved with their two children, ages three and five. The children resided with their mother who remarried and wanted to move to the United States with her new partner and a third child of the new relationship. The girl's mother was prepared to pay for the trips to visit with their father. The court held that there would be joint custody of the girls with primary residence with their mother. The court also ordered that the mother pay for three access visits with their father annually. In another case, *Fasan v. Fasan*,[64] the court also allowed the mother to move from Windsor to Ottawa. In this case the mother, a law student, was offered a clerkship with the Supreme Court of Canada. The mother requested the court to allow her to move with their four-year-old son. The boy was close with his father and extended family in Windsor. The court held that both parties earned good salaries and that the child could visit his father regularly in Windsor. Additionally, the court believed that the job offered to the mother would indirectly benefit the child.[65]

There are several cases where the court would not allow a move. For example, in *O'Brien v. Thomson*[66] the mother had sole custody of the child. There was an oil spill in the mother's home and she moved the child to the maternal grandmother's home without informing the father. When the father found out about the move, he requested custody of the child as did the maternal grandmother. The court found that the father was not made aware of the move and that his right to custody should not be lightly set aside. Custody was awarded to the father. In another case, *Karpodinis v. Kantos*[67] the mother's employment was going to be terminated unless she relocated to Houston, Texas from British Columbia. The Court of Appeal held that the child's best interest was to remain in British Columbia and have a relationship with his father and extended family.[68] In final anaylsis, the court stated that it will always base the decision on the best interest of the child.[69]

(10) SUPERVISED ACCESS

High conflict[70] post-separation family law cases usually involve se-rious allegations of domestic violence, child abuse and neglect, and/or other safety concerns such as parental psychopathology and substance abuse.[71] Even after court-ordered visitation agreements have been issued, one-fourth to one-third of these families still report ongoing hostilities about children's custody and access arrangements.[72]

Many of the common interventions, such as parent education pro-grams,[73] impasse mediation,[74] and parent coordination,[75] are shown to be inappropriate for high conflict families due to their entrenched personality characteristics.[76] As child custody and visitation[77] disputes have become an increasingly difficult issue before the courts, supervised visitation programs have proliferated across Canada. Supervised visitation is designed to pro-vide a means to continue and maintain the relationship between a child and his or her non-custodial parent[78] after separation and/or divorce when con-flict between parents requires a safe outside resource.

Judges order supervised visitation for a variety of reasons, including, but not limited to, an underdeveloped parent-child relationship, access de-nial by one parent towards the other, substance abuse problems, mental health problems of the parent, allegations of child abduction, and domestic violence. The courts have generally accepted that it is in the best interests of children to have regular and frequent contact with both parents.[79]

Many jurisdictions have provided space where visits between the non-custodial parent and the child take place under supervised conditions. Supervised access may be ordered for a variety of reasons and under various circumstances. In general, supervised access services have been designed for those cases where a non-custodial parent may "pose a threat, either to a child or to a former spouse; alcohol or drug abuse, or psychiatric disturbance; risk of abduction of the child by the non-custodial parent; a history of concern about abusive behaviour; poor parenting skills; or a lengthy separation between the non-custodial parent and the child."[80] Often these situations involve "high conflict" cases. High conflict families post-separation typically involve domestic violence and/or concurrent substance/alcohol abuse, and raise serious concerns about parenting deficits against the other parent.[81]

Supervised access is one way of responding to contentious issues surrounding custody by providing a safe and neutral place for children to visit parents and systematically providing arrangements in which ex-partners do not have to confront each other. In short, supervised access programs provide services that make it possible for children to visit parents with whom they may not have been able to have contact with otherwise.

Supervised access centers vary in the services they offer. While supervised access programs are set up at supervised visitation facilities, many centers also offer exchange services where parents are able to visit their children off-site and without supervision, although children are picked-up and dropped off under supervised conditions. Ancillary services that accompany some access centers include mediation interventions, educational interventions, and short-term counselling/therapy.[82] These services aim at reducing conflict and resolving access problems so that over-reliance on supervised visitation/exchange is minimized, as such programs were not designed for long-term usage.

(11) CONCLUDING THOUGHTS

Family law is unique in every aspect because it not only deals with child and spousal support as well as property issues, but, more importantly, with the emotional, behavioural and physical arrangements of children's lives during, as well as after, the separation and/or divorce process. Children do not live in isolation from the family. Their well-being is inextricably linked to the parental relationship.

Family law reform struggles with the complex intertwining relationship between various systems and power relations (social, legal and political). The effects of laws and policies on children and their families at all stages of the separation and/or divorce process are socially, economically, and politically profound.

SELECTED READINGS

Bala, Nicholas & Jane Anweiler, "Allegations of Sexual Abuse in a Parental Custody Dispute: Smokescreen or Fire?" (1987/88) 2 Can. Fam. L.Q. 343.

Davies, Christine, "Access to Justice for Children: The Voice of the Child in Custody and Access Disputes" (2004) 22 Can. Fam. L.Q. 153.

Jaffe, Peter & Claire Crooks, "Assessing the Best Interest of the Child: Visitation and Custody in Cases of Domestic Violence" in Jeffrey Edelson & Oliver Williams, eds., *Parenting by Men who Batter* (New York: Guilford Press, 2004) 45.

Johnston, Janet, "Children of Divorce who Refuse Visitation" in Depner, Charlene & James Bray, eds., *Non-Residential Parenting: New Vistas in Family Living* (Newbury Park, California: Sage Publications, 1993) 109.

Johnston, Janet, "High Conflict Divorce" (1994) 4(1) The Future of Children: Children and Divorce 165.

Johnston, Janet, "Parental Alignments and Rejection: An Empirical Study of Alienation in Children of Divorce" (2003) 31 Journal of the American Academy of Psychiatry and Law 158.

Johnston, Janet & Joan Kelly, Commentary on Lenore Walker, Kristi Brantley & Justin Rigsbee, "A Critical Analysis of Parental Alienation Syndrome and its Admissibility in the Family Court" (2004) 1(4) Journal of Child Custody 77.

Johnston, Janet & Joan Kelly, "Rejoinder to Gardner's Commentary on Kelly and Johnston's "The Alienated Child: A Reformulation of Parental Alienation Syndrome"" (2004) 42(4) Fam. Ct. Rev. 622.

Johnston, Janet & Vivienne Roseby, *In the Name of the Child: A Developmental Approach to Understanding and Helping Children of Conflicted and Violence Divorce* (New York: The Free Press, 1997).

Joyal, Renee & Anne Quéniart, "Enhancing the Child's Point of View in Custody and Access Cases in Quebec" (2002) 19(1) Can. J. Fam. L. 173.

Kelly, Joan & Michael Lamb, "Using Child Development Research to Make Appropriate Custody and Access Decisions for Young Children" (2000) 38(3) Family and Conciliation Courts Review 297.

Kelly, Joan & Robert Emery, "Children's Adjustment following Divorce: Risk and Resilience Perspectives" (2003) 52(4) Family Relations 352.

Keough, William, *Child Representation in Family Law* (LBC Information Services: Carswell Publishing International, 2000).

Pruett, Marsha et al., "Critical Aspects of Parenting Plans for Young Children: Interjecting Data into the Debate about Overnights" (2004) 42(1) Fam. Ct. Rev. 39.

Warshak, Richard, "Blanket Restrictions: Overnight Contact between Parents and Young Children" (2000) 38(4) Family and Conciliation Courts Review 422.

Warshak, Richard, *Divorce Poison: Protecting the Parent-Child Bond from a Vindictive-Ex* (New York: Regan Books, 2001).

Warshak, Richard, "Payoffs and Pitfalls of Listening to Children" (2003) 52(4) Family Relations 373.

ENDNOTES

1. Parliament of Canada, *Government of Canada's Response to the Report of the Special Joint Committee on Child Custody and Access: Strategy for Reform* (Ottawa: Department of Justice, 1999).
2. Parliament of Canada, *Final Federal-Provincial-Territorial Report on Custody and Access and Child Support: Putting Children First* (Ottawa: Department of Justice, 2002).
3. Department of Justice Canada, *The Early Identification and Streamlining of Cases of High Conflict Separation and Divorce: A Review* by Ron Stewart (Ottawa: Family, Children and Youth Section, Department of Justice Canada, 2001).
4. This term has been advanced by Janet Johnston, a sociologist in the U.S.A. She is a leading academic scholar and researcher in the area of children and families pre- and post-separation and divorce.
5. Department of Justice Canada, *An Analysis of Options for Changes in the Legal Regulation of Child Custody and Access* by Brenda Cossman (Ottawa: Family, Children and Youth Section, Department of Justice Canada, 2001).
6. Department of Justice Canada, *The Voice of the Child in Divorce, Custody, and Access Proceedings* by Rhonda Bressner (Ottawa: Family, Children and Youth Section, Department of Justice Canada, 2002).
7. Department of Justice Canada, *Child Access in Canada: Legal Approaches and Program Supports* by Pauline O'Connor (Ottawa: Family, Children and Youth Section, Department of Justice Canada, 2002).
8. Department of Justice Canada, *Divorce Reform and the Joint Exercise*

of Parental Authority: The Quebec Civil Law Perspective by Dominque Goubau (Ottawa: Family, Children and Youth Section, Department of Justice Canada, 2000).

9. R.S.C. 1985, c. 3 (2nd Supp.).
10. Rachel Birnbaum, "Rendering Children Invisible: The Forces at Play During Separation and Divorce in the Context of Family Violence" in Ramona Alaggia & Cathy Vine, eds., *Cruel But not Unusual: Violence in Canadian Families* (Waterloo: Wilfrid Laurier University Press, 2006) at 267.
11. See *supra* note 9 at s. 16(1).
12. See *supra* note 9 at s. 2(1).
13. See *supra* note 9 at s. 16(8).
14. See Barbara Fidler & Rachel Birnbaum, "Child Custody Disputes: Public and Private Assessments" (2006) 25 Can. Fam. L.Q. 137.
15. (1995), 11 R.F.L. (4th) 432, 22 O.R. (3d) 481, 123 D.L.R. (4th) 562, 84 O.A.C. 349, [1995] O.J. No. 770, 1995 CarswellOnt 90 (C.A.).
16. *Ibid.* at para. 27.
17. See *supra* note 9 at s. 16(9).
18. R.S.O. 1990, c. C.12.
19. See Table of Concordance.
20. Department of Justice, *An Analysis of Options for Changes in the Legal Regulation of Child Custody and Access* by Brenda Cossman (Ottawa: Department of Justice Canada, Family, Children and Youth Section, 2001) available at the Department of Justice website.
21. See *supra* note 9 at s. 16(10).
22. James McLeod & Alfred Mamo, *Annual Review of Family Law 2004* (Toronto: Thomson Carswell Professional Publishing, 2004).
23. Jonathan Gould, *Conducting Scientifically Crafted Child Custody Evaluations* (Thousand Oakes, Calif.: Sage Publications, 1998); and Philip Stahl, *Conducting Child Custody Evaluations: A Comprehensive Guide* (Thousand Oakes, Calif.: Sage Publications, 1994).
24. The Office of the Children's Lawyer is an independent law office within Ontario's Ministry of the Attorney General. The Office represents the interests of children before the court in custody and access disputes, child welfare proceedings, and civil litigation and estate matters.
25. The court before which an application is brought in respect of custody of or access to a child, by order, may appoint a person who has the technical or professional skill to assess and report to the court on the needs of the child and the ability and willingness of the parties or any of them to satisfy the needs of the child.
26. R.S.O. 1990 c. C.43. In a proceeding under the *Divorce Act* (Canada) or the *Children's Law Reform Act* in which a question concerning

custody of or access to a child is before the court, the Children's Lawyer may cause an investigation to be made and may report and make recommendations to the court on all matters concerning custody of or access to the child and the child's support and education. See Rachel Birnbaum, Barbara J. Fidler and Katherine Kavassalis, *Child Custody Assessments: A Resource Guide to Mental Health and Legal Professionals* (Toronto: Carswell, forthcoming) for a review of how to conduct custody and access assessments.

27. Nicholas Bala, "Mental Health Professionals in Child-Related Proceedings: Understanding the Ambivalence of the Judiciary" (1996) 13 Can. J. Fam. L. 261.

28. See (2005), 43(2) Fam. Ct. Rev. in its entirety for an excellent discussion on the pros and cons of these debates. See also Rachel Birnbaum & Helen Radovanovic, "Brief Intervention Model for Access-Based Post-Separation Disputes: Family and Court Outcomes" (1999) 37(4) Family and Conciliation Courts Review 504.

29. See Jonathan Gould, *Conducting Scientifically Crafted Child Custody Evaluations* (Thousand Oaks, Calif.: Sage Publications, 1998); Arthur Leonoff & Robert Montague, *Guide to Child Custody Assessments* (Scarborough, Ont.: Carswell Publishing, 1996); Gary Melton, John Petrila, Norman Poythress, & Christopher Slobogin, *Psychological Evaluations for the Courts: A Handbook for Mental Health Professionals and Lawyers* (New York: Guilford Press, 1987); and Philip Stahl, *Conducting Child Custody Evaluations: A Comprehensive Guide* (Thousand Oaks, Calif.: Sage Publications, 1994).

30. Rachel Birnbaum, Elizabeth McCarty & Willson McTavish, "*Haider v. Malach*: Child Custody Guidelines Gone Awry" (2001) 18 Can. Fam. L.Q. 357.

31. In Ontario, there are three independent professional bodies. The Ontario College of Social Workers and Social Service Workers, the Ontario College of Psychologists, and the Ontario Interdisciplinary Association of Custody/Access Assessors. Presently only the Ontario College of Psychologists have mandatory guidelines and standards to carry out custody and access evaluations.

32. The Canadian Association of Social Workers (CASW) does not have any mandatory practice guidelines for social workers involved in custody and access matters before the court. In Ontario, the College of Social Workers and Social Service Workers is presently drafting guidelines for those who practice in this area.

33. Personal Communication, January 25, 2007, C. McKnight. It was offered as a pilot course in early November, 2002 funded by the Department of Justice, Canada. The course is offered on a fee basis as a long

distance Internet based course from the Justice Institute in British Columbia.

34. William Austin, "Assessing Credibility in Allegations of Marital Violence in the High Conflict Child Custody Case" (2000) 38(4) Family and Conciliation Courts Review 462.

35. The Office of the Children's Lawyer in Ontario has and continues to provide training for clinical investigators, lawyers, and panel agents engaged in custody and access matters. This is the only interdisciplinary training that is offered in Canada.

36. *MacKenzie v. Beaver*, 33 R.F.L. (6th) 450, 2006 CarswellNS 513, 2006 NSSC 344 (S.C.); *Ampuero v. Ampuero* (2006), 34 R.F.L. (6th) 208, 2006 CarswellOnt 7457 (Ont. C.J.).

37. *Griffiths v. Griffiths* (2005), 2005 ONCJ 235, 2005 CarswellOnt 3209 (Ont. C.J.).

38. *Van de Perre v. Edwards*, [2001] 2 S.C.R. 1014, 2001 SCC 60, 19 R.F.L. (5th) 396, [2001] 11 W.W.R. 1, 204 D.L.R. (4th) 257, (sub nom. *P. (K.V.) v. E. (T.)*) 275 N.R. 52, (sub nom. *K.V.P. v. T.E.*) 156 B.C.A.C. 161, 255 W.A.C. 161, 94 B.C.L.R. (3d) 199, [2001] S.C.J. No. 60, 2001 CarswellBC 1999, 2001 CarswellBC 2000, REJB 2001-25876.

39. *Young v. Young*, [1993] 4 S.C.R. 3, [1993] 8 W.W.R. 513, 108 D.L.R. (4th) 193, 18 C.R.R. (2d) 41, 84 B.C.L.R. (2d) 1, 160 N.R. 1, 49 R.F.L. (3d) 117, 34 B.C.A.C. 161, 56 W.A.C. 161, [1993] R.D.F. 703, [1993] S.C.J. No. 112, EYB 1993-67111, 1993 CarswellBC 264, 1993 CarswellBC 1269.

40. *Stevenson v. DeRose* (2001), 2001 CarswellOnt 1724 (Ont. S.C.J.).

41. See *supra* note 14; also see *supra* note 10.

42. Online: <www.unhchr.ch/html/menu3/b/k2crc.htm>. Article 3 of the Convention provides that: "In all actions concerning children, whether undertaken by public or private social welfare institutions, courts of law, administrative authorities, or legislative bodies, the best interests of the child shall be a primary consideration." Article 9 of the Convention provides that "where the parents are living separately and a decision must be made as to the child's place of residence" the determination shall be made in "accordance with applicable law for the best interests of the child." Article 9(3) specifies that governments "shall respect the right of the child who is separated from one or both parents to maintain personal relationships and direct contact with both parents on a regular basis, except if it is contrary to a child's best interests." Article 12 provides that children have the right to express their views freely in matters concerning them [1992] C.T.S. 3. See also Parliament of Canada, *Report of the Special Joint Committee on Child Custody and*

Access, For the Sake of the Children (Ottawa: Department of Justice, 1998).

43. In Ontario, the *Children's Law Reform Act* explicitly states in subs. 24(2)(b) that judges must consider "the child's views and preferences, if they can reasonably be ascertained." Also see Nicholas Bala, "Child Representation in Alberta: Role and Responsibilities of Counsel for the Child in Family Proceedings" (2006) 43(4) Alta. L. Rev. 845; and regarding child legal representation in the Province of Alberta, see Dale Hensley, "Role and Responsibilities of Counsel for the Child in Alberta: A Practitioner's Perspective and a Response to Professor Bala" (2006) 43(4) Alta. L. Rev. 871.

44. Rachel Birnbaum & Dena Moyal, "Visitation Based Disputes Arising on Separation and Divorce: Focused Child Legal Representation" (2002) 20 Can. Fam. L.Q. 37; Rachel Birnbaum, "Independent Child Legal Representation: A concept in the Making" (2005) 20 J.L. & Soc. Pol'y 131.

45. *Children's Law Reform Act,* R.S.O. 1990, c. C.12, s. 28(a); *Divorce Act*, R.S.C. 1985, c. 3 (2nd Supp.), s. 16(4).

46. Rachel Birnbaum, "Hearing the Voices of Lawyers and Clinical Investigators who Represent Children in Child Custody and Access Disputes" (2005) 24(3) Can. Fam. L.Q. 281; Rachel Birnbaum & Barbara Jo Fidler, "Commentary on Epstein and Madsen's 'Joint Custody with a Vengeance: The Emergence of Parallel Parenting Orders'" (2005) 24 Can. Fam. L.Q. 338; see also Brahm Siegal, "Considering *Kaplanis*: Who's Your (Sole) Daddy?" (2006) 25 Can. Fam. L.Q. 39, for case law on sole and joint custody decisions from January, 2005 to November, 2005 in Ontario.

47. *Merriam v. McGee*, 2007 NSFC 7, 2007 CarswellNS 42 (Fam. Ct.) at para. 19.

48. *Ladisa v. Ladisa* (2005), 11 R.F.L. (6th) 50, 2005 CarswellOnt 268, [2005] O.J. No. 276, 193 O.A.C. 336 (C.A.); *Stewart v. Stewart*, 204 Man. R. (2d) 298, 2006 MBQB 175, 2006 CarswellMan 273, 32 R.F.L. (6th) 434 (Q.B.), affirmed 214 Man. R. (2d) 199, 395 W.A.C. 199, 40 R.F.L. (6th) 1, 2007 CarswellMan 201, 2007 MBCA 66 (C.A.).

49. Joan Kelly, "Children's Adjustment in Conflicted Marriage and Divorce: A Decade Review of Research" (2000) 39(8) Journal of the American Academy of Child Adolescent Psychiatry 963.

50. *Gordon v. Goertz*, [1996] 2 S.C.R. 27, 1996 CarswellSask 199, [1996] S.C.J. No. 52, [1996] 5 W.W.R. 457, 19 R.F.L. (4th) 177, 196 N.R. 321, 134 D.L.R. (4th) 321, 141 Sask. R. 241, 114 W.A.C. 241, (sub nom. *Goertz c. Gordon*) [1996] R.D.F. 209, 1996 CarswellSask 199F at para. 24.

51. *South v. Tichelaar* (2001), 20 R.F.L. (5th) 175, [2001] O.J. No. 2823, 2001 CarswellOnt 2447 (Ont. S.C.J.).
52. *Ibid.*; see also *Broz v. Broz* (2001), 18 R.F.L. (5th) 3, 2001 CarswellOnt 1641 (Ont. S.C.J.) [*Broz*].
53. *Ibid., Broz* at para. 21.
54. (2002), 2002 CarswellOnt 4435, [2002] O.J. No. 4889 (Ont. S.C.J), affirmed (2003), 2003 CarswellOnt 3234, [2003] O.J. No. 3297 (Ont. C.A.), additional reasons at (2003), 2003 CarswellOnt 100, [2003] O.J. No. 96, 37 R.F.L. (5th) 77 (Ont. S.C.J.).
55. *Ibid.* at para. 25.
56. 27 R.F.L. (6th) 159, 2005 CarswellOnt 7576, 2005 ONCJ 329 (C.J.).
57. *Ibid.* at para. 26.
58. See *supra* note 50.
59. *Ibid.* at para. 37.
60. *Ibid.* at para. 116.
61. See *supra* note 50.
62. *MacGyver v. Richards* (1995), 123 D.L.R. (4th) 562, 11 R.F.L. (4th) 432, 22 O.R. (3d) 481, 84 O.A.C. 349, [1995] O.J. No. 770, 1995 CarswellOnt 90 (C.A.) at para. 35.
63. (1997), [1997] B.C.J. No. 2081, 1997 CarswellBC 1914 (B.C. S.C.).
64. (1991), 32 R.F.L. (3d) 121, [1991] O.J. No. 745, 1991 CarswellOnt 256 (Ont. Gen. Div.).
65. *Ibid.* at para. 41.
66. (sub nom. *C.J.M. v. A.T.*) 221 N.S.R. (2d) 297, 697 A.P.R. 297, 1 R.F.L. (6th) 318, 2004 NSCA 34, 2004 CarswellNS 65 (C.A.).
67. (2006), 27 R.F.L. (6th) 254, 2006 CarswellBC 1319, [2006] B.C.J. No. 1209, 55 B.C.L.R. (4th) 90, 227 B.C.A.C. 192, 374 W.A.C. 192, 2006 BCCA 272 (C.A.), additional reasons at 2006 CarswellBC 2259, 2006 BCCA 400 (C.A.), leave to appeal refused (2006), [2006] S.C.C.A. No. 318, 2006 CarswellBC 2797, 2006 CarswellBC 2798, 362 N.R. 390 (note) (S.C.C.).
68. *Ibid.* at para. 27.
69. *Ibid.* at para. 25.
70. A term frequently used to describe multi-problem families in which partner violence, alleged physical and child sexual abuse and/or neglect, substance abuse, mental illness, or questionable parenting practices. See Saini & Birnbaum, "Unraveling the Label of "High Conflict": What Factors really count in Separated and Divorced Families (Part 1)" (2007) 51(1) Ontario Association of Children's Aid Societies 14 for a systematic review of the high conflict literature to date.
71. Janet Johnston & Vivienne Roseby, *In the Name of the Child: A De-*

velopmental Approach to Understanding and Helping Children of Conflicted and Violent Divorce (New York: Free Press, 1997).

72. Rachel Birnbaum, "Rendering Children Invisible: The forces at Play during Separation and Divorce in the Context of Family Violence" in Ramona Alaggia & Cathy Vine, eds., *Cruel But not Unusual: Violence in Canadian Families* (Waterloo: Wilfrid Laurier University Press, 2006) at 264.

73. Jack Arbuthnot & Donald Gordon, "Does Mandatory Divorce Education for Parents Work? A Six-Month Outcome Evaluation" (1996) 34 Family and Conciliation Courts Review 60. See also, Jack Arbuthnot, Kevin Kramer & Donald Gordon, "Patterns of Re-Litigation Following Divorce Education" (1997) 35 Family and Conciliation Courts Review 269; and Brenda Bacon & Brad McKenzie, "Parent Education after Separation/Divorce: Impact of the Level of Parental Conflict on Outcomes" (2004) 42(1) Fam. Ct. Rev. 85.

74. Janet Johnston, Report to the State-wide Office of Family Court Services, AOC, *Developing and Testing Group Interventions for Families at Impasse* (San Francisco, Judicial Council of California, 1999).

75. Christine Coates, Robin Deutsch, Hugh Starnes, Matthew Sullivan & BeaLisa Sydlik, "Parenting Coordination for High-Conflict Families" (2004) 42(2) Fam. Ct. Rev. 246.

76. Peter Jaffe & Robert Geffner, "Child Custody Disputes and Domestic Violence: Critical Issues for Mental Health, Social Service, and Legal Professionals" in George Holden, Robert Geffner & Ernest Jouriles, eds., *Children Exposed to Marital Violence: Theory, Research and Applied Issues* (1998) American Psychological Association 371.

77. Child visitation and child access are being used interchangeably. Both terms are defined as the legal arrangement by which the non-custodial parent visits with the child/ren following separation and/or divorce. The social science literature uses the terms interchangeably depending on the country where the author is from. For example, in Australia and Great Britain, access is referred to as "contact" and supervised access centres are referred to as "contact centres."

78. While children can and do have supervised visitation with individuals who may not be part of their immediate family, this chapter refers solely to children involved in supervised visitation with their non-custodial parent in a government sponsored supervised visitation center in Ontario.

79. *Children's Law Reform Act*, R.S.O. 1990, c. C.12, s. 34(1).

80. Norman Park, Michele Peterson-Badali & Jennifer Jenkins, "An Evaluation of Supervised Access I: Organizational Issues" (1997) 35(1) Family and Conciliation Courts Review 37.

81. See *supra* note 10. See also, Jessica Pearson & Nancy Thoennes, "Supervised Visitation: The Families and their Experiences" (2000), 38(1) Family and Conciliation Courts Review 123; Helen Radovanovic, "Parental Conflict and Children's Coping Styles in Litigating Separated Families: Relationships with Children's Adjustment" (1993) 21(6) Journal of Abnormal Child Psychology 697; Andrew Schepard, "The Evolving Judicial Role in Child Custody Disputes: From Fault Finder to Conflict Manager to Differential Case Manager" (2000) 22 U. Ark. L. Rev. 395.

82. These ancillary services are usually provided on a fee-for-service basis by private contracted services (*i.e.* Bartemaeus Inc. in Toronto) and are not offered in government funded centers throughout Canada.

16

Rethinking Child Welfare Issues

(1) INTRODUCTION

Hillary Rodham wrote, "[T]he phrase, 'children's rights' is a slogan in search of a definition."[1] Historically, children had few rights. In nineteenth-century Canada, children were expected to work as soon as they were physically able. Children as young as seven years of age could be subjected to the same punishments as adults in the criminal justice system, including hanging. The Court of Equity recognized its *parens patriae* (parent of the country) authority which included the responsibility to "cause the performance of anything essential to the welfare or the benefit of infants and their properties."[2] However, at the time, the courts were focused on the protection of the property and estate interests of infants, which led to an Ontario court appointing a lawyer for an infant in 1827.

In 1881, the Office of the Official Guardian (now known as the Office of the Children's Lawyer)[3] was established to protect the property interests of infants in Ontario. However, as times changed and the view of childhood as a distinct and vulnerable period in a child's life evolved, children began to be perceived as persons with independent rights and interests.

As a result of the tragic death of Kim Ann Popen in 1976,[4] the Attorney General of Ontario established the Child Representation Program to be administered by the Office of the Official Guardian. In 1989, the United Nations *Convention on the Rights of the Child*[5] recognized the right of children to be heard in proceedings that affect their future.[6]

The intense focus on childhood derives from the development of psychology as a social science coupled with the notion that children have rights as individuals. Principles of psychology assert that early childhood experiences influence one's behaviour later on in life, and that adverse experience, physical or emotional deprivation, or abuse can limit or impede a child's present and future functioning in every sphere. Since serious consequences, both personal and public, can flow from early child-rearing difficulties, a notion developed that the state had a vested interest in protecting children from parents or caregivers whose behaviour might be dangerous to their well-being. Although a significant development, it is limited and narrow in scope; designed to intervene only when a breakdown in the standard or quality of care can be demonstrated, the legislation expressing the state's concern for protecting children is reactive.

The deaths of several children in Ontario[7] and across Canada[8] were a turning point that brought about a closer examination of child welfare practice and public policy. As they were deaths at the hands of child caregivers, the need for a proactive policy that would effectively assess the safety of children and address the basic needs of child-rearing was specifically highlighted: freedom from poverty; adequate nutrition; accessible day care when one or both parents worked; safe shelter; and supportive community services. Children need nurturing parents, and parents need access to social and financial resources to assist them when necessary. Until society demands more social policies that adequately provide basic resources (housing, education) to children and their families, society will remain deficient in its commitment to child welfare and protection.

In Ontario, child welfare matters fall under the provisions of the *Child and Family Services Act,*[9] which was substantially amended in 1999 and several times since.[10] Each province in Canada has its own corresponding legislation to protect children.[11] There will always be controversy within the legal and human-service professions about the intent and consequences of child welfare policy and to what extent the state or its agents are authorized to intervene in family life. Controversy will also continue over the roles of lawyers as protectors of children's rights, and mental health professionals as protectors of the physical and social well-being of children at risk. Also at issue are the rights of parents as decision-makers for their children, such as voluntary placement in a treatment facility, the right of a child to provide an informed consent, and third-party review of such decisions, to name a few.

We seem to be struggling to find a balance between the guarantees of fairness in proceedings involving children and parents and the rights of children to adequate care, protection and, in some cases, treatment intervention, all of which are generally considered necessary for healthy growth and development. It should be self-evident that both legal rights and physical and emotional protection are necessary, but it remains unclear which aspect, if any, should be given greater importance. For example, where a child is neglected, abandoned, or abused, it seems obvious that someone should intervene to protect the child from harm. But, from a legal perspective, what do "neglect" and "abandonment" and "emotional abuse" mean? When and how is intervention justified and who shall decide—parent, child, mental health professional, or the court?

In Chapter 15, we discussed what can happen to children involved in custody and access disputes resulting from the dissolution of the marriage. In Chapter 17, we consider those aspects of law concerned with the welfare of children when they appear to require protection from parents, caregivers, or sometimes from themselves.

(2) BEST INTERESTS OF THE CHILD

The overriding concern of judges in courts across Canada is finding out what serves the best interests of the child. This principle, which now guides all court decisions involving children,[12] has replaced the conflicting traditional assumption that fathers have unquestionable rights of control over their children or that all children of tender years belong with their mothers. The best interests test, as discussed in Chapter 15, remains difficult to define. As has been stated, the best interests of the child embodies a myriad of factors, and despite heavy use of the term throughout different legislation (child welfare and child custody and access) it is still a concept in search of meaning.[13]

Compare the definition of "best interest of the child" as stated in the *Child and Family Services Act*[14] (*CFSA*) with that found in the *Children's Law Reform Act*[15] (*CLRA*). It is important to note that the *CFSA* takes precedence over the *CLRA*. The *CFSA* requires consideration of all factors in light of individual circumstances, including:

1. The child's physical, mental and emotional needs, and the appropriate care or treatment to meet those needs.
2. The child's physical, mental and emotional level of development.
3. The child's cultural background.
4. The religious faith, if any, in which the child is being raised.
5. The importance for the child's development of a positive relationship with a parent and a secure place as a member of a family.
6. The child's relationships and emotional ties to a parent, sibling, relative, other member of the child's extended family or members of the child's community.
7. The importance of continuity in the child's care and the possible effect on the child of disruption of that continuity.
8. The merits of a plan for the child's care proposed by a society, including a proposal that the child be placed for adoption or

adopted, compared with the merits of the child remaining with or returning to a parent.

9. The child's views and wishes, if they can be reasonably ascertained.
10. The effects on the child of delay in the disposition of the case.
11. The risk that the child may suffer harm through being removed from, kept away from, returned to or allowed to remain in the care of a parent.
12. The degree of risk, if any, that justified the finding that the child is in need of protection.
13. Any other relevant circumstance.

Moreover, subsection 37(4) provides that,

> (4) Where a person is directed in this Part to make an order or determination in the best interests of a child and the child is an Indian or native person, the person shall take into consideration the importance, in recognition of the uniqueness of Indian and native culture, heritage and traditions, of preserving the child's cultural identity.[16]

However, it should be noted that the "best interests" definition in the *Child and Family Services Act* is applicable only after a child has been found by the court to be in need of protection, or when a child's placement or supervision by the Children's Aid Society is being reviewed by the court under the *Act*.[17]

In contrast, the *Children's Law Reform Act* states that the court shall consider all the circumstances of the child including:

1. love, affection, and emotional ties between the child and,
    a) each person entitled to or claiming custody of or access to the child,
    b) other members of the child's family who reside with the child, and
    c) persons involved in the care and upbringing of the child;

2. the views and preferences of the child, where such views and preferences can be reasonably ascertained;
3. the length of time the child lived in a stable home environment;
4. the ability and willingness of each person applying for custody of the child to provide the child with guidance and education, the necessaries of life and any special needs of the child;
5. any plans proposed for the care and upbringing of the child;
6. the permanence and stability of the family unit with which it is proposed that the child will live, and
7. the relationship by blood or through adoption order between the child and each erson who is a party to the application.[18]

The "best interests" test as outlined in the *Children's Law Reform Act* has a much broader application than the *Child and Family Services Act* and applies in all circumstances under provincial jurisdiction where the legal interests of children may be affected. Words uncommon to legislative drafting, such as "love," "affection," and "emotional ties," charge the court with the responsibility of considering the emotional as well as the physical needs of the child.[19]

The "best interests" test is the standard guide for child welfare decisions in every province. The overriding importance of the "best interests" doctrine is demonstrated by the following case.

In *B.(R.) v. Children's Aid Society of Metropolitan Toronto*,[20] the Supreme Court of Canada considered the nature and permissible extent of state intervention. The Children's Aid Society apprehended a child of Jehovah's Witness parents in order for the child to receive a blood transfusion deemed necessary by a pediatrician. Since the parents' religion forbade blood transfusions, they objected on two grounds: freedom of religion guaranteed by section 2(a) of the *Charter of Rights and Freedoms*, and the right to raise their children as they saw fit, a protected liberty interest under section 7 of the *Charter*.[21] A majority of Supreme Court judges found that the *Child and Family Services Act,* in giving the Society the right to intervene in these circumstances, was a reasonable limit on parental authority. While the right to raise one's children as one sees fit is indeed a liberty right guaranteed by section 7 of the *Charter*, the state has the right to intervene to protect the child when parental conduct falls below a standard seen as acceptable by the community.[22]

In *Winnipeg Child & Family Services (Northwest Area) v. G. (D.F.)*,[23] a Manitoba judge ordered a pregnant Native mother to be placed in the custody of the Director of Child and Family Services and detained in a hospital until the birth of the child, in order to stop her from glue-sniffing.[24] Ultimately, the majority of the Supreme Court judges refused to invoke their *parens patriae* jurisdiction to force the mother into treatment as they believed the State had no authority to 'apprehend' a fetus.[25]

Many cases continue to be litigated over the rights of children and their best interests as opposed to the rights of parents. The issues are complex and each case is usually decided on its own set of particular facts. The state should be the last resort in taking responsibility for the care and upbringing of children. As the late Dr. Paul Steinhauer stated,

> [R]emoval is no panacea. . .and should only be considered when: the family environment is so inadequate and/or damaging that the child is in immediate physical danger, or ongoing developmental and future adjustment are seriously and chronically at risk; or all possibility of improving the family situ-

ation, either through direct work with the child and family without removal, or through the provision of appropriate support services. . .[26]

More often than not, child welfare workers across Canada are caught between their duty to protect children from further abuse or neglect at home and their attempt, paradoxically, to integrate children back into those same families, a task that is both complex and challenging.

In Ontario the number of child abuse and neglect cases investigated has tripled since 1993 from an estimated 45,000 investigations to almost 130,000 in 2003.[27] The numbers continue to grow. In part, the rise in numbers can be attributed to several changes in our collective understanding of abuse, neglect, emotional harm, and the effects of children witnessing domestic violence, along with increased attention from the media and the obligation of the public at large (especially amongst professionals) to report suspected child abuse.

In Ontario, the introduction of the Eligibility Spectrum, the Child Welfare Well-Being Scales, and the Ontario Risk Assessment Model (2000) added additional assessment tools to agencies in determining whether a child is in need of protection. While these instruments have greatly enhanced the ability to identify when children may or may not be at risk, they have also added to the already increased workload of agency workers. Child protection work can be stressful and the pressures (internal and external) on social workers in this area of practice, while rewarding, can also be taxing.[28]

(3) CHILD AND FAMILY SERVICES ACT

The *Child and Family Services Act* sets out a declaration of principles,[29] which will be elaborated on in Chapter 18. However, the paramount purpose of the *Act* is to promote the best interests, protection and well-being of children. The *Act* sets out a series of steps which the Children's Aid Society must take before removing a child from the care of parents. A parent is entitled to a hearing within five days from the date a child is apprehended.[30] Before a child can be removed from his or her caregivers, the court must be assured that less intrusive measures have been offered but refused, have not worked, or are not likely to be effective. Even with a finding that a child is in need of protection, the court must be satisfied that its intervention is also required to protect the child;[31] that is, the court must be satisfied that the parents are unwilling or unable to make and maintain required changes.

SELECTED READINGS

Belsky, Jay, "Etiology of Child Maltreatment: A Developmental-Ecological Analysis" (1993) 114(3) Psychological Bulletin 413.

Blythe, Betty et al., "A Review of Intensive Family Preservation Services Research" (1994) 18(4) Social Work Research 213.

Corcoran, Jacqueline, "Family Interventions with Child Physical Abuse and Neglect: A Critical Review" (2000) 22(7) Children and Youth Services Review 563.

Jones, David, "The Untreatable Family" (1987) 11(3) Child Abuse and Neglect 409.

For an excellent source of research reports in child welfare across Canada see, Faculty of Social Work, University of Toronto, online: <http://www.cecw-cepbca>. Centre of Excellence for Children's Well-Being Centres, funded by Public Health Agency of Canada.

ENDNOTES

1. Hillary Rodham, "Children under the Law" (1973) 43(4) Harvard Educational Review 487.
2. Joseph Chitty, *Treatise on the Law of Prerogatives of the Crown and the Relative Duties and Rights of the Subject* (London: J. Butterworth, 1820) at 155-156.
3. The name has since been changed to what is now known as the Office of the Children's Lawyer. This office provides legal representation to children in child protection matters pursuant to *CFSA,* s. 38. It also provides independent legal representation to children in custody and access matters as described in Chapter 12.
4. The headline read from: Jennifer Coutts, "Baby's Death Sparked Changes in the Way Aid Societies Operate" *The Globe and Mail* (11 August 1994) A11. Kim Ann Popen died tragically at 19 months old after habitual beatings by her mother.
5. Resolution 44/25 (September, 1990) online: <http://www.unhchr.ch/html/menu3/b/k2crc.htm>. Canada is a party to the United Nations Convention on the Rights of the Child. Article 12 provides that children have a right to express their views freely in matters concerning them.
6. *Ibid.* at Article 12.
7. In addition to the Popen case cited above, see: M. Welsh & K. Donovan, "How the System Failed these Kids" *The Toronto Star* (18 September

1996) AI. This was a story of six children who died despite signs of abuse. The article was followed by yet another headline, Christie Blatchford, "Heikamp Visits Judge who ended her Criminal Trial Baby Jordan Starved to Death, Charges Dismissed" *National Post* (14 July 2001), online: <http://www.fathers.ca/baby_jordan.htm> (downloaded July 11, 2006). Baby Jordan died of chronic starvation in the City of Toronto while many professionals were supposedly watching out for him. For a more in-depth discussion of this case, see Chapter 26.

8. The death of Matthew Vaudreuil, who was killed by his mother, resulted in *The Gove Report* in British Columbia (1995) and the creation of a Ministry for Children and Families.

9. R.S.O. 1990, c. C.11 [*CFSA*].

10. Bill 6 (1999) in Ontario was introduced as an amendment to the *CFSA* to increase protection to children from parental abuse and neglect. This was later followed by the government's introducing child welfare transformation in 2006 with Bill 210. Bill 210 is meant to allow greater flexibility in long-term placement of children, permit extended family and community placement for children, and allow for continued contact post-adoption. Child protection mediation (alternative dispute resolution) is also part of the new amendments that have taken effect. See *Child Welfare in Canada* (1994), National Clearinghouse on Family Violence, Health Canada for a description of child welfare legislation and services prior to the 1990's. Also, see Nicolas Bala et al., *Canadian Child Welfare Law* (Toronto, Ontario: Thompson Educational Publishing, 1991), for additional reading on the background and history of child welfare in Canada.

11. See Ontario, *supra* note 10 and the Table of Concordance.

12. The *Children's Law Reform Act,* R.S.O. 1990, c. C.12, s. 24.

13. See Joan Kelly, "The Best Interests of the Child: A Concept in Search of Meaning" (1997) 35(4) Family and Conciliation Courts Review 377.

14. R.S.O. 1990, c. C.11.

15. See *supra* note 12.

16. See *supra* note 14 at s. 37(3) and (4).

17. *Ibid.*

18. See *supra* note 12 at s. 24(2).

19. *Ibid.* The *CFSA* adopts the criteria for "best interests" of both the old *Child Welfare Act* and *the Children's Law Reform Act*, and adds these additional significant criteria to the determination of "best interests": cultural and religious background, Indian or Native heritage, and the relative merits of plans proposed by a society, the effects on the child of delay in disposition, the relative risk to a child of removal from,

prolonged absence from, or return to the parents, and the degree of risk, if any, that justified the finding that the child is in need of protection.

20. (1994), 9 R.F.L. (4th) 157, 21 O.R. (3d) 479 (note), 122 D.L.R. (4th) 1, [1995] 1 S.C.R. 315, 26 C.R.R. (2d) 202, (sub nom. *Sheena B., Re*) 176 N.R. 161, 78 O.A.C. 1, 1995 CarswellOnt 105, 1995 CarswellOnt 515, EYB 1995-67419, [1994] S.C.J. No. 24.
21. *Ibid.*
22. *Ibid* at para. 86.
23. (1997), 152 D.L.R. (4th) 193, 121 Man. R. (2d) 241, 158 W.A.C. 241, 31 R.F.L. (4th) 165, 1997 CarswellMan 475, 1997 CarswellMan 476, [1998] 1 W.W.R. 1, (sub nom. *Child & Family Services of Winnipeg Northwest v. D.F.G.*) 219 N.R. 241, [1997] 3 S.C.R. 925, 39 C.C.L.T. (2d) 155 (Eng.), 3 B.H.R.C. 611, 39 C.C.L.T. (2d) 203 (Fr.).
24. *Ibid.* at para. 89.
25. *Ibid.* at paras. 56 and 57.
26. Paul Steinhauer, *The Least Detrimental Alternative* 1st ed., (Toronto, Ont.: University of Toronto Press, 1991) at 113.
27. Child Welfare Secretariat, *Child Welfare Transformation 2005: A strategic plan for a flexible, sustainable and outcome oriented service delivery model* (Toronto: Ontario Ministry of Children and Youth Services, 2005).
28. See Cheryl Regehr et al., *Stressors in Child Welfare Practice* (Toronto, Ont.: University of Toronto, 2000). This document can be accessed on the Centre of Excellence for child welfare website available at: www.cecw-cepb.ca (accessed on August 1, 2007).
29. See *supra* note 9.
30. *Ibid.* at s. 46(1)(a).
31. *Ibid.* at s. 57(1).

17

Child Protection

(1) INTRODUCTION

Part III of the *Child and Family Services Act (CFSA)*,[1] sets minimum standards of care for children in Ontario. Each province in Canada has enacted similar legislation designed to protect the welfare of children living within its jurisdiction. In this chapter we will examine the Ontario legislation, however readers should refer to the legislation in their respective provinces.[2] The *CFSA* enables the province to vest its authority in an approved agency. Fifty-three agencies throughout Ontario provide services to children and families when there is an allegation that care provided to a child has fallen below the standards prescribed by law. While they have different names, for purposes of this chapter, agencies will be referred to in each instance as the Children's Aid Society.

A Children's Aid Society is empowered to intervene in the care of the child and, where it is deemed necessary, remove the child from the care and custody of his or her parents to a place of safety. The Children's Aid Society's interference with the family occurs when the level of care the child is receiving falls below the minimum community standards set out in the legislation. Social workers employed by Children's Aid Societies in Ontario are empowered by law to act as agents of the Minister of Community and Social Services and are given the authority to take action to protect a child living in circumstances defined by the *Act* as constituting harm or risk of harm.[3]

The *CFSA* consists of the culmination of a long process on the part of the provincial government to solicit a broad range of discussion and opinion regarding the precise definition of a child in need of protection. The process began with the report *Protecting Vulnerable Children: Report of the Panel of Experts in Child Protection*,[4] chaired by Madam Justice Mary Jane Hatton in 1998.

There have since been significant amendments to the *Act*[5] and policy changes have in turn followed from these amendments. The intent of the policy changes to child welfare has stressed a transformation agenda that includes: (1) a more flexible intake and assessment model; (2) a court process strategy to reduce delays and encourage alternatives to court; (3) a broader range of placement options that will support more effective permanency planning; (4) a rational and accountable framework; (5) a sustainable and strategic funding model; (6) a single information system; and (7) a focus on child welfare research capacity. All of these approaches are based on strength-based assessments to support achievements of positive client outcomes through evidence-based practice.

The *Act* considers a child to be in need of protection where it can be demonstrated that he or she: (1) has suffered physical harm; (2) has been sexually molested or exploited; (3) requires medical treatment to cure, prevent or alleviate physical harm; (4) has suffered emotional harm, and parental incapacity to remedy the harm; or (5) is at risk of harm (sexual or emotional harm, abandonment, etc.).[6]

The balance between the protection of family privacy and the interest of the state in preventing the abuse of children has shifted slightly in each direction from decade to decade. For example, in the early 1980s maintaining the integrity of the family unit was a significant consideration for the court. Presently, although maintaining the family unit is important, it is not paramount, particularly, for children at risk.

Child protection agencies in all provinces, but notably in Ontario and British Columbia, are beset by reports in the media that children in their care are subject to continuing abuse and neglect, that, in some instances results in death (as reported in Chapter 16). Inquests, investigations, and recommendations aimed at preventing such tragic outcomes occupy public attention for brief periods and then drop when the glare of media attention fades.[7] Inadequate resources resulting from decreased provincial funding and too few workers responsible for too many children and families, as well as inadequate training and supervision of front line workers, are frequently cited as reasons for the failure of the province to protect children. In addition, legislation that favours protecting families—considering that as the least intrusive and onerous intervention—is often cited as the reason why some children are returned by the courts to families where risk is high.

All of these factors may be valid explanations for why children continue to slip through systems set up to protect them. However, we still do not have a federal or provincial policy that creates a comprehensive plan for child welfare and support. Such a policy would establish inter-disciplinary and cooperative links between health, education, legal and community and social services, and the youth criminal justice system. These linkages are essential to the provision of community based outreach services in order to work with families on a preventative, as well as a crisis based, level as envisioned by the recent transformation agenda (as discussed above) instigated in the child welfare system in Ontario.

Abusive and neglectful situations tend to have a long history of inactivity or inadequate response. Typically, investigations reveal that nothing had been done to prevent the abuse or neglect by providing necessary support services (such as housing, financial, educationl, legal) to the family. In some cases numerous services and professionals had been involved, but the profound lack of communication and coordination of services ended with the same result; little service. As a further consideration, the enormous cost of lengthy child welfare trials and appellate litigation might better be devoted to front-line child supervision and family support on behalf of children; these services, however, often fall victim to reduced agency budgets.

(2) THE FUNCTIONS OF CHILDREN'S AID SOCIETIES

Child welfare proceedings take place in the Ontario Court of Justice or the Superior Court of Justice (Family Court).

To fulfill their mandate of child protection, Children's Aid Societies across Ontario function to:

(a) investigate allegations or evidence that children, who are under the age of 16 years or in the Society's care or under its supervision, may be in need of protection;

(b) protect, where necessary, children who are under the age of 16 years or in the Society's care or under its supervision;

(c) provide guidance, counselling and other services to families for protecting children or for the prevention of circumstances requiring the proection of children;

(d) provide care for children assigned or committed to its care under the *Act*;

(e) supervise children assigned to its supervision under the *Act*;

(f) place children for adoption under Part VII of the *Act*; and

(g) peform any other duties given to it by this or any other *Act*.[8]

Each Children's Aid Society in the province has a broad mandate, which according to law, must be fulfilled in order to protect vulnerable children.

(3) DEFINITION OF A CHILD IN NEED OF PROTECTION

The *CFSA* defines a "child" as a person under 16 years of age for the purposes of child protection. Crown wardship remains until the child is 18 years of age and can continue, in some cases, until the child reaches his or her 21st birthday. A child in need of protection is defined by one or more of the following circumstances:

- (a) the child has suffered physical harm, inflicted by the person having charge of the child or caused by or resulting from that person's,
  - (i)   failure to adequately care for, provide for, supervise or protect the child; or
  - (ii) pattern of neglect in caring for, providing for, supervising or protecting the child;
- (b) there is a risk that the child is likely to suffer physical harm inflicted by the person having charge of the child or caused by or resulting from that person's,
  - (i)   failure to adequately care for, provide for, supervise or protect the child; or
  - (ii) pattern of neglect in caring for, providing for, supervising or protecting the child;
- (c) the child has been sexually molested or sexually exploited, by a person having charge of the child, or by another person where the person having charge of the child knows or should know of the posssibility of sexual molestation or sexual exploitation and fails to protect the child;
- (d) there is a risk that the child is likely to be sexually molested or sexually exploited as described in clause (c);
- (e) the child requires medical treatment to cure, prevent, or alleviate physical harm or suffering and the child's parent or the person having charge of the child does not provide, or refuses or is unavailable or unable to consent to, the treatment;
- (f) the child has suffered emotional harm, demonstrated by serious,
  - (i)   anxiety;
  - (ii) depression;
  - (iii) withdrawal;
  - (iv) self-destructive or aggressive behavior; or
  - (v)   delayed development;

  and there are reasonable grounds to believe that the emotional harm suffered by the child result from the actions, failure to act or pattern of neglect on the part of the child's parent or the person having charge of the child;

(f.1) the child has suffered emotional harm of the kind described in subclause (f)(i), (ii),(iii), (iv) or (v) and the child's parent or the person having charge of the child does not provide, or refuses or is unavailable or unable to consent to, services or treatment to remedy or alleviate the harm;

(g) there is a risk that the child is likely to suffer emotional harm of the kind described in subclause (f)(i), (ii), (iii), (iv), or (v) resulting from the actions, failure to act or pattern of neglect on the part of the child's parent or person having charge of the child;

(g.1) there is a risk that the child is likely to suffer emotional harm of the kind described in subclause (f)(i), (ii), (iii), (iv), or (v) and that the child's parent or person having charge of the child does not provide, or refuses or is unavailable or unable to consent to, services or treatment to prevent the harm;

(h) the child suffers from a mental, emotional or developmental condition that, if not remedied, could seriously impair the child's development and the child's parent or the person having charge of the child does not provide, or refuses or is unavailable or unable to consent to, treatment to remedy or alleviate the condition;

(i) the child has been abandoned, the child's parent has died or is unavailable to exercise his or her custodial rights over the child and has not made adequate provision for the child's care and custody, or the child is in a residential placement and the parent refuses or is unwilling to resume the child's care and custody;

(j) the child is less than 12 years old and has killed or seriously injured another person or caused serious damage to another person's property, services or treatment are necessary to prevent a recurrence and the child's parent or the person having charge of the child does not provide, or refuses or is unavailable or unable to consent to, those services or treatment;

(k) the child is less than 12 years old and has on more than one occasion injured another person or caused loss or damage to another person's property, with the encouragement of the person having charge of the child or because of that person's failure or inability to supervise the child adequately; or

(l) the child's parent is unable to care for the child and the child is brought before the court with the parent's consent and, where the child is 12 years of age or older, with the child's consent, to be dealt with under this Part.[9]

(4) HOW PROTECTION PROCEEDINGS ARE INITIATED

A child who is believed to be in need of protection may be apprehended with or without a warrant depending on the situation, and brought to a place of safety.[10] A child protection worker with a warrant has the authority to enter any premises specified in the warrant and by force, if necessary, search for and remove a child.[11] Child protection proceedings can be initiated when no apprehension has taken place.

(5) BY WHOM AND WHEN A CHILD MAY BE APPREHENDED

Persons who have the right to apprehend a child include: a police officer; a Director of Child Welfare; a local Director of a Children' s Aid Society; or a person authorized by a Director or local Director.[12] These persons have the right in some circumstances to enter premises by force, if need be, and to apprehend a child with or without a warrant. Within five days of apprehension, the acting Children's Aid Society must commence a Protection Application, return the child to the person having charge prior to the apprehension, or enter into a voluntary care agreement with the child's parents. If none of these options has been initiated within five days, the child must be returned to the person from whom he or she was taken. However, as stated previously, an apprehension is not necessary to commence a protection application.

During adjournments, the court has no authority to remove a child from his or her legal caregivers if the court is satisfied that the child will be adequately protected and is not likely to suffer a risk of harm in his or her own home. The onus is on those who apprehend to persuade the court otherwise.

In general, the courts have held that apprehension should be undertaken only when a child is confronted by real and immediate danger. Subsection 40(7) of the *CFSA* deals with the right of a worker, who has reasonable and probable grounds to believe that a child is in need of protection, to apprehend the child without a warrant and take the child to a place of safety, which includes a hospital. Where a child is too young to consent to a physical examination, the worker may on the child's behalf authorize the examination where a parent's consent would otherwise be required.

In one Ontario case, *M. (J.). v. Toronto Board of Education*,[13] a father's action for assault and battery against a worker who apprehended a child did not succeed. A worker is immune from civil prosecution where a child is removed to a place of safety before a warrant can be obtained if that worker was acting in good faith. In another case, *R. v. Daniels*,[14] child welfare workers entered a house because of their concerns about a mother and her three children. The concerns were based on the mother's prior attempt to commit suicide with a gun that was in the house. The police did not believe a warrant could be obtained to enter the house. The mother came to the door with her children and granted access to the police and the child welfare workers. The father was charged with careless storage of firearms and ammunition; he later argued that he was subject to an unreasonable search. During the criminal proceedings the court found that given that the mother opened the door and showed no signs of danger, the police were prohibited from entering the house without a warrant. Because of their entry, the evidence collected was inadmissable in court. This finding seems to be consistent with s. 40(7) of the *CFSA*.

Of interest is a further case in which a trial judge dismissed a Society's protection application, a decision—along with a judgment awarding costs against the Society—that was upheld by the appeal court. The trial judge did not believe the allegations of sexual abuse and had questioned the child extensively; this judicial questioning formed the basis of the appeal. The appeal court noted that a protection proceeding is not the same as a two-party litigation, that the community also has an interest in the proceedings, and that the judge must inquire into the facts to determine whether the child is in need of protection.[15]

As in many areas of law, having children give evidence in child protection proceedings or undergo judicial interviews in custody and access proceedings raises not only legal challenges, but also social and emotional challenges for children, irrespective of age. Having their own legal representation helps to facilitate the protection of children and their rights.

(6) TEMPORARY CARE AND SPECIAL NEEDS AGREEMENTS

The *Act* provides for temporary care by agreement. These agreements include: (1) a temporary care agreement for children under the age 16 if the Society has an appropriate placement available and is satisfied that no less disruptive course of action, such as care in the child's own home, is possible; (2) a special needs agreement in those instances where the parents are unable to provide the child with the necessary services required for special needs created by physical, mental, emotional, behavioural or other handicaps; and (3) a special needs agreement where the person is 16 or 17 years of age and requires special services.[16]

Consent of the child involved is required where the child is 12 years of age or older unless he or she is unable to consent because of a developmental handicap. The consent of the Director of Child Welfare is required for an extension of any temporary care agreements. No initial temporary care agreement may exceed six months, and extensions, if granted, must not exceed 12 months and in no circumstance shall they ever extend 24 months. If a child is under the age of six the agreement cannot exceed 12 months. A special needs agreement may not extend beyond the child's 18th birthday.[17]

Either the parent or the Society may terminate a temporary care or special needs agreement by giving at least 21 days written notice. A child who is 12 years of age or older and the subject of an agreement may make a written request for a review of the agreement by the Society or the Minister. If no new agreement is reached, the existing agreement automatically terminates at the end of the 21-day period. If this occurs, the Society must either return the child to the previous custodian or submit the matter to the court for a determination of the child's need for protection. If the aggreement has not been terminated by someone and no extension is signed, the Society must return the child or bring an application as soon as is practical, but within 21 days.

In order to ensure that both parties comply with the terms, a social worker must make certain that the agreement for temporary care and custody contains a statement about the Society's responsibilities and the parents' responsibilities during the time of the agreement. In addition, the agreement must state that responsibility for the child is transferred to the Society by the voluntary agreement of all parties on the basis that the legal caregiver is temporarily unable to provide care. The Society, for its part, must keep parents informed of the child's progress, notify the parents of any emergency concerning the child, and help the parents and the child to plan for their reunion. The parents are obliged to maintain contact with the child.

Special needs agreements must be for a specified period of time, but may be extended. In the case of a child 16 to 18 years old who has a special need and is not in the care of his or her parent, the agreement can be entered into by the child on his or her own behalf.[18] A 16 or 17 year old not yet before the courts is permitted under the *Act* to obtain service from the Society only if he or she has a special need and is not in the care of a parent.

(7) PARTIES TO A CHILD WELFARE PROCEEDING AND NOTICE[19]

"Parties" always include the Children's Aid Society, and the child's parents, and/or actual caregivers. The Director of Child Welfare may also be added as a party on the application. A child aged twelve or more is entitled to notice but is not a party to the application. Where the child is an Indian or a Native person, a representative chosen by the child's band or Native community is also a party to the application. The band/First Nation's rights include the rights to seek access, apply for a status review, receive notice of proceedings (including adoption), and the right to appeal any court decision. The declaration of principle in the *Act* recognizes the distinct culture and heritage of Native children, including the concept of extended family.[20]

The complexity of cultural identity in our acculturated society is demonstrated in the following case.[21] A Native mother left her child with her brother who placed the child with the local Children's Aid Society after he could no longer care for him. After the child became a Crown Ward, every effort was made to find him a Native home, but to no avail. The court concluded that the child's need for a continuing relationship with his Native heritage did not outweigh the close family relationship he had developed with his foster parents.

(8) HEARINGS AND ORDERS

A proceeding may be initiated by filing an application, whereupon the clerk must set a date and issue a Protection Application or Status Review Application. Persons entitled to have notice include:

1. parents or legal caregivers having actual custody of the child;
2. foster parents who have been caring for the child for a continuous period of more than 6 months;
3. a child over 12, unless the Court directs that the child not be served because the hearing might negatively affect the child's emotional health;
4. a child under 12, at the discretion of the Court;
5. the Society (if it is a status review application); and
6. the Band is also entitled to notice as are any added parties.[22]

The *Act* defines a parent as:

(a) the child's mother;
(b) an individual described in one of paragraphs 1 to 6 of subsection 8(1) of the *Children's Law Reform Act*,[23] unless it is proved on a balance of probablities that he is not the child's natural father;
(c) the individual having lawful custody of the child;
(d) an individual who, during the 12 months before the intervention under this Part, has demonstrated a settled intention to treat the child as a child of his or her family, or has acknolwedged parentage of the child and provided for the child's support;
(e) an individual who, under a written agreement or court order, is required to provide for the child, has custody of the child or has a right of access to the child; and

(f) an individual who has acknowledged parentage of the child in writing under section 12 of the *Children's Law Reform Act*, but does not include a foster parent.[24]

(9) CUSTODY OF CHILD PENDING A HEARING

Pending final disposition of the protection application, the onus is on the Children's Aid Society to demonstrate and present evidence as to why a child should remain in temporary care and custody. Unless this motion is made, or if it fails, the child will be returned to the person who had charge before his or her apprehension. In order to determine where the child will live pending a full hearing, the court may consider any evidence as long as the source is identified and the court determines it is credible and trustworthy, and the other party has a fair opportunity to correct or contradict it. The court may also consider the legal caregivers' past conduct toward any child in his or her care in reaching a decision about continuing residence of the child.

(10) THE HEARING

Since the Ontario Court of Justice is a statutory court where judges are provincially appointed, it holds no *parens patriae* [literally meaning, 'parent of the country'] power; no provincially appointed judge can exercise this power because such authority arises out of the equitable jurisdiction of the old Courts of Chancery. However, many inferior court judges seem to act on the basis of the *parens patriae* doctrine. Child protection hearings pursuant to the *CFSA* are always held in private unless the court orders a public hearing. They must also always be held separately from hearings in criminal matters, including those under the *Youth Criminal Justice Act*.[25] Two representatives of the news media are entitled to be present at a hearing, but the court may exclude them if their presence would be injurious to the child's emotional health. In addition, no person is permitted to make public or publish information that can identify a child in such proceedings.

(11) THE COURT PROCESS

A child is brought before the courts by one of the following procedures:

1. an application/status review application;
2. an order to produce, which compels the parent or guardian to attend the court hearing;

3.   apprehension;
4.   termination of an agreement for temporary care; or
5.   a third party application.

In general, the Children's Aid Society elects to proceed by an order to produce rather than by apprehending the child if the child is not in immediate danger. The Society may seek an order of supervision in an effort to keep the child with the family.

(a) The Two Part Nature of the Hearing

The hearing in child protection matters has two distinct stages, with the Children's Aid Society carrying the burden of proof in both. In the first stage, the Society must establish that the child is in need of protection, which means that it has to prove that the parent having care of the child has failed to maintain minimum community standards in one of the ways listed in the *Act*. The second stage is the disposition, which cannot be made unless there is a finding at the first stage that the child is in need of protection. The best interests test only applies at the second or disposition stage of the proceeding, after the court has found that the child is in need of protection.

(b) Temporary Care and Custody Hearing

In general, after the first hearing before the court, the proceedings may be adjourned to give the Children's Aid Society time to assess the situation, which may include a medical examination of the child without parental consent, and to give the parties time to retain counsel and provide written responses to the Society's allegations. This adjournment can not exceed 30 days without the consent of all parties. While the court hearing is adjourned, the court has four options in providing for the child. According to subsection 51(2) of the *CFSA*, the child may:

(a) remain in or be returned to the care and custody of the person who had charge of the child immediately before intervention. . .;

(b) remain in or be returned to the care and custody of the person referred to in clause (a), subject to the society's supervision and on such reasonable terms and conditions relating to the child's supervision as the court considers appropriate;

(c) be placed in the care and custody of a person other than the person referred to in clause (a), with the consent of that other person, subject to the society's supervision and on such reasonable terms and conditions as the court considers appropriate; or

    (d) remain or be placed in the care and custody of the society, but not
        be placed in,
        (i) a place of secure custody as defined in Part IV (Young Justice),
           or
        (ii) a place of open temporary detention as defined in that Part that
           has not been designated as a place of safety.[26]

The onus is on the Society to demonstrate why the child should not remain with the custodial parent.

(c) Case Conference

A temporary hearing, case conference or settlement conference may be convened. These out-of-court efforts are made to reduce both the number of trials and, to the child's benefit, the delays in disposing of a child welfare proceeding. As discussed in Chapter 6, case conferences are very informal; counsel summarize their cases, indicate what evidence they intend to present, and hear an opinion from the judge about the probable legal outcome, all of which may facilitate a settlement without going to trial.

(d) Dispositions

The following are possible dispositions of a hearing for a protection application where the court has found that a child is in need of protection.

(i) No Order

The Court may find that the child is in need of protection but at the same time determine that no order is necessary.

(ii) Supervision Order

A supervision order places the child with the parent or another person subject to the supervision of the Children's Aid Society. The minimum period of supervision is three months and the maximum is 12 months. A supervision order will expire when the duration is finished or upon the child's marriage or 18th birthday. The court may also impose terms and conditions in the order relating to the method of supervision. The courts have interpreted subsection 57(8) very broadly and have used it to impose detailed conditions on the parent or person in charge of the child.[27]

(iii) Society Wardship Order

A Society wardship order commits a child to the care and custody of the Society that initiated the proceedings. No order may exceed 12 months, but if a previous order was in place, no period of continuous temporary care may exceed 24 months for children over six years of age. For children under six, the period of temporary care is reduced to 12 months. The order expires upon completion of the duration, or upon the child's marriage or 18 birthday. The order gives the Society the authority to secure a licensed placement for the child where it feels that his or her needs will best be met by doing so. It is important to note that the temporary care periods are cumulative; that is, the court will count all the periods of time in care including a temporary care agreement.

The Society must also ensure not only that the child receives a proper education in accordance with both Ontario law and his or her intellectual capacity, but that provision is made for the child's occupational training and total development such as any good parent would be expected to provide.

(iv) Crown Wardship Order

A Crown wardship order commits the child to the care of the Society that brought him or her before the court. It can expire upon the child's marriage, 18th birthday, adoption, or a determination by the court. Where a Crown wardship order expires as a result of a child reaching his or her 18th birthday and that child is either enrolled as a full time student in an educational institution or is mentally or physically handicapped, the Society may provide continuing care and maintenance for those particular circumstances.

Under the terms of each of the above four dispositons, the court is enjoined from removing a child from the care of legal caregivers unless it is satisfied that less restrictive alternatives, including non-residential services and other alternatives, have either been tried and proven unsuccessful, were refused by the legal caregiver, or would not adequately protect the child. The court must also consider placement with a relative, neighbour, community, or the extended family. Native children must always be placed with a member of the child's extended family, band, Native community or another Native family unless a substantial contrary reason exists.[28]

(e) Consecutive Orders of Society Wardship and Supervision

Under a consecutive order, the child is made a ward of the society for a specified period of time. The child would then be returned to a parent or another person for a period of time not exceeding an aggregate of 12 months.[29]

(f) Status Review Proceedings

For supervision and Society wardship, the court must review all orders prior to their expiration. Orders for Crown wardship may be reviewed providing the child has not been placed for adoption.[30] The Children's Aid Society can apply for a review at any time, but the parent of a child or a child who is 12 years of age or over can apply for a review only after the expiration of six months time from the making of the Crown wardship order. The parent and/or child can apply for other reviews at any time. The Director of the Society must review the status of every child who is a Crown ward at least once in each calendar year.[31]

Once a finding of the need for protection has been established, the question of disposition must be dealt with by the court. The following cases demonstrate the reasoning used in making distinctive dispositions.

By statute, children can only be in the care of the Society for two years in the case of children over six years of age, and 12 months for children under six years. In one Ontario case the children were orginally taken into care because of the mother's physical neglect and unclean living conditions. However, the children were healthy and well-adjusted, and had bonded with the mother. Although the Society asked for Crown wardship to clear the way for adoption, evidence was produced that the mother had taken steps to improve herself and her housekeeping skills. The court was satisfied that the minimum standards in which protection of children could be demonstrated were met and there was no evidence that the children faced a substantial risk of harm if returned to the mother if supervision from the Society was provided for a 12 month period.[32]

In another case, a child was placed with foster parents at birth. As the case took nearly two years to come to trial, the child had already bonded with the foster parents and they wanted to adopt. The court refused to consider the question of the child's best interests until the initial question of the need for protection from the birth parents had been decided.[33]

In a further case, a child, having suffered physical abuse from the birth mother, was apprehended and placed with foster parents. The father and paternal grandfather had access to the child, who developed an attachment to both of them as well as to the foster mother. The court found that the child's best interest would be served if he were placed with his extended family, who were the paternal grandparents in this case, in spite of his bonding with the foster mother as primary caregiver.[34]

(12) ASSESSMENTS

In Ontario, after a finding is made by the Court, or on consent, the court may order a child and family to undergo a psychological and psycho-social assessment, which includes medical, emotional, developmental, and educational assessments that then become evidence in the proceeding.[35] The court must also decide who will conduct the assessment. Interestingly, as the demand for parenting assessments from mental health professionals increases, the literature of both law and mental health reveals a parallel increase in scepticism about their value.[36]

Assessments, particularly those done to inform legal proceedings, must be wary of opinions that are not supported by evidence. Since lawyers present its contents to the court, objectivity of the assessment must be able to withstand scrutiny, particularly in areas of human interaction where ambiguity defies objective reporting. Some guidelines can be offered, how-ever, to provide structure in formulating assessments. For example, there should be a clear statement, mutually agreed to by all parties, about why the assessment was undertaken, where it took place, who was present, what reports were prepared, and who had access to those reports. It should also contain a statement of conclusions based on observed facts along with a professional interpretation of these facts.

The mental health professional preparing an assessment who is aware of ambiguous feelings will strive to create a climate in which a parent can express negative feelings and doubts. Parental ambivalence is a factor that underlies parent-child interaction, even in untroubled families, and such ambivalence is amplified when there is a custody dispute or when fitness for parenting is brought into question. Parents may appear to alternate between being warm and caring, and insensitive and rejecting, reflecting their conflicting desires to both win and lose.

In addition, mental health professionals conducting assessments should be aware of the admissibility of their expert opinions. As in all areas of law, the reader may wish to become familiar with the issues of admiss-ability of expert evidence and their presentation of written information to the court (also stated in Chapter 8).[37]

(13) APPEALS

Any decision made under the *Child and Family Services Act*, except for an assessment order, is subject to appeal to the Superior Court of Justice if the matter was heard in the Ontario Court of Justice or to the Divisonal Court if the matter was heard in the Superior Court of Justice (Family Court).[38] An appeal may be launched by: (a) the child, if he or she is entitled to participate; (b) any parent; (c) the person who had charge of the child prior to intervention; (d) the Director of Child Welfare; (e) a local director of a Society; or (f) a representative of the child's Native band or Native community. The appeal must be filed within 30 days of the decision. There is a positive obligation to expedite child protection appeals. If the parents had custody of the child at the time the original hearing granted them custody, then the child would automatically remain in their custody pending the appeal.

The grounds on which the appellate court can take action depend upon whether the appeal judge finds any error either in fact or in law in the decision of the trial judge. The appellate court's responsibility is not to re-try the protection application. There must be a specific error in law or in fact presented that would change the initial decision made by the judge.

The appellate court judge has several options. If no error is found to exist, the appeal will be dismissed. If the appeal is allowed on the basis of a demonstrable error, the appellate court can substitute its decision and return the child to the person in whose care he or she was apprehended. The court may also rule that a new trial take place. If a litigant is unhappy with the decision of the appellate court, whether it is the Superior Court of Justice or the Divisional Court, it is possible to appeal to the Court of Appeal and with leave, ultimately to the Supreme Court of Canada.

(14) LEGAL REPRESENTATION FOR THE CHILD: THE ROLE OF THE OFFICE OF THE CHILDREN'S LAWYER

A child may be represented by counsel at any stage of any proceeding under the *Child and Family Services Act*,[39] which provides that the child must have legal representation if any of the circumstances presented in subsection 38(1) are present. One exception is if the court is satisfied that the child's interests are adequately protected without legal counsel. Subsection 38(1) of the *CFSA* states:

(1) A child may have legal representation at any stage in a proceeding under this Part;

(2) Where a child does not have legal representation in a proceeding under this Part, the court,

(a) shall, as soon as practicable after the commencement of the proceeding; and

(b) may, at any later stage in the proceeding,

determine whether legal representation is desirable to protect the child's interests.

The circumstances under which this would occur include occasions where:

(a) the court is of the opinion that there is a difference of views between the child and a parent or a Society, and the Society proposes that the child be removed from a person's care or be made a Society or Crown ward under paragraph 2 or 3 of subsection 57(1);

(b) the child is in the society's care and,

    (i) no parent appears before the court, or

    (ii) it is alleged that the child is in need of protection within the meaning of clause 37(2)(a), (c), (f), (f.1) or (h); or

(c) the child is not permitted to be present at the hearing,

Legal representation shall be deemed to be desirable to protect the child's interests, unless the court is satisfied, taking into account the child's views and wishes if they can be reasonably ascertained, that the child's interests are otherwise aedquately protected.[40]

If the child is not represented, the judge must determine whether separate representation is needed to protect the child's interests and make an order for independent legal representation. The child will be assigned a staff lawyer from the Office of the Children's Lawyer, or the matter will be referred to a lawyer in private practice who is a member of the Child Representation Programme Panel.[41]

Accessibility of counsel to the child and the capacity of the child to express views and preferences are essential to the provision of representation to a child. All children irrespective of age (including newborns) are entitled to independent legal representation in child protection matters in Ontario. This issue of legal representation was highlighted by Justice Little when she noted in a case where the child's voice needed to be heard,

> In so far as her Charter rights may be affected, Heather M. has counsel who may raise constitutional claims on her behalf, if the circumstances justify doing so. This case illustrates the appropriateness of representation for non-verbal children, depending on the circumstances of the case, despite their inability to give instructions. It is absolutely essential, in my view, that Heather M. be represented in this case.[42]

The approach assumed by the lawyer is also of crucial importance. The possible approaches are *adversarial*, in which the lawyer takes instruction from the child as from an adult client, a *guardianship* role, in which the lawyer examines the available information and then advocates a position which he or she sees as being in the child's best interests in spite of the child's instructions, and that of *amicus curiae*, in which the lawyer maintains neutrality and acts as an intermediary between the child and the court while providing the court with facts, reports, and important information. Decisive factors are, of course, the age of the child, the child's capacity to understand the proceedings and their consequences, and ability to express their views and preferences. In general, children ten years of age or older are considered capable of expressing wishes and understanding consequences, while younger children may be more or less capable of such understanding. The lawyer of a young child might therefore serve as an advocate of the child's legal rights and social needs.

As Justice Steinburg, in his Royal Commission report:

> [T]he development of a valid concept of child law advocacy requires meaningful interaction between the legal and social work professions . . . [I]t is a joint function of both the legal and social work professions to define and to strike a proper balance of the legal and social rights of children both within the family and before the courts in order to make our concept of child advocacy work.[43]

The following cases are instructive on the role of legal counsel as interpreted by the courts. A Society had applied for supervised access. At the hearing, counsel for the child advised that the child wished to return to her parents but did not want supervised visits. Counsel then added her own opinion that the child was emotionally incompetent to instruct counsel and so counsel would call witnesses in the child's best interests. The respondent parents' counsel objected. The court held that counsel for the child was an advocate and so her personal opinions about the child's best interests should be disregarded. If the child could give instructions, it stated, they should be presented; if the child was unable to give instructions, counsel might apply for removal from the case but could not act as *amicus curiae*.[44] In another matter Justice Czutrin ruled:

> It is for the children's counsel, ultimately, to present whatever evidence they have or to review the evidence and make submissions to protect the children's best interests. These should not be personal views, but based on a position the Children's Lawyer takes, based on the evidence and the law, to advance a position to protect the children. It is not for counsel to stand up and give personal views or to give evidence from the counsel table...Ultimately, it is for the court to decide the issues in this case. Counsel is not the legal guardian in this case or amicus curiae, but the legal representative. The relation between the child's counsel and the child is one of solicitor and client. . .[45]

(15) RIGHTS OF CHILDREN

The concept of children's rights is relatively new to our thinking about children. Those involved with traditional social agencies such as Children's Aid Societies may feel that they alone can represent the child's best interests. They may fear that legal representation will create delays and will fail to appreciate the child's situation as understood by a social worker through long involvement with the child.

It has been observed that the social service system has developed as a quasi-legal system; in part because of deficiencies in the court system, such as overloaded dockets and delays that were costly and damaging to the parties involved. In addition, it has also been demonstrated that social agencies, because of bureaucratic concerns and restrictive administrative policies, do not always represent a child's best interests. Nor are parents always reliable to represent a child's best interests because of the primacy of their own needs and the fear of self-incrimination.

The discretion of the social service system, which went unexamined for so long, has now been brought under scrutiny by the introduction of legal representation for children. The current belief of many child advocates is that there is a need for procedural safeguards protected by a lawyer. There must also be persons who can produce an appropriate investigation of a child's physical, social, and emotional needs and compatibility of these needs with the resources of the competing parties, and then be able to provide expert opinion evidence to the court. Obviously, both legal and social work skills are required.

(a) Rights of Children in Care

There are certain sections of the *CFSA* that define the rights of children in care. The children referred to in these sections on rights are those receiving residential services, such as care from foster parents, and those in temporary detention placement, or in secure or open custody under the *Youth Criminal Justice Act.* Child rights to care include:

(a) to participate in the development of the child's individual plan of care and in any changes made to it;
(b) to be able to receive meals that are well-balanced, of good quality and appropriate for the child;
(c) to be provided with clothing that is of good quality and appropriate for the child, given the child's size and activities and prevailing weather conditions;
(d) to receive medical and dental care, subject to section 106, at regular

intervals and whenever required, in a community setting whenever possible;

(e)   to receive an education that corresponds to the child's aptitudes and abilities, in a community setting whenever possible; and

(f)   to participate in recreational and athletic activities that are appropriate for the child's aptitudes and interests, in a community setting whenever possible.[46]

The Office of Child and Family Service Advocacy has an obligation to coordinate and administer a system of advocacy for children.[47] Of particular importance is its role in monitoring Children's Aid Society workers. Since early 2007 this Office now reports solely to the Legislature of Ontario. This is a significant development, and the specific rights listed in the *Act* should be carefully noted by child welfare workers. Rights are meaningless unless enforced and monitored; if they are ignored or overridden, children in particular have little power to sound an alarm, even if aware that their rights have not been observed. Children in vulnerable situations need an advocate to ensure that these rights are protected and that the needs of a large care system do not obscure or ignore these rights.

The *Act* also provides specific complaint and review procedures that are available to children and families of children in care in order to ensure that the child's rights are protected where the Society takes an opposing view. An independent advocate for the child is essential to protect his or her rights.[48]

(16)   REPORTING SUSPICION OF CHILD ABUSE

The Ontario legislation requires that any person who has reasonable grounds to believe that a child has been abused or is at risk of abuse report it to a Society. Professionals who become aware of abuse in the course of their duties must immediately report their suspicions. This includes physicians, nurses, dentists, pharmacists, psychologists, teachers, principals, social workers, family counsellors, clergy, day nursery operators, youth workers (volunteers not listed, although they would still be included in the "everyone" clause), peace officers, coroners, lawyers, and service providers and their employees.

A Children's Aid Society worker who obtains information that a child in care or under Children's Aid Society supervision may be experiencing abuse must report the information to the Director. The *only* exception to the positive duty to report child abuse is provided by the solicitor-client privilege.

Failure of those who perform professional or official duties with children to report such suspicion is punishable by a fine of not more than $1,000[49]and could result in a charge of liability under the *Criminal Code*[50] if the child should subsequently suffer a predictable injury. To aid in making a report of abuse, the checklist "Indications of Abuse" may be obtained from a Children's Aid Society.[51]

In a well publicized case, a family physician was charged under the former *Child Welfare Act* with failure to report the sexual abuse of a child.[52] The child's mother had informed the doctor that the stepfather had repeatedly fondled the child over a period of time. The doctor did not question the child or report the incident to the Children's Aid Society, but did refer the family to counselling, from which, the stepfather had withdrawn after a few sessions. The Society was subsequently alerted; the stepfather was arrested and the doctor was charged for failing to report the abuse of a child to the Society. The court found that the law was unclear in its definition of child abuse and was therefore unable to make a finding that the doctor had failed to comply with the *Act*. In addition, the judge stated that the sketchy second-hand description reported by the mother was not sufficient to establish beyond a reasonable doubt that the doctor should have reported the abuse at that time. The court concluded that since there existed reasonable doubt, the matter had to be resolved in favour of the doctor.

The significance of this case lies in the dangers of a broad definition of sexual abuse that intrudes into the intricate and varied expressions of love found within families. Children do need legal protection against excess and assault within the family, but can the law deal with behaviour that moves into the grey areas of community moral standards? The second critical matter raised by the case is whether a professional, using his or her best judgment on information available, will be held liable for failure to report abuse according to an equivocal legal standard.

Legal action can only be taken against an informant if it can be shown that the information was given maliciously or in the absence of reasonable grounds to suspect that the information was true.

(a) Ontario Child Abuse Register

In Ontario, a central register with a minimum storage of 25 years was created by statute.[53] The register contains the names of those who have been verified by the Society as child abusers. A person whose name is entered in the register must be given written notice of this fact and may request a hearing to expunge his or her name from the register.[54] The hearing is subject to the requirements of procedural fairness and any decision may be appealed by the applicant.[55] Access to the register is limited to persons on staff at the ministry concerned, the Children's Aid Societies, inter-provincial child protection agencies, or a person providing treatment or service to a registered person.

There is much controversy about the value of the register; because it is limited to what is reported and tends to give the appearance that official action has been taken. As a result, the register is not considered helpful by workers concerned with case-by-case child protection.

(17) CONCLUSION

The critical issue for society is the balance between the right of the child to protection and the family's right to privacy and autonomy. This issue is further compounded in a country, such as Canada, where a pluralistic society makes difficult the task of determining acceptable community standards of child rearing practices. Since cultures vary in their attitudes toward physical discipline as a necessary part of child-rearing, confusion will persist unless the law clearly states that in this country physical force used against children is not condoned.

As stated in Chapter 16, protecting children from harm is a complicated and challenging endeavor for many of those working in the child welfare system. While social workers working for child welfare all strive to meet their legal obligations there is much room for human error when dealing with children and their families. Therefore, it is incumbent on those that work in this difficult area to have the necessary supports (such as proper training and supervision) made available through sufficient funding from the government.

SELECTED READINGS

Bennett, Marlyn, "Aboriginal Mothers' Involvement with Child Protection and Family Court Systems. Examining Alternative Court Processes" in *Canada's Children: Centre of Excellence for Child Welfare Update* (Child Welfare League of Canada, 2007) at 88.

Canada's Children: Centre of Excellence for Child Welfare Update (Child Welfare League of Canada, 2007).

Crush, Linda, "The State of Child Protection Mediation in Canada" (2007) 24 Can. Fam. L.Q. 5.

Tonmyr, Lil et al., "Policy Makers' Perspectives on the Utility of a National Study of Child Maltreatment" (2004) 9(3) Child Maltreatment 304.

Trocme, Nico et al., *Canadian Incidence Study of Reported Child Abuse and Neglect: Major Findings* (Public Health Agency of Canada, 2003).

WEBSITES

For ongoing practice and research studies in child welfare see the University of Toronto, Faculty of Social Work Centre of Excellence for Children's Well-Being, online: <http://www.cecw-cepb.ca/>.

Public Health Agency of Canada, www.phac-aspc.gc.ca

ENDNOTES

1. *Child and Family Services Act*, R.S.O. 1990, c. C.11. It is important to note that with the introduction of Bill 210, the *Act* in Ontario has been changed quite significantly. Of the many changes alternative dispute resolution has been introduced. Specifically, child protection mediation, family group conferencing, and aboriginal approaches (Talking Circles and First Nation Circles) are all part of the new *Act*. It will take some time to see what, if any, effect these new changes will have. Note that at the time of writing, not all amendments had been proclaimed.
2. See the Table of Concordance.
3. In order to use the title or present yourself as a social worker in Ontario you have to be a member of the College of Social Workers and Social Service Workers. However, in this chapter "child welfare workers" and "social workers" are used interchangeably. See Chapter 27 for a discussion of the regulation of social work in Canada.
4. Mary Jane Hatton, Ontario Ministry of Community and Social Services, *Protecting Vulnerable Children: Report of the Panel of Experts on Child Protection* (Toronto: The Panel, 1998).
5. See *supra* note 1, (Bill 210, *Child and Family Services Statute Law Amendment Act, 2005*).
6. See *supra* note 1 at s. 37(2).
7. The Child Mortality Task Force was established in 1996 to review the deaths of children receiving child welfare services in 1994-1995. This led to the Child Welfare Reform agenda initiated by the government in 1998.
8. See *supra* note 1 at s. 15(3).
9. *Ibid.* at s. 37(2).
10. *Ibid.* at s. 40(2) and (7).

11. *Ibid.* at s. 40(6).
12. *Ibid.* at s. 44(1)(2).
13. *M. (J.) v. Toronto Board of Education* (1987), (sub nom. *M. v. Toronto Bd. of Education*) 38 D.L.R. (4th) 627, 59 O.R. (2d) 649, 1987 CarswellOnt 859 (H.C.).
14. *R. v. Daniels* (2003), 2003 CarswellOnt 3001 (Ont. C.J.).
15. *Children's Aid Society of Hamilton-Wentworth v. M. (P.)* (1988), 17 R.F.L. (3d) 46, [1988] O.J. No. 1584, 1988 CarswellOnt 297 (Ont. H.C.).
16. See *supra* note 1 at ss. 29, 30. It should be noted that despite the *CFSA* stipulation that the agencies can sign Special Needs Agreements, there is also an administrative directive by the Ministry of Child and Youth Services to not sign these agreements with parents. Instead parents are redirected to other community based agencies for service. Special Needs Agreements are considered for children who are not deemed to be children in need of protection.
17. *Ibid.* at ss. 29 and 32.
18. *Ibid.* at s. 31.
19. *Ibid.* at s. 39.
20. *Ibid.* at s. 1(1) and (5).
21. *Children's Aid Society of London & Middlesex v. O. (M.)* (1997), 29 O.T.C. 265, 1997 CarswellOnt 1817, [1997] O.J. No. 1261 (Gen. Div.).
22. See *supra* note 1 at s. 39(1)-(8).
23. *Children's Law Reform Act,* R.S.O. 1990, c. C.12.
24. See *supra* note 1 at s. 37(1).
25. S.C. 2002, c. 1.
26. See *supra* note 1 at s. 51(2).
27. *Ibid.* at s. 57(1) and (8).
28. *Ibid.* at s. 57(1) and (5).
29. *Ibid.* at s. 57(1) and (4).
30. *Ibid.* at s. 64.
31. *Ibid.* at s. 66(1).
32. *Children's Aid Society of Haldimand-Norfolk v. L. (C.B.)* (1995), [1995] O.J. No. 1107, 1995 CarswellOnt 2135 (Ont. Prov. Div.).
33. *Children's Aid Society of Peel (Region) v. K. (D.)* (1991), 4 O.F.L.R. 121, 1991 CarswellOnt 1468, [1991] O.J. No. 159 (Prov. Div.).
34. *Children's Aid Society of Kingston (City) & Frontenac (County) v. C. (T.)* (1994), [1994] O.J. No. 1510, 1994 CarswellOnt 2150 (Ont. Prov. Div.).
35. See *supra* note 1 at s. 54(1).
36. For an excellent review of the issue of assessments see the entire journal (2005) 43(2) Fam. Ct. Rev.

37. *R. v. Mohan*, [1994] 2 S.C.R. 9, 18 O.R. (3d) 160 (note), EYB 1994-67655, 29 C.R. (4th) 243, 71 O.A.C. 241, 166 N.R. 245, 89 C.C.C. (3d) 402, 114 D.L.R. (4th) 419, 1994 CarswellOnt 1155, 1994 CarswellOnt 66, [1994] S.C.J. No. 36. Also see *Children's Aid Society of Toronto v. O. (K.)* (2004), 50 R.F.L. (5th) 298, [2004] O.J. No. 630, 2004 CarswellOnt 686 (Ont. C.J.).

38. See *supra* note 1 at s. 69(1) and (2).

39. *Ibid.* at s. 38(1).

40. *Ibid.* at s. 38(4).

41. See Ministry of Attorney General, Office of the Children's Lawyer website for the referral form and court order for obtaining child legal representation.

42. *Kenora-Patricia Child & Family Services v. M. (A.)* (2003), 45 R.F.L. (5th) 418, [2003] O.J. No. 3911, 2003 CarswellOnt 3804 (Ont. C.J.), affirmed 2004 CarswellOnt 750, 3 R.F.L. (6th) 368, [2004] O.J. No. 673, [2004] O.T.C. 216 (S.C.J.), affirmed (2004), 2004 CarswellOnt 2072, 5 R.F.L. (6th) 96, 187 O.A.C. 52, [2004] O.J. No. 2106 (C.A.) at para. 48 [C.J.] per Little J.

43. M. J. J. McHale, "The Proper Role of the Lawyer as Legal Representative of the Child" (1980), 18(2) Alta. L. Rev. 216 at 236, quoting Steinburg J., *Fifth Report of Royal Commission on Family and Children's Law, Part III: Children's Rights* (Vancouver, B.C., 1975) at 238-9.

44. *Children's Aid Society of Metropolitan Toronto v. S.D. and J.D.*, [1993] O.J. No. 148 (Ont. Prov. Div.).

45. *R. (C.) v. Children's Aid Society of Hamilton* (2004), 4 R.F.L. (6th) 98, [2004] O.J. No. 1251, 2004 CarswellOnt 2268 (Ont. S.C.J.) at para. 30, 31.

46. See *supra* note 1 at s. 105(2).

47. *Provincial Advocate for Children and Youth Act, 2007*, S.O. 2007, c. 9.

48. *Ibid.* at ss. 109-111.

49. *Ibid.* at s. 72(6.2).

50. R.S.C. 1985, c. C-46, ss. 218-219. Section 218 deals with "Abandoning a Child," which would potentially apply to Social Workers as, in accordance with s. 214, "abandon" (and "expose") includes: a) a wilful omission to take charge of a child by a person who is under a legal duty to do so; and b) dealing with a child in a manner that is likley to leave that child exposed to risk without protection. Section 219 deals with "Criminal Negligence," which would apply when failing to report amounts to the wanton or reckless disregard for the lives or safety of other persons (and this includes children).

51. Children's Aid Societies maintain current information, which is available to the public, on child abuse.
52. *R. v. Cook* (1983), 37 R.F.L. (2d) 93, 1983 CarswellOnt 349 (Ont. Fam. Ct.).
53. See *supra* note 1 at s. 72(1) and (2).
54. *Ibid.* at s. 75(1).
55. *Ibid.* at s. 76(2).
56. *Ibid.* at s. 76(7)-(9).

18

ADOPTION

(1) INTRODUCTION

> Sis, even if you were adopted,
> I'd still love you..
> . . .not that you are, of course.
> At least I don't think so.
> But, come to think of it,
> You don't really look like
> Mom and Dad. Gee, maybe
> You should get a DNA test
> Or something. Oh well,
> Don't worry about it.
> We all love you, even
> If your real parents don't.
> Happy Valentines Day.[1]

The word adoption continues to denote a negative stereotype, as illustrated by the above quote. While much of the empirical research on adoption has focused on the pathology of adoptees, others argue that there is great variability amongst adoptees and their mental health functioning.[2]

For some, adoption "creates a family that is *connected* to another family, the birth family, and often to different cultures and to different racial, ethnic, and national groups as well. Adoptive families might teach us something about the value for families of connection with the larger community."[3]

Adoption has never become part of the common law and as such, the regulations and practices governing it are statutory and vary in some respect from province to province. We will cover relevant aspects of Ontario law concerning adoption, and suggest that readers in other provinces consult their specific legislation.[4] In Ontario, the rights and obligations of adopted persons have dramatically changed in keeping with being *connected*.[5] These changes will be discussed below.

(2) ADOPTIONS IN ONTARIO

The best interests of the child remains the primary concern of the court in adoption matters in Ontario, as it is in all matters concerning the welfare of children under the province's *Child and Family Services Act.*[6] However, the circumstances governing adoptions have changed substantially over the years. Today there are far fewer children to adopt because more birth mothers are electing to keep their babies or an unwanted pregnancy may be terminated by abortion long before the possibility of adoption arises. No longer are there many unwanted infants awaiting adoption; adoption has become an option only for the fortunate few who are able to locate an eligible child. The notable exceptions are older children whose families can no longer care for them and children with physical, mental, or emotional disabilities.

There are four types of adoption proceedings in Ontario:

1. adoption of a child found to be in need of protection, where a Crown wardship order has been made;
2. a private adoption arranged through a licensee;
3. an adoption by a relative or other person known to the parents; and
4. adoption on consent as arranged through a child welfare agency.

A child can come into the adoption system through either a finding of the need for protection followed by an order for Crown wardship without access or by consent of the parents (subject to any order dispensing with the consent of a parent of the child) and where the child is over seven years of age, the child's consent.[7]

(a) Commencing an Adoption

All adoptions are initiated by filing an application, which is the formal document required by the court. An application may be filed personally by the adopters, their agents, or their lawyer. All applications are heard by the court *in camera*.[8] Part VII of the *Child and Family Services Act* deals with adoption; it addresses the licensing of private adoption agencies, the role of the Children's Aid Society ("Society") in the adoption of children, and the procedure for adopting a child.

(b) Residence of Adoptee

A child being considered for adoption (the adoptee) in Ontario must be a resident of the province.[9] The question of residence becomes important when the adoptee is a foreign national. The decision-maker may be aware of the possibility that the adoption is sought as a way to lend strength to a child's application to enter or remain in Canada as a permanent resident. Such "adoptions of convenience" have been viewed as an abuse where no genuine parent-child relationship can be demonstrated. For example, in *Kwan v. Canada (Minister of Citizenship & Immigration)*[10] the applicant was adopted at the age ten, in accordance with the laws of China, by her Aunt and Uncle who were Canadian residents. Four years later, she applied from China for permanent residence in Canada, and her adoptive Canadian father submitted an undertaking of financial support (as is required for family class sponsorships).[11] The regulations to the *Immigration and Refugee Protection Act*[12] define "adopted" as a person who is adopted in accordance with the laws of a country other than Canada where the adoption creates a genuine relationship of parent and child, but does not include a person who is adopted for the purpose of gaining admission to Canada.[13] On the facts of the case, the immigration officer found, and both the Immigration and Refugee Board and the Federal Court affirmed upon appeal, that there was no genuine parent-child relationship. As such, she was ineligible for admission to Canada as a sponsored family class member, as she was not truly a daughter of the sponsoring couple.

Moreover, the Court found that the natural parents' motives for adoption were to ensure a better future and educational opportunities for their daughter by gaining admission to Canada and thus that the adoption was really for the purpose of gaining admission to Canada. The Court concluded that the legislative provisions served three purposes: to prevent adoptions undertaken to circumvent immigration selection requirements; to prevent adoptions undertaken to sponsor a birth family member; and to promote family unity by ensuring that adopted children under the age of nineteen who are genuinely in need of parental care are allowed to immigrate to Canada.[14] A number of factors were also cited in this case to assist in assessing a relationship between a parent and child, including:

(a) motivation of the adopting parent(s) and;

(b) to a lesser extent, the motivation and conditions of the natural parent(s);

(c) authority and suasion of the adopting parent(s) over the adopted child;

(d) *supplanting of the authority of the natural parent(s) by that of the adoptive parent(s)*;

(e) *relationship of the adopted child with the natural parent(s) after adoption;*

(f) *treatment of the adopted child versus natural children by the adopting parent(s);*

(g) relationship between the adopted child and adopting parent(s) before the adoption;

(h) changes flowing from the new status of the adopted child such as records, entitlements, etc., including documentary acknowledgment that the adopted child is the son or daughter of the adoptive parents; and

(i) arrangements and actions taken by the adoptive parent(s) as it relates to caring, providing and planning for the adopted child.[15]

This list of factors is not exhaustive. Some factors may not be applicable to facts of a particular case while others not included in this list may be relevant.[16] (Emphasis in the original)

It is crucial to note that in *Kwan* it was accepted that the child in issue had been adopted in accordance with the law of China. The issue was whether she could gain entry to Canada as a member of the family class, a question determined solely by reference to immigration legislation, and not by provincial adoption legislation. Note, for example, in the above discussion of *Kwan* that no where in the decision is the best interests of the child considered. It is also important to mention that in Ontario, international adoption agencies are licensed to assist in the adoption of children from outside Canada.

Professionals whose clients are involved with questions regarding the status of prospective adoptees from other countries should advise their clients to seek legal assistance.

(c) Who May Apply

Single individuals or spouses, whether married or unmarried, and irrespective of sexual orientation can apply for the adoption of a child.[17] The primary concern of the adoption agency is that the adoptive home is able to provide a stable environment that closely meets the child's needs.

A Crown ward's foster parents may make application, with the approval of the local Director of the Children's Aid Society and the Director of Child Welfare, to adopt a child where that child is residing with them at the time of the application.

(d) Religion of the Applicant

It is not an absolute requirement of the *Act* that a child be placed with people of the same religious faith. However, where the natural parent expresses wishes regarding the religious affiliation of the adoptive parents, the adoption agency or licensed person, although not obligated to comply with these wishes, generally attempts to honour them where possible. Further, religious affiliation or proposed religious upbringing of the child is one factor the court will consider in granting an adoption order.

(3) VALID ADOPTION CONSENTS

Consent to adoption must be obtained from every person who is a parent or has had lawful custody of the child. This, of course, includes the biological father and mother but excludes foster parents.[18] Any person who has given consent may withdraw that consent in writing within 21 days of the time it was given.[19] In the case of a newborn infant, the consent cannot be taken until after the child is seven days old.[20]

The consent of a child, parent or person with lawful custody of the child must be in writing. An employee of a Society or licensee must ensure that the consent reflects the true and informed wishes of the person giving the consent. A clear explanation should be given by the worker of the possible alternatives to adoption and the legal consequences of the adoption consent. It is not enough to merely tell the person that he or she is giving up all parental rights to the child. It is essential that the following points be covered:

1. the person giving the consent to the child's adoption has the right to cancel that consent in writing within 21 days of the time the consent was given;
2. after the 21 day period has expired, consent can be withdrawn only if the court is satisfied that it is in the best interests of the child, and only if the child has *not* already been placed for adoption and is residing with the prospective adopters;
3. the person who consents has the right to consult an independent lawyer and must have had the opportunity to seek counselling;
4. the order for adoption, once made, will mean permanent surrender of all parental rights to the child, in other words, the child becomes the child of the adopting parents and ceases to be the child of the natural parents; and
5. the nature and operation of the voluntary disclosure registry and the right to participate.[21]

(a) Consent of the Child

The written consent of a child seven years of age or older is required for an adoption to proceed.[22] However, the child must have had the opportunity to obtain counselling and independent legal advice concerning the consent before consenting.

(b) Dispensing with a Person's Consent

Before the dispensing of a person's consent, the court must be satisfied that: (a) obtaining consent would cause the person emotional harm; or (b) the person is not able to consent because of a developmental disability.[23] In *A. (M.L.), Re*[24] the judge addressed the issue of affidavit evidence in lieu of a formal hearing and concluded:

> [t]he fact that the Court can accept affidavit evidence would lend weight to the argument that a formal hearing with *viva voce* evidence is not required. Thus the child's psychologist, psychiatrist, and/or social worker would, in my view, be capable of attesting in written form to the fact that the child is capable of appreciating the nature of the application. One would think that such a professional would be just as capable and reliable as the presiding Judge's momentary appraisal of the child in his/her Chambers.[25]

In one case, after an adoption of a child with the consent of both parents had occurred in Ontario, the child's paternal grandparents sought custody under the *Children's Law Reform Act.*[26] The application was dismissed on a finding that all matters concerning custody were controlled by the *Child and Family Services Act,* which provided jurisdiction only to the Ontario Court of Justice or the Superior Court of Justice. The Court of Appeal said that to permit the grandparents to assert a custodial claim under a provision of the *Children's Law Reform Act* would be inconsistent with subsection 143(2) of the *Child and Family Services Act,* which states that once a child has been placed for adoption but no adoption order has yet been made, no person shall interfere with the parties to that placement. This decision should, however, be approached with caution since the respective jurisdictions of the two statutes dealing with custody both rely on the best interests doctrine, and may be interpreted differently in another case.[27]

In *A. (R.) v. T. (L.J.)*[28] a child was placed in the applicants' home as a foster child at two and a half years of age. The applicants obtained joint guardianship of the child and the birth parents were granted supervised access to the child. The birth parents never exercised access and the applicants filed for adoption of the child. The applicants did not want to have to serve the father as they could not locate him. The court found that the *Act* is clear in that if service is dispensed with, it has to be in the child's best interest and all reasonable efforts must be made to locate the birth parent. The court found that all reasonable efforts to locate the father were not made and therefore, it was not in the child's best interest to dispense with service. However, the court only dealt with the father's service in this case.

(4) HOME STUDY REPORT OF THE DIRECTOR

The Director of Child Welfare must be notified of any proposed adoption. Upon notification, the Director is obliged to order that a home study be done and a report submitted before a child is placed in the adopting home. A home study is an inquiry into both the suitability of the home and the capacity of the applicants to provide a nurturing environment for the child. The home study is usually completed by a social worker and recommends either approval or refusal of the adoption placement. If the report is positive, the adoption can proceed. If it is negative, the applicants must be notified and informed of their right to a review of the decision of the Director and of their right to provide further evidence in support of the adoption.

(5) FAMILY ADOPTION ORDERS

There is a provision for inter-family adoption. The court may make an order for adoption of a child, if it is in his or her best interests, by: (a) a relative of the child; (b) the child's parent; or (c) the spouse of the child's parent.[29] The procedure for placement of children in family adoptions is far simpler than for extra-familial adoptions. Any family member may place a related child for adoption with a relative, a parent, or the parent's spouse within or outside Ontario. There is no longer a ban on bringing related children into Ontario for adoption without first notifying the Director or obtaining his or her prior approval; such adoptions, once granted, do not have to be registered.

(6) NATIVE ADOPTION ORDERS

The *Act* expressly provides that in considering the best interests of a child who is an "Indian or native person," regard must be given to the importance "in recognition of the uniqueness of Indian and native culture, heritage and traditions, of preserving the child's cultural identity."[30]

In the case of Native children, their band and Native community must be given advance notice of a proposed adoption. The Band or community then has 60 days to prepare and submit to the Society its own plan for the care of the child, and this plan must be considered by the Society.[31]

(7) TERMINATION OF ACCESS ORDERS

When a child is placed for adoption in Ontario by a Society or licensee, orders in regard to access to the child are terminated, *unless* that access order was made under child protection proceedings in Part III of the *Child and Family Services Act* and the continuation of the access order is felt by the court to be in the child's best interests.[32]

(8) ADOPTION ORDERS

The court may order the adoption of a child who is less than sixteen years of age, or is sixteen years of age, or is 16 years of age or older but has not withdrawn from parental control.[33] The court may also order a family adoption by the child's relative, parent or step-parent.[34] In every case the order must be based on the best interests of the child. However, where the consent of a person has been dispensed with, the court may not grant an adoption order until all appeal periods have elapsed.

There have been significant changes in who may adopt children as a result of the ever increasing recognition, social and legal, of same-sex relationships. Spouse is now defined to include same-sex couples for the purpose of adoption.

(a) Adoptive Parents' Right to Maternity and Parental Leave

In 1996, the Ontario Court (General Division) ruled that sections of the *Unemployment Insurance Act*[35] contravened the *Charter* by giving adoptive parents only ten weeks of maternity leave compared with fifteen weeks of maternity leave and ten weeks of parental leave for birth parents. Mr. Justice Donald Cameron ruled that "adopted children are indirectly denied equal benefit of the law to the extent that their parents may be economically constrained to return to work after only ten weeks."[36] He added that the distinction between adoptive and biological parents was based on "an assumption that since the adoptive mother is highly unlikely to breast-feed, neither she nor her husband needs comparable bonding time with their child."[37]

(b) Legal Effect of an Adoption Order

An order for adoption cannot obliterate emotional ties with a stroke of the pen, neither for the biological parents nor for an older child. However, the legal affect is abrupt, clear, and unequivocal. In Ontario, the adoptee becomes the child of the adopting parents for all purposes as though he or she had been born into that family, and ceases to be the child of his or her biological parents and family.

In *P. (M.A.R.) (Litigation Guardian of) v. Catholic Children's Aid Society of Metropolitan Toronto*[38], a child who was a Crown ward of the province and sought access to her sister who had been adopted. The Society refused her application on the grounds that the statute prohibits access to the former family once a child has been adopted. Nevertheless, the Society was aware that it also had a responsibility to act in the best interests of the child under its jurisdiction, namely the Crown ward applicant, who turned to the court. The Provincial Court held that there was no bar to access and awarded costs against the Society. This was affirmed in the General Division and in the Court of Appeal. Leave to appeal to the Supreme Court of Canada was refused but the question of the best interests of the child being served by contact with members of the former family after adoption has occurred has been opened.

With the new legislation that came into force on November 30, 2006 the issue of contact has now been opened up with "openness orders" and "openness agreements" as they allow for some contact, although not necessarily face to face.

In fact, Bill 183, the 2005 *Adoption Information Disclosure Act*[39] amended various statutes in Ontario to reflect disclosure of birth parents' information to adoptees and of adoptees' information to birth parents under certain conditions. The passing of this *Act* raised many political, philospohical, and academic debates of the right to know by the adoptee versus the privacy right of the birth parent. As of September 19, 2007, the law that allowed the opening of post adoption records was struck down by the Ontario Superior Court of Justice. New adoption information legislation was introduced on December 10, 2007. The new Bill, if passed, would enable adult adoptees and birth parents to apply for copies of their adoption orders and birth records, and to place a disclosure veto on file prior to September 1, 2008. Adult adoptees and birth parents will continue to be able to put a no contact notice and contact preferences in their files.

The provinces of Quebec, Nova Scotia, Prince Edward Island, and New Brunswick base their disclosure of adoption information on consent. In Manitoba and Saskatchewan, consent is required for adoption disclosure related to adoptions that took place prior to the passing of new adoption laws. Both provinces have disclosure vetoes that can be filed for information related to adoptions following the introduction of the new laws. Disclosure vetoes introduce an element of consent for the birth parents by allowing them to block access to birth registration information. British Columbia, Alberta, and Newfoundland are the only three provinces where adoption legislation can be applied retroactively. However, these provinces also have disclosure vetoes for earlier adoptions.[40]

In 1996, British Columbia became the first province to open its adoption records. Adoptees are thus entitled to gain access to their original birth registration and learn the identity of their birth parents, as well as their own names at birth. Parents who gave up children are able to obtain copies of the adoption orders and learn the child's adopted names. Names of the adoptive parents are deleted to protect their privacy. This is a reversal of the procedure in many other jurisdictions, where registries determine whether both parties wish to be identified. British Columbia has simplified the process by giving adoptees and birth parents the right to veto the release of information about them, rather than promising that their identities will be kept secret. The British Columbia law also creates a registry for birth fathers who may wish to be a party to an adoption proceeding, gives children over the age of seven a say in an adoption procedure and a right to consent to a change in their legal name, and recognizes the right of same sex couples and common law spouses to apply to adopt children.

(9) INTERNATIONAL ADOPTIONS

Canada has ratified the *Convention on Protection of Children and Co-operation in respect of Intercountry Adoption.*[41] The *Convention* establishes safeguards aimed at preventing the abduction, sale, or trafficking of children. It also establishes consistent lower cost adoption procedures and seeks to eliminate improper financial gains. Approximately 20,000 intercountry adoptions occur each year, of which 2,000 involve Canadians. The legislation creates a Central Authority to monitor the adoption process and coordinate requests to adopt children from other countries. Eleven provinces and two territories have passed implementing legislation, including British Columbia, Manitoba, New Brunswick, Prince Edward Island, Ontario, Saskatchewan, Alberta, Newfoundland and Labrador, Nova Scotia, Northwest Territories, Nunavut, Quebec, and the Yukon.

(10) CHANGE OF NAME

Most provincial legislation permits a child's name to be changed to that of the adopting parents. In Ontario, a given name or surname may be changed by that of the adopting parents at their request and with the written consent of a child who is twelve years of age or older. In Ontario the name on the birth registration is also changed.

SELECTED READINGS

Ambert, Anne-Marie, "The Negative Social Construction of Adoption: Its Effects on Children and Parents", online: York University Faculty of Arts <http://www.arts.yorku.ca/soci/ambert/writings/adoption.html>.

Baldassi, Cindy L., "The Quest to Access Closed Adoption Files in Canada: Understanding Social Science Context and Legal Resistance To Change" (2005) 21(2) Can. J. Fam. L. 211.

Weger, Katarina, *Adoption, Identity, And Kinship: The Debate Over Sealed Birth Records* (New Haven: Yale U.P., 1997).

WEBSITES

Adoption Counsel of Canada, www.adoption.ca

ENDNOTES

1. *Carlton Cards, 1997* as stated in K. Wegar, "Adoption, Family Ideology, and Social Stigma: Bias in Community Attitudes, Research, and Practice" (2000) 49 Family Relations 363.
2. David Brodzinsky et al., *Children's Adjustment to Adoption: Developmental and Clinical Issues* (Thousand Oaks, Calif.: Sage Publications, 1998).
3. Elizabeth Bartholet, *Family Bonds: Adoption and the Politics of Parenting* (Boston: Houghton Mifflin, 1993) at 186.
4. See Tables of Concordance.
5. In Ontario Bill 183, the *Adoption Information Disclosure Act*, 2005 amended the *Vital Statistics Act, Child and Family Services Act, Freedom of Information and Protection of Privacy Act, and Personal Health Information Act, 2004* to permit adopted persons to obtain personal information about their birth parents. The reader is advised to become familiar with each *Act* in its entirety to understand what information can be made available and how to obtain this information.
6. R.S.O. 1990, c. C.11.
7. *Ibid.* at s. 137.
8. *In camera*, meaning in chambers or away from public scrutiny.
9. See *supra* note 6 at ss. 141(1), (2), (3) and (5).
10. *Kwan v. Canada (Minister of Citizenship & Immigration)* (2001), 211 F.T.R. 33, 2001 FCT 971, 2001 CarswellNat 1933, [2001] F.C.J. No.

1333, 17 Imm. L.R. (3d) 167, 2001 CarswellNat 3518, [2002] 2 F.C. 99 (T.D.).

11. See Chapter 25 for a fuller discussion of Immigration law.

12. S.C. 2001, c. 27.

13. *Immigration Regulations, 1978*, SOR/78-172.

14. See *supra* note 10 at para. 44

15. *Ibid.* at para. 74, citing from *Guzman v. Canada (Minister of Citizenship & Immigration)* (1995), 33 Imm. L.R. (2d) 28, 1995 CarswellNat 1165 (Imm. & Ref. Bd. (App. Div.)) at para. 14.

16. See *supra* note 10 at para. 74.

17. See *supra* note 6 at s. 146(4).

18. *Ibid.* at s. 137(1) and (2).

19. *Ibid.* at s. 137(8).

20. *Ibid.* at s. 137(3).

21. *Ibid.* at s. 137(4)(b) requires that the birth parents be given the opportunity to seek counselling and independent legal advice before consenting to their child's adoption.

22. *Ibid.* at s. 137(6).

23. *Ibid.* at s. 137(9).

24. (1979), 25 O.R. (2d) 779, 1979 CarswellOnt 1504 (Prov. Ct.).

25. *Ibid.* at para. 10.

26. R.S.O. 1990, c. C.12.

27. *M. (R.) v. M. (S.)* (1994), 9 R.F.L. (4th) 372, 20 O.R. (3d) 621, 119 D.L.R. (4th) 757, 75 O.A.C. 1, [1994] O.J. No. 2505, 1994 CarswellOnt 478 (C.A.), affirmed (1995), 1995 CarswellOnt 3032 (Ont. C.A.).

28. *A. (R.) v. T. (L.J.)* (1999), 29 C.P.C. (4th) 323, 1999 CarswellMan 196, 45 R.F.L. (4th) 452, 137 Man. R. (2d) 312 (Master).

29. See *supra* note 6 at s. 146(2).

30. *Ibid.* at s. 136(3).

31. *Ibid.* at s. 141.2.

32. *Ibid.* at s. 143(1).

33. *Ibid.* at s. 146(1).

34. *Ibid.* at s. 146(2).

35. S.C. 1996, c. 23.

36. *Schafer v. Canada (Attorney General)* (1996), 135 D.L.R. (4th) 707, 1996 CarswellOnt 2150, 96 C.L.L.C. 210-031, 36 C.R.R. (2d) 236, 29 O.R. (3d) 496, 39 C.C.L.I. (2d) 33, 24 C.C.E.L. (2d) 1, [1996] O.J. No. 1915, 4 O.T.C. 20 (Gen. Div.), reversed (1997), 1997 CarswellOnt 2744, 149 D.L.R. (4th) 705, 45 C.R.R. (2d) 1, 102 O.A.C. 321, 35 O.R. (3d) 1, 49 C.C.L.I. (2d) 165, 97 C.L.L.C. 240-005, [1997] O.J. No. 3231, 33 O.T.C. 240 (note) (C.A.), leave to appeal refused (1998), 49

C.R.R. (2d) 186 (note), 113 O.A.C. 399 (note), 227 N.R. 87 (note) (S.C.C.) at para. 192 [Gen. Div.].

37. *Ibid.* at para. 199.

38. *P. (M.A.R.) (Litigation Guardian of) v. Catholic Children's Aid Society of Metropolitan Toronto* (1995), (sub nom. *V. (A.) v. P. (M.A.) (Litigation Guardian of)*) 122 D.L.R. (4th) 719, [1995] O.J. No. 421, 1995 CarswellOnt 80, 11 R.F.L. (4th) 95 (Ont. Gen. Div.), affirmed (1995), [1995] O.J. No. 2227, 1995 CarswellOnt 486, 15 R.F.L. (4th) 330, 126 D.L.R. (4th) 673, (sub nom. *Catholic Children's Aid Society of Metropolitan Toronto v. P. (M.A.R.)*) 84 O.A.C. 308 (C.A.), leave to appeal refused (1996), [1996] 1 S.C.R. v, 199 N.R. 239 (note), 92 O.A.C. 160 (note), 18 R.F.L. (4th) 217 (note), 130 D.L.R. (4th) vii.

39. S.O. 2005, c. 25.

40. *Making Adoption Bill Retroactive Break Promises and Invade Privacy of Thousands of Ontarians,* online: Newswire <http://www.newswire.ca/en/releases/archive/March2005/29/c9314.html> (accessed on March 4, 2007).

41. Online: Hague Conference on Private International Law <http://www.hcch.net/index_en.php?act=conventions.text&cid=69>.

PART III

CRIMINAL LAW

19

Structure of a Crime

(1) INTRODUCTION

The structure of Canadian criminal law and the workings of the criminal justice system deserve explanation because they exert a profound impact upon the lives of many of the clients of social workers. Victims of crime and their families, those charged with criminal offences, and those on probation or parole are among the many Canadians directly affected by the criminal justice system and who through a variety of routes, come into contact with social workers. An understanding of the nature of a crime, the necessary elements, the defences available, and the consequences which may flow from a conviction may help social workers provide appropriate assistance. However, it should be stressed again that legal knowledge is not a substitute for legal advice and representation.

(2) WHAT IS A CRIME?

Every society identifies particular conduct as unwanted and seeks to discourage it. Strategies for deterring unwanted conduct may be formal or informal and the criminal law is but one of the formal strategies available. Whether particular conduct should be regarded as "unwanted" and if so, whether such conduct should be defined as criminal, are frequently matters of considerable debate. Consequently, it is no surprise that the forms of conduct considered to be "crimes" are historically and socially contingent. In this sense, crime is itself a social construct, a matter of human agency. Consider, for example, gambling; long considered a crime, most forms of gambling have been decriminalized and gambling has now become a source of substantial income for provincial and territorial governments, as opposed to just organized crime as in the past. Conversely, conduct once regarded as legal—rape of one's wife for example—only came to be recognized as a crime in Canada in 1983.[1]

In Canada, as elsewhere in the western world, there has been a growing inclination to criminalize behaviour, often in response to the perception that crime is on the rise and thus personal security, increasingly, threatened. While there is substantial empirical evidence that suggests the contrary, this evidence has had little impact on the perception of crime. As such, the past few decades have witnessed many calls to "get tough on crime," for "zero tolerance" policies, and for more severe punishments. While some support this turn to criminal law, others express concern about its impact, particularly upon those who are socially marginalized and who are individually blamed and held responsible for what are often, at root, profound social problems.[2]

Others have asserted that while the criminal law now captures in its sweep a great deal of behaviour that does not result in significant harm to others, other forms of conduct that cause tremendous social harms are completely untouched by the criminal justice system. For example, many workers are killed or seriously injured every year in the workplace, yet rarely is this form of social harm treated as criminal.[3]

(a) Not Only a Crime

In addition to the question of whether particular conduct is regarded as a crime, it is also important to note that even if regarded as a crime, the criminal law is often not the exclusive form of social control governing that behaviour. At any given historical juncture, conduct may be simultaneously defined in multiple ways: as a crime; as a regulatory infraction; as a civil wrong; and/or as a health or educational issue. For example, the sale of cigarettes to young people is criminalized, consumption is discouraged through taxation, educational campaigns seek to curb use, and health professionals work with those addicted to help them quit.[4] As such, social control is produced through a complex web of relations.

The multiple ways in which particular behaviour is regulated also means that multiple avenues for redress may exist. For example, if one person assaults another, he or she may be charged with the criminal offence of assault. A criminal prosecution by the state may follow. If a conviction (finding of guilt) is made, the standard of proof is that the accused committed the assault beyond a reasonable doubt. As a result, he or she will be punished by the state through the imposition of a fine, probation, custody and/or other penalty. In a civil action, the victim may sue the assailant for "battery" (unconsented touching) and receive damages (money) from the assailant to compensate for the pain and suffering that resulted from the attack. If the assailant is found civilly liable for the attack, the judge would have based this decision on a balance of probabilities, which is the civil standard. A balance of probabilities means that it is more likely than not that the defendant caused the damages claimed by the plaintiff. Rather than the imposition of punishment, compensation is payable to the victim in a civil proceeding (note however that in some instances restitution may be ordered to the victim in the criminal context, but this will not be compensation for pain and suffering as in the civil context).

The differences between civil and criminal actions in the above scenario are four-fold: the way in which the assault/battery is defined; the method of proceeding against the assailant; the standard of proof required to find that the assailant committed the act; and the form of the disposition. Despite the differences, however, the two procedures respond to precisely the same act. Is there any sound reason why this should be so? What would happen if actions now defined as "crimes," with the exception of serious offences against the person, were treated as civil actions with financial penalties instead of criminal trials and incarceration? Note that many victims of crime have indicated a preference for civil proceedings because in that context they are responsible for developing the case and moving it forward, unlike the criminal context where carriage of the case is in the hands of the Crown Attorney and victims are witnesses only.[5]

(b) Differential Enforcement

Many commentators have noted the often large disparity between crime as defined by law and crime as operationalized on a daily basis (surveillance, prosecution, criminal justice processing, etc.). Some offences that exist on paper are, in practice, rarely if ever, enforced. Others are differentially enforced against particular populations. So, for example, forms of conduct that constitute criminal fraud may be ignored when committed by employers, addressed administratively (if at all) when dealing with over-billing by physicians, or prosecuted vigorously in dealing with social assistance recipients.[6] In fact, the most marginalized groups in society are more likely to be over-represented in charging, prosecution and prison statistics. Much research documents the disproportionate impact of the criminal justice system upon individuals who are socially marginalized and vulnerable: Aboriginal persons; persons with low incomes and racialized peoples in particular. For example, Aboriginal people represent 15-17% of the prison population but only 2% of the general population.[7]

Another example can be found in the legal response to domestic violence. Although forms of domestic violence that include physical assault,

sexual assault or threatening for example, have long been criminal offences—and indeed for a period in Canada's history there existed a particular offence of assaulting or beating one's wife[8]—the reality for a very long
time was that domestic violence was simply not treated as an offence. Indeed
June Callwood and Marvin Zuker wrote in 1976, in a handbook appropri-
ately entitled, *The Law is Not for Women,* that a husband may beat his wife
with moderation. As they explained, "policemen are reluctant to proceed
with such domestic disputes because of the high number of cases subsequently dropped. . . The obvious hazard here is that an abusive husband is
unlikely to be pleased that his wife has called the police. Unless you have
somewhere else to live you may be in danger of more beatings."[9] Over the
past two decades advocates have worked hard to change the criminal justice
system response, and to have domestic violence treated as other crimes.
While some advocates continue to push for more aggressive criminal justice
intervention, others express concerns about the impact of such interventions
in the lives of women, especially those who experience social marginalization.[10]

(c) Expectations of the Criminal Justice System

As noted above, the criminal justice system is just one of the many
tools used to obtain social control. While calls for more conduct to be
criminalized and for sentences to be made harsher imply that the criminal
justice system is an effective method of social control, the evidence does
not necessarily confirm this presumption. First, it is important to distinguish
between the varying ways in which the criminal justice system is thought
to operate as a device of social control: general deterrence; specific deterrence; and the educative or symbolic importance of reinforcing certain social
values. The evidence on deterrence suggests that there are at least three
important dimensions to consider: swiftness of punishment; the certainty of
being caught; and the severity of punishment. From the evidence to date, it
appears that it is, in fact, the certainty of being punished, rather than the
severity of punishment, that holds the strongest deterrent effect. Moreover,
the effects of deterrence are thought to vary depending on the nature of the
conduct in issue.[11] Research also indicates that the longer a person is separated from society, the less likely it is that he or she will make a successful
readjustment to society on release. In one particular study, prisoners who
had served only part of their sentences, but were released to considerable
community consternations, were more successful upon release than prisoners who served their full sentence.[12] Why then are our politicians, the
press, and the media proposing ever-longer and harsher sentences if they
do not achieve the desired result?

There are also potential risks to criminalization. For example, many are concerned that recent case law categorizing the failure to disclose one's positive HIV status to a partner when engaging in unprotected sex as aggravated sexual assault will have negative ramifications. The Canadian HIV/ AIDS Legal Network concludes that,

> [T]here is no good evidence that the criminal law is effective at preventing HIV transmission. Criminalization of HIV may drive people away from public health initiatives that have proven effective, such as HIV testing, counseling and support, and partner notification. The public attention given to criminal prosecutions may create a false sense of security that the law will protect people from HIV infection. It may also undermine the message that every person is responsible for his or her own sexual health, and lead to human rights abuses by increasing the stigma and discrimination faced by people living with HIV.[13]

(3) CANADIAN CRIMINAL LAW

(a) Jurisdiction

Canadian criminal law is created entirely by federal statutes, as it is enacted under the federal criminal law power. The most important of these statutes are the *Criminal Code*,[14] the *Controlled Drugs and Substances Act*,[15] and the *Youth Criminal Justice Act*.[16] Beyond the above statutes, many other pieces of federal legislation contain offence provisions; some of these are construed as full criminal offences (requiring proof of all of the elements of a true criminal offence as described below) and others as quasi-criminal or regulatory offences.

While criminal law is a matter of federal jurisdiction, and provinces are thus precluded from legislating in relation to the criminal law, provinces may create regulatory offences in relation to matters of proper provincial jurisdiction, which are often referred to as "provincial offences." In many instances, it is clear when a particular subject matter falls within one head of power or another, but this is not always the case. *Ontario's Safe Streets Act*[17] prohibits squeegee work and particular forms of panhandling, provides for arrests without warrants, substantial fines (up to $500 for a first conviction, $1,000 for subsequent convictions) and the possibility of incarceration for up to six months upon a subsequent conviction.[18] The *Act* has been legally challenged on several bases, including the argument that the provincial government has encroached upon the criminal law jurisdiction of the federal government. The competing characterization is that the law aims to control the flow of vehicular traffic (regulating streets, sidewalks and highways, a matter of provincial jurisdiction) and the suppression of conditions that give rise to harm (also a matter of provincial jurisdiction).[19] The courts have agreed with this latter characterization and have held that the legislation is properly within provincial jurisdiction.[20]

While "true crime" offences generally require subjective awareness (known as full *mens rea*, which means "guilty mind"), a distinction is made between full *mens rea,* strict liability, and absolute liability offences.[21] Full *mens rea* (a requirement for most but not all criminal offences) requires subjective appreciation, or intention, on the part of the accused at the time he or she is doing the act prohibited by law (this does not mean that he or she must know the act in question is illegal). Absolute liability, by contrast, simply requires proof of the act and thus, the accused's state of awareness is irrelevant to liability. Strict liability falls between full *mens rea* and absolute liability by requiring the prosecution to prove only the act in question, but placing an obligation on the accused to show due diligence (that she or he took all reasonable steps in the circumstances) to avoid a conviction. In contrast to *Criminal Code* offences, many regulatory offences (both provincial and federal) are strict or absolute liability offences. Significantly, irrespective of whether the offence is a criminal or regulatory offence the Supreme Court of Canada has held that where jail is a potential outcome of a conviction, a standard of absolute liability would infringe *Charter* rights.[22] In other words, where an offence is punishable by imprisonment there must be subjective *mens rea* or at a minimum, the availability of a defense of due diligence. The Court has reasoned that the severity of the punishment of imprisonment and the stigma attached to such offences requires a degree of moral blameworthiness, and this necessitates consideration of the accused's mental state.

(b) Types of Criminal Offences

As outlined in Chapter 5, there are three types of criminal offences: summary conviction offences; indictable offences; and hybrid offences. Summary conviction offences are comparatively less serious and generally carry penalties of no more than a fine of two thousand dollars or six months imprisonment, or both.[23] Recently, Parliament expanded the maximum potential punishment to eighteen months for some of the more common summary offences, such as sexual assault and assault causing bodily harm. An indictable offence, on the other hand, is a more serious crime and can carry a hefty jail sentence, such as an automatic life sentence in the case of first degree murder (with parole eligibility varying depending on whether it is first degree or second degree murder). The third type of offence is a hybrid offence; an offence which can either be prosecuted as a summary or an indictable offence depending on how the Crown Attorney prosecuting the offence elects to proceed.

(c) Necessary Elements of a Criminal Offence

> Peter, Paul and John, all aged nineteen, broke into an abandoned warehouse one night to get out of the cold, using a tire iron from John's car. They looked around, found some candles, which they lit, some boxes to sit on and some old maps and newspapers dating back to 1940. They were reading the papers and maps when they were interrupted by police sirens and whistles. In their panic to leave they kicked over a candle, igniting the papers and causing a fire. All three were caught and were charged with arson. All were convicted of arson. Peter, who had no previous criminal record, received two years probation and a community service order. Paul and John, who had previous records, received eighteen months in reformatory.

To constitute a criminal offence, the accused person must intend to commit a forbidden act (have the requisite "*mens rea*" or guilty mind), and must actually commit the act (have committed the "*actus reus*" or forbidden act). The two elements must co-exist and have a causal connection for an act to be considered criminal. In the above case, the three accused may not have intended to start a fire, yet they were convicted of arson. Were the two necessary elements of a crime present and did they co-exist?

(i) Intention

The mental element alone is not enough to convict one of a criminal offence.

> Arthur was furious at the storekeeper for ejecting him from the store. He intended to return with a baseball bat and teach the man a lesson by cracking the bat over his head, but he did nothing. The intent to commit a crime was present, but not the act; therefore, Arthur did not commit an offence.

Neither is the act alone a crime.

> Martha is pedalling her bicycle down the street. Suddenly a child darts out of an alley, directly in front of her. She cannot stop in time and strikes the child. The child is seriously injured. Assuming Martha was cycling in an entirely lawful manner, no offence was committed.

(ii) A Causal Connection

The mental element must cause the forbidden act to occur. There must be a causal connection between the intention to commit the offence and the forbidden act itself so that directly acting upon the intention led to the committing of the forbidden act.

> George intended to rob a bank. On his way to the robbery he hears sirens and sees police cars screech to a halt in front of the bank that he was planning to rob. Someone else robbed the bank moments before George arrived. Even though George had the requisite intention, there is no causal link between his *mens rea* and the robbery which was perpetrated by someone else. As a result, George did not commit robbery.

Where the intention is acted on and causes the offence, both necessary elements are present and co-exist:

> Andrea wanted a new sweater and planned to steal it. She went into Sears for that purpose, tried on sweaters until she found one she liked, put it on under her own clothing and left the store. The offence is complete. Andrea intended to take the sweater and did take the sweater. Andrea has committed theft.

(d)   Recklessness, Negligence and Omissions

In some circumstances, recklessness as to the consequences of an act is sufficient to show the requisite guilty mind and may constitute a criminal offence. In Canadian criminal law, "recklessness" has a special meaning. It is meant to capture circumstances where an individual adverts to a risk (turns his or her mind to it) of a certain act, but decides to charge ahead indifferent to the consequences of that act. So, for example,

> Paul is selling homes in a new development. A buyer inquires whether or not deposits on purchases are insured. Paul is unsure but rather than checking tells the purchaser that deposits are insured. It turns out they are not. The developer goes bust and the purchaser loses her deposit. Paul is guilty of fraud. The guilty mind requirement is satisfied by his recklessness in making a representation indifferent to its truth or falsity.

Recklessness is to be distinguished from what is known as criminal negligence. Unlike most crimes, which involve advertence on the part of the offender, criminal negligence is a crime of inadvertence. The most frequent example is criminal negligence in the operation of a motor vehicle, which results in injury or death to another person.[24] A person may be found guilty of criminal negligence causing either death or bodily harm where his or her behaviour leads to either result and exhibits wonton and reckless disregard for the lives and/or safety of other persons.[25] In other words, to establish criminal negligence in the operation of a motor vehicle, the prosecution need not establish a subjective intention to cause harm. However, the phrase "wanton or reckless disregard for the lives or safety of other persons" requires some behaviour that represents a marked and substantial departure from the standard of conduct that would be expected of a reasonable person in the circumstances.[26] For example:

> Two young men are street racing late one night in downtown Toronto. Each is travelling at a speed three times that of the speed limit. One of the drivers loses control and mounts the sidewalk, striking and killing two pedestrians. It will not matter that the driver did not intend to cause death, or serious bodily harm. Rather, the offence only requires the Crown to establish that the driver's conduct represented a marked and substantial departure from the standard of driving that would be expected from the reasonable motorist.

In a limited number of situations, negligence, or neglect of a legal duty, can also result in a criminal negligence offence. Where the law imposes a legal duty to act in a certain way and the person fails to do so, the omission may constitute a crime. For example, parents are under a legal duty to provide the necessaries of life for their children.[27] If they fail to do so, such failure may constitute an offence. When the Crown attempts to make out a case for failing to provide the necessaries of life, he or she must prove that the parent acted in a way that constituted a marked departure from the conduct of a reasonably prudent parent, in circumstances where it was objectively foreseeable that the failure to provide the necessaries of life would lead to a risk of danger to the life, or a risk of permanent endangerment to the health, of the child.[28] Should the child die as a result of the parent's neglect, beyond the offence of failing to provide the necessaries of life, the responsible parent could also be found guilty of criminal negligence causing death or even manslaughter. In such circumstances, the Crown has much discretion in choosing what charges will be brought against the accused.

Failure to obtain medical treatment that could preserve the life of a child could also constitute failing to provide the necessaries of life.[29] It is not an excuse under Canadian law for a parent to fail to provide necessary medical treatment because their religious faith does not permit such treatment.[30]

(e) Attempted Offences

Attempting to commit a forbidden act is an offence if the person not only intends the act, but does anything for the purpose of carrying out the offence beyond mere preparation.[31]

> Jim plans to break into Jonathan's house to steal his stereo equipment. He breaks in and begins to disconnect the stereo, but is interrupted by Jonathan's large dog. He panics and leaves. He is stopped by the police, who charge him

with breaking and entering and attempted theft. Although he took nothing, Jim has committed attempted theft because he did something substantial to further his intentions.

(4) *CHARTER* GUARANTEES

The *Canadian Charter of Rights and Freedoms* has had an enormous influence on the evolution of Canadian criminal law, and voluminous judgments have been written in which the parameters of protection afforded by the *Charter* have been shaped and re-shaped. While some of the provisions bearing upon criminal law and procedure are discussed elsewhere (see Chapters 2 and 5), here we highlight some of the rights that arise upon being charged. Section 11 of the *Charter* provides that a person charged with an offence has the right to be informed without unreasonable delay of the specific offence, to be tried within a reasonable time, not to be compelled to testify at his or her own trial and to be presumed innocent until proven guilty according to law in a fair and public hearing by an independent and impartial tribunal. This latter right, the presumption of innocence now enshrined in section 11(d), runs like a golden thread throughout the web of English Criminal Law. The section 11(d) presumption of innocence places the onus upon the state to prove that the accused is guilty beyond a reasonable doubt (a corollary of this right is that the accused cannot be compelled to testify, a right guaranteed in section 11(c)). The establishment of proof must be in accordance with "law in a fair and public hearing, by an independent and impartial tribunal" as expressly noted in section 11(d). A fair hearing is assumed to be a full adversarial hearing where the accused hears all evidence against him or her, has a full opportunity to challenge that evidence through cross-examination, has a full opportunity to tender evidence in support of his or her case, a full opportunity to make argument, and that all evidence tendered is properly admissible (see Chapter 8 regarding the rules of evidence).

(5) PROOF

(a) Burden of Proof

As in human existence, the absolute truth is elusive in criminal trials, if not impossible to determine. However, there must be a substantial degree of certainty, in the mind of the judge or jury, that the person intentionally committed the illegal act before he or she can be convicted. Therefore, the Crown prosecutor has the burden of proving guilt and he or she must prove the offence beyond a reasonable doubt. There is usually no requirement upon an accused to prove anything. The accused has an absolute right not to testify and the silence of the accused is not to be taken as an admission of guilt. Nevertheless, in some circumstances an accused may be asked to disprove an element of the offence, otherwise known as a reverse onus; where it is found that a reverse onus is a reasonable part of proving the offence, it will not be found to violate the *Charter*. For example, placing the onus on the accused to show that he or she is not promoting hate speech, but rather that there is a factual basis to his or her speech, is not a violation of the presumption of innocence provision of the *Charter*.[32]

(b) Standard of Proof

"Reasonable doubt" means different things to different people. Many judges have struggled with the meaning. Justice Cory, formerly a justice of the Supreme Court of Canada, has defined a reasonable doubt in the following terms:

> A reasonable doubt is not an imaginary or frivolous doubt. It must not be based upon sympathy or prejudice. Rather, it is based on reason and common sense. It is logically derived from the evidence or absence of evidence.

> Even if you believe the accused is probably guilty or likely guilty, that is not sufficient. In those circumstances you must give the benefit of the doubt to the accused and acquit because the Crown has failed to satisfy you of the guilt of the accused beyond a reasonable doubt.

> On the other hand you must remember that it is virtually impossible to prove anything to an absolute certainty and the Crown is not required to do so. Such a standard of proof is impossibly high.

> In short, if based upon the evidence before the court you are sure that the accused committed the offence, you should convict since this demonstrates that you are satisfied of his guilt beyond a reasonable doubt.[33]

(6) PRESUMPTIONS

In some cases, where the elements of the offence are hard to prove, the accused is presumed to have knowledge of the circumstances or to have the requisite illegal intention. Among these offences are breaking and entering[34] and care and control of a motor vehicle while under the influence of alcohol.[35] Significantly, a person is presumed not to suffer from a mental disorder so as to exempt him or her from criminal responsibility. If the mental fitness of the accused is in issue, the onus is on the party who raises the question to establish, on a balance of probabilities, the existence of such a disorder.[36]

Presumptions are legal fictions, but they do have a common sense basis; they speak to the obvious. For example, the intention to commit an indictable offence is inferred from evidence that a person broke into and entered a home. Intention is presumed unless and until the accused provides evidence to the contrary. Without presumptions, convictions for criminal acts could be relatively more difficult to obtain. Yet, at the same time, presumptions must be utilized with caution because they may threaten to weaken the presumption of innocence.

SELECTED READINGS

Criminal Law Issues, online: Canadian HIV/AIDS Legal Network <http://www.aidslaw.ca/EN/issues/criminal_law.htm>.

Grace, Elizabeth K.P. & Susan Vella, *Civil Liability for Sexual Abuse and Violence in Canada* (Toronto: Butterworths, 2000).

Law Commission of Canada, *What is a Crime? Challenges and Alternatives Discussion Paper* (Ottawa: Law Commission of Canada, 2003).

Menzies, Robert, Dorothy Chunn & Susan Boyd, *[Ab]Using Power: The Canadian Experience* (Halifax, NS: Fernwood Press, 2001).

Morris, Ruth, *Penal Abolition: The Practical Choice* (Toronto: Canadian Scholars Press, 1995).

Reiner, Robert, "Media Made Criminality: The Representation of Crime in the Mass Media" in Mike Maguire, Rodney Morgan & Robert Reiner, eds., *The Oxford Handbook of Criminology,* 3d ed. (Oxford: Oxford University Press, 2002).

Roach, Kent, *Essentials of Canadian Criminal Law,* 2d ed. (Toronto: Irwin Law, 2000).

Roach, Kent & Julian Roberts, *Community-Based Sentencing: Perspectives of Crime Victims an Exploratory Study* (Ottawa, Ont.: Department of Justice Canada, 2004).

Schneiderman, David, "The Constitutional Disorder of the Safe Streets Act: A Federalism Analysis" in Joe Hermer & Janet Mosher, *Disorderly People: Law and the Politics of Exclusion in Ontario* (Halifax, NS: Fernwood Press, 2002).

ENDNOTES

1. Law Commission of Canada, *What is a Crime? Challenges and Alternatives Discussion Paper* (Ottawa: Law Commission of Canada, 2003).
2. See for example Robert Menzies, Dorothy Chunn & Susan Boyd, *[Ab]Using Power: The Canadian Experience* (Halifax, NS: Fernwood Press, 2001); Robert Reiner, "Media Made Criminality: The Representation of Crime in the Mass Media" in Mike Maguire, Rodney Morgan & Robert Reiner, eds., *The Oxford Handbook of Criminology,* 3d ed. (Oxford: Oxford University Press, 2002); Law Commission of Canada (ed.), *What is a Crime? Defining Criminal Conduct in Contemporary Society* (Vancouver, BC: UBC Press, 2004).
3. Laureen Snider, "Resisting Neo-Liberalism: The Poisoned Water Disaster in Walkerton, Ontario" (2003) V5(2) Soc. & Leg. Stud. 27.
4. See *supra* note 1.
5. Kent Roach & Julian Roberts, *Community-Based Sentencing: Perspectives of Crime Victims an Exploratory Study* (Ottawa, Ont.: Department of Justice Canada, 2004); and Elizabeth K.P. Grace & Susan Vella, *Civil Liability for Sexual Abuse and Violence in Canada* (Toronto: Butterworths, 2000).
6. Janet Mosher, "Welfare fraudsters and tax evaders: the state's selective invocation of criminality" in Bernard Schissel & Carolyn Brooks (ed.), *Marginality and Condemnation: An Introduction to Criminology* 2d ed. (Halifax: Fernwood Press, 2007) and Janet Mosher, "The Construction of "Welfare Fraud" and the Wielding of the State's Iron Fist" in Elizabeth Comack (ed.) *Locating Law: Race/Class/Gender/Sexuality Connections* 2d ed. (Halifax: Fernwood Press, 2006).
7. Kent Roach, *Essentials of Canadian Criminal Law,* 2d ed. (Toronto: Irwin Law, 2000) at 2.
8. Section 292 of the *Criminal Code,* in effect from 1909 until 1953, created an indictable offence, punishable by up to two years' imprisonment and a whipping for an assault or beating or "his wife or any other female person and thereby occasions actual bodily harm."
9. June Callwood and Marvin Zuker, *The Law is Not for Women: A Legal Handbook for Women* (Toronto: Pitman Publishing, 1976) at 27-28.
10. There is an extensive literature debating these issues; see for example, Dianne Martin and Janet Mosher, "Unkept Promises: Experiences of Immigrant Women with the Neo-Criminalization of Women" (1995) 8 C.J.W.L. 3. See also, Jessica Dayton, "The Silencing of a Woman's Choice: Mandatory Arrest and No Drugs Prosecution Policies in Domestic Violence Cases" (2002-2003) 9 Cardozo L. Rev. 286; Linda Mills, "Intimate Violence as Intimate: The Journey and a Path (2002-

03) 9 Cardozo L. Rev. 461; Joanne C. Minaleer, "Evaluating Criminal Justice Responses Through the Lens of Women's Needs" (2001) 13 C.J.W.L. 74; and Jody Raphael, "Rethinking Criminal Justice Responses to Intimate Partner Violence" (2004) 10(11) Violence Against Women 1354.

11. See *supra* note 1.
12. Ruth Morris, "Penal Abolition: The Practical Choice" (Toronto, Ont.: Canadian Scholars Press, 1995).
13. *Criminal Law Issues*, online: Canadian HIV/AIDS Legal Network <http://www.aidslaw.ca/EN/issues/criminal_law.htm>.
14. R.S.C. 1985, c. C-46.
15. R.S.C. 1996, c. 19.
16. S.C. 2002, c. C-1.
17. S.O. 1999, c. 8.
18. *Ibid.* at s. 5(1)(b).
19. David Schneiderman, "The Constitutional Disorder of the Safe Streets Act: A Federalism Analysis" in Joe Hermer & Janet Mosher, *Disorderly People: Law and the Politics of Exclusion in Ontario* (Halifax, NS: Fernwood Press, 2002) at 79.
20. *R. v. Banks* (2007), 275 D.L.R. (4th) 640; leave to appeal to the Supreme Court of Canada was subsequently denied.
21. *R. v. Sault Ste. Marie*, [1978] 2 S.C.R. 1299.
22. *R. v. Wholesale Travel Group Inc.*, [1990] 3 S.C.R. 154 at para. 77; *Reference re s. 94(2) of the Motor Vehicle Act (British Columbia)* [1985] 2 S.C.R. 486 at para. 5.
23. See *supra* note 14 at s. 787(1).
24. *Ibid.* at s. 249.
25. *Ibid.* at s. 219.
26. *R. v. Tutton and Tutton*, [1989] 1 S.C.R. 1392 at paras. 26, 28.
27. See *supra* note 14 at s. 215(1).
28. *R. v. Naglik*, [1993] 3 S.C.R. 122 at para. 46.
29. *R. v. Cyrenne, Cyrenne and Cramb* (1981), 62 C.C.C. (2d) 238 at para. 15.
30. See *supra* note 26. See also *B.(R.) v. Children's Aid Society of Metropolitan Toronto*, [1995] 1 S.C.R. 315, EYB 1995-67419, [1994] S.C.J. No. 24, 9 R.F.L. (4th) 157, 21 O.R. (3d) 479 (note), 122 D.L.R. (4th) 1, 26 C.R.R. (2d) 202,1995 CarswellOnt 105, 1995 CarswellOnt 515, (*sub nom.* Sheena B., Re) 176 N.R. 161, (*sub nom.* Sheena B., Re) 78 O.A.C. 1 (S.C.C.).
31. See *supra* note 14 at ss. 24(2), 463.
32. *R. v. Keegstra*, [1990] 3 S.C.R. 697 at para. 15.
33. *R. v. Lifchus,* [1997] 3 S.C.R. 320 at para. 37.

34. See *supra* note 14 at s. 348(2).
35. *Ibid.* at s. 253.
36. *Ibid.* at s. 16(2).

20

A Field Guide to the *Criminal Code* and Related Statutes

(1) THE *CRIMINAL CODE*

The *Criminal Code*[1] is the major criminal statute, which has expanded greatly since its first enactment in 1892. As society attempts to regulate an ever-broader range of activities, it is particularly astonishing to see the growth in the number of minor offences. The *Code* creates offences, prescribes the rules of procedure for various criminal matters, and establishes the parameters and principles for sentencing. The *Code* is frequently revised through legislative amendments (several Bills are pending before Parliament at the time of writing) and the statutory provisions are themselves constantly subject to judicial interpretation and re-interpretation. In addition, criminal law has been, and continues to be, subjected to rigorous constitutional scrutiny to ensure compliance with the rights of accused persons under the *Canadian Charter of Rights and Freedoms*.[2]

The present *Code* is divided into some twenty-eight parts. Some parts are grouped together to form various categories of offences—for example, offences against public order, or offences against the person and reputation—while others delineate summary and indictable offences and the respective procedures for proceeding with each type of case. Below, some of the many categories of offences are briefly described and the offences that are more likely to be encountered by social workers, discussed.

(a) Offences Against Public Order—Part II

The grouping in Part II of the *Code* defines and prescribes penalties for a mixed array of crimes, including such acts as treason, sedition, sabotage, mutiny, passport offences, unlawful assemblies, riots and piracy. Of note in this category of offences are unlawful assembles and riots.[3] An unlawful assembly is defined as an assembly of three or more persons who, with intent to carry out a common purpose, assemble in such a manner or conduct themselves when they are assembled as to cause a person in the neighbourhood of the assembly to fear, on reasonable grounds, that they will disturb the peace tumultuously or will needlessly and without reasonable cause provoke others.[4] A riot is defined as an unlawful assembly that has begun to disturb (rather than merely threaten to disturb) the peace tumultuously.[5] In recent years, both provisions have been used to charge persons participating in demonstrations, including a demonstration in Montreal during World Trade Organization meetings, and an anti-poverty demonstration in Toronto. Some activists in particular worry that the use of these criminal provisions threatens the free speech rights of those who seek to express views contrary to the government of the day.

A new Part II.1 came into force January 17, 2002. This part creates several terrorism related offences, including a prohibition on the financing of terrorism.[6]

(b) Sexual Offences, Public Morals and Disorderly Conduct—Part V

Part V of the *Code* deals with a range of sexual offences, including incest, and various forms of sexual conduct with a child under the age of 14 (Bill C-22 presently before Parliament would raise the age to 16, but provides that consent is a defence if the complainant is 12 or 13 and the accused is less than two years older, or if the complainant is 14 or 15 and the accused is no more than five years older).[7] Part V also deals with child pornography, the distribution of obscene materials, and indecent acts. A controversial provision in this part is section 159, which makes anal intercourse an offence unless in private between husband and wife or between any two persons, each of whom is 18 or over, and both of whom consent. While the Supreme Court of Canada has yet to consider this provision, two provincial appellate courts have found this provision to be unconstitutional.

Note that sexual assault is not dealt with under this part, but rather under Part VIII, which among other things, deals with assaults generally.

(c) Offences Against the Person and Reputation—Part VIII

Offences ranging from criminal negligence, to murder, to the dangerous operation of a motor vehicle, to the failure to provide necessities of life, are all addressed in Part VIII of the *Code*. This is also the Part of the *Code* dealing with assaults and sexual assaults. Before turning to assaults it is important to note section 241, which makes it an offence for anyone to counsel a person to commit suicide or to aid and abet a person to commit suicide, irrespective of whether the suicide actually ensues. This is an indictable offence with a maximum term of 14 years imprisonment. Whether assisted suicide should be a criminal offence is very controversial, and there are strongly held views on both sides of this debate. In *Rodriguez v. British Columbia (Attorney General)*[8] the Supreme Court of Canada held that by prohibiting a physician from assisting suicide, section 241 did not violate the section 7 *Charter* rights of a terminally ill person who was physically incapable of ending her own life.[9] Another noteworthy offence is that of abduction in contravention of a custody order. It is an offence for a parent or other person with lawful custody to "take, entice away, conceal, detain, harbour" a child under 14, in contravention of a custody order with the intention of depriving a parent or guardian of his/her custody or access rights.[10]

Assault is governed by sections 265-268. There are three forms of assault which carry increasingly severe penalties upon conviction: assault[11] (often referred to as "common assault"); assault with a weapon or causing bodily harm;[12] and aggravated assault[13] (resulting in wounding, maiming, disfigurement or endangerment of life). The provisions dealing with sexual assault (sections 271-273) mirror these provisions: sexual assault; sexual assault with a weapon or causing bodily harm; and aggravated sexual assault. If a firearm is used in the commission of the offence of sexual assault with a weapon or aggravated sexual assault, there is a mandatory minimum sentence of four years, and up to a maximum of life for aggravated sexual assault. Whether an assault is "sexual" depends upon whether it is committed in circumstances of a sexual nature, such that the sexual integrity of the complainant has been violated. This is an objective test (how would it be regarded by the reasonable person, rather than how it is regarded by the complainant), to be applied having regard to all of the circumstances.

One of the most complex and controversial issues in relation to sexual assault has been, and continues to be, that of consent. Consent is addressed in section 265 and applies to all forms of assaults. Additional provisions regarding consent and sexual assaults are dealt with in sections 273.1, 273.2 and for those under the age of 14, in Part V (discussed above). Section 273.1 defines consent in the affirmative, as the voluntary agreement to engage in the sexual activity in question. Various other provisions provide express examples of where there is no consent because voluntary agreement is presumed to be absent. For example, subsection 265(3) provides that there is no consent if the complainant submits or does not resist because of the application of force to the complainant or to another person, because of fear that such force will be used, or because of the exercise of authority. Section 273.1 provides that there is no consent if the complainant is induced by the abuse of a position of trust or authority, is incapable of giving consent, or expresses a lack of agreement through words or conduct.

Two further issues are important to note: the accused's subjective belief regarding consent; and the evidence admissible regarding consent. Is there an offence if the accused honestly believed the complainant was consenting, even if the judge is satisfied on the evidence that the complainant did not consent? And must this belief be a reasonable one considering all the circumstances? These questions have vexed lawyers, judges and politicians for years and the law in this regard has changed significantly over time. The *Code* now provides that an honest belief in consent is a defence, but the honesty of this belief must be assessed by considering whether there were reasonable grounds to justify it.[14] Moreover, the *Code* provides some explicit guidance on the question of reasonableness; where the accused's belief in consent arose from his self-induced intoxication, from recklessness or wilful blindness, or from his failure to take reasonable steps in the circumstances known to him at the time to ascertain whether the complainant was consenting, his belief in consent will not be a defence to the charge.[15]

The evidentiary rules governing sexual assault have radically changed over the past few decades. Gone are the requirements that a sexual assault is to be corroborated by other evidence, and that the victim must have complained about the assault at the first reasonable opportunity.[16] Evidence of the complainant's sexual activity with others is not admissible except in very limited circumstances and is never admissible to support an inference that the complainant is more likely to have consented or is less worthy of belief (inferences for which historically such evidence had been used).[17] There are specific provisions to protect the identity of the complainant and to prevent publication of his or her name[18] and the presiding judge must so advise the complainant at the first reasonable opportunity.[19] The spouse of the person charged with sexual assault can be both a competent and compellable witness against the accused spouse.[20] This last amendment makes it possible for one spouse to testify against the other when he or she is the victim and only witness to a sexual assault, or when their child is the victim of incest. Recall as well from our earlier discussion that it has only been since 1983 that the legal concept of sexual assault within marriage has existed in Canada. Prior to that time, the *Code* included an offence of "rape," which was statutorily defined as "a male person commits rape when he has sexual intercourse with a female person who is not his wife a) without her consent [and] b) with her consent if the consent i) is extorted by threats, ii) is obtained by personating her husband, [or] iii) is obtained by fraud." The express exclusion of wives within the definition of "rape" derived both from the common law doctrine of coverture (which regarded a woman's legal identity as merging with that of her husband upon marriage), and from the view that upon marriage a woman gave irrevocable consent to sex with her husband at his pleasure.

An extremely important evidentiary issue in relation to sexual assault that has substantial implications for social work practice is that of the accused's access to, and the admissibility of, the complainant's therapeutic records. This issue is discussed in detail in Chapter 8.

(d) Drug-Related Offences

Drug-related offences and penalties are contained in the *Controlled Drugs and Substances Act*.[21] The *Act* contains eight schedules, each including a list of particular substances. Controlled substances are those substances listed in schedules I-V. It is an offence for anyone, except as authorized under the Regulations, to possess any of the substances listed in schedules I-III, or to "seek or obtain" a substance in schedules I-IV.[22] Other provisions prohibit the trafficking, production, and exportation of controlled substances. Punishment varies depending both upon the type of offence (possession versus trafficking for example), but also depending upon which schedule the drug is contained within, and in the case of possession of cannabis, the amount in one's possession. Cannabis related offences accounted for roughly 75% of all drug-related offences in 2000 and in the past few years there has been a sustained debate regarding the de-criminalization of possession of cannabis. Some argue that the criminalization of possession has created more social harm than good, especially given the very substantial numbers of young Canadians who every year acquire criminal records due to cannabis possession. The John Howard Society, for example, notes that as of 2002, some 1.5 million Canadians had criminal records for possession. Others point out that criminalization has not been effective in reducing use; in fact, use has risen over time.

In *R. v. Malmo-Levine*[23] the accused challenged the criminalization of the possession of marijuana. The Court rejected the accused's argument that the "harm principle" (only truly harmful conduct should be subject to criminal prohibition) constituted a principle of fundamental justice under section 7 of the *Charter*. In the subsequent case of *R. v. Parker*[24], the Ontario Court of Appeal did however find that the lack of a health exemption for the medical use of marijuana (an absolute prohibition on possession that threatened health) was a breach of fundamental justice. Parliament subsequently enacted the *Marijuana Medical Access Regulation*,[25] authorizing the use of marijuana in particular medical circumstances. These Regulations were challenged, and found to be unconstitutional in *Hitzig v. R.*[26]

Legal advice is necessary where a client is charged with a drug offence because of the consequences which may flow from a conviction. Unless an absolute discharge is granted, the person is left with a criminal record and possibly a term of imprisonment. A criminal record can have an adverse impact on an individual's ability to travel abroad, and this is especially true of a record related to drugs when entry is being sought to the United States.

(2) PARTIES TO AN OFFENCE

Main parties to an offence are often called principals. In addition to principals, other persons who contribute in some way to the commission of an illegal act may also be guilty of the offence. This can occur in several ways:

1. Aiding and Abetting—if one person assists or encourages another to commit a forbidden act, both may be equally guilty.[27]
2. Common Intention—if two or more people form a common intention to commit an illegal act, and in the course of that act one of them commits any other offence which was a probable consequence of carrying out the common purpose, all are parties to that offence.[28]
3. Counselling—a person who counsels (procures, solicits or incites) another to commit an offence is a party to that offence and to any further offence the person counselled commits in consequence of that counselling. Even if the offence is not committed, the person who counsels may be found guilty and subject to the same punishment as a person who attempts to commit that offence.[29]
4. Accessory after the Fact—anyone who assists a person who has committed a criminal act with the intention of assisting the perpetrator to escape becomes an accessory after the fact to the offence.[30]

(3) DEFENCES TO A CRIMINAL CHARGE

The most common defence strategy is to reveal the limitations and weaknesses of the Crown's case (both factually and legally) and thus raise a reasonable doubt as to the accused's guilt. The Crown's case may be challenged in a host of ways: by keeping out inculpatory evidence; by raising the possibility of mistaken identity; or by arguing that the Crown's case is simply insufficient to meet the threshold burden of proof beyond a reasonable doubt. In many instances, these sorts of challenges to the case can be made without the accused calling any evidence at all. In other instances, the accused will call evidence, perhaps to establish the existence of conditions that negate the required *mens rea* (for example, raising intoxication or mistake of fact). In yet other circumstances, the accused will concede that the act in question occurred, and with the requisite *mens rea*, but will lead evidence to attempt to establish that the conduct was provoked, excused or justified. Below is a brief overview of these three broad categories of argument open to the defence and some of the more specific defences that may be raised.

(a) Raising a Reasonable Doubt—Challenging Identity

The person who raises a reasonable doubt about the identity of the perpetrator will be acquitted. For example, his or her presence elsewhere, corroborated by one or more disinterested witnesses (an alibi), may raise such a doubt.

> Linda was charged with theft of a ring from a jewelry store. The prosecution asserts she is the perpetrator because she bears a strong resemblance to the thief who was caught on tape by the store's security cameras. At trial, several classmates testified that at the time of the offence she was writing a college examination in English. She also produced her mark from that examination.

A person charged may also raise a reasonable doubt about the identity of the person who committed the offence, perhaps by cross-examination of the Crown's witness regarding his or her opportunity or ability to observe.

> Louise is charged with theft from a store. A store security guard testifies that he saw her enter, take some sweaters to try on and later leave the store. Immediately afterwards, a cashmere sweater was missing. When she entered the store the next day, she was charged. She might question the state of the security guard's eyesight, where he was located at the time he made his observation, who else was in the store, how many young women were trying on sweaters, and what she was wearing that day in order to raise a reasonable doubt. It is then up to the judge to decide whether or not he or she has a reasonable doubt about the identity of the accused.

(b) Challenging *Mens Rea*

(i) Mistake of Fact (As Distinguished from Mistake of Law)

Here, what is challenged is not the identity of the perpetrator, nor the existence of the requisite act or omission, but rather the existence of the required *mens rea* (guilty mind).

> After a vigorous tennis match, Arnold picked up a tennis racquet which he thought was his and took it home. On closer inspection, he found that the grip size was different but otherwise it was exactly like his. In these circumstances, mistake of fact may be a complete defence. But if the racquet he took was a new oversized one, completely different from his own, he would have a problem claiming a mistake of fact. The less reasonable the purported mistaken belief, the less likely a judge is to believe it.

Mistake of fact must be distinguished from mistake of law. It has long been accepted in the criminal law that ignorance of the law by a person who commits an offence is not an excuse for committing that offence and this principle is now captured by section 19 of the *Criminal Code*. Essentially this means that it does not matter that the accused was unaware that particular conduct is, at law, a crime. Take, for instance, an accused who testifies that he did not know hitting his wife is a crime. Even if his testimony is accepted as truthful, it will not constitute an excuse or defense to the charge. That is, one's own ignorance that his or her conduct is a crime is not an excuse. This situation is distinguished from one where there is a mistake of fact. An example, in the context of welfare fraud, can illustrate the distinction. Assume that Stephen understands that he is required to report all income. He subsequently receives a student loan. He does not know that the welfare regulations define student loans as income (and indeed in most contexts, loans are treated as debts, not income) so he does not report the student loan. Commonly, in the administration of social assistance, the assertion is made that Stephen and others in similar positions are guilty of fraud, and the principle of "ignorance of the law" is invoked. But this is incorrect. If we believe Stephen's evidence, he has not committed fraud because he has not withheld information with the intention of depriving the state. Nor would this be a correct application of the principle "ignorance of the law is no excuse." Stephen is not claiming that he did not know fraud was a crime (he has not made a mistake of law) but rather he did not know the regulations defined loans as income (a mistake of fact). His mistake of fact demonstrates that he did not have the requisite *mens rea*; he did not have the intent to deprive the state.[31]

One final observation: in very narrow circumstances, one may be able to rely upon ignorance of the law. Where the accused establishes that he or she relied on advice regarding the law from a government official, that was in fact inaccurate advice, this may constitute a defence.

(ii) Intoxication

Intoxication may operate to negate *mens rea* in certain limited circumstances. For some crimes, like murder, intoxication can serve to raise a reasonable doubt as to whether the accused intended to cause death, resulting in a conviction for manslaughter and not murder. For most crimes of violence, however, the effect of section 33.1 of the *Code* is to limit the ability of the accused to argue that by reason of self-induced intoxication he or she lacked the intent or voluntariness necessary to commit the crime so as to provide a complete defence to the charge. For many other offences, extreme drunkenness akin to automatism may be a defence.

(iii) Mental Disorder

Section 16 of the *Code* provides that an accused is not criminally responsible if the offence was committed while the accused was suffering from a mental disorder (defined in section 2 as a "disease of the mind"), but only if the mental disorder rendered the accused incapable of appreciating the nature and quality of the act or omission or knowing that the act or omission is wrong. An accused is presumed not to suffer from a mental disorder and the party who puts the accused's mental state in issue must establish, on a balance of probabilities, the existence of a disorder at the time of the offence.

The test for determining the existence of a mental disorder is a legal rather than medical one. Over time, the criminal law has developed and codified a definition of mental disorder which is more restrictive than any definition commonly understood by psychiatry and social work. However, expert psychiatric and psychological evidence is virtually always tendered on the question of whether the accused suffers from a mental disorder that rendered him or her incapable of appreciating the nature and quality of the act or omission or knowing that the act or omission was wrong. Moreover, the court has the jurisdiction to seek out medical assistance. The court may order an assessment of the mental condition of an accused if there are reasonable grounds to believe that such evidence is necessary to determine whether the accused suffers from a mental disorder. The accused, and in more limited circumstances the prosecution, may apply to the court for an assessment order.[32] Social workers, particularly those working in psychiatric hospital settings, often play a role in these assessments.

Where an accused is found to suffer from a mental disorder of the sort contemplated by section 16, the verdict which must follow is that of not criminally responsible on account of mental disorder.[33] This does not mean, however, that the accused person necessarily goes free. Rather, three outcomes are possible: where the accused poses no threat to the safety of the public, he or she is to be discharged absolutely; she or he may be conditionally discharged; or she or he may be detained in a hospital.[34] The *Criminal Code* provides for the creation of provincially constituted Review Boards, whose statutory responsibilities include, among other things, the review of such dispositions (other than absolute discharges) every twelve months, and in some instances, will make the original disposition. If the mental disorder continues, the accused may be detained for a long period of time, perhaps longer than the maximum sentence for the offence with which he or she was charged. For this reason the mental disorder defence is only pleaded in the most serious cases or where the person's mental disorder is so extreme and obvious that it is raised by the judge.

The accused's mental capacity is often in issue when the court determines whether the accused is fit to stand trial. The test for an accused's fitness to stand trial is whether he or she is unable, on account of mental disorder, to conduct a defence to a charge, or to instruct his or her lawyer to do so. In particular, the court needs to know whether she or he understands the nature or object of the proceedings, the possible consequences of the proceedings, or is able to communicate with his or her lawyer.[35] The issue of fitness to stand trial can be raised by the accused person or prosecutor at any stage of the proceedings. The judge can also raise the issue of his or her own volition, at any time, and where the court has reasonable grounds to believe the accused may be unfit and the accused is unrepresented, it shall order representation by a lawyer.[36] As with the determination of the existence of a mental disorder, the court may order an assessment of the accused's mental condition to determine fitness to stand trial. Upon a finding that an accused is not fit to stand trial, he or she will usually be remanded to a psychiatric facility. The court may order the accused to undergo treatment for up to 60 days, but only where medical evidence supports the conclusion that a specific treatment should be administered to the accused for the purpose of making the accused fit to stand trial.[37] If the accused subsequently becomes fit to stand trial, he or she may then be tried.

Every two years the court must determine whether sufficient evidence can be adduced against an accused who is found unfit to stand trial, although the accused may apply for an earlier review if there is reason to doubt that the Crown is able to make out a *prima facie* case against the accused.[38]

(c) Justification and Excuse

(i) Provocation

Provocation means that the accused acted under the heat of passion caused by the words, gestures, or blows of another, and must be of such intensity as to deprive the ordinary person of self-control. The defence of provocation is only available to a charge of murder. Even if provocation is proved, it is not a complete defence, but has the effect of lessening the conviction from murder to manslaughter and thereby reducing the penalty.[39]

(ii) Self-Defence

The *Code* distinguishes two situations where self-defence may be available as a defence. In the first, self-defence to an unprovoked assault will be a complete defence, if the person assaulted uses no more than necessary force to repel the assault and the force used is not intended to cause death or grievous bodily harm.[40] The second situation arises where death or grievous bodily harm is caused to the perpetrator of the initial unlawful assault. Here, the accused may invoke self-defence if he or she was under a reasonable apprehension of death or grievous bodily harm from the initial perpetrator and he or she believed, on reasonable grounds, that there was no other way to preserve himself or herself from death or grievous bodily harm.[41]

The law of self-defence has been particularly important for abused women. In a landmark decision of the Supreme Court of Canada, *R. v. Lavallee*,[42] the court observed that while the *Code* itself did not include the requirement of an "imminent" attack, this had been read in by courts over time.[43] The reading of "imminent" into the *Code* was premised upon an understanding that only where an attack was imminent or under way would an accused reasonably apprehend death or grievous bodily harm and that there was no other way of preserving himself or herself.[44] Furthermore, the Court noted that the paradigmatic self-defence situation had historically been that of the bar-room brawl, a far cry from the facts before the Court in *Lavallee*. In *Lavallee*, the accused had endured a long and horribly abusive relationship. On the night in question the deceased had threatened the accused with death, and as he turned to leave the room she shot him. Significantly, the Court ruled that the expert evidence on battered woman syndrome which the accused sought to adduce was admissible. This evidence, the Court reasoned, was essential to properly assess the reasonableness of the accused's perception of grievous bodily harm or death. That is, that "reasonableness" needed to be assessed from the situation and experience of a woman in a lengthy abusive relationship, experiencing a cycle of violence, with increasingly severe physical assaults. Moreover, the evidence of battered woman syndrome, with its attention to learned helplessness, was critical to assessing the reasonableness of the accused's belief that she could not otherwise preserve herself.[45]

(d) Necessity

The defence of necessity may be invoked where there was no real opportunity to avoid breaking the law. The defence requires that there be urgent peril, no reasonable legal alternative to the criminal action taken, and reasonable proportionality between the peril avoided and the crime committed.

(e) Duress

An accused who commits an offence under threat of death or serious harm from a person who is present when the offence is committed, and which the accused believed would be carried out, is excused. Duress will afford no defence to the principal of a host of more serious criminal offences, including murder and sexual assault, but may be available to a party to such offences.[46]

> Mark and Margaret are at a party. Mark spots a bracelet and tells Margaret to pick it up and pocket it or he will break every bone in her hand. She believes him because he recently beat up her brother so severely that he is still in the hospital and she fears for her life. On their way home she is charged with theft. Margaret may be successful in pleading duress because she had been threatened with serious harm from a person present and had good reason to believe that the threat may be carried out.

(f) Justification

In very limited circumstances, the defence of justification may be available to an accused. For example, an assault upon an intruder who enters a person's home is justified if the force used is no greater than necessary to prevent entry.[47] Moreover, everyone is justified in using as much force as is reasonably necessary to prevent the commission of an offence that would likely cause immediate or serious injury to a person or to the property of the person.[48]

A particular and controversial species of justification is found in section 43 of the *Code*, which provides that a parent or teacher is justified in using force to correct a child, as long as the force is reasonable in the circumstances and is intended for corrective or educative purposes. In 2004, the Supreme Court of Canada ruled that this provision, which permits the use of "reasonable corrective force" against children, did not violate the *Charter* (see the discussion of this in Chapter 2). The Court observed that the requirement that the force be reasonable in the circumstances precluded the use of objects (belts, rulers), slaps or blows to the head or any use of force that results in harm or the prospect of harm. Moreover, the use of force upon a child under the age of two or upon a teenager could not be justified since the Court found that the application of force does not serve a corrective purpose when applied to children in these age brackets.[49] Implicit in the Court's ruling are the assumptions that the application of some degree of force to some children does indeed have a corrective impact on behaviour and that force can be applied to children without resulting in harm, or the prospect of harm. Both of these assumptions are questioned by others, who are concerned for example, that any force applied to a child, even if minor or trifling, can cause harm to the child.

(4) CRIMINAL PROCEDURE

Most Parts in the *Code* are devoted to criminal procedure, and address matters such as arrest, the laying of the charge, bail proceedings, trial process, and appeal provisions. Separate Parts deal with summary trials and accused persons with mental disorders, and another Part with the prescribed Forms for almost every eventuality. Also included are special powers respecting search warrants, seizure of goods, and forfeiture of weapons connected with an offence. Here we review only a few of these procedural issues.

(a) Jurisdiction

Two Parts define the power of superior and inferior courts to hear particular offences. For example, murder may only be tried in a superior court by a judge, while an inferior (provincial) court judge has absolute power to try offences such as theft and betting and gaming offences.[50] An accused charged with an indictable offence usually has the option of being tried by judge alone, or judge and jury.[51]

(b) Judicial Interim Release—Bail

In bail hearings, properly called "judicial interim release," there is a presumption in favour of releasing a person from custody until trial, unless the Crown prosecutor shows cause as to why the accused should be detained in custody until trial. In a certain class of offences or circumstances, the onus is on the accused to "show cause" why he or she should be released. Included in this class of offences are murder, offences committed while out on bail, narcotics offences, and connections with organized crime.[52] Section 11(*e*) of the *Charter* creates a constitutional right not to be denied reasonable bail without just cause.

(c) The Plea

The two most common pleas available in criminal law are "guilty" or "not guilty." There is no such thing as "guilty with an explanation." Only if a person actually committed the offence, intended to do so and all of the necessary elements are present should a person plead guilty. Even then, one of the legal defences may be available to the person charged. In any event, everyone charged with an offence is entitled to plead "not guilty" and to raise a defence at trial. The explanation for the offence may be a defence to the charge, or may mitigate the penalty if the accused person is found guilty at trial. Legal advice should be sought before entering a plea of guilty, yet as we discuss in Chapter 7, such advice is not always accessible, especially for less serious crimes. All too often accused persons enter a plea of guilty without the benefit of legal advice and representation.

A significant phenomenon within the criminal justice system is that of the plea bargain. Commonly defence counsel and the Crown enter negotiations, the outcome of which is often an agreed statement of facts and a joint submission regarding sentencing to present to the Court. The Court is not bound by the joint submission regarding the sentence, but will usually adopt such submissions. Most cases in the criminal justice system are dealt with in this manner, and the early guilty plea is considered an important mitigating factor in sentencing.

(5) SENTENCING

A sentencing hearing is less formal than a trial and a much greater range of information is admissible. A significant development in relation to sentencing has been the increased role accorded to victims. A sentencing judge is required to inquire whether the victim of the crime has been informed of the availability of victim impact statements and must permit the victim to give his or her impact statement orally if he or she so chooses. While many see this increased role for victims as long overdue, others are concerned that the "criminal" law is being used to redress "civil" wrongs against the individual. Victim statements are emotional appeals built on profound and personal hurt, but it is difficult to determine the weight to be given to such statements. In our system of law, crimes against the person are seen as crimes against the state and it is therefore the state that prosecutes the perpetrator on behalf of both the victim and society. The attempt to recognize the victim, some worry, may interfere with the objectivity of the criminal process which purports to provide justice and fairness to all parties.[53]

(a) Aboriginal Accused

In some instances involving Aboriginal accused, a sentencing circle may be employed.[54] Section 718.2(e) instructs judges to consider all available sanctions other than imprisonment that are reasonable in the circumstances, with particular attention to the circumstances of Aboriginal offenders. In *R. v. Gladue*[55] the Supreme Court of Canada held that the purpose of this provision is an attempt to remedy the over-incarceration of Aboriginal offenders and requires that judges attend to, among other relevant circumstances, the systemic discrimination experienced by Aboriginal persons, which may account for why the accused is before the court. It also requires the court to consider restorative justice and other approaches that may be more appropriate because of the offender's Aboriginal heritage.[56]

(b) Sentencing Objectives

Upon conviction, a judge must determine the sentence. In most instances judges have considerable discretion, fashioning a sentence within a maximum penalty framework. There is presently, however, a push to limit this flexibility by creating more and more mandatory minimum offences. The sentences available will, of course, depend upon the provisions of the particular statute that was violated by the convicted person. Here, we focus on sentencing pursuant to the *Criminal Code*.

Major sentencing reforms introduced in 1985 (Bill C-46) articulated for the first time in the *Code* the purpose and principles that were to govern sentencing (in many respects the reforms codified principles that had developed over time by the courts). Section 718 now provides that the fundamental purpose of sentencing is to "contribute . . .to respect for the law and the maintenance of a just, peaceful and safe society by imposing just sanctions" that have at least one of six objectives: denunciation; deterrence (specific and general); incapacitation; assistance in rehabilitation; reparations for harms done to victims or the community; or promotion of a sense of responsibility in the offender and acknowledgement of the harm to victims and the community. Section 718.1 further provides that a fundamental principle of sentencing is that the sentence must be proportionate to the gravity of the offence and the degree of responsibility of the offender.

Moreover, as noted above, this section provides that an accused should not be deprived of liberty if a less restrictive sanction may be appropriate in the circumstances.

(c) Sentencing Options

If an accused person pleads guilty or is found guilty by the court, a conviction may be registered and the resulting penalties may range from an absolute discharge to life imprisonment, depending on the penalty prescribed by law and the seriousness of the offence in all the circumstances. Sentencing is also impacted by section 12 of the *Charter*, which provides that everyone has the right not to be subjected to any cruel and unusual treatment or punishment.

(i) Absolute and Conditional Discharge

At the least punitive end of the scale is a discharge, wherein the accused is deemed not to have been convicted.[57] Discharges are available for all but very serious offences. The discharge must be in the best interests of the accused and must not be contrary to the public interest, which usually requires the person to be of reasonably good character in that a deterrent sentence is not required. The importance of an absolute discharge is that it is *not* a conviction. A person can therefore say truthfully that he or she was not convicted of an offence, although the court record of guilt remains. An absolute discharge has no conditions attached, whereas a conditional discharge requires the conditions to be fulfilled before it becomes final. These conditions may include probation, restrictions on movement, or other provisions as ordered by the court.

(ii) Fines

A fine may be levied by the court in lieu of or in addition to another punishment. Where there is a minimum term of imprisonment, however, the fine must be given in addition to this term of imprisonment. If the offence is indictable, the fine may be for any amount, but if the offence is prosecuted by summary conviction, the maximum is $2,000 for an individual and up to $100,000 for an organization.[58]

Unless a statute requires the payment of a fine upon conviction, a judge can order a fine only if the accused has the ability to pay or discharge a fine.[59] The discharge of the fine refers to another creature of the *Code*, the fine option program. While the *Code* creates the possibility of the discharge of a fine through participation in a fine option program, the creation of actual programs requires provincial action.[60] Unfortunately, many accused do not have access to such programs because they have not been created in all jurisdictions. This differential access to fine option programs creates fundamental problems, particularly given that default (failing to pay the fine by the date specified) results in imprisonment.

A form of Dickensian debtors' prison has survived into the twenty-first century, as noted by the Supreme Court of Canada in *R. v. Wu*.[61] Mr. Wu was fined $9600 for possession of 300 cartons of contraband cigarettes, a fine being mandatory ($0.16/cigarette) under the governing legislation, the *Excise Act*.[62] It was evident that Mr. Wu was impecunious and unable to pay the fine. No fine discharge programs were available to him in Ontario. Faced with this reality the trial judge ordered that Mr. Wu pay the fine, gave no time for payment of the fine, and ordered a conditional sentence of 75 days in default of payment, notwithstanding the trial judge's conclusion that the case did not warrant imprisonment. The Supreme Court of Canada overturned the trial judge on the grounds that a conditional sentence is a form of imprisonment (conditional sentences are discussed more fully below) and that the genuine inability to pay a fine is not a proper basis for a sentence of imprisonment. Imprisonment upon default, the Court observed, is intended to act as a serious motivation to those who have the funds to pay their fines.[63] However, imprisonment should not be used where default arises from a genuine inability to pay.[64] In the course of its decision, the Court noted with dismay the statistics before it regarding the significant percentages of persons incarcerated due to non-payment of fines.

> Debtors' prison, a dreadful institution excoriated by Charles Dickens in *Little Dorrit*, is no longer with us. But according to the most recent report from Statistics Canada, 17 percent of all people in custody in provincial or territorial institutions in 2000-2001 were jailed for default on unpaid fines, i.e., at least one of the causes for their committal arose from a fine default: see Canadian Centre for Justice Statistics, *Adult Correctional Services in Canada, 2000-2001* (2002), at Table 7. The numbers are fairly steady, if in slight decline, from 20 percent in 1998-1999 to 19 percent in 1999-2000.

> A similar picture was presented by the National Council of Welfare in its report *Justice and the Poor* (2000), at p. 76. The Council says that in 1989-1990, fine default "played a major role" in the imprisonment of women, especially of Aboriginal women in the Prairie provinces. At the time, 47 percent of female prisoners in Saskatchewan were admitted for fine default. On a provincial basis, the Council noted of the Quebec system, at pp. 76-77, for example:

> A 1994 Quebec survey found that 35 percent of the imprisoned defaulters had been fined for offences under the Criminal Code or other federal criminal laws (average fine of $262 or, in case of default, average of 26 days in prison),

10 percent for both federal and provincial offences (average $1,366 or 50 days), and 55 percent for violations of provincial laws (average $342 or 13 days) or municipal bylaws (average $116 or 8 days). The vast majority (65 percent) of the fines had been issued for driving/traffic offences, mostly under provincial laws (45 percent). The rest of the fines were for thefts and other property offences under the Criminal Code (5 percent), violations of drug laws and other federal statutes (3 percent), assaults and other offences against the person (2 percent), illegal hunting, poaching and other violations of provincial laws (2 percent), failure to appear in court and other Criminal Code violations (15 percent) as well as unspecified municipal offences (8 percent).

It is curious that, while a force behind the 1996 sentencing reforms to the *Code* was a reaction to the overuse of prison as a sanction (*R. v. Gladue*, [1999] 1 S.C.R. 688, at para. 57), prison as an enforcement mechanism for unpaid fines remains at such a high level. In its 1987 report, the Canadian Sentencing Commission had observed that "[t]he imposition of a 'semi-automatic' prison term for fine default has been the subject of relentless criticism in the sentencing literature. There is statistical evidence to support the conclusion that the imprisonment of fine defaulters without reference to their ability to pay discriminates against impoverished offenders": *Sentencing Reform: A Canadian Approach—Report of the Canadian Sentencing Commission* (1987), at p. 380. The Commission recommended that "a quasi-automatic prison term not be imposed for fine default and that offenders only be incarcerated for *wilful* breach of a community sanction" (p. 381), meaning probation or fines (p. 347). In its 1996 sentencing reforms, Parliament took these views into account.[65]

(iii) Suspended Sentence and Probation

Unless the offence provides for a minimum sentence, the judge may suspend sentence and release the accused on a probation order. The judge may also include a probation order as part of the sentence where the accused is ordered to pay a fine, or ordered to serve a term of imprisonment of less than two years.[66] Apart from the statutory requirements of good behaviour (to appear before the court as required and to notify the court or probation officer of any change of name, address or employment), the judge may prescribe a number of other conditions in the probation order, which may include supervision by a probation officer, an order to provide support for dependants, abstention from alcohol, drugs or possession of a weapon, an obligation to seek and maintain employment, a treatment order, an order for restitution, compensation or community service, or an order to remain within the jurisdiction of the court.[67] The term of a probation order is up to three years. Since a probation order is a court order, the terms must be complied with; if not, the person may be brought back before the court and where the sentence was originally suspended, sentenced on the original offence, as well as for breach of probation (itself an offence under section 733.1).

(iv) Conditional Sentences

Reforms in 1996 introduced the conditional sentence, a form of imprisonment within the community, and directed judges to incarcerate only where a community sentencing alternative was not feasible. Conditional sentences, often termed "house arrest," are available only where all of the circumstances warrant a period of incarceration, and only then may the judge consider whether the sentence may be served, with conditions, in the community. Two conditions apply: the period of imprisonment must be less than two years; and the offender must not pose a danger to the community. A Bill before Parliament would restrict the availability of conditional sentences, including where an offence is prosecuted by indictment and the maximum penalty is more than 10 years. This would include, among many other offences, the prosecution of cases of alleged welfare fraud over $5,000.

Although in many instances conditional sentences may be less harsh than jail time, this may well depend upon the conditions attached and the social location of the accused, as was tragically illustrated by the case of Kimberley Rogers in Ontario. Kimberley Rogers pled guilty to the crime of fraud, for having failed to disclose $13,468.31 in student loans she had received over a three-year period while in receipt of Ontario Works (welfare) benefits (note that not very long ago the rules permitted the dual receipt of Ontario Works and student loans).[68] Ms. Rogers was sentenced to house arrest for six months. At the time of her conviction, a three month ban on receipt of benefits was in effect for those convicted of welfare fraud (this preceded the introduction of a lifetime ban, which has also been subsequently revoked). Ms Rogers died in her apartment during a heat wave in August, 2001, eight months pregnant. Confinement to one's home, if that home is over-heated (as in the case of Ms Rogers), under-heated, infested with cockroaches or rodents, over-crowded, covered in mildew or shares any of the characteristic features of much low-income housing, will have significant and deleterious effects on both physical and mental health that would most likely not exist for a person who is adequately housed. So too, trying to acquire the other material necessities of life often requires much more time for a low-income person than for a person with adequate financial means. For many, trying to access food means visiting multiple food banks and/or other charities and/or buying products at several stores (where one can get the best buy), rather than a single stop at a supermarket. Similarly, acquiring clothing and other necessities is often time-consuming and complicated. Trying to find these necessities will often require long absences from the home; the three hours, one day per week during which Ms Rogers was permitted to leave her home was manifestly inadequate. Ms Rogers, even after her lawyers were successful in having the three month ban lifted pending a constitutional challenge, still had only eighteen dollars per month to live on after her rent was paid.

(v) Custodial Sentences

All sentences of two years or more are served in federally-operated penitentiaries.[69] Sentences under two years fall under provincial jurisdiction and are served in jails and correctional centers operated by the province.[70]

Where the sentence imposed is not more than 90 days, the court may order that it be served intermittently, for example, on weekends from Friday night until Monday morning.[71] While the person is out of custody, he or she is subject to a probation order. The purpose of such a sentence is to allow the convicted person to continue his or her employment or carry out his or her community responsibilities. However, once the sentence has been ordered, it cannot be varied except on appeal. This situation often creates serious problems and may defeat the purpose of the sentence. For example, if the prisoner is required to change working hours or work weekends, which conflicts with the order, he or she may end up losing the very job which the sentence was designed to preserve.

(vi) Conditional Releases

Once incarcerated, all offenders are required by law to be considered for some form of conditional release during their sentence. The *Corrections and Conditional Release Act*[72] provides for various forms of conditional release, ranging from temporary absences to full parole. Temporary escorted absences, governed by section 17, provide for releases of up to 5 days (up to 15 with approval of the Commissioner) for family, compassionate, or rehabilitative reasons, and for unlimited time if there are medical reasons. Unescorted temporary absences are also available under section 115, and work releases under section 18. Offenders are also eligible for day parole and later, full parole. The period of time which must pass prior to eligibility varies depending upon the nature of the offence, but most federal inmates are eligible for full parole after serving one third of the sentence. Decisions regarding eligibility for these various forms of release are, for federal inmates, made by the National Parole Board. Provincial Parole Boards in British Columbia, Ontario and Quebec make these decisions for provincial inmates; for the other provinces and territories the National Parole Board makes the decision. The primary decision-making criterion as to whether parole will be granted and the offender permitted to serve the remainder of the sentence in the community subject to conditions, is that of public safety. Conditions will attach to the release, and may include that the offender reside in a community-based residential facility, often called half-way houses or group homes. These facilities have been established across the country to assist in the reintegration of persons who have received and served custodial sentences. Unfortunately, the community has vacillated in their acceptance. When a violent incident occurs, it is not uncommon for a public outcry against such homes to be raised. The truth which tends to be overlooked is that offenders will be released on expiry of their sentences and that the community is better served by assisting than by rejecting the offender.

Social workers are aware that communities selected to contain such group homes have been exceedingly vocal in their opposition. Critics point to the danger placed on residents of the community with proof that innocent persons have been murdered by parolees living in half-way houses. Advocates have stressed the need for better trained staff and improved screening by the Parole Board while strongly supporting the continuation of such homes.

(vii) Statutory Release

Most federal inmates are statutorily released after serving two-thirds of the sentence (this does not apply to those serving a life or indeterminate sentence). This release does not turn upon an affirmative finding of the Parole Board, but rather is determined by statute. However, the Correctional Service of Canada may recommend to the Parole Board that an inmate not be statutorily released, and the Board may order that the inmate be detained until the end of the sentence.

(d) Pardons

Many citizens are not aware that the federal government has enacted legislation which allows pardons for those who have been convicted of criminal offences. Where the conviction was for a summary offence, the waiting period before application can be made is three years after completing the sentence; for an indictable offence, it is five years.[73]

To obtain a pardon, a person must apply to the Solicitor General of Canada through the local National Parole Board Office and it is the Parole Board that makes the determination. For indictable offences the Board must be satisfied that the applicant has been of good conduct throughout the five year period since completion of the sentence, and has not been convicted of any offence under a Federal Act or regulation thereto. For summary conviction offences, the applicant only need demonstrate that he or she has not been convicted of an offence during the period since completion of the original sentence.

The effect of a pardon is equivocal. The criminal record is to be kept separate and apart from other criminal records and may only be disclosed with permission of the responsible Minister. Except for certain sexual offences, all information pertaining to the conviction is removed from the Canadian Police Information Centre (CPIC). The *Criminal Records Act*[74] prohibits federally regulated employers from asking job applicants whether they have been convicted of offences for which a pardon has been granted, and the *Canadian Human Rights Code*[75] expressly forbids discrimination based on a pardoned conviction.[76] Similar protections against discrimination with respect to employment are found in at least some provincial jurisdictions.[77]

There is no need to apply for a pardon for an absolute or conditional discharge. One year after an absolute discharge and three years after the conditions of a conditional discharge have been satisfied the criminal record will be automatically treated in the same manner as if a pardon had been granted.

(e) Consequence of Conviction or Acquittal

If an accused person is found not guilty, he or she is discharged by the court and is free to go. No further proceedings may be taken against that person concerning *that* particular offence except on appeal, where a new trial may be ordered on the same offence. The underlying principle is that no person should be tried more than once for the same offence. The *Charter* now guarantees this right in section 11(h), which provides that if acquitted of the offence, the accused has the right not to be tried for it again, and if found guilty and punished for the offence, not to be tried or punished for it again. In some circumstances, the person who has been acquitted may subsequently be charged with another offence committed at the same time, which is a different offence. In a highly publicized case the accused was acquitted of a murder that had been committed during a robbery.[78] After acquittal, he confessed to the killing, was charged with robbery and perjury, and was convicted. The court decided that, since a finding by the jury about his commission of the robbery was not essential to acquittal on the murder charge, he could be tried for robbery.

SELECTED READINGS

Ferraro, Kathleen J., "Words Change, But the Melody Lingers: The Persistence of the Battered Women Syndrome in Criminal Cases Involving Battered Women" (2003) 9(1) Violence Against Women 110.

Huss, M.T. "Battered Womem Who Kill Their Abusers" (2006), 21(8) Journal of Interpersonal Violence 1063.

Roach, Kent. *Due Process and Victims' Rights: The New Law and Politics of Criminal Justice* (Toronto: University of Toronto Press, 1999).

Shaffer, Martha. "The Battered Woman Syndrome Revisited: Some complicating Thoughts Five Years After *R. v. Lavallee*" (1997), 47 University of Toronto Law Journal 1.

Stuart, Don. *Canadian Criminal Law: A Treatise* (Toronto: Carswell, 2001).

ENDNOTES

1. R.S.C. 1985, c. C-46.
2. Part I to *The Constitution Act, 1982*, Schedule B to the *Canada Act, 1982* (U.K.), 1982, c. 11.
3. See *supra* note 1 at ss. 63 and 64.
4. *Ibid.* at s. 63(1).
5. *Ibid.* at s. 64(1).
6. *Ibid.* at ss. 83.01-83.33.
7. Bill C-22, House of Commons, 2nd Session, 37th Parliament, 51 Elizabeth II, 2002.
8. [1993] 3 S.C.R. 519, 1993 CarswellBC 1267, EYB 1993-67109, [1993] S.C.J. No. 94, 82 B.C.L.R. (2d) 273, 85 C.C.C. (3d) 15, 107 D.L.R. (4th) 342, 17 C.R.R. (2d) 193, 24 C.R. (4th) 281, 158 N.R. 1, 34 B.C.A.C. 1, 56 W.A.C. 1, [1993] 7 W.W.R. 641, 1993 CarswellBC 228.
9. *Ibid.* at paras. 247 and 248.
10. See *supra* note 1 at s. 282.
11. *Ibid.* at s. 265.
12. *Ibid.* at s. 267.
13. *Ibid.* at s. 268.
14. *Ibid.* at s. 273.1.
15. *Ibid.* at ss. 265(4), 273.2.
16. Ibid. at ss. 274, 275.
17. *Ibid.* at s. 276. See also *R. v. Seaboyer*, [1991] 2 S.C.R. 577, 7 C.R.

(4th) 117, EYB 1991-67624, 128 N.R. 81, 6 C.R.R. (2d) 35, 66 C.C.C. (3d) 321, 83 D.L.R. (4th) 193, 1991 CarswellOnt 109, [1991] S.C.J. No. 62, 4 O.R. (3d) 383 (headnote only), 48 O.A.C. 81, 1991 CarswellOnt 1022.

18. *Ibid.* at s. 486(3).

19. *Ibid.* at s. 486(4).

20. *Canada Evidence Act,* R.S.C. 1985, c. C-5 at s. 4(2).

21. S.C. 1996, c. 19.

22. *Ibid.* at s. 4(2).

23. (2003), 233 D.L.R. (4th) 415, [2003] S.C.J. No. 79, [2004] 4 W.W.R. 407, 191 B.C.A.C. 1, 314 W.A.C. 1, 16 C.R. (6th) 1, [2003] 3 S.C.R. 571, 114 C.R.R. (2d) 189, REJB 2003-51751, 2003 CarswellBC 3133, 2003 CarswellBC 3134, 2003 SCC 74, 179 C.C.C. (3d) 417, 314 N.R. 1, 23 B.C.L.R. (4th) 1 at para. 113.

24. (2000), 49 O.R. (3d) 481, 188 D.L.R. (4th) 385, 146 C.C.C. (3d) 193, 75 C.R.R. (2d) 233, 37 C.R. (5th) 97, 135 O.A.C. 1, 2000 CarswellOnt 2627, [2000] O.J. No. 2787 (C.A.).

25. P.C. 2001-1146 (14 June 2001).

26. (2003), (sub nom. *Hitzig v. Canada*) 231 D.L.R. (4th) 104, 177 O.A.C. 321, 111 C.R.R. (2d) 201, 2003 CarswellOnt 3795, [2003] O.J. No. 3873, 14 C.R. (6th) 1, 177 C.C.C. (3d) 449, 231 D.L.R. (4th) 104 (C.A.), leave to appeal refused (2004), 2004 CarswellOnt 1830, 2004 CarswellOnt 1831, 112 C.R.R. (2d) 376n, 197 O.A.C. 400 (note), [2004] S.C.C.A. No. 5, 331 N.R. 394 (note) (S.C.C.).

27. See *supra* note 1 at ss. 21(1), 463.

28. *Ibid.* at s. 21(2).

29. *Ibid.* at ss. 22(1), 22(2) and 464.

30. *Ibid.* at s. 23(1).

31. For an excellent analysis of *mens rea* in the context of welfare fraud see *R. v. Maldonado* (1998), [1998] O.J. No. 3209, 1998 CarswellOnt 3151 (Ont. Prov. Div.).

32. See *supra* note 1 at s. 672.11.

33. *Ibid.* at s. 672.34.

34. *Ibid.* at s. 672.54.

35. *Ibid.* at s. 672.23.

36. *Ibid.* at s. 672.24.

37. *Ibid.* at ss. 672.58, 672.59.

38. *Ibid.* at s. 672.33.

39. *Ibid.* at s. 232.

40. *Ibid.* at s. 34(1).

41. *Ibid.* at s. 34(2).

42. [1990] 1 S.C.R. 852, EYB 1990-67181, [1990] 4 W.W.R. 1, 67 Man.

R. (2d) 1, 108 N.R. 321, 76 C.R. (3d) 329, 55 C.C.C. (3d) 97, 1990 CarswellMan 198, 1990 CarswellMan 377, [1990] S.C.J. No. 36, 132 W.A.C. 243.

43. *Ibid.* at para. 46.

44. *Ibid.*

45. *Ibid.* at para. 50; see also *R. v. M. (M.A.)*, [1998] 1 S.C.R. 123, 36 O.R. (3d) 802 (headnote only), 106 O.A.C. 132, 1998 CarswellOnt 419, 1998 CarswellOnt 420, 12 C.R. (5th) 207, 222 N.R. 4, 155 D.L.R. (4th) 513, 121 C.C.C. (3d) 456, [1998] S.C.J. No. 12; Martha Shaffer, "The Battered Woman Syndrome Revisited: Some Complicating Thoughts Five Years After *R. v. Lavallee*" (1997) 47 University of Toronto Law Journal 1; M.T. Huss, "Battered Womem Who Kill Their Abusers" (2006) 21(8) Journal of Interpersonal Violence 1063; and Kathleen J. Ferraro, "Words Change, But the Melody Lingers: The Persistence of the Battered Women Syndrome in Criminal Cases Involving Battered Women" (2003) 9(1) Violence Against Women 110.

46. See *supra* note 1 at s. 17.

47. *Ibid.* at s. 41(1).

48. *Ibid.* at s. 27.

49. *Canadian Foundation for Children, Youth and the Law v. Canada (Attorney General)*, (sub nom. *Canadian Foundation for Children v. Canada*) [2004] 1 S.C.R. 76, 2004 SCC 4, 2004 CarswellOnt 252, 2004 CarswellOnt 253, 315 N.R. 201, 183 O.A.C. 1, [2004] S.C.J. No. 6, 70 O.R. (3d) 94 (note), (sub nom. *Canadian Foundation for Children v. Canada*) [2004] 1 S.C.R. 76, 115 C.R.R. (2d) 88, REJB 2004-53164, 16 C.R. (6th) 203, 46 R.F.L. (5th) 1, 234 D.L.R. (4th) 257, 180 C.C.C. (3d) 353 at para. 45.

50. See *supra* note 1 at ss. 469, 553.

51. *Ibid.* at ss. 471 and 473.

52. *Ibid.* at ss. 515-523.

53. Kent Roach, *Due Process and Victims' Rights: The New Law and Politics of Criminal Justice* (Toronto: University of Toronto Press, 1999).

54. *Ibid.* at 298.

55. [1999] 1 S.C.R. 688, [1999] S.C.J. No. 19, 1999 CarswellBC 778, 1999 CarswellBC 779, 23 C.R. (5th) 197, 238 N.R. 1, 133 C.C.C. (3d) 385, 171 D.L.R. (4th) 385, 121 B.C.A.C. 161, 198 W.A.C. 161, [1999] 2 C.N.L.R. 252.

56. *Ibid.* at para. 31.

57. See *supra* note 1 at s. 730.

58. *Ibid.* at ss. 787 and 735(1).

59. *Ibid.* at s. 734(2).

60. *Ibid.* at s. 736.
61. [2003] 3 S.C.R. 530, [2003] S.C.J. No. 78, 113 C.R.R. (2d) 297, REJB 2003-51514, 2003 SCC 73, 2003 CarswellOnt 5099, 2003 CarswellOnt 5100, 182 O.A.C. 6, 16 C.R. (6th) 289, 180 C.C.C. (3d) 97, 313 N.R. 201, 234 D.L.R. (4th) 87.
62. R.S.C. 1985, c. E-14.
63. See *supra* note 59 at para. 3.
64. *Ibid.*
65. *Ibid.* at paras. 34-36.
66. See *supra* note 1 at s. 731.
67. *Ibid.* at s. 732.1.
68. *R. v. Rogers* (April 25, 2001), Rodgers J., [2001] O.J. No. 5203 (Ont. C.J.).
69. See *supra* note 1 at s. 743.1(1).
70. *Ibid.* at s. 743.1(3).
71. *Ibid.* at s. 732.
72. S.C. 1992, c. 20.
73. *Criminal Records Act*, R.S.C., 1985, c. C-47 at s. 4.
74. R.S.C. 1985, c. C-47.
75. R.S.O. 1990, c. H.19.
76. *Ibid.* at s. 5(1).
77. *Ibid.*
78. *R. v. Gushue* (1979), (sub nom. *Gushue v. R.*) [1980] 1 S.C.R. 798, 1979 CarswellOnt 70, 16 C.R. (3d) 39, 30 N.R. 204, 50 C.C.C. (2d) 417, 106 D.L.R. (3d) 152, 1979 CarswellOnt 697.

21

Youths in Conflict with the Law

(1) HISTORICAL APPROACHES

Influenced by shifts in understandings of child development, in causal theories of youth law-breaking, and in views regarding the efficacy of treatment and/or punishment, dramatically different models of legal intervention have come and gone over the past century in Canada. At common law, youthful law-breaking was governed by the doctrine of *doli incapax* ("the incapacity to do wrong"), according to which children under seven were immune from prosecution on the basis that they were assumed to be developmentally incapable of forming the *mens rea* (mental requirement) essential to a criminal offence. Those aged seven to 13 inclusive, were also presumed to lack capacity, however this presumption was open to rebuttal if the prosecution could establish that the child appreciated the nature and consequences of the conduct and that it was wrong.[1] Prior to the mid-nineteenth century, and consistent with the view that children are different from adults only in size, there is little evidence of children over the age of seven being treated differently than adults in relation to the application of the criminal law, although on occasion, mercy was shown in the punishment of children.[2]

(a) The *Juvenile Delinquents Act*

The first comprehensive statute regulating youthful offenders appeared in 1908, in the form of the *Juvenile Delinquents Act (JDA)*.[3] In effect for more than 75 years, the *JDA* emerged at a time when a broader reform movement, focused upon "rescuing" or "saving" children, flourished.[4] Applicable to children between the ages of seven and 16, those brought before the court were regarded not as criminals, but as misguided or misdirected youths. Their environments, and in particular, their families, were regarded as the cause of delinquency. Through the exercise of its *parens patriae* ("father of the people") jurisdiction, the court stepped in as the stern, kind father to provide the guidance assumed to be lacking in the family home; such guidance was also deemed necessary to the proper reformation of the young person before the court. The reach of the *Act* extended beyond alleged infractions of the *Criminal Code*,[5] to include other behaviour that violated norms of acceptable youthful behaviour: truancy; sexual promiscuity (applied predominately in relation to girls); and running away. The central inquiry of the courts was focused not upon whether there existed proof beyond a reasonable doubt of a criminal infraction, but rather, whether the young person was in need of guidance and treatment. As the *Act* itself explained, a juvenile was to be treated "not as a criminal, but as a misdirected and misguided child" and that "the care and custody and discipline of a juvenile delinquent shall approximate as nearly as may be that which should be given by its parents."[6] Significantly, the *JDA* embraced a view of children as distinct from adults, with special needs, requiring not only a separate court system, but also the assurance that children would be detained separate and apart from adults.

Given the child welfare orientation of the legislation, little attention was paid by the courts to procedural formality when hearing matters of youthful offending, and virtually no attention was accorded to the rights of those alleged to be delinquent. Youths were not convicted of an offence, but adjudged to be "delinquent", and often sentenced to indeterminate periods of state custody—indeterminate since the length of necessary treatment to reform the child could not be predicted in advance. Thus outcomes were not proportionate to the gravity of the infraction but rather, tied to the nature and length of treatment perceived to be necessary and to the reformation of the child.

The model of juvenile justice embraced by the *JDA* came under mounting criticism; criticism informed by an array of rights-based social movements, an increasing rights-based consciousness (leading in part to the *Canadian Charter of Rights and Freedoms* in 1982), and by the more particular evolution of conceptions of children's rights (for example, the *United Nations Convention on the Rights of the Child*).[7] Beyond the concerns regarding the lack of respect for children's rights was mounting evidence that the model was not, in fact, delivering what had been promised. In some instances, rather than treatment, children were virtually warehoused in training schools or reformatories. In the worst of cases, children were subject to systemic, institutional abuses by those entrusted with their care. Moreover, support grew for the view that it was profoundly unfair to hold youths who had committed no criminal offences, or who were guilty of only minor infractions, for long periods in training schools or reformatories for treatment purposes.

(b) The *Young Offenders Act*

After years of debate, new youth justice legislation, the *Young Offenders Act*[8] was proclaimed in 1984. While certainly not abandoning notions of the particular and special needs of youths, nor a role for treatment, the *YOA* much more closely approximated an adult criminal justice model by acknowledging the due process rights of those accused. The age jurisdiction expanded at the upper end to include 17 year olds, and retracted at the bottom end to exclude those under 12 years of age. Unlike its predecessor, the offence jurisdiction under the *Act* was confined to the prosecution of offences under the *Criminal Code* or other federal legislation.[9] With sentences to be proportionate to the gravity of the offence, the right to counsel (including state-appointed and funded counsel if required), a due process model of procedure, and an emphasis on accountability through punishment, the *YOA* reflected a marked disjuncture from its predecessor.

But this shift in direction did not stem the tide of criticism regarding the state's approach to youthful offending for long. Many argued that the *Act* was not tough enough, and calls for longer sentences were vocalized across the country. Fueled by sensationalized media accounts of youth violence, a growing number of citizens and politicians came to hold the view that youth crime was on the increase and that the *YOA* was partly to blame. Yet this view regarding the increase of youth crime belied the actual statistics, and the call for harsher, longer sentences ran contrary to the accumulated body of research showing the potential criminogenic impact of criminal justice processing. At the same time, others critiqued the *Act* as too punitive, having resulted in a dramatic increase in the resort to custodial sentences, even for minor infractions. Indeed Canada's rate of incarceration of youths—four times that of adults and twice that of many American states—placed it as the world leader in the incarceration of youths.[10] In the view of many, youths were often inappropriately processed through the criminal justice system because of a lack of resources in the child welfare and children's mental health systems.[11]

(c) The *Youth Criminal Justice Act*

In April, 2003, the *YOA* was repealed and replaced by the *Youth Criminal Justice Act*[12] *(YCJA)*. In many respects, the new legislation responded to the concerns regarding the over-reliance on custody and the harshly punitive approaches developed under the *YOA*. However, in at least one important respect, some argue it simultaneously responded to the call to "get tough" by expanding the circumstances in which a youth may be given an "adult sentence", rather than the considerably shorter "youth sentence" available under the *YCJA*. But perhaps its most significant feature is its embracement of a restorative justice approach, an approach that moves youth justice beyond the rigid dichotomy of treatment or punishment, which has for so long dominated the field.

(2) *YOUTH CRIMINAL JUSTICE ACT*

(a) Purpose

The *YCJA*, in its preamble, acknowledges a shared societal responsibility to address the developmental challenges and needs of young persons, to provide guidance and support to those at risk of committing crimes, and through multi-disciplinary approaches, to take "reasonable steps to prevent youth crime by addressing its underlying causes." The *Act*'s stated purpose is that of fostering responsibility and accountability through meaningful consequences and effective rehabilitation and reintegration. Elsewhere, the *Act* makes clear that timeliness is critical to the concept of "meaningful consequences" and to rehabilitation and reintegration, as is particular attention to gender, ethnic, cultural and linguistic differences, and to the needs of Aboriginal young persons and young persons with special requirements.

(b) Age

While there had been calls to lower both the maximum and minimum ages of the *YOA,* the *YCJA* does neither, instead retaining jurisdiction over youths between the age of 12 and 17 inclusive. Children under 12 who commit criminal or other offences are, as under the *YOA*, to be dealt with through the child welfare system.

(c) Alternative Measures; Alternative Sanctions

The *Act* creates numerous vehicles available to both police and Crown attorneys to address the behaviour of a young person without resorting to formal court processes. Early evidence indicates that as a result of the new initiatives, there has been a substantial increase in the numbers of cases diverted from the courts under the *YCJA*.[13] The police are mandated, prior to laying a charge, to consider extrajudicial measures. Among such measures are: taking no action; giving a warning; issuing a caution (where provincial or territorial attorneys-general have created a program authorizing police or Crowns to administer such cautions); and the making of a referral to a program or agency (with the young person's consent). Section 4(a) of the *Act* makes clear that the above measures are "often the most appropriate and effective way to address youth crime" and section 4(c) creates a presumption that such measures are adequate to hold accountable first time non-violent offenders. As Barnhorst suggests, Parliament has sent a clear message that it expects first time, non-violent offenders to be dealt with outside of the formal justice system.[14]

In addition to extrajudicial measures are extrajudicial sanctions, which include community service and restitution (s.10). These sanctions may only be considered if: the matter cannot be adequately dealt with through a warning, caution or referral; they are part of a program of sanctions created by the province; the young person consents to participation (after being given a reasonable opportunity to consult with counsel); the young person "accepts responsibility" (which is not a formal admission of legal guilt); and in the opinion of the Attorney General, there is sufficient evidence to proceed.

The emphasis placed upon extra-judicial interventions is consistent with research which has found that placing low risk, low need youths in correctional programming may increase, rather than decrease, their chances of re-offending. Reid notes of this research that, "the best preventative strategy may be to restrain the use of the youth justice system, to do less criminal justice processing not more, and to let parents and community resources outside the justice system deal with the young person."[15]

(d) Restorative Justice

Broadly speaking, restorative justice refers to processes wherein the objective is to heal relationships, repair harm, and restore harmony. Unlike the traditional court-based, adversarial model in which the accused is pitted against the state in a bi-polar battle to determine a "winner," restorative justice processes involve a wider array of players—victims, offenders, family members and members of relevant communities of interest—in a dialogue that seeks to foster deeper awareness and understanding, active participation, and ultimately, reconciliation and restoration of harmony.

The *YCJA* stipulates that both extrajudicial sanctions and extrajudicial measures are to be administered in a manner that encourages young persons to acknowledge and repair the harm caused to the victim and the community, encourages families of young persons and the community to become involved in their design and implementation, and provides an opportunity for victims to participate in decisions related to the measures selected and to receive reparation. In other words, the *YCJA* must be administered in a manner consistent with restorative justice practices.

The *Act* also creates two other vehicles that offer additional potential for restorative justice practices: the conference; and youth justice committees. Under section 19, conferences (a group of people) may be convened by any decision-maker under the *Act* (be it a judge, a youth court worker, a police officer, etc. but note, controversially, not defence counsel), for the purpose of giving advice. While much depends upon how conferences are in fact utilized by various decision-makers, they certainly offer a vehicle for restorative justice approaches.[16] Youth justice committees, comprised of citizens appointed federally or provincially, have both advisory functions (*e.g.* to make recommendations regarding sentence) and educative functions (*e.g.* providing information to the public on the *Act*). The *Act* also contemplates a role for committees in supporting the victim of an alleged offence, facilitating the reconciliation of the victim and the young person and in coordinating any child welfare intervention with that of the criminal justice system.[17]

The enhanced potential for the use of restorative justice practices under the *YCJA* is particularly important for Aboriginal communities and Aboriginal youths, who are over-represented at every stage of the youth justice system, a system which has, through discriminatory practices, contributed to that over-representation.[18]

(e) Rights

Young persons charged under the *YCJA* are entitled to not only all of the rights (both statutory and constitutional) of an adult accused person, but also to special protection of those rights. Upon arrest or detention, a youth must be advised, in language appropriate to his or her age and understanding, of the right to remain silent,[19] warned of the potential use of any statement made against him or herself,[20] told of the right to consult with counsel and a parent or other adult,[21] and advised of the right to have one or more of those persons present when he or she makes a statement.[22] Any waiver of these rights must be in writing or recorded on video tape or audio tape.[23]

The right to counsel, protected not only by the *Act* but by the *Constitution*, is further enhanced by section 25, which creates an obligation upon the court to advise an unrepresented youth of his or her right to counsel and if the youth is unable to retain counsel, to direct that counsel be provided. Section 25 also makes clear that young persons have the right to personally exercise the right to counsel. In other words, counsel represents and takes instructions from the youth, not from the youth's parent(s) or guardian(s).

(f) Pre-Trial Detention

A youth who is detained has the right to be brought before a judge within 24 hours to determine whether he or she will be held pending trial.[24] The test for "bail" or "judicial interim release" is the same as for adults: whether detention is necessary for the protection or safety of the public, or to ensure the accused's attendance in court. The *Act* also attempts to address the concern that pre-trial detention was being used inappropriately for child welfare or mental health purposes by explicitly precluding its use for such ends (s. 29(1)). A youth who is detained must be held separate and apart from adults unless to do so would compromise his or her safety or the safety of others, or there is no place of detention for young persons within a reasonable distance.

(g) Sentencing

The *Act* sends several clear messages regarding sentencing: custody should generally not be used for non-violent young persons; over-reliance on custody should be reduced; all available sanctions other than custody that are reasonable in the circumstances must be considered; sentences should promote rehabilitation and reintegration and must be meaningful to the young person; timely dispositions are critical; and sentences must be proportionate to the gravity of the offence.[25] It is also significant to note the absence of particular sentencing principles found in the adult system: specific deterrence; general deterrence; denunciation; and incapacitation.[26] Despite their absence from the legislation, there continues to be a debate as to whether such principles may be invoked in sentencing.[27]

A range of dispositions exist under the *YCJA*: reprimand; absolute discharge; conditional discharge; a fine of up to $1,000; monetary restitution to the victim(s); restitution of property; performance of personal service (with the victim's consent); up to 240 hours of community service; probation of up to two years; participation in a community based program of intense community supervision or support; attendance at a non-residential program of up to six months; deferred custody and supervision for a period not exceeding 6 months (similar to an adult conditional sentence); and custody. As with the *YOA*, provinces are to maintain two levels of custody: open and secure. However, responsibility for the determination of which level of custody applies now rests presumptively with the provincial director, rather than the sentencing judge (although a province may opt to retain the *YOA* approach of having the sentencing judge make this determination).

The maximum combined length of sentence is ordinarily two years, and any custodial sentence must be followed by a supervision order which is one half as long as the period of custody (custody plus supervision cannot exceed two years). More severe sentences are reserved for first degree murder (a maximum of ten years of which no more than six are to be served in custody, with the balance under supervision in community),[28] second degree murder (seven years with a maximum of four years in custody),[29] attempt to commit murder, manslaughter or aggravated sexual assault (three years),[30] and for "presumptive offences" (an "adult sentence").

Presumptive offences have proven to be a controversial part of the new legislation. Under the *YOA*, as amended in 1995, youths aged 16 and 17 charged with murder, attempted murder, manslaughter or aggravated sexual assault would be tried as adults in ordinary courts, unless the young person or Crown applied to have the matter proceed within youth court. The *YCJA* eliminated transfers, but in their place created the "presumptive offence," defined as an offence committed by a person aged 14 or older (provinces can raise the minimum age to 15 to 16) under one of the following provisions of the *Criminal Code*: first or second degree murder; attempted murder; manslaughter; aggravated sexual assault; or any serious violent offence for which an adult is liable to a term of more than two years if the youth has two previous judicial determinations that he or she has committed a serious violent offence.[31] If convicted of a presumptive offence, the youth court will issue an "adult sentence" (any sentence that could be imposed on an adult convicted of the same offence) unless the youth is able to persuade the court that a youth sentence would be sufficient to hold him or her accountable.[32] In so doing, the *YCJA* has expanded both the age range (now covering fourteen and fifteen year olds) and the list of offences for which an adult sentence will be presumptively meted out. It is in this regard that Bromwich and others argue that Parliament has responded to the calls to "get tough" on youthful offenders, anticipating increased numbers of youths serving adult sentences.[33] Beyond the presumptive offences, the Crown may also apply to have a youth aged 14 or over sentenced as an adult if the youth is convicted of any "serious violent offence" (defined as an offence causing or attempting to cause serious bodily harm) for which an adult would be liable to more than two years of imprisonment.[34] In these cases, the Crown bears the burden of establishing that a youth sentence would be insufficient to hold the accused accountable.[35]

The presumptive offence provisions have been constitutionally challenged in at least three provinces. Appellate courts in Ontario and Quebec (see *R. v. D. (B.)*[36] and *Québec (Ministre de la Justice) c. Canada (Ministre de la Justice)*[37]) have found the provisions to be unconstitutional, while the British Columbia Court of Appeal came to the contrary result (*R. v. T. (K.D.).)*[38] Significantly, the Ontario Court of Appeal found that the need to treat young persons separately and not as adults in administering criminal justice is a principle of fundamental justice within section 7 of the *Charter*, as is the burden upon the Crown to prove aggravating circumstances when a more severe penalty is sought.[39] The Court concluded that the presumption of an adult sentence, wherein the youth bears the onus of dislodging that presumption, violates both these principles of fundamental justice and is therefore unconstitutional. No doubt, the disagreement between appellate courts will ultimately result in the issue making its way before the Supreme Court of Canada for final resolution.

Another significant issue relates to the use of custody. As noted, much concern was expressed regarding the over-use of custody under the *YOA*, particularly as a response to non-violent, and often minor, infractions. There was a specific concern about the use of custody for system-generated breaches, such as breaches of existing orders or failing to appear in court. Statistics Canada data for 1998-99 reveal the magnitude of the concern; 31% of youth in custody were there for failing to appear in court or for breaching their original sentence disposition, usually probation.[40] While the *Act* gives many signals that custody is to be reserved primarily for "violent offences" (a phrase that the Supreme Court of Canada has indicated must be interpreted narrowly as "causing, attempting to cause, or threatening bodily harm," *R. v. D. (C.)*;[41] *R. v. R. (C.D.)*[42]) and used only as a last resort (only if no other alternative will be sufficient to hold the young person accountable), section 39 also contemplates its use where a youth has failed to comply with non-custodial sentences. Thus, it remains to be seen whether section 39 will be relied upon to incarcerate youths for the breach of existing dispositions, the conditions of probation in particular. Here it is also crucial to note that often the conditions attached to probation are ambiguous (*e.g.* be of good behaviour), or compliance lies outside of the control of the young person alone (*e.g.* attend school or reside in a particular location). These features mean that conditions can be easily breached and thus, the circumstances surrounding a potential breach need to be very carefully considered.

(h) Publication of Names

Like its predecessor, the *YCJA* precludes, subject to particular exceptions, the publication of the name of a young person or any other information related to a young person, if it would identify the young person as a young person dealt with under the *Act*.[43] The exceptions to this general prohibition arise presumptively where a young person receives an adult sentence, or where a young person receives a youth sentence for a presumptive offence. As with the presumptive offence provisions, these exceptions to the general prohibition have also come under constitutional scrutiny. Courts of appeal in both *Québec (Ministre de la Justice) c. Canada (Ministre de la Justice)* and *R. v. D. (B.)* ruled that the exceptions to non-disclosure violated section 7 of the *Charter,* holding that the stigmatization and labeling of youths that can result from publication compromises the psychological security of the young person (bringing the conduct with section 7),[44] and finding the bar on publication to be a "cornerstone of Canadian youth justice."[45]

In addition to the presumptive publication provisions, a peace officer may also apply to the court for an order permitting publication of information that identifies a young person if the young person is alleged to have committed an indictable offence, there is reason to believe she or he is a danger to others and publication of the information is necessary to assist in apprehending him or her.

Information identifying a young person as a victim or witness is similarly barred from publication.

(i) Role of Parents

The *YCJA* contains several provisions requiring that notice be given to parents (*e.g.* notice of arrest and detention and of extrajudicial sanctions administered). The *Act* also contemplates that for those parents who participate in the proceedings, or otherwise demonstrate an active interest, various additional sources of information will be shared with them (*e.g.* any medical reports or pre-sentence reports). Opportunities for parents to be heard are structured into various dimensions of the legal process, but with few exceptions it is the youth, rather than his or her parents, with whom the decision rests as to whether a procedure available under the *Act* will be initiated (*e.g.* whether to seek a "youth sentence" for a presumptive offence). If of the opinion that a parent's presence is necessary or in the best interests of the young person, the court may also compel the attendance of a parent. Beyond this, parental involvement is encouraged in the design of extrajudicial measures and certainly, in many restorative practices, one would imagine that parents will often be important participants.

While the *Act* envisions a strong parental role, it also makes clear that young persons are entitled to exercise *their* rights, in their own right, independently of their parents, including their right to counsel. While most parents may see themselves as the client, who ought to instruct counsel, in fact, it is the young person who instructs counsel and who enjoys a confidential and privileged relationship with counsel.[46]

A new provision of the *Act* enables provinces and territories to set up a program to recover, from parents and/or young persons, the costs of state-ordered legal representation.[47] While earlier case law under the *YOA* indicated that a youth court judge should inquire into the ability of parents to pay for counsel for the young person, an order requiring parents to pay could not be made. The effect of the new provision may well be, in some instances, to create a parental obligation to fund counsel. As Wilson notes, this gives rise to a concern that parents may encourage their children to plead guilty in order to minimize the potential legal costs, which could be very substantial.[48] But beyond this possibility, the additional financial exposure created for families, many of whom simply cannot afford counsel, will place further strain on what is often already a fraught parent-child relationship.[49]

(3) THE ROLE OF COUNSEL AND OF SOCIAL WORKERS

While social workers were key players within the child welfare model of the *JDA,* and lawyers were rarely participants, the due process model of the *YOA* led to a greatly enhanced role for legal counsel and a less prominent role for social workers. The *YCJA,* especially given its embracement of extrajudicial measures and sanctions, as well as the use of restorative practices, seems to invite a wider array of both professional and non-professional players into the task of rehabilitating and reintegrating young persons into the community.

The role of legal counsel in youth criminal justice proceedings has long been controversial. For ardent defenders of the due process model, counsel's duty is virtually the same as that owed to adult defenders: to advance all arguments, and put forward all defences, that will most likely secure the acquittal of the accused, or if found guilty, that will lead to the least intrusive sentence. By contrast, those aligned with a child welfare or treatment approach maintain that counsel should act in the best interest of a child, which may lie in not having a charge dismissed, but in a long period of custody for treatment purposes. Although some lawyers continue to support a "guardian" role, the lawyer as zealous advocate has come to dominate the field.[50] Nevertheless, the zealous advocate role does not mean that counsel should ignore obvious treatment needs of a young person (or any other client for that matter). Attention to these needs in making suggestions for sentence (not advocating for a longer sentence, but rather, on the young person's instructions, the particular form of sentence) or quite apart from the criminal process, facilitating the youth's ability to access services, are important dimensions of counsel's role. At the disposition stage, a lawyer who is knowledgeable about resources and services in the community can be of tremendous assistance to a client in obtaining a beneficial disposition. Many lawyers, however, may not be familiar with the range of resources in the community. This is an arena that would benefit from fruitful collaboration between social workers and lawyers.

Social workers play many roles in relation to youth criminal justice: in the preparation of pre-sentence reports addressing not only the needs of the young person, but also the resources available to address those needs; assisting in the preparation of medical or psychological reports; working with community based organizations that deliver services including those organizations funded to provide alternative sentencing programs; and as designated youth workers under the legislation. Importantly, a designated youth worker is assigned to every youth placed in custody and is charged with the task of planning and implementing a reintegration plan, including linking the youth with the most effective programs to meet his or her needs.

SELECTED READINGS

Anand, Sanjeev, "Crafting Youth Sentences: The Roles of Rehabilitation, Proportionality, Restraint, Restorative Justice, and Race Under the Youth Criminal Justice Act" (2003) 40 Alta. L. Rev. 943.

Bala, Nicholas, "Dispositions & Sentencing Under the Y.C.J.A: A Review of Principles & Case Law" (2005) available at http://law.queensu.ca/faculty/bala/papers/ycsasentencing.htm.

Barnhorst, Richard, "The Youth Criminal Justice Act: New Directions and Implementation Issues" (2004) 46 Canadian Journal of Criminology and Criminal Justice 231.

Bittle, Steven, Nathalie Quann, Tina Hattem, & Danielle Muise, "A One-Day Snapshot of Aboriginal Youth in Custody Across Canada" (2001) available online at http://canada.justice.gc.ca/en/ps/rs/rep/2001/snap1/index.html.

Bromwich, Rebecca Jaremko, "Compassion, Human Rights and Adult Sentencing Under the Y.C.J.A." (2002) 14 W.R.L.S.I. 71.

The Evolution of Juvenile Justice in Canada (2004), online: Department of Justice Canada International Co-operation Group <http://www.justice.gc.ca/en/ps/inter/juv_jus_min/JuvenileJusticeEvolution-EN.pdf>.

Doob, Anthony & Carla Cesaroni, *Responding to Youth Crime in Canada* (Toronto: University of Toronto Press, 2004).

Green, Ross Gordon & Kearney F. Healy, *Tough on Kids: Rethinking Approaches to Youth Justice* (Saskatoon: Purich Pub., 2003).

Hillian, Doug & Marge Reitsma-Street, "Parents and Youth Justice" (2003) 45(1) Canadian Journal of Criminology and Criminal Justice 19.

Hillian, Doug, Marge Reitsma-Street & Jim Hackler, "Conferencing in the Youth Criminal Justice Act of Canada: Policy Developments in British Columbia" (2004) 46 Canadian Journal of Criminology & Criminal Justice 343.

Latimer, Jeff, "A Meta-Analytic Examination of Youth Delinquency, Family Treatment and Recidivism" (2001) 43(2) Canadian Journal of Criminology and Criminal Justice 237.

Latimer, Jeff & Laura Casey Foss, "The Sentencing of Aboriginal and Non-Aboriginal Youth under the YOA" (2005) 47(3) Canadian Journal of Criminology and Criminal Justice 481.

Mann, Ruth, *Juvenile Crime and Delinquency: A Turn of the Century Reader* (Toronto: Canadian Scholars' Press, 2000).

Olivo, Laurence, David Goldstein & Ralph Cotter, *Youth and the Law: New Approaches to Criminal Justice and Child Protection* (Toronto: Emond Montgomery Pubs., 2001).

Schissel, Bernard, *Blaming Children: Youth Crime, Moral Panics and the Politics of Hate* (Halifax: Fernwood, 1997).

Sprott, Jane, "The Development of Early Delinquency: Can Classroom and School Climates Make a Difference?" (2004) 46(5) Canadian Journal of Criminology and Criminal Justice 553.

Tustin, Lee & Robert Lutes, *A Guide to the Youth Criminal Justice Act* (Toronto: LexisNexis Butterworths, 2004).

Wilson, Larry, "The Role of Counsel in the *Youth Criminal Justice Act*" (2003) 40(4) Alta. L. Rev. 1029.

Winterdyk, John, ed., *Issues and Perspectives on Young Offenders in Canada,* 3d ed. (Toronto: Thomson Canada Ltd., 2005).

ENDNOTES

1. *The Evolution of Juvenile Justice in Canada* (2004), online: Department of Justice Canada International Co-operation Group <http://www.justice.gc.ca/en/ps/inter/juv_jus_min/JuvenileJusticeEvolution-EN.pdf>.
2. *Ibid.*
3. S.C. 1908, c. 40.
4. Susan Reid, "Youth at Risk in the Youth Criminal Justice System" in

John Winterdyk, ed., *Issues and Perspectives on Young Offenders in Canada,* 3d ed. (Toronto: Thomson Canada Ltd., 2005) at 110. See *supra* note 1.

5. R.S.C. 1985, c. C-46.
6. See *supra* note 3 at s. 38.
7. General Assembly of the United Nations, Resolution 44/25 of November 20, 1989.
8. S.C. 1995, c. 19.
9. For example, the *Controlled Drugs and Substances Act,* S.C. 1996, c. 19.
10. Ross Gordon Green & Kearney Healy, *Tough on Kids: Rethinking Approaches to Youth Justice* (Saskatoon: Purich Publishing, 2003). Also, see *supra* note 4 at 115.
11. *Ibid.*
12. S.C. 2002, c. 1.
13. Nicholas Bala, "Dispositions & Sentencing Under the Y.C.J.A: A Review of Principles & Case Law" (2005) online: <http://law.queensu.ca/faculty/bala/papers/ycsasentencing.htm>.
14. Richard Barnhorst, "The Youth Criminal Justice Act: New Directions and Implementation Issues" (2004) 46 Canadian Journal of Criminology and Criminal Justice 231 at 232.
15. See *supra* note 4 at 115-6.
16. For a description of various conferences, see *supra* note 13.
17. See *supra* note 12 at s. 18.
18. Linda Fisher & Hannele Jantti, *Aboriginal Youth and the Youth Justice System,* in John Winterdyk, ed., *Issues and Perspectives on Young Offenders in Canada,* 3d ed. (Toronto: Thomson Canada Ltd., 2005) at 268-9, 279.
19. See *supra* note 12 at s. 6.
20. *Ibid.*
21. *Ibid.* at s. 25.
22. *Ibid.*
23. *Ibid.* at s. 146.
24. See *supra* note 5 at s. 503.
25. See *supra* note 13 for a thorough overview of sentencing.
26. See *supra* note 14.
27. See *supra* note 13.
28. See note 12 at s. 42(2)(q)(i).
29. *Ibid.* at s. 42(2)(q)(ii).
30. *Ibid.* at s. 42(r)(i)(B).
31. *Ibid.* at s. 69.
32. *Ibid.* at s. 62.

33. Rebecca Jaremko Bromwich, "Compassion, Human Rights and Adult Sentencing Under the Y.C.J.A." (2002) 14 Windsor Rev. Legal Soc. Issues 71.

34. See *supra* note 12 at s. 62.

35. *Ibid.* at s. 72(2)

36. *R. v. D.(B.)* (1986), 11 O.A.C. 236, 49 C.R. (3d) 283, 24 C.C.C. (3d) 187, 1986 CarswellOnt 93 (C.A.).

37. 175 C.C.C. (3d) 321, 2003 CarswellQue 538, 10 C.R. (6th) 281, 228 D.L.R. (4th) 63, [2003] R.J.Q. 1118, (sub nom. *Reference re: Bill C-7 respecting the criminal justice system for young persons*) 108 C.R.R. (2d) 189, [2003] J.Q. No. 2850, REJB 2003-39418, [2003] Q.J. No. 2850, 2003 CarswellQue 14745 (C.A.).

38. [2006] B.C.J. No. 253, 206 C.C.C. (3d) 44, 37 C.R. (6th) 243, 2006 BCCA 60, 2006 CarswellBC 287, 138 C.R.R. (2d) 336, 222 B.C.A.C. 160, 368 W.A.C. 160 (C.A.).

39. *Ibid.* at para. 62.

40. See *supra* note 10.

41. (2005), 261 D.L.R. (4th) 257, 2005 SCC 78, 2005 CarswellAlta 1869, 2005 CarswellAlta 1870, 343 N.R. 1, 34 C.R. (6th) 323, 203 C.C.C. (3d) 449, [2005] 3 S.C.R. 668, [2006] 5 W.W.R. 195, 376 A.R. 258, 360 W.A.C. 258, [2005] S.C.J. No. 79, 54 Alta. L.R. (4th) 67.

42. 110 W.A.C. 94, 1995 CarswellAlta 713, 178 A.R. 94, [1995] A.J. No. 1072 (C.A.).

43. See *supra* note 12 at s. 110(1).

44. *Québec (Ministre de la Justice) c. Canada (Ministre de la Justice)* and *R. v. D. (B.)* both ruled that exceptions to non-disclosure violated s. 7 of the *Charter*.

45. *Ibid.*

46. Larry Wilson, "The Role of Counsel in the *Youth Criminal Justice Act*" (2003) 40(4) Alta. L. Rev. 1029 at 1034.

47. See *supra* note 12 at s. 25(10).

48. See *supra* note 46 at 1036.

49. *Ibid.* at 1037.

50. *Ibid.* at 1033.

PART IV

SELECTED TOPICS IN "SOCIAL LAW"

22

Consent, Capacity, and Substitute Decision-Makers

(1) INTRODUCTION

Across a range of social work practices, issues of consent and capacity will arise. As we review below, issues of consent and capacity are regulated not only by the law but also by the ethical guidelines and standards of practice of social work.[1] Not only must social workers be constantly vigilant to ensure ongoing consent, they need to understand what may happen when a person lacks the capacity to give consent or to manage his or her personal care or property.

(2) CONSENT

At the core of the concept of consent are the rights to self-determination and autonomy, both of which are values central to social work practice. The rights to self-determination and autonomy engage fundamental issues such as bodily integrity, meaningful participation in decisions affecting us, and the control of information about ourselves. This ethical foundation of social work practice requires that social workers obtain consent of their clients to proceed with virtually any and every form of proposed intervention. The obtaining of consent is not only a fundamental ethical principle, it is a legal duty. In many instances, the failure to obtain consent where the intervention entails physical contact constitutes both the criminal offence of assault (touching without consent) and the tort of battery. The failure to obtain consent for the disclosure of confidential information may, in some circumstances, give rise to civil liability. Moreover, proceeding without consent, whether it be to an intervention or to the disclosure of information, may give rise to the possibility of a disciplinary proceeding against a social worker for the failure to meet established standards of practice.[2]

(a) Components of a Valid Consent

To be valid, consent must be informed, voluntary, not obtained through misrepresentation or fraud, and given by a person who has the capacity to do so.[3] The adequacy of the information provided is assessed on an objective standard: what would a reasonable person in similar circumstances require in order to make a decision? It is also important to note that consent can be withdrawn at any time.[4]

(b) Scope and Application of the *Health Care Consent Act*[5]

In Ontario, the *Health Care Consent Act, 1996 (HCCA)* regulates the conduct of "health practitioners" in regard to obtaining consent to treatment.[6] The *Act* applies consistently in all settings including hospitals for both psychiatric and acute care, homes for the aged, nursing homes, and long term care homes. Social workers are not included in the statutory definition of "health practitioners," so the provisions of the *Act* that deal with health care practitioners in obtaining consent to treatment are not directly applicable to social workers. However, the *HCCA* explicitly states that the *Act* does not affect the law relating to giving or refusing consent to anything not included in the definition of treatment. This means that the common law, described below, continues to apply.

The *Act* also provides that where there is a plan of treatment, one health practitioner may, on behalf of others involved in that treatment plan, determine capacity and obtain consent. As members of multi-disciplinary teams, social workers often work in settings where a "health practitioner," as defined by the *Act*, has determined capacity and obtained consent from the person who is the subject of the treatment plan.

The *Act*'s definition of consent very much tracks the common law: it must be informed, voluntarily given, and obtained without misrepresentation or fraud. To be informed, information must be provided regarding the nature of the treatment, the expected benefits, the material risks, the material side effects, the alternative courses of action, and the likely consequences of not having the treatment.[7]

(c) When Consent is Not Required

In limited circumstances social workers may proceed without consent. It is recognized that in emergencies, where immediate intervention is required and consent cannot be obtained, a social worker may proceed without consent (*e.g.* if the individual is delirious or unconscious and there is no other person available at that time to provide consent).

(d) Consent and Court-Ordered Assessments

Social workers in a variety of practice contexts work with clients who have been court-mandated to undergo an assessment (*e.g.* custody and access, persons charged criminally including youths in conflict with the law). It is important to recognize that the client has been ordered by a court to undergo the assessment. Participation is not volitional, but coerced, and thus runs contrary to a fundamental tenet of informed consent. Moreover, because it is often impossible to predict in advance what information may be revealed during an assessment or what the legal implications of that information may be, providing full information about the potential risks and benefits of the assessment in advance may prove difficult.

When undertaking a court ordered assessment, the social worker's ethical duty to advance the client's best interests is confounded by the duty owed to the court and to other parties (for example, children) involved in the court proceeding. The Guidelines for Ethical Practice of the Canadian Association of Social Workers indicate that in these situations, the social worker's primary duty is to the court (Guidelines 1.4.3).[8] Clients need to be informed of this duty to the court and that the social worker's assessment may not be in the client's best interests. Clients also need to be advised of the limits on confidentiality (Guidelines 1.4.3). While full disclosure of the duty to the court and of the limits of confidentiality may undermine the ability to develop a therapeutic alliance and may ultimately impair the quality of the assessment, the obligations (both ethical and legal) owed to the client appear to require it.

(e) Consent and the Disclosure of Client Information

Social workers are obligated to protect the confidentiality of all professionally acquired information. Disclosure is permitted only with client consent (which must be informed, voluntary, and given by a person with the capacity to do so) or where required or allowed by law to do so.[9] Two important exceptions to this general obligation are relevant to social work practice: the duty to report that a child may be in need of protection; and the duty to protect innocent third parties from harm (discussed in Chapter 26).

Social workers in Ontario are obligated under the *Child and Family Services Act*[10] *(CFSA)* to report "reasonable grounds to suspect" that a child may be in need of protection (as defined by the *CFSA)* and the information upon which the suspicion is based.[11] The failure to do so is an offence under the *CFSA*, with a maximum fine of $1,000 upon conviction.[12] The *CFSA* makes clear that this obligation applies notwithstanding confidentiality.[13] The Supreme Court of Canada in *Bella v. Young*[14] has also made it clear that statutory reporting obligations do not override all duties owing to the client.[15] In that case the Court found Memorial University and its professors to be negligent in reporting a social work student to child welfare authorities based solely upon a fact situation she had described in an appendix to a term paper. The fact situation, although not footnoted properly, was taken directly from a textbook and was not a confessional of the student—a fact that could have been readily determined by the University but was not. The Court held that the University owed a duty of care to the student, and that that duty had been breached because there was no information that, interpreted by a reasonable person, would suggest a child was in need of protection from the student.

The "public safety" exception is reflected in, for example, the Ontario College of Social Workers and Social Service Workers Standards of Practice, which permit the disclosure of client information without the client's consent, provided the disclosure is essential to the prevention of physical injury to self or others.[16] In some instances, the failure to do so may also give rise to a civil claim against a social worker, although the law in this area remains unsettled (see generally Chapter 26). It is generally accepted that many professionals have a "duty to protect" where they have information regarding a clear threat of serious harm to an identifiable victim. The Supreme Court of Canada has not yet considered this precise issue, but has considered when a solicitor-client privilege (a principle fundamental to the administration of justice) may be set aside because of public safety concerns. In that case, *Smith v. Jones*,[17] the Court identified three necessary elements: 1) a clear risk to an identifiable person or group of persons 2) a risk of serious bodily harm or death and 3) imminent danger.[18] The Court expressly noted that it was not addressing the issue of the establishment of a tort duty on doctors (or other professionals) to disclose confidential information when a public safety concern arises, as that issue was not squarely before the Court.[19] However, given that these considerations were seen by the Court to be sufficiently weighty to set aside the solicitor-client privilege, they are also likely to displace an obligation of confidentiality.

It is also important to distinguish the potential of *legal* liability for the failure to disclose or otherwise warn a victim and the *ethical* obligation to act to protect innocent parties from harm. In a given situation, although disclosure may not be required to avoid legal liability, it may be ethically required.

(3) CAPACITY

(a) The Concept of Capacity/Capable

Capacity (a term that has the same legal meaning as "capable") is essential to informed consent and more broadly, to the ability to be able to make decisions about such things as the management of property or of personal care. Capacity is not static, rather a person may have capacity to make one kind of decision but not another; or may have the requisite capacity at one time, yet not at another. Any assessment of capacity must therefore be context and time specific.

In Ontario, the *HCCA* addresses capacity in relation to consent to treatment (by health practitioners), admission to care facilities, and personal assistance services, while the *Substitute Decisions Act*[20] *(SDA)* speaks to capacity to manage property and to manage personal care.[21] Both these statutes, as well as the common law, include in the concept of capacity the ability to understand the information that is relevant to making a decision (*e.g.* about treatment or about the management of personal property) and the ability to appreciate the reasonably foreseeable consequences of a decision or lack of a decision. The law presumes capacity and social workers are entitled to rely on that presumption unless there are reasonable grounds to believe that capacity may be lacking. Significantly, the *HCCA* does not set a minimum age of consent, although many jurisdictions assume capacity at either sixteen or eighteen years of age.

(b) Capacity Assessments

It is helpful to distinguish three contexts in which capacity assessments occur: under the *HCCA* under the *SDA*; and in situations caught by neither the *HCCA* nor the *SDA*. Under the *HCCA*, various health professionals are designated as "capacity evaluators" for specific purposes: consent to treatment; consent to admission to a care facility; and consent to personal assistance service. A Regulation to the *HCCA* (O. Reg. 264/00) designates social workers as capacity evaluators for the purpose of determining whether a person is capable with respect to his or her admission to a care facility and with respect to a personal assistance service, but not regarding treatment.[22]

Under the *SDA*, assessors for the purposes of undertaking assessments of capacity (to manage property or personal care) are designated by Regulation. Social workers who have successfully completed a qualifying course and who comply with continuing education requirements and minimum annual numbers of assessments are assessors for purposes of the *SDA*. Such assessments can ordinarily only be carried out with the consent of the person to be assessed, however, in some limited instances, courts may order that a person undergo an assessment.

For matters not covered by either the *HCCA* or the *SDA*, social workers must be attentive to the existence of capacity to give consent. While they are entitled to rely upon a presumption of capacity, there will be circumstances where reasonable grounds exist to question capacity. The Canadian Association of Social Workers Guidelines for Ethical Practice indicate that social workers are to evaluate a client's capacity to give informed consent as early in the relationship as possible.[23]

(c) Importance of Personal Context to Capacity Assessment

In all assessments of capacity it is important for social workers to be aware of the client's beliefs, values, interests, and cultural context. It is important to monitor one's own attitudes and feelings and to be vigilant in order to avoid a finding of incapacity on the basis that the choices made are, from one's own vantage point, poor ones.

(4) SUBSTITUTE DECISION-MAKERS

(a) What is a Substitute Decision-Maker?

If a client/patient is found to be incapable for the purposes of decision-making regarding treatment, care facilities, or personal assistance service (decisions covered by the *HCCA*), a substitute decision-maker will be the one to give or refuse consent. While there are some modest differences in how decisions in each of these areas are addressed by the *Act*, in most material respects they are the same.

The *HCCA* creates a hierarchy of potential substitute decision-makers:

- guardian of the person (a person appointed under the *SDA*);
- attorney for personal care (a person designated in a power of attorney for personal care to make personal care decisions on someone else's behalf in the event of incapacity);
- representative appointed by the Consent & Capacity Board;
- spouse or partner;
- child or parent of the incapable person;

- brother or sister;
- any other relative;
- as a last resort, the Public Guardian and Trustee.[24]

(b) Obligations of Substitute Decision-Makers

Persons acting as substitute decision-makers are to act in accordance with any known wishes given by the incapable person while they were capable. If those wishes are not known, the substitute decision-maker is to act in the incapable person's best interests (and in this regard is required to consider a range of factors including whether the condition of the incapable person will be improved, his or her values and interests, and whether the benefits outweigh the risks).

Wishes may be expressed in a variety of ways, such as through a power of attorney or in any other written form, orally or in any other manner. Later wishes prevail over earlier wishes. A centrally important role that social workers play in enhancing the autonomy interests of their clients is to work with them, while capable, to make their wishes clearly known. Social workers are also an important resource to other health professionals in communicating information about the values, interests, beliefs, and wishes of persons who have been found to be incapable. Moreover, social workers are critical to the advancement of one of the express objectives of the *HCCA*—ensuring a significant role for supportive family members when a person lacks capacity to make a decision.

(c) Review of Findings of Incapacity

Persons found to lack capacity under the *HCCA* or under the *SDA* are entitled to apply to the Consent and Capacity Board for a review of that finding and may also apply to the Board to request that a representative of their choice be appointed to make decisions on their behalf regarding treatment, care facility admission, and personal assistance service.

(d) *Substitute Decisions Act*

The *SDA* addresses issues of capacity to manage property (capacity is assumed if aged eighteen years or older) and personal care (capacity is assumed if aged sixteen years or older), and also creates some of the vehicles through which particular substitute decision-makers listed in the *HCCA* are created: powers of attorney for property, powers of attorney for personal care; appointment by the Court of a guardian of property or a guardian of the person; and the appointment of a statutory guardian.

(e) Powers Of Attorney

Powers of attorney may relate to the management of property or personal care (including health care, nutrition, shelter, clothing, hygiene or safety). Powers of attorney for property may authorize the person named as attorney to do anything in respect of property that the person granting the power of attorney could do if capable, except make a will. A person may give a written power of attorney for personal care, authorizing the attorney(s) to make decisions on the grantor's behalf regarding personal care (including with respect to admission to a care facility or the use of personal assistance services) and may give specific instructions. The attorney is a fiduciary who must act in good faith and for the incapable person's benefit, follow his or her expressed wishes if known, and alternatively, act in his or her best interests. Like the *HCCA*, and consistent with social work values, attorneys are required to encourage the incapable person to participate, to the best of his or her abilities, in decisions about property or care, whichever the case may be. Attorneys are also required to foster regular personal contact between the incapable person and supportive family members and friends and to consult, from time to time, with them and with the person(s) from whom the incapable person receives personal care.

(f) Guardians of Property and of the Person

Any person may apply to the court for the appointment of a guardian of property or a guardian of the person. The court will only make such appointment if satisfied that the person is incapable and that no alternative course of action that would be less restrictive of the person's decision-making rights exists. A guardian owes the same duties and has the same obligations as those for attorneys described above. The Public Guardian and Trustee (PGT) is appointed as guardian only as a last resort.

(g) Statutory Guardian of Property

The PGT or someone approved by the PGT will become the statutory guardian of property if a person has no continuing power of attorney and is assessed as incapable. For those in the community or facilities other than a psychiatric facility, the PGT will become statutory guardian upon receipt of a certificate of incapacity from a qualified assessor. The assessor must explain to the person whose capacity is in issue the purpose of the assessment, the effect of the finding, and the right to refuse to be assessed. If a certificate is issued under the *Mental Health Act*[25] *(MHA)* certifying that a person who is a patient of a psychiatric facility is incapable of managing property, the PGT is the person's statutory guardian of property.

(h) Temporary Guardianship

If concerned that a client is incapable and that a significant loss to his or her property has or may result or that he or she may not be accessing the necessities of life or that serious illness, injury, deprivation of liberty, or personal security has or may result, the social worker should contact the PGT, who is required to investigate. If the PGT determines that a risk of this sort exists, the PGT will request a capacity assessment and may apply to the court for temporary guardianship.

SELECTED READINGS

Doron, Israel, "Mental Incapacity, Guardianship and the Elderly: An Exploration of Ontario's Consent and Capacity Board" (2003) 18(1) C.J.L.S. 131.

Hiltz, D'Aray and Anita Szigeti, *A Guide to Consent and Capacity Law in Ontario*, 2008 edition (Toronto: Butterworths, 2007).

Saks, Elyn R. & Dilip V. Jeste, "Capacity to Consent: A Snapshot of Contemporary Legal and Clinical Issues (2006) 24(4) Behav. Sci. & L. 409.

Schneider, Richard D., *The Annotated Ontario Mental Health Statutes*, 4th Edition (Toronto: Irwin Law, 2007).

ENDNOTES

1. See also Chapter 27.
2. *Ibid.*
3. *Health Care Consent Act, 1996*, S.O. 1996, c. 2, Sched. A at s. 11.
4. *Ibid.* at s. 14.
5. S.O. 1996, c. 2, Sched. A.
6. *Ibid.* at s. 13.
7. *Ibid.* at s. 11.
8. Social workers should also consult the guidelines of the associations or colleges in their respective provinces.
9. In Chapter 8 we discuss situations where the court may order disclosure of a confidential record.

10. R.S.O. 1990, c. C.11.

11. *Ibid.* at s. 72(1).

12. *Ibid.* at s. 72(6.2).

13. *Ibid.* at s. 72(7).

14. [2006] 1 S.C.R. 108, [2006] S.C.J. No. 2, 343 N.R. 360, 2006 SCC 3, 2006 CarswellNfld 19, 2006 CarswellNfld 20, 21 C.P.C. (6th) 1, (sub nom. *Young v. Bella*) 261 D.L.R. (4th) 516, 254 Nfld. & P.E.I.R. 26, 764 A.P.R. 26, 37 C.C.L.T. (3d) 161, [2006] R.R.A. 1.

15. *Ibid.* at para. 49.

16. *Code of Ethics and Standards of Practice, Principle 5.1.6*, online: Ontario College of Social Workers and Social Service Workers <http://206.221.245.198/sections/membership_info/current_members/ethicsandpractice.html>.

17. [1999] 1 S.C.R. 455, 132 C.C.C. (3d) 225, 169 D.L.R. (4th) 385, 22 C.R. (5th) 203, [1999] S.C.J. No. 15, (sub nom. *Jones v. Smith*) 60 C.R.R. (2d) 46, 236 N.R. 201, 1999 CarswellBC 590, 1999 CarswellBC 591, 120 B.C.A.C. 161, 196 W.A.C. 161, 62 B.C.L.R. (3d) 209, [1999] 8 W.W.R. 364, 1999 SCC 16.

18. This case is also discussed in Chapter 27.

19. See *supra* note 17 at para. 59.

20. S.O. 1992, c. 30.

21. For a helpful overview, see *A Guide to the Substitute Decisions Act*, online: Ministry of the Attorney General <http://www.attorneygeneral.jus.gov.on.ca/english/family/pgt/sdaact.asp>; and *The Role of the Office of the Public Guardian and Trustee in Providing Property Guardianship Services*, online: Ministry of the Attorney General <http://www.attorneygeneral.jus.gov.on.ca/english/family/pgt/ISBN-0-7794-5323-9.pdf>.

22. The Ontario College of Social Workers and Social Service Workers has established standards of practice for social workers undertaking these assessments.

23. See *supra* note 16 at principle 1.3.2.

24. See *supra* note 3 at s. 20.

25. R.S.O. 1990, c. M.7.

23

Mental Health and the Law

(1) CONFLICTING INTERESTS AND DUTIES

The last quarter of a century has seen growing recognition of the need to achieve a delicate balance between the rights to autonomy and the public duty to treat and protect those who may be at risk. The conflict weighs the right of the individual to be protected from state imposed restriction on freedom and the public interest in safety. Mental health professionals too, have an interest in providing care to those who may benefit from that care. A complicating factor is the extent to which one believes in the efficacy of psychiatric treatment and decision-making.

On the one hand, social workers seek to enhance self-determination and personal liberty, yet on the other, they are acutely aware of the need for treatment and anxious to protect both the individual and others from harm. This tension is not unique to social workers, but rather pervades the field of mental health.[1] This tension also relates to a debate within mental health with respect to the balance between responding to crisis or near-crisis situations through coercive state intervention and the provision of supports and services necessary for the integration of persons with significant mental illness into mainstream society. In this latter approach, the focus is on matters such as adequate housing, employment, and access to health care and other social services. The Canadian Mental Heath Association has noted that "although serious mental illness will remain traumatic, removing the crippling factors that often accompany it—poverty, social exclusion, stigma—and offering real support in a context of social acceptance will create the opportunity for consumers to live as valued citizens."[2]

(2) MENTAL HEALTH LEGISLATION

V In Ontario, the *Mental Health Act*[3] *(MHA)* identifies the different ways in which an individual can be admitted voluntarily or involuntarily to a psychiatric facility/ detailing both the criteria for admission and the procedures to be followed. It also articulates the rights of psychiatric patients and responsibilities of mental health service providers. Moreover, it provides the legislative framework for Community Treatment Orders (CTOs).

Persons are admitted to psychiatric facilities through a variety of different channels: as voluntary patients; as involuntary patients; as informal patients; and as remanded by the Criminal Justice System.

(a) Voluntary Patients

As the term implies, voluntary patients are those who are voluntarily admitted to psychiatric facilities. The *Act* specifically provides that none of its provisions authorize a psychiatric facility to detain or restrain a voluntary patient.[4]

(b) Involuntary Patients

The process of involuntary admission may be initiated by an examining physician, by a police officer, or by a justice of the peace acting upon information sworn before him or her, who may order an examination of the person by a physician. The initial process (Form 1) permits apprehension by the police and detention for up to 72 hours for the purposes of examination. Once examined, the person must be released or admitted as a voluntary or informal patient, or involuntarily admitted (Form 3). At its most basic, the test for involuntary admission focuses upon the potential of serious bodily harm to the person to be detained or to another person, or of serious physical impairment of the person to be detained.[5]

(c) Informal Patients

An informal patient is a person admitted to a psychiatric facility with the consent of another person under the *Health Care Consent Act*[6] (*"HCCA"*).[7] As with voluntary patients, nothing in the *Act* authorizes a psychiatric facility to detain or restrain an informal patient. The *HCCA* gives the substitute decision-maker authority to consent to the incapable person's admission to a psychiatric facility for purposes of treatment.[8] However, if the incapable person is sixteen years of age or older and objects, consent to his or her admission may only be given by a guardian of the person (if the guardian has this authority) or an attorney for personal care.[9] The latter will only apply where the power of attorney authorizes the attorney to use force that is necessary and reasonable in the circumstances to admit the incapable person to the psychiatric facility.[10]

(3) CRIMINAL JUSTICE SYSTEM

Persons with mental health issues are over-represented in the criminal justice system and in Canada's correctional institutions. Moreover, there are significant concerns regarding the frequency with which police are called upon to deal with persons suffering from serious mental illness. A recent study in London, Ontario found, for example, a significant upward trend in the number of hours police spent responding to largely non-violent nuisance type offences allegedly committed by persons with serious mental illness.[11] The study questioned, as have others, the appropriateness of a police response in these circumstances, rather than a community mental health response. In Ontario the deaths of persons suffering from mental illness caused by police interventions have given rise to additional concerns, including police use of lethal force and the inadequacy of police training in relation to mental illness. The Coroner's Jury in the case of the death of Otto Vass recommended, among other things, police use of and training in Tasers, improved training of police officers regarding mental illness (training that includes the active participation of psychiatric consumers/survivors), the creation of a specialized mobile crisis intervention team, and the opening of a structured dialogue between the police and mental health service providers.[12]

Ontario now has a Mental Health Diversion program that permits formal legal proceedings to be held in abeyance and for accused persons to undergo treatment in the community. There is also a specialized Mental Health Court that operates in Toronto and which has mental health workers on site.[13] Persons with mental health disabilities who are charged with criminal offences may be admitted to a psychiatric facility for assessment or treatment. For example, the *MHA* authorizes a judge who has reason to believe that an accused suffers from a mental disorder to order him or her to attend a psychiatric facility for examination or to remand that person for admission for a period of up to two months.[14] Part XX.1 of the *Criminal Code*[15] also enables judges to order assessments of an accused in a variety of circumstances, including where there is an issue of the accused's fitness to stand trial, and where the accused was at the time of the offence suffering from a mental disorder that might support a verdict of "not criminally responsible on account of mental disorder."[16]

(4) COMMUNITY TREATMENT ORDERS

The introduction of community treatment orders has been described as the "single most hotly contested event in the mental health legislative history" in Ontario.[17] Viewed from one vantage point, CTOs are a less restrictive alternative to hospitalization, enabling those with serious mental health problems to live in the community. Yet from another perspective, CTOs are seen as coercive by compromising the freedom of some of those who live in the community through the constant threat of involuntary hospitalization for failing to follow the treatment plan.

A CTO may be issued if during the previous three years a person was a patient in a psychiatric facility on two or more separate occasions or for a total cumulative time of 30 days during that 3 years, *or* has previously been under a CTO *and* several other requirements are satisfied.[18]

The person who is the subject of the CTO or the assigned substitute decision-maker must consent to the CTO.[19] Some question whether consent can be volitional in this context given that one's consent is expressed under pain of involuntary hospitalization.

The community treatment plan is developed by the physician, the person subject to the CTO and/or his or her substitute decision-maker, and others involved in aspects of the care, commonly social workers.[20] The plan will include requirements such as taking medication, keeping medical appointments, as well as other aspects of care. All those named in the Plan have a responsibility to implement the plan. The CTO's duration is six months, but it may be renewed.[21] Persons subject to a CTO may also request a review at any time to determine whether they are now capable of living in the community with a CTO.[22]

If the plan is not being followed, the physician must contact the person subject to the CTO, remind the person of his or her responsibilities, and provide assistance to meet those responsibilities. If the person still fails to comply, the physician may order an examination and the police will bring the person to the physician for assessment. The physician may then issue a new CTO, detain the person in a psychiatric facility for assessment, or release him or her.[23]

(5) RIGHTS ADVISORS

Rights advisors are designated to perform certain duties under the *MHA*. Among these duties, rights advisors are required to contact a person who is subject to a CTO and his or her substitute decision-maker to give information about the person's rights and obligations under the plan.[24] Rights advisors must also meet with patients when a certificate of involuntary admission or of incapacity has been issued to explain the significance of the certificate and the right to have it reviewed.[25]

(6) PERSONAL HEALTH INFORMATION

The *Mental Health Act* contains particular provisions regarding personal health information.[26] A psychiatric facility may use or disclose personal health information, with or without consent, for the purposes of examining, assessing, observing or detaining a patient. In addition, information may be disclosed to a physician who is considering a CTO, to another person named in a CTO, and to a prescribed person providing advocacy services. The *Act* also makes specific provision for court-ordered disclosure. In this regard, the *Act* directs facilities not to comply with a summons or order for production if a physician indicates in writing that disclosure would likely result in harm to the treatment or recovery of the patient or injury to the mental condition or bodily harm to a third party.[27] The court or decision-making body issuing the summons or order is directed to then hold a hearing, and may only order disclosure if satisfied that it is essential to the interests of justice.[28]

SELECTED READINGS

Kaiser, Archibald, "Imagining An Equality Promoting Approach to the Status Quo of Canadian Mental Health Law" (2003) 11 Health L.J. 185.

Gray, John & Richard O'Reilly, "Protecting the Rights of People with Mental Illness: Can We Achieve Both Good Legal Process and Good Clinical Outcomes?" (2002) 23(2) Health L. Can. 25.

Lawson Health Research Institute & Lisa Heslop, "Trends in Police Contact with Persons with Serious Mental Illness in London, Ontario" (London, Ont.: London Police Service, 2002).

Ontario Court of Justice, Mental Health Court Toronto, online: <http://www.ontariocourts.on.ca/ontario_court_justice/mentalhealth/index.htm>.

Szigeti, Anita, "Ontario's Community Treatment Orders: How Did We Get There and Where Do We Go Now? An Advocate's Perspective" (2001) 21 Health L. Can. 66.

ENDNOTES

1. Archibald Kaiser, "Imagining An Equality Promoting Approach to the Status Quo of Canadian Mental Health Law" (2003) 11 Health L.J. 185 and John Gray & Richard O'Reilly, "Protecting the Rights of People with Mental Illness: Can We Achieve Both Good Legal Process and Good Clinical Outcomes?" (2002) 23(2) Health L. Can. 25.
2. CHMA study, 1993 as quoted in Kaiser, *ibid.* at 190.
3. R.S.O. 1990, c. M.7 as amended by *Brian's Law (Mental Health Legislative Reform)*, proclaimed on December 1, 2000.
4. *Ibid.* at s.14.
5. *Ibid.* at ss. 15-17 and 20.
6. S.O. 1996, c. 2, Sched. A.
7. *Ibid.* at s. 1(c)(ii).
8. *Ibid.* at s. 24(1).
9. *Ibid.* at s. 24(2).
10. *Ibid.* at s. 24(2)(b).
11. Lawson Health Research Institute & Lisa Heslop, "Trends in Police Contact with Persons with Serious Mental Illness in London, Ontario" (London, Ont.: London Police Service, 2002).
12. See the verdict and recommendations of the Coroner's jury in the case of Otto Vass, online: <http://www.ppao.gov.on.ca/pdfs/sys-tas-vass.pdf>. The use of Tasers has recently become a matter of grave concern in light of the death of Robert Dziekanski in October, 2007.
13. See <http://www.ontariocourts.on.ca/ontario_court_justice/mental-health/index.htm>.
14. See *supra* note 3 at s. 21(1).
15. R.S.C. 1985, c. C-46.
16. *Ibid.* at s. 672.11.
17. Anita Szigeti, "Ontario's Community Treatment Orders: How Did We Get There and Where Do We Go Now? An Advocate's Perspective" (2001) 21 Health L. Can. 66.
18. See *supra* note 3 at s. 33.1(4).
19. *Ibid.* at s. 33.1(4)(f).
20. *Ibid.* at s. 33.1(4)(b).
21. *Ibid.* at s. 33.1(11).
22. *Ibid.* at s. 33.2(1).
23. *Ibid.* at s. 33.3.
24. *Ibid.* at s. 33.1(4)(e).
25. *Ibid.* at s. 38 (3).
26. *Ibid.* at s. 35.
27. *Ibid.* at s. 35(6).
28. *Ibid.* at s. 35(7).

24

Financial Safety Nets

(1) HISTORICAL BACKGROUND

In the post-World War II period, new social policies were developed and introduced at both the provincial and federal levels of government.[1] Many of these policies removed certain matters entirely from the play of market forces, while others regulated the market to minimize and/or socialize risk. The provision of education and health care, for example, became the responsibility of the state, and all citizens, irrespective of wealth, were entitled to them by virtue of their status as citizens. Legislation creating welfare and disability benefits, unemployment insurance, old age security, and compensation for injured workers acknowledged the vulnerability of each citizen to potential unemployment, ill health and disability, and material deprivation.

The benefit programs attaching to employment—such as unemployment insurance and workers' compensation—have long been more generous and less stigmatizing than residual, needs-tested social assistance ("welfare") programs. This differentiation has had a markedly gendered impact; men, due to their stronger labour market attachment, have had greater access to the more generous, less stigmatizing programs than have women.

Since the 1970s there has been a marked shift in economic and social policy; one which has significantly re-shaped the financial safety nets available to Canadians. This shift has affected virtually all income maintenance policies and programs, but has had the most dramatic impact upon social assistance programs.

(a) Revocation of *CAPA*

The federal government has staged a marked retreat from the social policy arena and its present day spending on social programs is the lowest since 1949.[2] Perhaps the most significant of the federal government's actions was its repeal of the *Canada Assistance Plan Act* (*CAPA*) in 1996.[3] *CAPA* had provided the legislative framework through which the federal government flowed money to the provinces for matters such as social assistance (a provincial head of power). Significantly, *CAPA* had operated both to create a statutory right to basic assistance and to establish some national standards. The legislation required provinces, in calculating benefits, to "take into account" the basic requirements of a person in need.[4] When called upon to interpret this provision, the Supreme Court of Canada found that provinces were required to do more than merely consider individuals' basic requirements.[5] Provinces were instead required to set benefit levels that were "compatible" with an individual's basic requirements, but not obligated to "fulfil" or "equal" basic requirements.[6] While the decision of the Supreme Court granted provinces considerable leeway in determining benefit levels, importantly, it did require that provinces set levels that approximated (were compatible with) basic requirements.

CAPA had also required that provinces provide an appeal process from decisions regarding assistance, that they not require a period of residency in the province as a condition of benefit receipt, and that they not deny assistance because an applicant refused to take part in a "work activity project."[7]

CAPA was replaced in 1996 with the Canada Health and Social Transfer (CHST), a block grant from the federal government to the provinces to cover health, education and social services with no conditions attached and no requirements that any percentage of the funds be dedicated to the provision of social assistance. In 2004 the CHST was replaced by the Canada Health Transfer and the Canada Social Transfer. For social assistance purposes, the critical moment was the introduction of the CHST, as the removal of conditions on funding opened the door for the provinces to substantially amend their welfare programs. Ontario and British Columbia both introduced sweeping reforms.

In addition to the revocation of *CAPA*, at both the federal and provincial level reforms were introduced to a variety of government benefit programs. Many of these reforms shared common features, including: the tightening of eligibility requirements (making it harder to qualify); reduction in benefit levels; reduction in the period of time benefits could be received; and increased surveillance for "fraud" and "abuse."

(b) Increasing Poverty Gap

These changes to the benefit programs that frequently provide support to the most vulnerable citizens have occurred at a time when the gap between rich and poor in Canada, [8] as well as the racialization of that gap, is growing.[9]

Persons who experience other forms of social disadvantage, based upon race, citizenship status, disability, single parent status, gender and Aboriginal ancestry experience disproportionately high rates of poverty and dependence upon social assistance regimes. Particular groups are more likely to experience persistent poverty, among them are lone parents (the vast majority of lone parents are women, and lone female parents experience much higher rates of poverty than do lone male parents—in 2003, 48.9% versus 20.0%)[10], Aboriginal people (Aboriginal women experience poverty at more than double that of non-Aboriginal women (36% versus 17%)), and persons with work-limiting disabilities.[11]

(2) ONTARIO'S SOCIAL ASSISTANCE REGIME

While we focus here upon Ontario's social assistance regime, we attempt to draw out the themes and issues which are common across many provincial social assistance regimes; and indeed which characterize many income support programs, both at the provincial and federal level.

As noted above, Ontario experienced significant reforms following the revocation of *CAPA*. For decades Ontario's social assistance regime was made up of two programs: family benefits (available to single parents and persons with disabilities); and general welfare assistance (available to the able-bodied, temporarily unemployed). Family benefits were higher than general welfare assistance, and persons in receipt of family benefits were also free of the requirement to search for work as was required of those in receipt of general welfare assistance, creating categories of what some have described as deserving and undeserving poor.

The *Social Assistance Reform Act, 1997* transformed this landscape, creating two new programs and re-drawing the line between the deserving and undeserving poor. "Ontario Disability Support Program" benefits are available to those who meet the definition of "disability" provided in the governing statute, the *Ontario Disability Support Program Act, 1997*.[12] All others who satisfy a needs test and other conditions are eligible, under the *Ontario Works Act, 1997,* for Ontario Works benefits; benefits that are even less generous than those available to persons with disabilities.[13]

In Ontario, 35% of the Ontario Works (welfare) caseload is comprised of single parents, the vast majority of whom are women[14] and persons who have satisfied the statutory definition of "disability" under the *Ontario*

Disability Support Program Act make up 51% of the overall social assistance caseload (Ontario Works and Ontario Disability Support Program combined).[15]

(a) Eligibility

Eligibility for either form of benefits is needs-based, and the total income and assets of a "benefit unit" is assessed in determining eligibility.[16] This means that if a person is living with his or her spouse (which itself has a particular definition for welfare purposes discussed later in the chapter), the income and assets of both spouses are assessed. In addition, prescribed personal and financial information must be provided by the applicant and by each dependent of the applicant.

To qualify for disability benefits, an applicant must, additionally, satisfy the statutory test of "disability." This test requires that:

(a)   the person has a substantial physical or mental impairment that is continuous or recurrent and expected to last one year or more;

(b)   the direct and cumulative effect of the impairment on the person's ability to attend to his or her personal care, function in the community and function in a workplace, results in a substantial restriction in one or more of these activities of daily living; and

(c)   the impairment and its likely duration and the restriction in the person's activities of daily living have been verified by a person with the prescribed qualifications. [17]

The difficulties of satisfying this test, and the problems presented by the application process itself, have been of ongoing concern. *Denial By Design. . .The Ontario Disability Support Program*, a 2003 report of the Income Security Advocacy Centre, details the "arduous and unrealistic barriers" the application process poses for the very people the legislation is ostensibly intended to benefit.[18]

(b) Benefit Levels

Across the country, welfare rates leave recipients well below Statistics Canada Low-Income Cut-Offs (LICOs). The National Council of Welfare, in its annual *Welfare Incomes* for 2005, notes that welfare incomes are woefully inadequate, and those in receipt of welfare, among the poorest of the poor.[19] Benefit levels as a percentage of the LICOs range from a low of 19% for a single employable in New Brunswick ($3,427/year) to a rare high of 73% for a lone parent with one child in Newfoundland and Labrador. The inadequacy of benefit levels means that persons in receipt of welfare regularly go without adequate food, accommodation and access to services (including phone and utilities).[20] In addition, inadequate income often generates a host of legal problems, including consumer debts, risk of eviction and family breakdown.[21]

In addition to associated legal problems, inadequate income leads to significant health problems. Ontario M.P.P. Deb Matthews, in a report prepared for the responsible Minister noted that under current rates it is impossible to provide children with the proper nutrition necessary for optimal brain development and readiness to learn.[22] In a survey of single parents in receipt of Ontario Works in Toronto two out of three indicated that they had run out of food, and one in two had used a food bank.[23] A recent report by Toronto Social Services, *Systems of Survival, Systems of Support* documents that after paying rent, many individuals and families are left with less than $5.00/day to meet all other basic requirements, and that "nutritious eating is simply not affordable for many people on social assistance in Toronto, making it difficult, particularly for children, to meet the energy and nutrient needs that are basic requirements of health."[24]

(c) Workfare

The revocation of *CAPA* also facilitated the introduction of workfare—the conditioning of benefit receipt upon participation in employment or work-readiness activities, the details of which are contained in individual contracts called "Participation Agreements."

In Ontario, the failure to comply with the conditions of eligibility regarding mandated employment assistance activities or to make "reasonable efforts" renders a person ineligible for income assistance, in the first instance for a period of three months, and thereafter, for periods of six months.[25] In addition, the legislation requires recipients to make reasonable efforts to become employed, if employed part-time to find full-time employment and if employed full-time and still eligible for benefits, to find higher paying waged work. Indeed, one of the articulated purposes of the *Ontario Works Act*, revealed by its title, is to recognize individual responsibility and promote self-reliance through paid employment.[26]

Ontario Works redefines most single mothers as workers; women are exempted from workfare only until their children reach school age (age three or four). In some jurisdictions, women are exempted only until their children are three months of age.[27]

(d) Spouses

As noted above, "spouse" has a particular definition for welfare purposes; a definition which in Ontario has changed radically over time and one which varies from province-to-province. While for a brief period from 1987-1995 the definition largely tracked the definition in the *Family Law Act* (simply put, married, had a child together, or cohabited for a period of three years), this definition was changed in 1995. The definition introduced in 1995 created a presumption that any two persons of the opposite sex who co-resided in the same residence were spouses.[28] If they challenged this conclusion, a determination of spousal status turned upon whether one provided financial support to the other *or* there existed a "mutual agreement or arrangement regarding their financial affairs" *and* the extent of the social, familiar and financial aspects of the relationships were consistent with cohabitation."[29] The new regulations were introduced on October 1, 1995 and by April, 1996, 10,013 recipients had been declared ineligible directly due to the new definition. Of these 89% were women, 79% were sole support parents, and of the sole support parents rendered ineligible, 96% were single mothers.[30]

This definition of "spouse" was subject to a constitutional challenge in *Falkiner et al. v. Director, Income Maintenance Branch, Ministry of Community and Social Services and Attorney General of Ontario.*[31] Ultimately the Ontario Court of Appeal found the definition to violate section 15 of the *Charter,* discriminating against the applicants (four women in receipt of social assistance) on the basis of their sex, marital status and their receipt of social assistance.[32] In coming to this conclusion, the Court found that the new definition disproportionately and adversely affected women, and perpetuated the historical disadvantage experienced by single mothers.[33] Importantly as well, the court concluded that the definition of spouse forced women to become financially dependent upon men "with whom they have at best a try-on relationship" and is so doing, "strikes at the core of human dignity."[34]

The government of Ontario subsequently introduced a new definition of spouse, one which many advocates believe fails to adequately honour the ruling of the Ontario Court of Appeal. The most significant feature of the new definition is that couples may now co-reside for a three month period before presumed to be spouses. The new definition of spouse provides that,

> "spouse", in relation to an applicant or recipient, means . . .
>
> (d) a person who has been residing in the same dwelling place as the applicant or recipient for a period of at least three months, if,

> (i) the extent of the social and familial aspects of the relationship be-tween the two persons is consistent with cohabitation, and
>
> (ii) the extent of the financial support provided by one person to the other or the degree of financial interdependence between the two persons is consistent with cohabitation.[35]

It is important to observe that the definition is now no longer hetero-sexual. In addition to the *Falkiner* case, the definition was impacted by the Supreme Court of Canada's decision in *H. (D.) v. M. (H.).*[36] In that case the Court found the definition of spouse under Ontario's *Family Law Act* sup-port provisions to violate the equality rights of gays and lesbians. Formerly governing relationships between "two persons of the opposite sex," the welfare regime now governs relationships between "any two persons" who co-reside.

The ambiguity of the definition makes it difficult in many situations for women (who as the statistics noted above reveal, bear the brunt of this new definition) to know at just what point in a relationship they will be found to be "co-residing" with a "spouse" (two separate, but inter-related, inquiries).

As with so many areas of social assistance law, this ambiguity opens a great deal of room for interpretation in its application. A detailed Minis-terial policy directive provides some guidance here, listing a number of relevant sources of information to determine co-residency: driver's license history; employment records; common phone numbers; and credit checks.[37] Factors to be considered for "spousal" determinations include an agreement about joint financial arrangements, contributions toward shared costs of necessities, shelter and services, money given or loaned, whether they are known by public authorities as a couple, arrangements for sharing household chores, groceries or meals, sharing childcare, caring for the other when ill, and receipt or acceptance of invitations as a couple. However, as the policy directive itself indicates, "there is no correct number of questions that must be answered a certain way" to conclude either spousal status or co-residency; rather all factors must be weighed together. In practice, situations vary widely as to when persons are deemed to be spouses, and/or deemed to be co-residing. For those in receipt of social assistance, the ambiguity and uncertainty can generate fear and indeed a reticence to become involved in intimate relationships.[38]

(e) Obligation to Pursue Support

Persons in receipt of social assistance are required to take all reason-able steps to secure other sources of financial support.[39] While this usually entails pursuing child support, it may also entail pursuing support owing under an immigration sponsorship (see Chapter 25). If it is concluded that all reasonable steps have not been taken, then the Director may deny benefits altogether, or reduce benefits by the amount that he or she determines would have been available if reasonable efforts had been expended.[40]

(i) Discretion

This provision regarding support provides a good illustration of a common feature of many income maintenance regimes; the vesting of a large amount of discretion in those charged with the administration of the regime. Discretion is often contrasted with "rules"; the latter unequivocally directing the outcome in defined circumstances and the former creating room for the consideration of various contextual factors to determine the outcome in a given case. Here the statutory language creates discretion in at least three ways: the director "may" (not "shall") deny or reduce benefits; the director interprets what is "reasonable" in a given case; and the director is given the choice between a complete denial of benefits, or a reduction (and if the latter, determines how much of a reduction). While discretion has the advantage of fashioning a response that is attentive to the particulars and dynamics of a situation, it also creates the potential for arbitrary or capricious decision-making. In the legal context, discretion is to be exercised in good faith, uninfluenced by irrelevant considerations or motives, reasonably, and within the statutory bounds of the discretion.[41]

In many respects, the Ministerial policy directives, such as the one addressing spousal status referred to above, provide some structure to the exercise of discretion granted under the governing legislation. In the context of the obligation to seek support, the governing policy directive itself indicates that its role is to provide "direction" on the treatment of cases where child or spousal support may be available.[42] The directive articulates a number of standards, among them that,

- individuals at risk of domestic violence are not expected to pursue support;
- if there is potential for support, the target for having support provisions in place is within 120 days from the date of application for assistance. In cases where entering into an agreement for support is not possible or appropriate, court proceedings are initiated in a timely fashion;
- delivery agents defend their own and Ministry arrears, including negotiating settlements where appropriate, with due diligence; and
- searches are conducted for spouses or same-sex partners whose whereabouts are unknown.

As described in the standards, individuals at risk of domestic violence are not expected to pursue support. The Directive provides further details to operationalize this policy.

> A temporary waiver of support for three months shall be granted to those applicants or participants who have left the home because of violent situations. . . . If at application there is no clear evidence to establish abuse, the applicant is expected to participate in establishing a claim of abuse, i.e. obtaining third party verification within three months. . . . After three months, the situation is reviewed. Where domestic violence can be verified (by police, doctor, counsellor, etc.), a further temporary waiver or extended temporary waiver of up to 12 months should be considered. There is flexibility to permit waivers of a period longer than 3 months when it is reasonable to do so under all of the circumstances.[43]

Importantly, the policy directive provides some structure to those exercising discretion in assessing the reasonableness of efforts to obtain support and whether benefits should be denied or reduced. Note as well that a matter of fundamental importance—whether and how domestic violence should be factored into decision-making—is not addressed at the level of the governing statute nor regulations, but rather through policy directives. Troubling, however, is research that indicates that many of those who apply for welfare, and often many of their advocates, are unaware of these policy directives, and frequently not advised of them even when they apply for welfare.[44]

(3) NEGATIVE STEREOTYPING

A pervasive feature of the Canadian landscape has been the stereotyping of those in receipt of social assistance as lazy, immoral, untrustworthy and if women, promiscuous and inadequate mothers. As noted in Chapter 3, The Canadian Human Rights Act Review Panel reported that in undertaking its review it heard more about poverty than any other issue. In its report the Panel documents the stereotypes and consequent discrimination routinely experienced by those living in conditions of poverty and strongly recommends the inclusion of social condition as a prohibited ground of discrimination to redress these conditions.

Similarly, in 1988, the Social Assistance Review Committee (a committee that undertook the most comprehensive review ever undertaken of Ontario's social assistance regime) noted the "widespread stigma experienced by recipients" and observed that misconceptions about both the programs and their beneficiaries abound: about the needs and aspirations of recipients; their reasons for requiring assistance; how long they required assistance; and whether they were genuinely in need. The Committee concluded that social assistance is probably the most poorly understood of Canada's social programs.[45]

Additionally, the Ontario Court of Appeal, in its decision in *Falkiner* (discussed above) observed that "persons on social assistance are often stigmatized and feel themselves unworthy. The serious invasions of their privacy and the unwarranted assumption of their dependency upon a man occasioned by the Regulation can only reinforce this unfortunate aspect of their lives."[46]

These forms of stereotyping are experienced routinely by many clients of social workers; they are denied access to housing, to goods and services, and to employment. Moreover the stereotypes are often invoked within the legal system to judge their ability as parents or their credibility as witnesses and within the political process to justify shrinking welfare programs and aggressive surveillance measures.

(4) FRAUD/ABUSE

Certainly one issue that has received a great deal of attention in the past decade has been that of welfare "fraud." Here we put quotations around the word "fraud," because although this is the term commonly used, in fact the vast majority of conduct that is being referred to is not in fact "fraud," as defined by the *Criminal Code*. Rather, commonly all over-payments made, even where they arise through error or misunderstanding, are attributed to the "fraudulent" behaviour of welfare recipients. The tremendous complexity of the welfare regime—and thus the potential for significant numbers of errors—has been widely acknowledged. Yet many of these errors are wrongly characterized as "fraud," and vulnerable citizens who often have no access to legal advice or representation all too often accept blame (either civilly through agreeing to repay an overpayment or criminally by pleading guilty to a fraud charge).

"Fraud" has been portrayed as an extensive problem and several measures introduced in Ontario to address it, including new powers to Eligibility Review Officer (EROs), whose role it is to investigate allegations of fraud. An ERO may conduct searches of non-dwelling places without a warrant or obtain a warrant to investigate a dwelling. If an ERO wishes to question a neighbour or relative about someone suspected of breaking the regulations, the person being questioned risks being charged with an offence if she or he does not co-operate.[47] Additionally, an ERO is empowered to question and demand answers from the subject of the investigation. While there is a good argument that in some circumstances these interviews constitute a *de facto* criminal investigations and that as such, the *Charter* rights of the person being questioned come into play, currently it seems that these rights are ignored.

For a period of time, Ontario also implemented a ban on welfare receipt if convicted of welfare fraud. The government first introduced a three-month ban on receipt of benefits for a first conviction for welfare fraud; six months for subsequent convictions. These provisions were changed to a lifetime ban effective April 1, 2000. From then until November 27, 2002 the lifetime ban was imposed in 106 cases of welfare fraud; 58 of these involved a parent(s) with children. This was revoked in January, 2004 and at the same time a new Policy Directive introduced, making referral to the police mandatory in every case where there exist reasonable grounds to suspect the intent to commit fraud.[48]

The attention given to fraud within welfare programs has fundamentally altered the relationship between workers (many of whom are social workers) and their clients. In research under taken by Herd & Mitchell, welfare recipients they interviewed reported that the climate in their relationship with welfare offices and workers was permeated with suspicion and hostility.

> The new system is more concerned with surveillance and deterrence, than it is with assisting people to find employment. . . .[o]verall the mood of the focus groups was that the new system was inspiring a greater degree of suspicion and hostility. . . more concerned with constant surveillance and treating "everybody like they're cheating the system"". [49]

SELECTED READINGS

Broad, Dave & Wayne Antony, eds., *Citizens or Consumers? Social Policy in a Market Society* (Halifax: Fernwood, 1999).

Burstein, Meyer, "Combating the Social Exclusion of At-Risk Groups" PRI Project, *New Approaches for Addressing Poverty and Exclusion,* Policy Research Initiative (Government of Canada, November, 2005).

Currie, Ab, *A National Survey of the Civil Justice Problems of Low and Moderate Income Canadians: Incidence and Patterns* (Ottawa: Research and Statistics Division, Department of Justice, December, 2005).

Galabuzi, Grace-Edward, *Canada's Creeping Economic Apartheid* (Toronto: Centre for Social Justice Foundation for Research and Education, 2001).

Herd, Dean & Andrew Mitchell, *Discouraged, diverted and disentitled: Ontario Works New Service Delivery Model* (Toronto: Community Social Planning Council of Toronto and the Ontario Social Safety Network, 2002).

Matthews, Deb, *Report to the Honourable Sandra Pupatello, Minister of Community and Social Services: Review of Employment Assistance Programs in Ontario Works and Ontario Disability Support Program, December* (Toronto: Ministry of Community and Social Services, December, 2004) at 17.

Mosher, Janet, Pat Evans & Margaret Little. *Walking on Eggshells: Abused Women's Experiences of Ontario's Welfare System* (2004), is available online: Woman and Abuse Welfare Research Project, http://dawn.thot.net/walking-on-eggshells.htm.

National Council of Welfare, *Poverty Profiles, 2005* (Ottawa: National Council of Welfare, 2006).

Yalnizyan, Armine, *Canada's Great Divide: The Politics of the Growing Gap Between Rich and Poor in the 1990s* (Toronto: Centre for Social Justice, 2000).

ENDNOTES

1. See generally Dave Broad and Wayne Antony, eds., *Citizens or Consumers? Social Policy in a Market Society* (Halifax: Fernwood, 1999).
2. Janine Brodie, "The Politics of Social Policy in the Twenty-First Century" in Broad and Antony, eds., *supra* note 1.
3. *Canada Assistance Plan Act*, R.S.C. 1985, c. C-1.
4. *Ibid.* s. 6(2)(a).
5. *Finlay v. Canada (Minister of Finance)*, [1993] 1 S.C.R. 1080, (sub nom. *Finlay v. Canada*) 63 F.T.R. 99 (note), 1993 CarswellNat 1381, 1993 CarswellNat 1887, EYB 1993-67291, 150 N.R. 81, 101 D.L.R. (4th) 567.
6. *Ibid.* at para. 81.
7. See *supra* note 3 at s. 6(2)(d), 7(e) and s. 15(3). Section 15(3) provided that, "[e]very agreement made pursuant to this section shall (a) provide that no person shall be denied assistance because he refuses or has refused to take part in a work activity project."
8. Armine Yalnizyan, *Canada's Great Divide: The Politics of the Growing Gap Between Rich and Poor in the 1990s* (Toronto: Centre for Social Justice, 2000).
9. Grace-Edward Galabuzi, *Canada's Creeping Economic Apartheid* (To-

ronto: Centre for Social Justice Foundation for Research and Education, 2001).

10. National Council of Welfare, *Poverty Profiles, 2002 and 2003* (Ottawa: Summer 2006) at 39.

11. Meyer Burstein, "Combating the Social Exclusion of At-Risk Groups" PRI Project, *New Approaches for Addressing Poverty and Exclusion*, Policy Research Initiative (Government of Canada, November, 2005).

12. S.O. 1997, c. 25, Sched. B.

13. S.O. 1997, c. 25, Sched. A.

14. See Social Assistance Statistical Report: out of an overall caseload of 204,222 cases as of March, 2006, 71,347 were sole support parents. http://www.mcss.gov.on.ca/NR/MCFCS/OW/Caseload/en/OW-MAR2006_En.pdf.

15. Adding 204,222 cases of Ontario Works recipients as of March, 2006, and the 215,268 cases in the Ontario Disability Support Program caseload (419490), online: <http://www.mcss.gov.on.ca/NR/MCFCS/ODSP/Caseload/en/ODSPMAR2006_en.pdf>.

16. See *supra* note 13.

17. See *supra* note 12 at s. 4(1).

18. Online: <http://www.incomesecurity.org/paytherent/resources/pdf_R/ISAC.pdf>.

19. National Council of Welfare, *Welfare Incomes, 2005* (Ottawa: National Council of Welfare, 2006).

20. Janet Mosher, Pat Evans & Margaret Little, *Walking on Eggshells: Abused Women's Experiences of Ontario's Welfare System* (2004), online: Woman and Abuse Welfare Research Project, <http://dawn.thot.net/walking-on-eggshells.htm>.

21. Ab Currie, *A National Survey of the Civil Justice Problems of Low and Moderate Income Canadians: Incidence and Patterns* (Ottawa: December, 2005).

22. Deb Matthews, *Report to the Honourable Sandra Pupatello, Minister of Community and Social Services: Review of Employment Assistance Programs in Ontario Works and Ontario Disability Support Program, December* (Toronto: Ministry of Community and Social Services, December, 2004) at 17.

23. Toronto Community & Neighbourhood Services, *Social Assistance & Social Exclusion: Findings from Toronto Social Services 2003 survey of single parents on Ontario Works* (Toronto: Community & Neighbourhood Services) at 17. See also Kate Bezanson, "Gender and Household Insecurity in the Late 1990s" in Kate Bezanson & Meg Luxton (eds.), *Social Reproduction* (Montreal: McGill-Queens, 2006) at 188-90.

24. Toronto Social Services, *Systems of Survival, Systems of Support* (Toronto: Toronto Social Services, April, 2006) at 24, 28.

25. O. Reg. 134/98, ss. 3, 33.

26. *OWA*, see *supra* note 13 at s. 1.

27. Lauren A. Smith et al., "Implications of Welfare Reform for Child Health: Emerging Challenges for Clinical Practice and Policy" (2000) 6 Pediatrics 1117.

28. R.R.O. 1990, Reg. 366, s. 1(1)(d) amended.

29. *Ibid.*

30. *Falkiner et al v. Director, Income Maintenance Branch, Ministry of Community and Social Services & Attorney General of Ontario*, decision of Ontario Court of Appeal (May 13, 2002), online: <http://www.ontariocourts.on.ca/decisions/2002/may/falkinerC35052.htm>.

31. *Ibid.*

32. *Ibid* at para. 3. The government defended its new definition, arguing that rather than detracting from equality as the applicants alleged, it promoted equality as between "common law" and married couples.

33. *Ibid* at para. 96.

34. *Ibid* at para.101.

35. O. Reg. 134/98 as amended. The definition of spouse also includes those who have declared themselves to be spouses, and those who have actual support obligations pursuant to family law legislation or a domestic contract.

36. *H. (D.) v. M. (H)*, [1999] 1 S.C.R. 328, 169 D.L.R. (4th) 604, (sub nom. *N.H. v. H.M.*) 236 N.R. 173, 120 B.C.A.C. 252, 196 W.A.C. 252, [1999] S.C.J. No. 8, 45 R.F.L. (4th) 270, [1999] 2 C.N.L.R. iv, 1999 CarswellBC 281, 1999 CarswellBC 282, reconsideration refused 1999 CarswellBC 908, 121 B.C.A.C. 146, 198 W.A.C. 146, 238 N.R. 80, 172 D.L.R. (4th) 305, 45 R.F.L. (4th) 273, 1999 CarswellBC 909, [1999] 2 C.N.L.R. iv (note), [1999] 1 S.C.R. 761, [1999] S.C.J. No. 22.

37. Ontario Ministry of Community and Social Services, Ontario Works Policy Directive # 19, September, 2001.

38. See *supra* note 20.

39. O. Reg. 134/98, s. 13(1).

40. *Ibid.*

41. J.H. Grey, "Discretion in Administrative Law" (1979) 17 Osgoode Hall L.J. 107 at 114.

42. Ministry of Community and Social Services, Ontario Works Policy Directive #23, January, 2004.

43. *Ibid.*

44. See *supra* note 20.

45. *Report of the Social Assistance Review Committee: Transitions* (Toronto: Queen's Printer, 1988) at 27.
46. See *supra* note 30 at para.100.
47. O. Reg. 134/98, s. 65.
48. Ministry of Community and Social Services, Ontario Works Policy Directive #45, August, 2003.
49. Dean Herd & Andrew Mitchell, *Discouraged, diverted and disentitled: Ontario Works New Service Delivery Model* (Toronto: Community Social Planning Council of Toronto and the Ontario Social Safety Network, 2002) at 8, 9 and 33.

25

Immigration

(1) INTRODUCTION

The immigration system, governed by the *Immigration and Refugee Protection Act[1] (IRPA)*, regulates admission to, and removal from, Canada. While the *IRPA* provides principles and a general framework, many of the details regarding the operation of the system are found within the regulations and thus can be amended much more readily. Timely and accurate legal information and advice are absolutely critical; inaccurate advice may have dramatic consequences, including deportation. As we noted in Chapter 5, longstanding concerns about the quality of advice and representation provided by some immigration consultants has resulted in a new regulatory environment. However, even within the context of the new regulatory environment, there continue to be concerns regarding the quality of work of some consultants. Citizenship and Immigration Canada ("CIC") will not deal with a paid representative who is not a lawyer or a member of the Canadian Society of Immigration Consultants. Therefore, if making a referral to a consultant, it is important to ensure that he or she is a member in good standing with the Society.

(2) ADMISSION TO CANADA

IRPA carves out three basic methods of entry to Canada: the independent or economic class; the family class; and the protected person (or refugee) class.[2] No matter the class, in addition to meeting the criteria of the relevant class, in order to secure permanent resident status and entry to Canada applicants must not fall into any of the categories of inadmissibility.

(a) Economic Class

The economic class, as defined by *IRPA*, is comprised of foreign nationals selected "on the basis of their ability to become economically established in Canada."[3] This assessment is conducted using a points system, where points are awarded in six areas: age; education; proficiency in the official languages of Canada; adaptability; work experience; and arranged employment in Canada. There are also special provisions, with particular requirements, for sub-categories within this class, including the skilled worker class,[4] the investor class,[5] the entrepreneur class,[6] and the self-employed class.[7]

(b) Family Class

One express goal of the *IRPA* is to "see that families are reunited in Canada", and admission to Canada through the family class is a primary vehicle to accomplish this end.[8] A Canadian citizen or permanent resident who is eighteen years of age or over may apply to sponsor a member of the family class. The sponsor cannot have been convicted of a sexual offence or of a *Criminal Code* offence against any relative or family member, cannot be in receipt of social assistance, and cannot be in default of a previous sponsorship, government loan, or court ordered support.[9] The bar on sponsorship, if convicted of an offence against a family member, has important implications for women experiencing domestic violence. While on the one hand the prohibition may send a strong message that domestic violence is not tolerated, on the other, women who are dependent upon their spouses to sponsor other family class members are reluctant to call the police for assistance due to the potential of conviction and the bar to sponsorship.

Members of the family class who may be sponsored include a spouse, common law partner (of at least one year's duration), conjugal partner, parent or grandparent, dependent child (under 22 years of age or in full-time attendance in school since turning 22), an orphaned brother, sister, niece, nephew or grandchild who is unmarried and under 18 years of age, and children under 18 who have been or will be adopted by the sponsor.[10]

If the sponsorship is of a spouse, common law partner, or an adopted child, CIC must be satisfied that the relationship is genuine and not entered into primarily for the purpose of acquiring immigration status.[11]

An important feature of the family class is a required "sponsorship" and "undertaking." The undertaking is a binding contract between the Minister of Citizenship & Immigration Canada and the sponsor, in which the sponsor undertakes to provide for the sponsored person's basic requirements and accepts an obligation to repay the government concerned if the sponsored person should receive social assistance benefits.[12] The period of sponsorship is for up to ten years, except for spouses for whom the term was reduced (in 2002) to three years.[13] The sponsorship agreement is one between the sponsor and the sponsored person wherein the sponsor commits to meeting the basic requirements of the sponsored person, and the sponsored person undertakes to make reasonable efforts to provide for his or her basic requirements and those of their family members.

(c) Refugee Class

The third method of admission to Canada is through the protected person or refugee class. A refugee is defined by the *Act* as a Convention refugee (referring to the 1951 Geneva Convention) or a person in similar circumstances.[14] A Convention refugee is defined further as,

> a person who, by reason of a well-founded fear of persecution for reasons of race, religion, nationality, membership in a particular social group or political opinion,
>
>   (a) is outside each of their countries of nationality and is unable or, by reason of that fear, unwilling to avail themselves of the protection of each of those countries; or
>   (b) not having a country of nationality, is outside the country of their former habitual residence and is unable or, by reason of that fear, unwilling to return to that country.[15]

Persons in need of protection are defined as persons whose removal to their country or countries of nationality, or country of former habitual residence, would personally subject them to a danger of torture, risk to their life or to cruel and unusual treatment or punishment, and who are unable or unwilling because of that risk to avail themselves of the protection of that country.[16]

The determination of refugee status may be made either within or outside of Canada's borders. Each year the government of Canada selects for sponsorship refugees from abroad to settle in Canada, and provides settlement assistance upon arrival. In 2004, the government sponsored 7,411 refugees.[17] Groups may also apply to sponsor refugees from abroad and many groups do so, often working under the umbrella of the Canadian Council for Refugees. In 2004 there were some 3,115 privately sponsored refugee landings in Canada.[18]

Many persons apply for refugee status from within Canada, often upon arrival at a port of entry. Once the application is made it is referred to the refugee protection division of the Immigration Review Board and a determination is made as to whether the applicant is eligible to make a refugee claim. Those who have already been accepted or refused as a refugee in Canada, those who have been accepted as refugees in another country to which they could return, and those who have come to Canada through a "safe third country" are ineligible to apply. Significantly, Canada has entered a "safe third country" agreement with the United States, the consequence of which is that a person who crosses the border from the United States into Canada will ordinarily be required (although there are exceptions) to make his or her claim for refugee status in the United States. While this agreement was found to be invalid by the Federal Court in November, 2007, there is likely to be ongoing litigation regarding its validity.

A claim for refugee status is ultimately heard by a single member of the Refugee Protection Division. If the person is found to be a refugee, he or she is then eligible to apply for permanent resident status. If not found to be a refugee or protected person, it may be possible to have the decision reviewed by the Federal Court. Additionally, it may be possible to proceed with a humanitarian and compassionate application (discussed below) and/or with a Pre-Removal Risk Assessment. It is really important to have legal advice and representation in these matters. In Ontario, legal aid certificates to retain a private bar lawyer are sometimes issued in refugee matters. In addition, representation may be available through the Refugee Law Office (based in Toronto) or through one of Ontario's community legal aid clinics (only some of whom provide representation in immigration matters).

(d) Humanitarian and Compassionate Grounds

While a cornerstone of the *IRPA* is that persons who wish to live permanently in Canada must submit their application, qualify for, and obtain a permanent resident visa outside of Canada prior to arrival, it can and does happen that persons within Canada wish to make an application for permanent resident status.[19] Where this situation occurs for spouses, they may be able to apply under the "spouse and common-law partner in Canada class" without the non-resident spouse having to leave the country. This class was extended in February, 2005 to all spouses and common-law partners of one-year duration, irrespective of whether that spouse/partner has temporary legal status.[20] It is important to secure legal advice if seeking to apply under this category.

The other possibility, and indeed the only option for some, is to make a "humanitarian and compassionate" ("H & C") application. The H & C application process involves two steps: step one entails a determination of whether the hardship of having to obtain a permanent resident visa from outside Canada would be unusual (not contemplated by the *Act*), undeserved, or disproportionate; and in the second step it is determined whether the applicant meets the requirements for permanent resident status.[21] The grant-ing of permanent resident status on a humanitarian and compassionate basis is discretionary, but in exercising this discretion, the best interests of a child who is directly affected must be taken into account.[22]

An H & C application may arise in different situations where a person seeking permanent resident status does not meet any of the three broad categories of admission discussed above: a failed refugee claimant; a person without status who has a long term financial or emotional attachment to a Canadian citizen or permanent resident; and a person whose family class sponsorship has broken-down before permanent resident status has been granted. The last of these categories raises issues of particular concern.

While ordinarily a member of the family class will apply from outside of Canada for permanent resident status and arrive in Canada only after that status has been conferred, in other situations, as briefly noted above, the application may be initiated from within Canada. Where the application is initiated from within Canada the sponsored family class member will be without status for a significant period of time, and unable to obtain either a work or study permit until "approved in principle" (a six-to-seven-month wait, according to Citizenship and Immigration Canada, but often closer to one-to-two years in Toronto). A sponsor may withdraw his or her sponsor-ship any time prior to the granting of permanent resident status. If the sponsorship is withdrawn, the only option for the sponsored family class member to avoid removal from Canada is to initiate an application on H & C grounds.[23]

It is important to appreciate the difficulties faced by sponsored family class members who experience violence or abuse at the hands of their sponsors. It is widely recognized that in abusive relationships, a common tactic of abuse is for the sponsor to threaten to withdraw his or her spon-sorship and/or threaten to have the sponsored person deported.[24] This type of threat is commonly reported in spousal relationships, but also where elderly parents or in-laws are sponsored. In most cases the sponsored person already has permanent resident status and even if the sponsor were to withdraw his or her sponsorship, it would not put the sponsored family class member(s) at risk of deportation. However, the sponsored individual often has little or no information about neither his or her actual status nor the legal implications of it, and so the sponsored person has no basis upon which to challenge the sponsor's claims. If the sponsored family class member does not yet have permanent residence status and the sponsor withdraws the sponsorship (which can be done any time up until permanent resident status is granted), then the only option to remain in Canada is to file an H & C application. Not surprisingly, given the unpredictable results of the H & C process, many women and other family members who experience abuse remain in the abusive family context because their immigration status is in jeopardy. We hasten to add that for women who are in Canada without any legal status, but in relationships with abusive men who both promise to sponsor them and simultaneously threaten to report them to CIC for deportation, the situation is exceptionally perilous. Moreover, since in many parts of the country a call to the police will mean inquiries about one's immigration status and a report to CIC, women without legal status will often not call the police for assistance.[25]

Several elements for consideration under the H & C process are especially pertinent in cases of sponsorship breakdown where there has been abuse in the relationship. Guideline 13.10 specifically addresses situations of domestic violence, noting that family members in abusive relationships may feel compelled to stay in the abusive relationship in order to remain in Canada. Guideline 13.10 also directs decision-makers to be "sensitive" to situations where a woman has left an abusive situation and, as a result, does not have an approved sponsorship (sponsorship being a positive factor in the overall assessment). Furthermore, decision-makers are to consider, amongst other things: information indicating that there was abuse, such as police incident reports, charges or convictions, reports from shelters for abused women, and medical reports; whether there is a significant degree of establishment in Canada; the hardship that would result if the applicant had to leave Canada; support of relatives and friends in the applicant's home country; the length of time in Canada; and whether the marriage or relationship was genuine.[26]

Significantly, elsewhere the guidelines indicate that considerations relevant to degree of establishment include: a history of stable employment; a pattern of sound financial management; integration into the community through involvement in community organizations, voluntary services or other activities; the undertaking of professional, linguistic or other study that shows integration; and a good civil record (for example, no interventions by police or other authorities for child or spouse abuse, or criminal charges).[27] Given the realities of the lives of many newcomers to Canada, particularly those who experience abuse, meeting the threshold of a "significant degree of establishment" can be enormously difficult. Moreover, if in receipt of social assistance, he or she will be barred from permanent resident status. While the guidelines indicate that the final determination should be made at the end of the application process to "allow time for the applicant to take advantage of employment opportunities that come with a positive humanitarian and compassionate finding and employment authorization," when all is said and done, if the applicant is in receipt of social assistance after all other processing has been completed, the application for permanent residence will be refused.[28]

(3) INADMISSIBILITY

To gain permanent resident status, not only must an applicant fit one of the three broad categories of admission or succeed on humanitarian and compassionate grounds, he or she must not fall into any of the categories of inadmissibility.[29] While below we review the general categories of inadmissibility, these apply differently for applicants in different categories; so again, securing legal advice is crucial.

One broad category of inadmissibility relates to health: if the applicant poses a risk to public health or safety or might reasonably be expected to cause excessive demand on health or social services, he or she is inadmissible. [30] Some exceptions apply to the excessive demand basis for inadmissibility; for example, it does not apply to a spouse, common law partner or dependent child.[31]

The person seeking admission must also be able to demonstrate that he or she can be self-supporting without resorting to social services in Canada. If this ability is not evident, admission will be denied.

An increasingly complex area of inadmissibility relates to threats to security, organized crime, violation of human or international rights, and criminality. While all are pertinent issues, we will focus on one in particular; criminality. *IRPA* distinguishes between serious criminality and criminality. With respect to "serious criminality," the *Act* provides that both a permanent resident and a foreign national are inadmissible on the grounds of serious criminality if convicted in Canada of an offence under an *Act* of Parliament punishable by a maximum term of imprisonment of at least ten years, or of an offence for which a term of imprisonment of six months or greater has been imposed.[32] This means that even a person with permanent resident status can be removed from Canada if convicted of such an offence. Moreover, the *Act* deems hybrid offences (see Chapter 5) to be indictable offences, irrespective of how the Crown elects to proceed in the actual case.[33]

The "criminality" provisions, by contrast, apply only to foreign nationals and not to permanent residents. A foreign national is inadmissible to Canada if convicted of an offence punishable by way of indictment, or of any two offences under any *Act* of Parliament not arising from a single occurrence.[34]

Once CIC learns of the conviction, the person convicted will receive a call in notice, to be examined to determine whether he or she is inadmissible. It is critical to have legal representation at this juncture. After the examination, the examining officer will determine whether the person is inadmissible considering the facts. The officer has no discretion in making a removal order if the person has been convicted of an offence carrying the penalties described above. Moreover, if the sentence was for two years or more (including time served pending trial), there is no right of appeal.

The criminality provisions obviously have important ramifications for all non-citizens charged with criminal offences. They have also had an important impact in cases of domestic violence. Again, some women are reluctant to contact the police for assistance in situations of abuse. While they want the abuse to stop, they frequently do not want their partners/spouses deported. Abused women fear that if the police lay charges and the man is convicted, he may face removal under the criminality provisions of the *IRPA*. Moreover, there is a documented concern regarding dual charging in cases of domestic violence, where the police lay charges against both the man and woman or only against the woman. A recent study undertaken by Pollack *et al.* suggests that both police and Crown attorneys may be inattentive to the context of particular acts of criminal misconduct, missing the crucial distinction between aggressive and defensive acts.[35] The partners of the women in the study were able to successfully manipulate the criminal justice system to avoid charges themselves and to shift the blame to their female partners, often employing the knowledge they had acquired from having been previously charged and convicted. This is all the more likely to happen when one spouse —and it will often be the abusive husband —has better command of English than the other.

Deeply troubling in the Pollack *et al.* study is not only the finding of women being charged with assault, but that many women (six of 19 in the study) were charged with "assault with a weapon." The weapons used by the women to defend themselves were items readily at hand, including an empty plastic bottle, an empty tape dispenser, and a telephone. Assault with a weapon is a hybrid offence, so may be prosecuted at the election of the Crown either by indictment (carrying a penalty of up to ten years) or by way of summary conviction (a penalty of up to 18 months).[36] The offence range and the deeming provisions of the *IRPA* place an assault with a weapon offence within the category of "serious criminality" and thus women—even those who are permanent residents—face the very real possibility of removal from Canada.[37] Given the Pollack *et al.* additional finding that women felt tremendous pressure to plead guilty, often because they lacked financial resources, there is a grave concern that abused immigrant women who have acted to defend themselves will be charged, convicted, and potentially, rendered inadmissible to Canada.

(4)   INTERSECTIONS WITH SOCIAL ASSISTANCE

When applying for social assistance benefits (Ontario Works ("OW") or Ontario Disability Support Program ("ODSP") in Ontario), applicants are required to provide information to verify their status in Canada, and Citizenship and Immigration Canada is contacted.[38] While the provisions vary from province to province, visitors, tourists and persons without current legal status are generally ineligible for benefits.[39] However, those who have filed an application for permanent resident status are generally eligible (but note receipt of social assistance is a bar to the granting of permanent resident status).

In Ontario, for those under an immigration sponsorship, there is an obligation to make "reasonable efforts" to obtain the compensation due under the sponsorship agreement. The policy directive that addresses matters related to immigration provides that:

> a sponsored immigrant is expected to have his/her needs met by the sponsor. However, when the sponsorship agreement has broken down because the sponsor is in default and the sponsored immigrant agrees to pursue support from the sponsor, the immigrant may be eligible for financial assistance.[40]

The policy directive provides that an applicant/recipient can be exempted from the obligation to make reasonable efforts to pursue compensation available under the sponsorship agreement if there "is a breakdown in the sponsorship by reason of family violence verified by a third party."[41] The directive goes on to note that verification may come from the police, a lawyer, or a community or health-care professional and that "[i]f verification is not immediately available, it may be necessary to make a referral to an appropriate person or agency to obtain this verification."[42] This exemption is only temporary and must be reviewed to determine if the circumstances that warranted the exemption continue. Careful attention to, and documentation of domestic violence on the part of social workers can help women access the verification that is required.

OW and ODSP offices notify CIC of any default of the sponsorship. The sponsor will receive notification of the default, and will be asked to attend a meeting with OW or ODSP officials to determine his or her ability to honour the sponsorship undertaking and agreement. British Columbia's policy provides that where there are "concerns about possible abuse, *no* contact is to be made with the sponsor, including by letter" (bolded in original).[43] Importantly, the approach in British Columbia recognizes that pursuit of a batterer for economic support by his ex-partner, whether directly or indirectly through an arm of the state, may trigger further and potentially more dangerous forms of violence.

Until the sponsor's debt is repaid to social assistance (all monies paid to support the sponsored person), he or she is precluded from sponsoring any other person. As noted, this bar on sponsorship serves to lock some family members into abusive relationships, particularly if they depend upon their sponsoring family member to sponsor or co-sponsor other members of their family.

In addition to the problems caused by categorical ineligibility, lack of knowledge of the availability of social assistance or of other routes to immigration status is a problem in many cases. Both the welfare and immigration systems are notoriously complex and it is extremely difficult for even a well-resourced English-speaker to access timely and accurate information. Profound social isolation experienced by many newcomers and especially those experiencing abuse, language barriers, the opaqueness of the systems, and the control and blatant manipulation of information by abusive sponsors all create obstacles to timely and accurate information about rights and avenues of redress.[44]

SELECTED READINGS

Citizenship and Immigration Canada, *Canada's Refugee System: What you Should Know* (Ottawa, Ont.: Citizenship and Immigration Canada, 2006).

Côté, Andreé et al., *Sponsorship. . .For Better or Worse: The Impact of Sponsorship on the Equality Rights of Immigrant Women* (Ottawa, Ont.: Status of Women Canada, March, 2001).

Dauvergne, Catherine, *Gendering Canada's Refugee Process* (Ottawa, Ont.: Status of Women Canada, 2006).

Dauvergne, Catherine, *Humanitarianism, Identity, and Nation: Migration Laws of Australia and Canada* (Vancouver, British Columbia: UBC Press, 2005).

Khosla, Punam, *If Low Income Women of Colour Counted in Toronto*, Final Report of the Action-Research Project, Breaking Isolation, Getting Involved (Toronto, Ont.: Community Social Planning Council of Toronto, 2003).

Martin, Dianne & Janet Mosher, "Unkept Promises: Experiences of Immigrant Women with the Neo-Criminalization of Wife Abuse" (1995) 8 C.J.W.L. 3.

National Association of Women and the Law et al., *Brief on the Proposed Immigration and Refugee Protection Act (Bill C-11)*, April, 2001.

Orloff, Lesley, "Lifesaving Welfare Safety Net Access for Battered Immigrant Women and Children: Accomplishments and Next Steps" (2001) 7 Wm. & Mary J. Women & L. 597.

Pollack, Shoshana et al., *Women Charged with Domestic Violence in Toronto: The Unintended Consequences of Mandatory Charge Policies* (Ottawa, Ont.: Status of Women Canada, March, 2005).

Randall, Melanie, "Refugee Law and State Accountability for Violence against Women: A Comparative Analysis of Legal Approaches to Asylum Claims based on Gender Persecution" (2002) 25 Harv. Women's L.J., 25th Anniversary Issue 281.

Razack, Sherene, "The Perils of Storytelling for Refugee Women" in Wenona Giles, Helene Moussa & Penny Van Esterik, eds., *Development & Diaspora: Gender and the Refugee Experience* (Dundas, Ont.: Artemis Enterprises, 1996).

Smith, Ekuwa, *Nowhere to Turn? Responding to Partner Violence against Immigrant and Visible Minority Women* (Ottawa, Ont.: Canadian Council of Social Development, 2004).

Waldman, Lorne, *Canadian Immigration & Refugee Law Practice, 2007* (Markham, Ont.: LexisNexis Butterworths, 2006).

Wayland, Sarah, *Unsettled: Legal and Policy Barriers for Newcomers to Canada* (Law Commission of Canada, Community Foundations of Canada, 2006).

WEBSITES

Citizenship and Immigration Canada, www.cic.gc.ca

CLEONet, www.cleonet.ca

Don't Ask Don't Tell Toronto, www.dadttoronto.org

Human Resources and Social Development Canada, www.hrsdc.gc.ca/en/workplaceskills/publications/index.shtml

Live-in Caregivers, www.cic.gc.ca/English/work/caregiver/index.asp

ENDNOTES

1.   S.C. 2001, c. 27.
2.   *Ibid.* at s. 12.

3.   *Ibid.* at s. 12(2).
4.   *Immigration and Refugee Protection Regulations*, SOR/2002-227 at ss. 73-87.
5.   *Ibid.* at ss. 88-96.
6.   *Ibid.* at ss. 97-99.
7.   *Ibid.* at ss. 100-101.
8.   *Ibid.* at s. 3(1)(d).
9.   *Ibid.* at ss. 130(1) and 133(1).
10. *Ibid.* at s. 12.
11. See *supra* note 4 at s. 4. See Chapter 18 for a discussion of this issue in the context of adoption.
12. Canada, Citizenship and Immigration Canada, *Processing Applications to Sponsor Members of the Family Class IP 2* (Citizenship and Immigration Canada, 2007) at s. 5.18.
13. *Ibid.* at s. 5.22.
14. See *supra* note 1 at s. 12(3).
15. *Ibid.* at s. 96(1).
16. *Ibid.* at s. 97(1).
17. Annual Report to Parliament on Immigration (Ottawa: Citizenship and Immigration Canada, 2005), online: <http://www.cic.gc.ca/English/resources/publications/annual-report2005/section4.asp>.
18. *Ibid.*
19. Canada, Citizenship and Immigration Canada, *Immigrant Applications in Canada Made on Humanitarian and Compassionate Grounds IP 5* (Citizenship and Immigration Canada, 2007) at s. 5.2.
20. For information on the extension of the spouse in Canada application process see the CIC website, www.cic.gc.ca.
21. See *supra* note 4 at ss. 64-69, 72.
22. See *supra* note 1 at s. 25(1); see also *Baker v. Canada (Minister of Citizenship & Immigration)*, [1999] 2 S.C.R. 817, 1 Imm. L.R. (3d) 1, 14 Admin. L.R. (3d) 173, 174 D.L.R. (4th) 193, [1999] S.C.J. No. 39, 1999 CarswellNat 1124, 1999 CarswellNat 1125, 243 N.R. 22.
23. See *supra* note 1 at s. 25; enables a person to apply from within or outside of Canada for Permanent Residence status on a humanitarian and compassionate basis.
24. Andreé Côté et al., *Sponsorship. . .For Better or Worse: The Impact of Sponsorship on the Equality Rights of Immigrant Women* (Ottawa, Ont.: Status of Women in Canada, March, 2001) and Ekuwa Smith, *Nowhere to Turn? Responding to Partner Violence Against Immigrant and Visible Minority Women* (Ottawa: Canadian Council of Social Development, 2004).
25. These concerns have lead to the creation of "Don't Ask Don't Tell"

campaigns in major cities throughout North America and some resulting policies. See www.dadttoronto.org for more information.

26. See *supra* note 19 at s. 13.10.
27. *Ibid.* at s. 11.2.
28. *Ibid.* at s. 16.14.
29. *Ibid.* at ss. 34-42.
30. See *supra* note 1 at s. 38(1).
31. *Ibid.* at s. 38(2)(a).
32. *Ibid.* at s. 36(1); a similar provision deals with offences committed outside of Canada.
33. *Ibid.* at s. 36(3); note that offences for which one has been pardoned, and offences under the *Youth Criminal Justice Act* are excluded.
34. *Ibid.* at s. 36(2)(a).
35. Shoshana Pollack et al., *Women Charged with Domestic Violence in Toronto: The Unintended Consequences of Mandatory Charge Policies* (Ottawa: Status of Women Canada, March, 2005).
36. *Criminal Code of Canada*, R.S.C. 1985, c. C-46 at s. 267.
37. See *supra* note 1 at s. 36(3)(a); and Citizenship and Immigration Canada, Manual ENF 1 Inadmissibility, A36 (1) (a) pp15-16 (2005-08-26) available at http://www.cic.gc.ca/english/resources/manuals/enf/enf01e.pdf.
38. *Ontario Works Act 1997*, O. Reg. 134/98 at s. 17(2).
39. Note that eligibility for other forms of social support and financial assistance vary tremendously.
40. Ontario, Ministry of Community and Social Services, Policy Directive #25, *Immigrants, Refugees and Deportee* (Ontario Works: September, 2001).
41. *Ibid.* at 14.
42. *Ibid.*
43. *Employment and Assistance Act*, S.B.C. 2002; *Employment and Assistance Regulation* at ss. 41, 43; and policies thereto Hardship Assistance, Sponsorship Undertaking Default, Ministry of Employment, available at http://www.gov.bc.ca.
44. Punam Khosla, *If Low Income Women of Colour Counted in Toronto*, Final Report of the Action-Research Project, Breaking Isolation, Getting Involved (Toronto, Ont.: Community Social Planning Council of Toronto, 2003).

PART V

LEGAL AND REGULATORY ISSUES FOR SOCIAL WORKERS

26

Legal Accountability of Social Workers

(1) INTRODUCTION

Professional regulation, civil liability and criminal liability each play a role in the legal accountability of social workers. Social workers, regardless of their level of training, hold themselves out to the public as having particular knowledge and skill, or the fact of their employment implies it. Private practitioners and some agencies charge a fee for service, which implies a contractual relationship between worker or agency and client for service according to a particular standard. Other social workers practice under statutory authority, notably those employed by Children's Aid Societies, correctional systems, and mental health and educational facilities. As a consequence, social workers may at some point in their careers be at risk of civil liability for acts or omissions in their dealings with clients. Workers may also face criminal prosecution if they are charged with intentional or negligent disregard of a professional duty. And finally, social workers may find themselves charged with professional misconduct or incompetence and compelled to appear before professional disciplinary bodies for, among other things, failing to meet the standards of practice.

Liability may arise from acts of omission as well as commission. In the last decade only a relatively small number of social workers, both American and Canadian, have been sued civilly, and even fewer have been criminally prosecuted. Criminal prosecutions have rarely succeeded and civil claims are usually settled without ever coming to court. More common, however, are disciplinary proceedings against social workers within the context of professional regulation.

(2) PROFESSIONAL REGULATION

On August 15, 2000 Ontario became the last province to enact legislation regulating social workers.[1] As with other provinces, this legislation governing the profession of social work is intended to enhance the public accountability of social workers in a variety of ways, including through the creation of educational requirements, restrictions on the use of the title "social worker," and "social service worker" establishment of standards of practice against which conduct can be assessed, and the creation of public complaints' processes.[2] In Ontario, the College of Social Workers and Social Service Workers is empowered to make determinations of a member's competency to practice social work or social service work and of whether a member has engaged in professional misconduct.

Pursuant to subsection 26(3) of Ontario's *Social Work and Social Service Work Act*,[3] a discipline committee may, after a hearing, find a member to be incompetent if, " the member has displayed in his or her professional responsibilities a lack of knowledge, skill or judgment or disregard for the welfare of a person or persons of a nature or extent that demonstrates that the member is unfit to continue to carry out his or her professional responsibilities. . . ." The regulations to the *Act* define misconduct to include, among other things:

- failing to meet the standards of the profession;
- doing anything to a client in the course of practising the profession in a situation in which consent is required by law, without such a consent;
- failing to supervise adequately a person who is under the professional responsibility of the member and who is providing a social work service;
- abusing a client physically, sexually, verbally, psychologically or emotionally;
- discontinuing professional services that are needed, except where particular preconditions are met;
- failing to keep records as required by the regulations and standards of the profession; and
- giving information about a client to a person other than the client or his or her authorized representative except,
  - i.   with the consent of the client or his or her authorized representative,
  - ii.   as required or allowed by law, or
  - iii. in a review, investigation or proceeding under the *Act* in which the professional conduct, competency or capacity of the member is in issue and only to the extent reasonably required by

the member or the College for the purposes of the review, investigation or proceeding.

As noted above, one of the grounds upon which a finding of professional misconduct can be made is that the social worker has failed to meet the standards of the profession. The Ontario College of Social Workers and Social Service Workers has published a *Code of Ethics and Standards of Practice* which delineates these standards. The *Standards of Practice* identify eight governing principles, and each is followed by a more detailed and specific set of "interpretations." While many of the principles are open to further interpretation and while questions will undoubtedly arise regarding the application of the principles in specific instances, the standards of practice are extremely important not only in the determination of professional misconduct or incompetency but in relation to civil and criminal liability, as described below.

Significantly, if a discipline committee finds a member guilty of professional misconduct or to be incompetent, its powers include those of revoking a certificate of registration, suspending registration for a period of up to 24 months, and imposing terms, conditions or limitations on a certificate of registration.[4] Additionally, where there is a finding of misconduct, the Committee may reprimand a member, require the member be counseled by the Committee, impose a fine to a maximum of $5,000 and order publication of the finding and order, with or without the name of the member.[5]

(3) CIVIL RESPONSIBILITY AND LIABILITY

(a) Negligence/Malpractice

One can speak only in broad concepts when defining civil responsibility and liability. In general terms, when persons hold themselves out to have professional knowledge or skill, and have academic credentials or some experience to support their professional status, they are assumed to have the requisite knowledge and skill. Those deemed to have the requisite knowledge and skill are responsible for work in accordance with a generally accepted standard of performance for that profession. If the person fails or neglects to do what a reasonable professional in similar circumstances would have done, or fails or neglects to carry out a statutory duty, and harm is caused to a client as a result (it is the proximate cause of the harm), he or she may be liable for civil damages. An English case establishes an important principle:

> [I]t should now be regarded as settled that if someone possessed of a special skill undertakes, quite irrespective of contract, to apply that skill for the

assistance of another person who relies on such skill, a duty of care will arise. The fact that the service is to be given by means of . . . words can make no difference. Furthermore, if . . . others could reasonably rely on his judgment or his skill or on his ability to make careful inquiry . . . to give information or advice to . . . another person who, as he knows or should know, will place reliance on it, then a duty of care will arise.[6]

The concept of the "duty of care" refers to the obligation to take reasonable care to avoid acts or omissions that one could reasonably foresee would be likely to cause injury or harm to another. The duty is owed where a relationship of sufficient proximity to another exists so that one could reasonably contemplate his or her acts or omissions may be likely to cause damage to the other; that is, it is not a duty owed to the world at large. In professional relationships, such as between social worker and client, there is little doubt that the relationship would be one of sufficient proximity to give rise to a duty of care.

The following fictitious situation illustrates circumstances in which civil liability may arise.

> Jason, a social worker, lives with and is responsible for the care and super-vision of four developmentally delayed adults in a community apartment. Peter, one of the residents, has not returned home from the sheltered workshop by dinner time nor by bedtime. Jason is tired and does nothing, expecting Peter will come home. Peter is lost and wanders the streets. He is hit by a car and severely injured. Peter's family sues Jason for negligence in his care of Peter. In these circumstances, Jason has failed to exercise the reasonable care for Peter's safety that another social worker in similar circumstances would have exercised. As a result of Jason's neglect, Peter suffered injury, which may be directly attributable to Jason's failure to provide the necessary super-vision. Damages could be awarded to Peter's family.

Here all the elements of negligence on the social worker's part are present: there is a duty of care; that duty has been breached by failing to live up to the standard expected of a reasonable social worker in such circumstances; and harm has resulted to the client, which was reasonably foreseeable. In any law suit, the court would look to the prevailing community standard of practice to determine whether or not the conduct was negligent. To discern this standard, the court will have careful regard of the standards of practice articulated by the governing body, but will also frequently hear from expert witnesses who offer their respective opinions as to the standard of practice expected in the particular situation. The plaintiff will be required to establish, on a balance of probabilities, that the worker was negligent.

Situations where negligence might arise are extremely diverse and could include such matters as a negligent or improper diagnosis, the rendering of inappropriate therapy or other treatment, the failure to maintain proper records, or the improper discontinuance of treatment. The failure to conduct a proper investigation may also give rise to a claim in negligence. In an Ontario case, a child protection worker concluded that a father had abused his child, and initiated an action against the father. The father claimed that the social worker believed the mother's story and so had not conducted an objective investigation as a result of a biased opinion. After three years of attempting to clear his name, a court found in the father's favour and awarded him damages.[7]

(b) Battery

In addition to these situations of negligence (where a duty of care has been breached and damages incurred as a result), liability may also arise as a result of what is termed an "intentional tort." Perhaps most relevant here is the intentional tort of "battery," which is defined as the touching of another person without that person's consent. In *Norberg v. Wynrib*,[8] the Supreme Court of Canada directed its attention to the relevance of the inequalities of power in professional relationships to the matter of informed consent. In that case the appellant brought an action for damages against her physician, who had supplied her with painkillers, to which he knew she was addicted, in exchange for activities of a sexual nature. At issue was whether the appellant had consented to these acts. The court noted that the factors which might vitiate consent are not limited to force, threat of force, fraud or deceit. The court observed, "our notion of consent must. . . be modified to appreciate the power relationship between the parties," since disparity in the relative positions of the parties may mean that the weaker party is not in a position to choose freely. Here the court found there to be a marked inequality in the powers of the parties and that the relative power of the physician had been exploited to pursue his own personal ends.

(c) Breach of Fiduciary Duty

While four of the judges analyzed the case of *Norberg* in terms of the tort of battery (three finding no consent, one finding there to be consent), two others preferred to approach the case as one of a breach of a fiduciary duty. While speaking of the physician-patient relationship, the words of Justice McLachlin are equally applicable to social workers. In the quote immediately below, Justice McLachlin first observes the multiple legal conceptualizations of the conduct in issue.

The relationship of physician and patient can be conceptualized in a variety of ways. It can be viewed as a creature of contract, with the physician's failure to fulfil his or her obligations giving rise to an action for breach of contract. It undoubtedly gives rise to a duty of care, the breach of which constitutes the tort of negligence. In common with all members of society, the doctor owes the patient a duty not to touch him or her without his or her consent; if the doctor breaches this duty he or she will have committed the tort of battery. But perhaps the most fundamental characteristic of the doctor-patient relationship is its fiduciary nature (underlining in original).[9]

Justice McLachlin goes on to note that the hallmark of a fiduciary relationship is one in which there is a relationship of trust; a trust placed by a person with inferior power in another person who has assumed superior power and responsibility. The trust requires that the person with superior power exercise that power for the good of the other and "only for his or her good and in his or her best interests."[10] It is an obligation that requires loyalty, good faith, and avoidance of a conflict of duty and self-interest. Applying the concept of fiduciary duty on the facts of *Norberg* led to the conclusion that the duty was breached when Wynrib:

prescribed drugs which he knew she should not have, when he failed to advise her to obtain counselling when her addition became or should have become apparent to him, and most notoriously, when he placed his own interest in obtaining sexual favours from Ms. Norberg in conflict with and above her interest in obtaining treatment and becoming well.[11]

Note how the concept of fiduciary duty led to a much more expansive scope for breach of duty than did the application of the concept of battery. This is significant for social workers, since in many, many instances, their relationships with clients are ones of a fiduciary nature, where they are obligated to exercise their power to advance and protect the interests of their clients.

(d) Duty to Protect

As we discussed in Chapter 8, communications between social workers and their clients are confidential, although generally not privileged. The duty of confidentiality is both an ethical and legal duty, and it is certainly possible that a breach of confidentiality could give rise to either or both a claim of negligence and an allegation of professional misconduct.

However, there are circumstances in which at least a limited breach of confidentiality may be permissible. One of the difficulties is that neither the legal nor the ethical parameters of permissible breaches of confidentiality are very clear. The *Code of Ethics and Standards of Practice* of the

Ontario College of Social Workers and Social Service Workers recognizes, as does the *Code of Ethics* and the *Guidelines for Ethical Practice* of the Canadian Association of Social Workers, that a breach of confidentiality may be allowed or required by law, but neither provides much guidance.[12] In Chapter 8, we discussed the situation where a court may compel disclosure of confidential records and the tests employed in both the criminal and civil context. Mandatory reporting of child abuse is another area in which the law compels the disclosure of information that may have been obtained in confidence.

The duty to protect arises in a different context; imagine that a client discloses information to you that reveals a detailed and chilling plan to kill his girlfriend. He has disclosed this information to you in confidence. Are you permitted, or indeed required, to do anything with this information? While there is no mandatory reporting obligation, if you do nothing with this information and your client does kill his girlfriend, might you be liable civilly? Among the treating professions, there is a great deal of discussion of this issue, arising largely from an American case called *Tarasoff*.[13] In that case a young man had disclosed to his treating psychologist that he intended to kill his girlfriend. The psychologist contacted campus police, who interviewed but did not detain the young man. Shortly thereafter, tragically, he killed his girlfriend. Her parents subsequently sued the psychologist, among others. The court was required to consider whether the parents could maintain a lawsuit against the psychologist and the court ruled that they could, holding that a psychologist has an obligation to use reasonable care to protect identifiable third party victims from harm.

The closest Canadian precedent on point is *Wenden v. Trikha*,[14] a case in which a young man, hospitalized in a psychiatric facility, fled the institution without permission and subsequently caused a serious car accident. The court recognized that when a psychiatrist becomes aware that a patient poses a serious danger to the physical well-being of a third party or parties, a duty arises to take reasonable steps to protect. Here, since no victim was identifiable by the psychiatrist, the court found there to be no negligence.

The case of *Smith v. Jones*, discussed in Chapter 8, addressed the question of the exceptions to privilege. Although in that case a detailed plan involving the deaths of innocent third parties was revealed to a psychiatrist, it was the court observed that the question of civil liability for the failure to protect was not in issue and would need to be addressed in future cases. The Court confined itself to the question of whether a solicitor-client privilege (which here applied to the psychiatrist because he had been retained by counsel for the accused) was subject to a public safety exception. In language that is quite similar to the decision of the Court, the *Code of Ethics* of the Canadian Association of Social Workers provides that "the general expectation that social workers will keep information confidential does not apply when disclosure is necessary to prevent serious imminent harm to a client or others.

(e) Vicarious Liability

Once a suit has been initiated, the tendency is to sue everyone: worker; supervisor; director; agency board members; and whoever else may be considered to share accountability. Social workers may find that they are considered liable, not only for their own acts, but also for the acts of those they supervise, both workers and volunteers.

In general, volunteers and students in training will not be held to the standard of care expected of fully trained professionals but rather to what can be reasonably expected of a student or volunteer. They are, however, expected to be competent for their assigned position and to possess more skills than a lay person. They are also expected to know their limitations and to seek help from staff or supervisors, or, where appropriate, to refer the situation to qualified persons.

Vicarious liability equates with organizational liability, in which an aggrieved party may chose to sue not only the person directly providing a service but supervisors, administrators, and members of the board of directors. Even when the direct practitioner assumes that the agency liability insurance will cover civil matters, the employer may still sue that practitioner through the insurance provider taking control of the litigation and suing the practitioner directly.

(4) DUTY AND LIABILITY UNDER THE *CRIMINAL CODE*

While the prosecution of social workers under the *Criminal Code*[15] for conduct undertaken in the execution of their professional duties is extremely rare, the potential of a criminal charge does form an important part of the legal backdrop in the practice of social work. The *Criminal Code* contains several sections which may pertain to social workers.

The *Code*, for example, imposes a positive duty to provide the necessities of life upon anyone who has legal guardianship of a child under the age of 16 years, or has charge of any person who is unable by reason of detention, age, illness, mental disorder or other case to withdraw himself or herself from that charge and is unable to provide himself or herself with the necessaries of life.[16] An offence is committed when a person under such a legal duty fails, without lawful excuse, to perform that duty and such failure endangers the life of the person to whom the duty is owed or causes or is likely to cause the health of that person to be injured permanently. With respect to a child, the offence can also be established if the child "is in destitute or necessitous circumstances," irrespective of whether endangerment to life occurs.[17]

The *Criminal Code* also renders it a crime to abandon or expose a child under the age of ten, so that the child's life is or is likely to be endangered or the child's health likely to be permanently injured.[18] As it is a hybrid offence, it may be prosecuted by way of indictment and subject to a term of imprisonment of up to five years, or by way of summary conviction and punishable by a term of up to 18 months.[19] This offence was at issue in an Ontario case brought against a caseworker, supervisor and agency director of the Brockville, Ontario Children's Aid Society.[20] The facts disclosed that the child had been returned to his mother's care after a period of Society wardship, with an order for close supervision. The court found the mother was capable of distorting the truth, was uncooperative and was difficult to work with. The father was at work and left care and control of the child to the mother. The assigned social worker maintained close and regular contact, obtained medical and social work assistance and kept close collateral contact by providing intellectual disability and psychological services, while carrying a heavy additional caseload. Nevertheless, the placement was not successful, a court review was planned and the baby's mother notified. The day before the hearing, the child was seriously abused by his mother. The judge held:

> The Crown must prove in this case, as it is a criminal trial, . . . not only the *actus reus* but also *mens rea* . . . or to put the matter in another way, an 'intention to bring about the forbidden result or forbidden state of affairs.'. . . . [The judge went on to quote from Justice Vannini regarding the concept of 'wilful'] ""Wilful" means by deliberate or purposeful conduct with full knowledge of, or reckless of or indifferent to the consequences of his act or omission; a callous disregard; a complete and utter disregard for the safety of children."

> The Crown must, therefore, prove that the conduct of [the worker] was so negligent as to constitute a reckless or callous disregard for the safety of [the child]. The same onus is on the Crown with respect to the other two accused. . ..[21]

The court found no evidence whatsoever against the other two accused, the Director of the C.A.S. or a supervisor, and then went on to consider the evidence against the social worker.

> This leaves me with [the social worker], the remaining accused, and on the whole of the evidence . . . I cannot find any acts of commission or omission

on her part that even approach the requirement of *mens rea* required in this case. It is true that, from the evidence, some visits were missed by [the worker] but these are quite easily explained by [the mother's] non-cooperation, holiday on the part of [the worker] and, no doubt, her heavy caseload. She was on the firing line, to put it bluntly; she had to make her own decisions with whatever assistance she could get and hope that her decisions were correct and, to my mind, she did the best she could under the circumstances, and I so find. I, also find that she followed the guidelines laid down by the Ministry to the best of her ability. Certainly there is no evidence that any omissions on her part amounted to wilful conduct amounting to a reckless or callous disregard for [the child's] safety.

In summary, I find that the Crown's evidence has fallen far short of proving beyond a reasonable doubt that any of the three accused are guilty of the offence charged. Therefore, all three accused are acquitted.[22]

The criminal negligence provisions of the *Code* are also potentially relevant. Criminal negligence is defined as doing anything, or omitting to do anything, that it is his or her duty (as imposed by law) to do and which shows wanton or reckless disregard for the lives or safety of other persons.[23] Criminal negligence is then further divided between negligence resulting in death (punishable by imprisonment for life) and negligence resulting in bodily harm (punishable by imprisonment for up to ten years).[24] In 1997 a social worker in Ontario was charged with criminal negligence in the death of Jordan Heikamp, who had starved to death while living in a shelter with his young mother some 35 days after his birth. In *R. v. Heikamp*,[25] Angie Martin, a social worker with the Toronto Catholic Children's Aid Society (C.C.A.S.) was charged with criminal negligence causing death, but those charges were dismissed at the conclusion of a preliminary hearing. The judge accepted the submission of Ms. Martin's counsel that there must be evidence of each of the following three elements to support a conviction: "a) a marked and substantial departure from the standard of a reasonable C.C.A.S. intake worker in the circumstances; b) a wanton and reckless disregard for the life and safety of Jordan in the manner in which she handled the matter; and c) that Martin's acts or omissions were a contributing cause of Jordan's death by chronic starvation."[26] The court found no evidence that Ms. Martin had acted in a manner that constituted a marked and substantial departure from the standards; to the contrary, she had complied with all policies and procedures in negotiating the difficult balancing of a child's right to be free of harm and taking the least intrusive measures, while dealing with a high caseload and few resources. The court also concluded that Ms. Martin had not exhibited a wanton or reckless disregard for Jordan's life and safety,[27] and that there was no evidence that her acts or omissions were a contributing cause of Jordan's death.[28] An inquest into Jordan's death resulted in several recommendations by the jury for change, including specific recommendations for the training of C.A.S. workers, the timing of risk assessments, and the gathering and verification of information.[29]

SELECTED READINGS

Alexander, Rudolph Jr., "Social Workers and Immunity from Civil Lawsuits" (1995) 40(5) Social Work 648.

Barker, Robert & Douglas Branson, *Forensic Social Work: Legal Aspects of Professional Practice* (New York: Haworth Press, 1993).

Dickens, Bernard, "Implications of Health Professionals Legal Liability" (1993) 1 Health L.J. 1.

Mactavish, Anne, "Mandatory Reporting of Sexual Abuse under the Regulated Professions Act" (1994) 14(4) Health L. Can. 89.

Reamer, Frederic, *Social Work Malpractice and Liability: Strategies for Prevention* (New York: Columbia University Press, 1994).

Samuels, Marilyn & Elayne Tanner, *Managing a Legal and Ethical Social Work Practice* (Toronto: Irwin Law, 2003).

Truscott, Derek & Kenneth Crook, *Ethics for the Practice of Psychology in Canada* (Edmonton: University of Alberta Press, 2004).

ENDNOTES

1. *Social Work and Social Service Work Act, 1998,* S.O. 1998, c. 31; the *Act* also regulates social service workers.
2. For a much more detailed explication of professional regulation see Marilyn Samuels & Elayne Tanner, *Managing a Legal and Ethical Social Work Practice* (Toronto: Irwin Law, 2003).
3. See *supra* note 1.
4. *Ibid.* at s. 26(4).
5. *Ibid.* at s. 26(5).
6. *Hedley Byrne & Co. v. Heller & Partners Ltd.* (1963), [1964] A.C. 465, 107 Sol. Jo. 454, [1963] 3 W.L.R. 101, [1963] 1 Lloyd's Rep. 485, [1963] 2 All E.R. 575 (U.K. H.L.).
7. *B. (D.) v. Children's Aid Society of Durham (Region)* (1996), 30 C.C.L.T. (2d) 310, 1996 CarswellOnt 2351, 136 D.L.R. (4th) 297, 92 O.A.C. 60, [1996] O.J. No. 2502 (C.A.).
8. *Norberg v. Wynrib*, [1992] 2 S.C.R. 226, [1992] S.C.J. No. 60, EYB

1992-67036, [1992] 4 W.W.R. 577, 92 D.L.R. (4th) 449, 12 C.C.L.T. (2d) 1, 9 B.C.A.C. 1, 19 W.A.C. 1, 138 N.R. 81, 68 B.C.L.R. (2d) 29, 1992 CarswellBC 907, 1992 CarswellBC 155, [1992] R.R.A. 668, additional reasons at (1992), EYB 1992-67037, [1992] 2 S.C.R. 318, 74 B.C.L.R. (2d) 2, [1992] 6 W.W.R. 673, 1992 CarswellBC 338, 1992 CarswellBC 908.

9. *Ibid.* at para. 64.
10. *Ibid.* at para. 65.
11. *Ibid.* at para. 84.
12. *Code of Ethics & Standards of Practice*, Ontario Association of Social Workers and Social Service Workers, online: <http://206.221.245.198/sections/membership_info/current_members/ethicsandprac-tice.html>; *Code of Ethics* and *Guidelines for Ethical Practice 2005*, Canadian Association of Social Workers, online: <http://www.casw-acts.ca/>.
13. For an excellent discussion of these issues see Derek Truscott & Kenneth Crook, *Ethics for the Practice of Psychology in Canada* (Edmonton: University of Alberta Press, 2004); *Tarasoff v. Regents of the University of California* (1974), 118 Cal. Rptr. 129 and (1976), 17 Cal. Rptr. 3d 425.
14. *Wenden v. Trikha* (1991), 8 C.C.L.T. (2d) 138, 116 A.R. 81, 1991 CarswellAlta 408, [1991] A.J. No. 612 (Q.B.), amended (1991), 118 A.R. 319, 1991 CarswellAlta 426 (Q.B.), additional reasons at (1992), 1 Alta. L.R. (3d) 283, 124 A.R. 1, 6 C.P.C. (3d) 15, [1992] A.J. No. 217, 1992 CarswellAlta 20 (Q.B.), affirmed (1993), 14 C.C.L.T. (2d) 225, 135 A.R. 382, 33 W.A.C. 382, 1993 CarswellAlta 528 (C.A.), leave to appeal refused 17 C.C.L.T. (2d) 285 (note), 149 A.R. 160 (note), 63 W.A.C. 160 (note), 159 N.R. 80 (note), [1993] 3 S.C.R. ix.
15. R.S.C. 1985, c. C-46.
16. *Ibid.* at s. 215(1).
17. *Ibid.* at s. 215(2).
18. *Ibid.* at s. 215.
19. *Ibid.* at s. 215(3).
20. *R. v. Leslie* (1982), 1982 CarswellOnt 1736 (Ont. Co. Ct.).
21. *Ibid.* at para. 23-25.
22. *Ibid.* at para. 23-28.
23. See *supra* note 17 at s. 219; see also the discussion of criminal negligence in Chapter 22.
24. *Ibid.* at s. 220.
25. *R. v. Heikamp* (1999), 1999 CarswellOnt 4721 (Ont. C.J.).
26. *Ibid.* at para 8.
27. *Ibid.* at para. 27.

28. *Ibid.* at para. 46.
29. The recommendations can be found online: <http://www.mcscs.jus.gov.on.ca/french/pub_safety/office_coroner/verdicts_and_recs/2001%20Inquests/HEIKAMP%20Recommendations.pdf>.

27

Self-Regulation of Social Workers

(1) INTRODUCTION

The hallmarks of an autonomous profession include public account-ability and the willingness and ability to demonstrate that accountability in legislation. The key concepts associated with professional self-regulation include the establishment of entry-to-practice requirements, the establish-ment and enforcement of professional standards of practice, the establish-ment of a complaint/discipline process, and the establishment and enforce-ment of continuing competence requirements, sometimes referred to as quality assurance.

In Canada, the regulation of professions is a provincial responsibility. The legislature of each province determines to whom it will delegate this responsibility, and more often than not, it devolves to the profession itself. For example, lawyers are regulated by law societies, medical doctors by medical colleges, chiropractors by chiropractic colleges, and so forth. In seven of the ten provinces,[1] the responsibility for regulation of the social work profession has been delegated to the professional association attached thereto. In the other three provinces—Prince Edward Island, Ontario, and British Columbia—the responsibility has been delegated to the profession through the establishment of a social work regulatory body that is separate from and independent of the provincial association of social workers.[2]

Each provincial jurisdiction, through legislation, has restricted the use of specific titles—for example, in Ontario it is Registered Social Worker, in Quebec it is Travailleur Social Professionnel in Quebec, and in New Brunswick it is Travailleur Social Immatricule—to persons who meet spec-ified criteria, and has made it an offence to use the title without authorization. All of the country's regulatory colleges and associations except for Newfoundland and Labrador signed a Mutual Recognition Agreement on Labour Mobility[3] to allow social workers to qualify for registration in other provinces to practice social work.

(2) STATUS OF SOCIAL WORK LEGISLATION IN CANADA: A SUMMARY[4]

(a) Alberta

(i) Legislation—Health Professions Act[5]

(A) Type of Regulation/Regulatory Framework

The *Health Professions Act* provides for the restricted use of the title registered social worker or the abbreviation of such title. It requires mandatory registration for all social workers (regardless of title used), continuing competency requirements, the practice of restricted activities, and a specialty register for clinical social workers.

(B) Penalty

The *Health Professions Act* and, specifically, the Social Worker Profession Regulations detail how to file a complaint to the Alberta College of Social Workers (ACSW). Every effort is made to resolve complaints before they proceed to discipline. Disciplinary measures by the Board include, but are not limited to, reprimand, suspension or cancellation of registration, and limitation of the right to practice social work.

(C) Governing Body

The council of the ACSW consists of ten members elected by its membership in accordance with the bylaws, four public members appointed by the government, the chair of the Aboriginal Social Work Committee, and the chairs of the regulatory committees (Registration, Professional Social Work Education, Clinical, and Competence).

(D) Entry to Practice Requirements

According to the *Health Professions Act*, the entry to practice requirements are:

    (a) (i)   an undergraduate degree or diploma in social work from an approved social work program; or

           (ii) a combination of education, experience, practice, or other qualifications that demonstrate the competence required for registration as a regulated member; or

    (iii) being registered as a social worker in another jurisdiction recognized as having substantially equivalent competence and practice requirements.

  (b) 1500 hours of practice experience supervised by a Registered Social Worker (RSW);

  (c) evidence of character and reputation suitable to the practice of the profession.[6]

(E) Minister Responsible

The Minister of Health and Wellness.

(b) British Columbia

(i) Legislation—Social Workers Act[7]

(A) Type of Regulation

The *Act* provides for control of the use of the titles social worker and registered social worker; social workers employed by the public sector are exempted from the title restriction. The Board of Registration for Social Workers also provides for a voluntary Private Practice Roster. To be qualified as a private practitioner, the social worker must have a master's degree in social work, two years post degree experience, and must have been approved by the Board for private practice.

(B) Penalty

A person who is not registered under the provision of this *Act* or who is not employed by Canada, the Province, or other employers as provided under this *Act*, shall not represent himself or herself as a social worker or a registered social worker; whoever contravenes these provisions commits an offence and is liable to a fine of not more than $1,000.[8]

(C) Governing Body

The Board of Registration for Social Workers is composed of ten to 12 members appointed by the Lieutenant Governor in Council, of whom two persons are not social workers while the remainder is made up of R.S.W.s.

(D) Entry to Practice Requirements

> a)   a bachelor's, master's, or doctoral degree in social work; or
> b)   a degree or certificate deemed by the Board to be equivalent to a bachelor's degree in social work or postgraduate degree in social work; or
> c)   a bachelor's degree in a related field and a combination of knowledge, skills, and abilities substantially equivalent to a social work degree.[9]

In addition to academic qualifications, an applicant must provide a clean criminal record check and evidence of good character consistent with the responsibilities and standards of a registered social worker.

(E) Minister Responsible

The Minister for Children and Family Development.

(c) Manitoba

(i) Legislation—*The Manitoba Institute of Registered Social Workers Incorporation Act*[10] *(MIRSW)*

(A) Type of Regulation

The *Act* provides for voluntary registration and control of the designation R.S.W., and the initials corresponding to that designation, or abbreviations thereof. The MIRSW is the regulatory body for the Manitoba Association of Social Workers (MASW).

(B) Penalty

A fine of not less than $100 and not more than $200 and costs.[11]

(C) Governing Body

The Board of the Manitoba Institute of Registered Social Workers.

(D) Entry to Practice Requirements

B.S.W., M.S.W., or an equivalent degree issued by a university or college accredited by the Council on Social Work Education or which, in the opinion of the head of the Faculty of the School of Social Work of the University of Manitoba, is an accredited university or college.

(E) Minister Responsible

No Minister responsible.

(d) New Brunswick

(i) Legislation—*New Brunswick Association of Social Workers Act (NBASW)*[12]

(A) Type of Regulation

The *Act* provides for the regulation of practice and control of the use of the title social worker or registered social worker, or abbreviations thereof.

(B) Penalty

For a first offence, a fine of not less than $500 and not more than $2,000 plus costs.[13] For any subsequent offence, a fine of not less than $1,000 and not more than $5,000 plus costs, or imprisonment for not more than six months, or both.[14] Upon failure to pay a fine, imprisonment for not more than six months.[15]

(C) Governing Body

The Board of the NBASW consists of the president, vice-president, immediate past president, secretary, treasurer, other members as established by the bylaws, and one other person who is not a member of the Association but is appointed by the Minister of Health and Community Services from a list of three names submitted by the Association of Social Workers. The Committee of Examiners consists of seven members, of whom six are appointed by the Association and one by the minister from a list of three names submitted by the Association.

(D) New Brunswick Association of Social Workers

  a) The association regulates the practice of social work in the province and governs its members; it also determines standards of professional conduct. The association appoints six members of the Com-

mittee of Examiners and submits names to the Minister for appointment of the seventh member.[16]

(E) Entry to Practice Requirements

a)   a bachelor's, master's, or doctoral degree in social work or the
     equivalent from a School of Social Work approved by the Com-
     mittee of Examiners;
b)   passing grade on the examination prescribed by the committee and
     sufficient experience; or
c)   registration as a member of an association of social workers ap-
     proved by the committee.[17]

(F) Discipline

The Complaints Committee is composed of a member of the Board,
who acts as chairperson, and two other members of the Association appointed by the Board. There is also a Discipline Committee that includes
five persons, four members appointed by the Board and a non-member
appointed by the Minister. Disciplinary measures include, but are not limited
to, revocation, suspension, and limitation of right to practice social work,
and a fine to a maximum of $5,000.[18]

(G) Minister Responsible

The Minister of Health and Community Services.

(e) Newfoundland and Labrador

(i) Legislation—Social Workers Association Act[19]

(A) Type of Regulation

The *Act* provides for control of the practice of social work and use of
the title social worker or registered social worker, or abbreviations of such
titles.

(B) Penalty

Section 54 of the *Act* provides the penalties for "holding out as a social
worker." For a first offence a fine of not less than $500 and not more than
$2,000 plus costs is levied, and for subsequent offences a fine of not less

than $1,000, a term of imprisonment of not more than six months, or both a fine and imprisonment.

(C) Governing Body

The Board of the Newfoundland and Labrador Association of Social Workers is comprised of a president, president-elect, secretary, treasurer, a member of the Board of CASW who is also a member of the Board, the immediate past president, other members as provided by the bylaws, and a member appointed by the Minister. The Board of Directors is empowered as the regulatory body and professional association for social workers. The Committee of Examiners consists of six persons appointed by the Board and a seventh person appointed by the Minister.

(D) Entry to Practice Requirements

a) a bachelor's, master's or doctoral degree, or other equivalent education in social work from an educational institution approved by the Committee of Examiners and completion of the examination prescribed;[20]

b) temporary registration is provided for up to seven years to persons without social work degrees who are asked to work in areas of the province where a duly qualified social worker is not available;[21]

c) to remain registered, a temporary registrant must agree to acquire a social work degree within seven years of the initial registration.[22]

(E) Discipline

A Discipline Committee is composed of five members of the association appointed by the Board.

Disciplinary measures by the Board include, but are not limited to, reprimand, revocation, suspension, and limitation of the right to practice social work.

(F) Minister Responsible

The Minister of Health and Community Services.

(f) Nova Scotia

(i) Legislation—*Social Workers Act*[23]

(A) *Type of Regulation*

The *Act* provides for control of the practice and use of the title social worker or registered social worker, or abbreviations thereof.

(B) *Penalty*

For a first offence a fine is levied of not less than $500 plus costs.[24] For any subsequent offence, a fine of not less than $1,000 plus costs, a term of imprisonment of not more than six months, or both.[25]

(C) *Governing Body*

The council of the Nova Scotia Association of Social Workers (NSASW) consists of the president, vice-president, secretary, treasurer, immediate past president, and other members as provided by the bylaws and the chair of the Board of Examiners. The Board of Examiners includes:

(a) seven social workers, appointed by the council, who represent the diversity of various fields of social work practice and who reflect the gender, racial, and ethnic composition of the Association, one of whom is teaching at an approved school of social work;

(b) three persons, as appointed by the Governor in Council, who are neither social workers nor social work candidates.

(D) *Nova Scotia Association of Social Workers*

The Association regulates the practice of social work and governs the profession, creates bylaws and regulations, and appoints seven members to be on the Board of Examiners.

(E) *Entry to Practice Requirements*

a) A doctoral or master's degree or a graduate-level diploma in social work from an approved faculty of social work, along with:
   (i) two years of experience;
   (ii) a passing grade in the examination required by the Board.

b) A bachelor's degree in social work from an approved faculty of social work, and:

       (i)   at least three years of experience;

       (ii) a passing grade in the examination required by the Board.

    c)   Registered membership and in good standing at an association of social workers approved by the council.[26]

(F) Discipline

The Complaints Committee is composed of three members of the Board, one of whom shall be a person appointed to the Board by the Governor in Council. The Discipline Committee is comprised of five persons appointed by the Board, three of whom are members of the Board, one a member of the Association, and one appointed to the Board by the Governor in Council. Disciplinary measures include, but are not limited to, revocation, suspension, and limitation of the right to practice social work.

(G) Minister Responsible

No Minister responsible.

(g) Ontario

(i) Legislation—*Social Work and Social Service Work Act*[27] *(SWSSWA)*

(A) Type of Regulation

The *SWSSWA* restricts the use of the title social worker and social service worker, and/or registered social worker or registered social service worker, and/or abbrevations of the titles, as well as holding out to be a social worker or social service worker. Ontario is the only province to also regulate social service workers. Furthermore, membership is required for social workers who perform specific functions under the *Health Care Consent Act*[28] and the *Substitute Decisions Act*.[29]

(B) Penalty

It is a provincial offence to contravene the title protection section of the *Act*. Upon conviction, a person found guilty is liable to a fine of not more than $5,000 for a first offence and not more than $10,000 for a subsequent offence.[30]

(C) Governing Body

The governing body of the profession is the Ontario College of Social Workers and Social Service Workers. The college is governed by a 21-member council composed of seven elected social work members, seven elected social service workers, and seven public members appointed by the government.

(D) Entry to Practice Requirements

1. A social work applicant must demonstrate that he or she has obtained:

   a) a degree in social work from a social work program accredited by the Canadian Association of Schools of Social Work, or a degree from a social work program or an equivalent program offered in Canada and approved by council as equivalent to a social work program accredited by the Canadian Association of Schools of Social Work;

   b) a degree from a social work program or an equivalent program offered outside Canada and approved by council as equivalent to a social work program accredited by the Canadian Association of Schools of Social Work; or

   c) a combination of academic qualifications and practical experience that the registrar determines is substantially equivalent to the qualifications required for a degree in social work from a social work program accredited by the Canadian Association of Schools of Social Work.[31]

2. The applicant must have successfully completed the examination or examinations in social work, if any, set or approved by council.[32]

3. A social service work applicant must demonstrate that he or she has obtained:

   a) a diploma in social service work from a social service work program offered in Ontario at a College of Applied Arts and Technology;

   b) a diploma from a program offered in Ontario at a College of Applied Arts and Technology that is equivalent to a social service work program and approved by council as equivalent to a social service work program offered in Ontario at a College of Applied Arts and Technology;

   c) a diploma from a social service work program or an equivalent program offered outside Ontario and approved by council as equivalent to a social service work program offered in Ontario at a College of Applied Arts and Technology; or

d)   a combination of academic qualifications and practical experience that the registrar determines is substantially equivalent to the qualifications required for a diploma in social service work from a social service work program offered in Ontario at a College of Applied Arts and Technology.[33]

(E) Complaints and Discipline

The Complaints Committee is composed of not less than six persons, of whom two are members of the public. The chairperson is a member of the council. This committee investigates complaints; there is a screening function and many different avenues that a referral to complaints can undergo. Manadatory referrals are also made to the Executive Committee by employers. Moreover, there is a Discipline Committee of not less than six persons, of whom two are members of the public. This committee conducts hearings and may impose sanctions (for example, it can revoke any certificate of registration, suspend, or impose terms and conditions, to name a few).

(F) Minister Responsible

Minister of Community and Social Services.

(h) Prince Edward Island (P.E.I.)

(i) Legislation—Social Work Act[34]

(A) Type of Regulation

The Act provides for the control of the practice of social work and the use of the title social worker or registered social worker, or abbreviations of such titles.

(B) Penalty

A fine not exceeding $500.[35]

(C) Governing Body

The P.E.I. Social Work Registration Board includes five members nominated by the P.E.I. Association of Social Workers and appointed by the Minister; four are registered social workers and members of the Association, with one additional person representing the perspective of the general public.

(D) Prince Edward Island Association of Social Workers

The executive of the association consists of a president, vice-president, secretary, treasurer, and other members as prescribed by the bylaws. The Association nominates members to the Board.

(E) Entry to Practice Requirements

a)   a degree from a school of social work recognized by the Board;
b)   practical training as prescribed;
c)   professional competency demonstrated by examination;
d)   good standing under any existing legislation; and
e)   currency of professional knowledge and skills.[36]

(F) Discipline

The Board serves as a complaints and discipline committee. The role of the Board in this respect is under review, and changes are anticipated for the end of 2008. Disciplinary measures by the Board include, but are not limited to, reprimand, suspension, cancellation and limitation of the right to practice social work.

(G) Minister Responsible

The Minister of Health and Social Services.

(i) Quebec

(i) Legislation—Professional Code[37]

(A) Type of Regulation

The Code provides for control of the use of the title social worker or other titles that suggests this designation or an equivalent one, or the use of the initials P.S.W., T.S.P., S.W., or T.S. The title "professional social worker" is also reserved.[38]

(B) Penalty

Between $600 and $6,000.[39]

(C) Governing Body

Ordre Professionnel des Travailleurs Sociaux du Québec, comprises a board of 20 Directors elected on a regional basis and four Directors appointed by the Office des Professions du Québec.

(D) Ordre Professionnel des Travailleurs Sociaux

The main function of the order is to ensure the protection of the public and to supervise the practice of its members. It also stipulates the skills and conditions required to practice and appoints the Inspection and Discipline committees.

(E) Qualifications[40]

B.S.W., M.S.W., or an equivalent diploma if obtained outside the province.

(F) Discipline

The Professional Inspection Committee is composed of not less than three members appointed by the bureau. At present, there are five members; this will be increased to nine by the end of 2007. The Discipline Committee comprises at least two members appointed by the bureau and one member, appointed by the government, who is a lawyer with at least ten years experience and who acts as chairperson. The Discipline Committee may impose, but is not limited to, the penalties as follows: reprimand; temporary or permanent striking off the roll; a fine of not less than $600 and not more than $6,000 for each offence; revocation of the permit; revocation of the specialist certificate; and restriction or suspension of the right to engage in professional activities.[41]

(G) Minister Responsible

The Minister of Justice.

(j) Saskatchewan

(i) Legislation—*The Social Workers Act*[42]

(A) *Type of Regulation*

The *Act* provides for control of the use of the title social worker.

(B) *Penalty*

For a first offence a fine is levied of up to $2,000, for a second offence, up to $4,000, and for each subsequent offence, up to $6,000 or imprisonment.[43]

(C) *Governing Body*

The Council of the Saskatchewan Association of Social Workers (SASW) consists of:

a)   the number of members prescribed in the bylaws, but not less than five, elected by the members; and

b)   a person appointed by the Lieutenant Governor in Council.

According to the bylaws, the officers are the past president, the president, the president-elect, the secretary, and the treasurer. The council consists of seven persons, including two members at large and the officers of the Association.

(D) *Saskatchewan Association of Social Workers*

The Assocation establishes, maintains and develops standards of knowledge, skills and competence for the purpose of serving and protecting the public interest. It also makes bylaws.

(E) *Entry to Practice Requirements*

A certificate or a bachelor's, master's or doctoral degree in social work from a university approved in the bylaws.

(F) *Discipline*

The Discipline Committee is composed of five members of the Association appointed by the Board. Disciplinary measures by the Discipline Committee include, but are not limited to, expulsion, suspension and limitation of the right to practice social work, or reprimand. In addition, the Discipline Committee may order that the member pay: a) a fine not exceeding $2,000 for each finding and $6,000 in the aggregate for all findings; and b) the costs of the investigation and hearing and other related costs.[44]

(G) Minister Responsible

The Minister of the Department of Community Resources (DCR).

(3) CODE OF ETHICS

The Canadian Association of Social Workers (CASW) Social Work Code of Ethics forms the basis for the standard of professional conduct and practice for social workers. Many social workers, while wishing to comply with the Code of Ethics, may fail to appreciate its significance. In the event of a complaint against a social worker concerning their professional conduct, the complaint/discipline committee or board of the respective provincial professional body will refer to the Code of Ethics[45] as the primary standard against which the complaint will be measured. Social workers are thus urged to read the Code and to ensure that their professional behaviour falls within its boundaries.

In 2005,[46] the Canadian Association of Social Workers Code of Ethics replaced the extant, 1994 code. The previous Code was viewed as prescriptive to the profession as it set standards for ethical behaviour. The new Code recognizes the individual and personal diversity of the profession and is based on situational ethics. That is, the social worker can work to determine what is right in a specific situation rather than what is "always" right. In additon, the 2005 Code explicitly highlights the importance of the client's ethno-cultural background and belief systems when examining ethical questions. The Code is accompanied by a companion document called Guidelines for Ethical Responsibilities in Common Practice Situations.[47]

The preamble to the Code states that the profession of social work is "dedicated to the welfare and self-realization of all people, the development and disciplined use of scientific and professional knowledge, the development of resources and skills to meet individual, group, national and international changing needs and aspirations, and the achievement of social justice for all."[48]

The Social Work Code of Ethics comprises certain core principles expressed as values, namely:

1) Respect for Inherent Dignity and Worth of Persons;
2) Pursuit of Social Justice;

3)   Service to Humanity;
4)   Integrity to Profesional Practice;
5)   Confidentiality in Professional Practice; and
6)   Competence in Professional Practice.[49]

The updated Code describes each of these values and practice principles. The companion document details the ethical responsibilites of social workers in various roles and practice areas of their profession. Each province has a copy the Code of Ethics on its website. It is encouraged that every social worker be aware of the Code in whatever area of practice in which he or she engages.

SELECTED READINGS

Aguilar, Gloria et al., "A Comparative Study of Practitioners and Students in the Understanding of Sexual Ethics" (2004) 1 Journal of Social Work Values and Ethics 10.

Antle, Beverly, CASW-ACTS Project to Research and Develop a National Statement of Ethical Principles: Phase 1: Critical Appraisal of the Literature, September, 2002.

Birnbaum, Rachel, "Code of Ethics as Control: Is it?" in Turner & Turner, eds., *Canadian Social Welfare Sixth Edition* (Pearson Publishing, in press).

CASW-ACTS; Companion document to the *Social Work Code of Ethics* (2005).

CASW-ACTS; *Social Work Code of Ethics* (2005).

Mittendorf, Susan & Julie Schroeder, "Boundaries in Social Work: The Ethical Dilemma of Social Worker-Client Sexual Relationships" (2004) 1 Journal of Social Work Values and Ethics 2.

Mullaly, Robert, "Foreward to the Past: The 2005 *CASW* Code of Ethics" (2007) 23(1-2) Canadian Social Work Review 145.

Reamer, Frederic, "Ethical Issues in Social Work" in Albert Roberts & Gilbert Greene, eds., *Social Worker's Desk Reference* (New York: Oxford University Press, 2002) at 65.

Reamer, Frederic, *Ethical Standards in Social Work* (NASW Press: Washington, D.C. 1998).

ENDNOTES

1. Alberta, Saskatchewan, Manitoba, New Brunswick, Nova Scotia, New-foundland and Labrador, Quebec, and the Association of Social Workers of Northern Canada.
2. The role of the regulatory colleges is to protect the public. The role of the provincial associations is to support and be a voice for the profession of social work.
3. The purpose of the MRA is to establish the conditions under which a social worker who is registered in one Canadian province will have his or her qualifications recognized in another Canadian province which is a party to the agreement. Every social worker should check with each individual regulatory body and/or association to obtain the current terms of conditions for qualification in each province.
4. Social workers may access each individual college and/or association website across Canada for the most current information on registration and entry to practice conditions. This summary is not meant to be exhaustive or inclusive. As with all legislation discussed throughout the book, social workers may wish to read each province's rules and regulations in their entirety.
5. R.S.A. 2000, c. H-7, Sched. 27.
6. Email discussions with Alison MacDonald, Associate Registrar, dated February 15, 2007.
7. R.S.B.C. 1996, c. 432.
8. Email discussions with Susan Irwin, dated February 23, 2007.
9. *Ibid.*
10. R.S.M. 1990, c. 96.
11. *Ibid.* at s. 15.
12. S.N.B. 1988, c. 78.
13. *Ibid.* at 18.
14. *Ibid.*
15. *Ibid.*
16. Email discussions with Suzanne McKenna, dated January 22, 2007.
17. *Ibid.*
18. *Ibid.*
19. S.N.L. 1992, c. S-18.1.
20. *Ibid.* at s. 17.
21. *Ibid.* at s. 20.
22. *Ibid.*
23. S.N.S. 1993, c. 12.
24. *Ibid.* at s. 55(1)(e).
25. *Ibid.*

26. *Ibid.* at s. 22.
27. S.O. 1998, c. 31.
28. S.O. 1996, c. 2, Sched. A.
29. S.O. 1992, c. 30.
30. *Ibid.* at s. 55(1).
31. *Ibid.* at s. 59.
32. Personal discussion with Glenda McDonald, Registrar, dated February 16, 2007.
33. *Ibid.* at s. 18.
34. R.S.P.E.I. 1988, c. S-5.
35. *Ibid.* at s. 19.
36. *Ibid.* at s. 9(1).
37. R.S.Q., c. C-26.
38. *Ibid.* at s. 36(d).
39. *Ibid.* at s. 188.
40. A new regulation on equivalence training that would enable a person whose education is substantially equivalent to a social work degree to receive a permit as a social worker should be operative in the fall of 2007. Email communication, dated February 14, 2007 with Mr. Richard Silver, Registrar.
41. See *supra* note 37 at s. 156.
42. S.S. 1993, c. S-52.1.
43. *Ibid.* at s. 29(2).
44. *Ibid.*
45. In Ontario, the College of Social Workers and Social Service Workers regulates two professions: social workers and social service workers. The Ontario Code of Ethics and Standards of Practice guide social workers' and social service workers' codes of conduct and ethical behaviour. When complaints are made against a member of the college, they must conform to the Ontario Code.
46. The new Code of Ethics, 2005 was developed under the leadership of Dr. Beverly Antle, who died tragically in a car accident on November 11, 2006. She was the president of the Ontario Association of Social Workers at the time.
47. *Companion document to the Social Work Code of Ethics* (Ottawa: Canadian Association of Social Workers-ACTS, 2005).
48. *Social Work Code of Ethics* (Ottawa: Canadian Association of Social Workers-ACTS, 2005) at 2.
49. *Ibid.*

TABLES OF CONCORDANCE

Topic	Alberta	British Columbia	Manitoba	New Brunswick	Newfoundland	Nova Scotia	Ontario	Prince Edward Is.	Quebec	Saskatchewan	N.W.T. Yukon
Adoption	Adult Adoption Act, R.S.A. 2000, c. A-4 Child Welfare Act, R.S.A. 1984, c. C-8.1, Part 6	Adoption Act, R.S.B.C. 1996, c. 5	Child and Family Services Act, S.M. 1985-86, c. 8 The Adoption Act, S.M. 1997, c. 47	Family Services Act, S.N.B. 1980, c. F-2.2, Part V	Adoption Act, S.N. 1999, c. A-2.1, s. 1	Children and Family Services Act, S.N.S. 1990, c. 5 Adoption Infromation Act, S.N.S. 1996, c. 3 Intercountry Adoption Act, S.N.S. 1998, c. 15	Child and Family Services Act, R.S.O. 1990, c. C.11, Part VII Intercountry Adoption Act, 1998, S.O. 1998, c. 29	Adoption Act, S.P.E.I. 1992, c. 1	Art. 543-584 C.C.Q.	Adoption Act, S.S. 1998, c. A-5.2	Children's Law Act, S.N.W.T. 1997, c. 14 Children's Act, R.S.Y. 2002, c. 31 Adoption Act, S.N.W.T. 1998, c. 9 Child Welfare Act, R.S.N.W.T. 1988, c. C-6
Children Who Break the Law	Youth Justice Act R.S.A. 2000, c. Y-1	Correction Act, S.B.C. 2004, c. 46 Youth Justice Act S.B.C. 2003, c. 85	Child and Family Services Act, S.M. 1985-86, c. 8	Custody & Detention of Young Persons Act, S.N.B. 1985, c. C-40	APPLIES TO ALL Youth Criminal Justice Act; S.C. 2002, c. 1	Children and Family Services Act, S.N.S. 1990, c. 5	Children and Family Services Act, S.N.S. 1990, c. C.11, Part IV	Child Status Act, R.S.P.E.I. 1988, c. C-6 Youth Justice Act, R.S.P.E.I. 1988, c. Y-3	Youth Protection Act, R.S.Q. c. P-34.1	Age of Majority Act, R.S.S. 1978, c. A-6 Private Vocational Schools Regulation Act, S.S. 1995, c. P.26.2	Youth Justice Act, S.N.W.T. 2003, c. 31 Young Persons Offences Act, R.S.Y. 2002. c. 232
Form of Marriage	Marriage Act, R.S.A. 2000, c. M-5	Marriage Act, R.S.B.C. 1996, c. 282	Marriage Act, R.S.M. 1987, c. M50	Marriage Act, R.S.N.B. 1973, c. M-3	Solemnization of Marriage Act, R.S.N. 1990, c. S-19	Solemnization of Marriage Act, R.S.N.S. 1989, c. 436	Marriage Act, R.S.O. 1990, c. M.3	Marriage Act, R.S.P.E.I. 1988, c. M-3	Art. 356-377 C.C.Q.	Marriage Act, S.S. 1995, c. M-4.1	Marriage Act R.S.Y. 2002, c. 146 Marriage Act, R.S.N.W.T. 1988, c. M-4

Topic	Alberta	British Columbia	Manitoba	New Brunswick	Newfoundland	Nova Scotia	Ontario	Prince Edward Is.	Quebec	Saskatchewan	N.W.T. Yukon
Education	Department of Education Act, R.S.A. 1980, c. D-17 / School Act R.S.A. 2000, c. S-3	School Act, R.S.B.C. 1996, c. 412	Public Schools Act, R.S.M. 1987, c. P250	Education Act, S.N.B. 1997, c. E-1.12	Schools Act, 2007, S.N. 1997, c. S-12.2	Education Act, S.N.S. 1995-96, c. 1	Education Act, R.S.O. 1990, c. E-2	School Act, S.P.E.I. 1993, c. 35	Education Act, R.S.Q. c. I-13.3	Education Act, S.S. 1995, c. E-0.2	Education Act, S.N.W.T. 1995, c. 28 / Education Act, R.S.Y. 2002, c. 61
Human Rights Canadian Human Rights Act, R.S.C. 1985, c. H-6	Alberta Bill of Rights, R.S.A. 2000, c. A-14 / Individual's Rights Protection Act, R.S.A. 1980, c. I-2	Human Rights Code, R.S.B.C. 1996, c. 210 / Civil Rights Protection Act, R.S.B.C. 1996, c. 49	Human Rights Code, S.M. 1987-88, c. 45	Human Rights Act, R.S.N.B. 1973, c. H-11	Human Rights Code, R.S.N. 1990, c. H-14	Human Rights Act, R.S.N.S. 1989, c. 214 / Blind Persons' Rights Act, R.S.N.S. 1989, c. 40	Human Rights Code, R.S.O. 1990, c. H.19	Human Rights Act, R.S.P.E.I. 1988, c. H-12	Charter of Human Rights and Freedoms, R.S.Q. c. C-12	Saskatchewan Human Rights Code, S.S. 1979, c. S-24.1	Human Rights Act, R.S.Y. 2002, c. 116 / Human Rights Act, S.N.W.T. 2002, c. 18
Evidence Canada Evidence Act, R.S.C. 1985, c. C-5	Alberta Evidence Act, R.S.A. 1980, c. A-21	Evidence Act, R.S.B.C. 1996, c. 124	Manitoba Evidence Act, R.S.M. 1987, c. E-150	Evidence Act, R.S.N.B. 1973, c. E-11	Evidence Act, R.S.N. 1990, c. E-16	Evidence Act, R.S.N.S. 1989, c. 154	Evidence Act, R.S.O. 1990, c. E.23	Evidence Act, R.S.P.E.I. 1988, c. E-11 / Electric Evidence Act, S.P.E.I. 2001, c. 32	Art. 2803-2810 C.C.Q.	Evidence Act, S.S. 2006, c. E-11.2	Evidence Act, R.S.Y. 2002, c. 78 / Evidence Act, R.S.N.W.T. 1988, c. E-8
Child Welfare (Child Protection, Children Born Outside Marriage)		Infants Act, R.S.B.C. 1996, c. 223 / Family Maintenance Enforcement Act, R.S.B.C. 1996, c. 127 / Child, Family and Community Service Act, R.S.B.C. 1996, c. 46	Child and Family Services Act, S.M. 1985-86, c. 8 / Family Maintenance Act, R.S.M. 1987, c. F20	Child and Family Services and Family Relations Act, S.N.B. 1980, c. C-2.1	Children's Law Act, R.S.N. 1990, c. C-13 / Child Care Services Act, S.N. 1998, c. C-11.1	Children and Family Services Act, S.N.S. 1990, c. C.5	Children's Law Reform Act, R.S.O. 1990, c. C.12, Part II / Child and Family Services Act, R.S.O. 1990, c. C.11, Part III	Child Status Act, R.S.P.E.I. 1988, c. C-6 / Victims of Family Violence Act, S.P.E.I. 1996, c. 47	Youth Protection Act, R.S.Q. c. P-34.1 / Art. 523-542 C.C.Q.	Child and Family Services Act, S.S. 1989-90, c. C-7.2 / Children's Law Act, 1997, S.S. 1997, c. C-8.2	Children's Act, R.S.Y. 2002, c. 31 / Child Welfare Act, R.S.N.W.T. 1988, c. C-6

Topic	Alberta	British Columbia	Manitoba	New Brunswick	Newfoundland	Nova Scotia	Ontario	Prince Edward Is.	Quebec	Saskatchewan	N.W.T. Yukon
Family Law Matters (Maintenance, Property Division, Custody, Enforcement) Divorce Act, R.S.C. 1985 (2nd Supp.), c. 3 Family Orders and Agreements Enforcement Assistance Act, R.S.C. 1985, c. 4	Matrimonial Property Act, R.S.A. 2000, c. M-8 Extra-provincial Enforcement of Custody Orders Act, R.S.A. 2000, c. E-14 International Child Abduction Act, R.S.A. 2000, c. I-4	Family Relations Act, R.S.B.C. 1996, c. 128 Family Maintenance Enforcement Act, R.S.B.C. 1996, c. 127	Family Maintenance Act, R.S.M. 1987, c. F20 Parents' Maintenance Act, R.S.M. 1987, c. P10 Child Custody Enforcement Act, R.S.M. 1987, c. C360 Dower Act, R.S.M. 1988, c. D-100 Marital Property Act, R.S.M. 1987, c. M45 Married Women's Property Act, R.S.M. 1987, c. M70	Child and Family Services and Family Relations Act, S.N.B. 1980, c. C-2.1 Extra-Provincial Custody Orders Enforcement Act, S.N.B. 1977, c. E-15 Marital Property Act, S.N.B. 1980, c. M-1.1	Family Relief Act, R.S.N. 1990, c. F-3 Family Law Act, R.S.N. 1990, c. F-2 Support Orders Enforcement Act, R.S.N. 1990, c. S-31 Children's Law Act, R.S.N. 1990, c. C-13	Testators' Family Maintenance Act, R.S.N.S. 1989, c. 465 Matrimonial Property Act, R.S.N.S. 1989, c. 275 Maintence Enforcement Act, S.N.S. 1994-95, c. 6 Reciprocal Enforcement of Custody Orders Act, R.S.N.S. 1989, c. 387 Maintenance and Custody Act, R.S.N.S. 1989, c. 160	Children's Law Reform Act, R.S.O. 1990, c. C.12 Family Law Act, R.S.O. 1990, c. F.3 Reciprocal Enforcement of Judgements Act, R.S.O. 1990, c. R.5 Family Responsibility and Support Arrears Enforcement Act, S.O. 1996, c. 31	Family Law Act, S.P.E.I. 1995, c. 12 Maintenance Enforcement Act, R.S.P.E.I. 1988, c. M-1 Custody Jurisdiction and Enforcement Act, R.S.P.E.I. 1988, c. C-33 Reciprocal Enforcement of Judgments Act, R.S.P.E.I. 1988, c. R-6	Act Respecting Reciprocal Enforcement of Maintenance Orders, R.S.Q. c. E-19 Art. 597-612 C.C.Q. Art. 431-492 C.C.Q. Art. 401-430 C.C.Q. Art. 585-596 C.C.Q. An Act to Facilitate the Payment of Support, R.S.Q. c. P-2.2 Act Respecting the Civil Aspects of International and Interprovincial Child Abduction, R.S.Q. c. A-23.01	Children's Law Act, S.S. 1997, c. C-8.2 Family Maintenance Act, 1997, S.S. 1997, c. F-6.2 Parents' Maintenance Act, R.S.S. 1978, c. P-1 International Child Abduction Act, 1996, S.S. 1996, c. I-10.11 Enforcement of Maintenance Orders Act, 1997, S.S. 1997, c. E-9.21 Reciprocal Enforcement of Judgments Act, 1996, S.S. 1996, c. R-3.1	Family Property and Support Act, R.S.Y. 2002, c. 83 Maintenance Enforcement Act, R.S.Y. 2002, c. 145 Reciprocal Enforcement of Maintenance Orders Act. R.S.Y. 2002, c. 191 Maintenance Orders Enforcement Act, R.S.N.W.T. 1988, c. M-2 Children's Law Act, R.S.Y. 2002, c. 31 Reciprocal Enforcement of Maintenance Orders Act, R.S.Y. 2002 c. 191. Children's Law Act, S.N.W.T. 1997, c. 14

Topic	Alberta	British Columbia	Manitoba	New Brunswick	Newfoundland	Nova Scotia	Ontario	Prince Edward Is.	Quebec	Saskatchewan	N.W.T. Yukon
Landlord and Tenant	Landlord and Tenant Act, R.S.A. 1980, c. L-6	Residential Tenancy Act, S.B.C. 2002, c. 78 Rent Distress Act, R.S.B.C. 1996, c. 403	Landlord and Tenant Act, R.S.M. 1987, c. L70 Reenacted Statutes of Manitoba Act, S.M. 1987, c. 9, Sched. A. Pt. II Residential Rent Regulation Act, R.S.M. 1987, c. R118	Landlord and Tenant Act, R.S.N.B. 1973, c. L-1 Residential Tenancy Act, S.N.B. 1975, c. R-10.2	Residential Tenancies Act, 2000, S.N. 2000, c. R-14.1	Residential Tenancies Act, R.S.N.S. 1989, c. 401 Overholding Tenants Act, R.S.N.S. 1989, c. 329 Rental Property Conversion Act, R.S.N.S. 1989, c. 399 Rent Review Act, R.S.N.S. 1989, c. 398 Tenancies and Distress for Rent Act, R.S.N.S. 1989, c. 464	Residential Rent Regulations Act, R.S.O. 1990, c. R.29 Landlord and Tenant Act, R.S.O. 1990, c. L.7 Residential Tenancies Act, 2006, S.O. 2006, c. 17	Landlord and Tenant Act, R.S.P.E.I. 198, c. L-4 Rental of Residential Property Act, S.P.E.I. 1988, c. 58	Art. 1851-2000 C.C.Q.	Landlord and Tenant Act, R.S.S. 1978, c. L-6 Residential Tenancies Act, R.S.S. 1978, c. R-22 Distress Act, R.S.S. 1978, c. D-31	Landlord and Tenant Act, R.S.Y. 2002, c. 131. Residential Tenancies Act, R.S.N.W.T. 1988, c. R-5
Legal Aid		Legal Services Society Act, S.B.C. 2002, c. 30	Legal Aid Manitoba Act, R.S.M. 1987, c. L105	Legal Aid Act, R.S.N.B. 1973, c. L-2	Legal Aid Act, R.S.N. 1990, c L-11	Legal Aid Act, R.S.N.S. 1989. c. 252	Legal Aid Services Act, 1998, S.O. 1998, c. 26		Legal Aid Act, R.S.Q. c. A-14	Legal Aid Act, S.S. 1983, c. L-9.1	Legal Services Act, R.S.N.W.T. 1988, c. L-4 Legal Services Society Act, R.S.Y. 2002. c. 135.
Social Work	Health Professions Act, R.S.A. 2000, c. H-7	Social Workers Act, R.S.B.C. 1996, c. 432	An Act to Incorporate the Manitoba Institute of Registered Social Workers, S.M. 1996, c. 104	An Act to Incorporate the New Brunswick Association of Social Workers, S.N.B. 1988, c. 78	Social Workers Association Act, S.N. 1992, c. S-18.1	Social Workers Act, S.N.S. 1993, c. 12	Social Work and Social Service Work Act, 1998, S.O. 1998, c. 31.	Social Work Act, R.S.P.E.I. 1988, c. S-5	Act Respecting Health Services and Social Services, R.S.Q. c. S-4.2 Professional Code, R.S.Q. c. C-26	Social Workers Act, S.S. 1993, c. S-52.1	

Topic	Alberta	British Columbia	Manitoba	New Brunswick	Newfoundland	Nova Scotia	Ontario	Prince Edward Is.	Quebec	Saskatchewan	N.W.T. Yukon
Mental Health	Mental Health Act, R.S.A. 2000, c. M-1	Mental Health Act, R.S.B.C. 1996, c. 288	Mental Health Act, S.M. 1998, c. 36	Mental Health Act, R.S.N.B. 1973, c. M-10	Mental Health Act, R.S.N. 1990, c. M-9	Hospitals Act, R.S.N.S. 1989, c. C.208 Nova Scotia Hospital Act, R.S.N.S. 1989, c. 313 Incompetent Persons Act, R.S.N.S. 1989, c. 218 Adult Protection Amendment Act, R.S.N.S. 1989, c. 2	Mental Health Act, R.S.O. 1990, c. M.7	Mental Health Act, S.P.E.I. 1994, c. 39 Adult Protection Act, R.S.P.E.I. 1988, c. A-5	Mental Patients Protection Act, R.S.Q. c. P-41 Art. 11-15 C.C.Q.	Mentally Disordered Persons Act, R.S.S. 1978, c. M-14 Mental Health Services Act, S.S. 1984-85-86, c. M-13.1	Mental Health Act, R.S.Y. 2002, c. 150. Mental Health Act, R.S.N.W.T. 1988, c. M-10

COURTS (BY NAME, AUTHORITY AND APPOINTMENT OF JUDGES)

Name of Court	Enabling Statutes	Judges Appointed Under	Alberta	British Columbia	Manitoba	New Brunswick	Newfoundland	Nova Scotia	Ontario	Prince Edward Island	Quebec	Saskatchewan	Yukon & N.W.T.
A. FEDERAL COURTS													
Supreme Court of Canada	s. 101, B.N.A. Act Supreme Court Act	Minister of Justice (Fed.)											
Federal Court —Appeal Division —Trial Division	s. 101, B.N.A. Act Federal Court Act	Minister of Justice (Fed.)											
B. PROVINCIAL SUPERIOR COURTS													
Appeal Court	s. 91(14) B.N.A. Act Judicature Act (Prov.)	s. 96 B.N.A. Act	Appellate Division of the Supreme Court (Court of Appeal)	Court of Appeal	Court of Appeal	Court of Appeal	Court of Appeal	Appeal Division of the Supreme Court	Court of Appeal	Supreme Court	Court of Appeal	Court of Appeal	Court of Appeal
Superior Trial Court Divisions of the Superior Court			Court of Queen's Bench	Supreme Court	Court of Queen's Bench Matrimonial Causes	Court of Queen's Bench Divorce & Matrimonial Causes	Supreme Court (Trial Division)	Supreme Court (Trial Division) Divorce & Matrimonial Causes	General Division Divisional Court Small Claims Court Provincial Division	Supreme Court	Superior Court	Court of Queen's Bench	Supreme Court
C. PROVINCIAL, COUNTY, OR DISTRICT AND SURROGATE COURTS													
County or District Courts	s. 92(14) B.N.A. Act County or District Courts Act (Prov.)	s. 96 B.N.A. Act (Except Quebec)	District Court	County Court	County Court	County Court	District Court Unified Family Court	County Court	County or District Court	Division of the Supreme Court	Court of the Sessions of the Peace (Similar to District Courts)	District Court	
Surrogate Court	Surrogate Courts Act (Prov.)	s. 96 B.N.A. Act	Surrogate Court Division of Court of Queen's Bench		Division of County Courts				Surrogate Court	Division of Supreme Court			

| COURTS (BY NAME, AUTHORITY AND APPOINTMENT OF JUDGES) | | | | | | | | | | | | | |
Name of Court	Enabling Statutes	Judges Appointed Under	Alberta	British Columbia	Manitoba	New Brunswick	Newfoundland	Nova Scotia	Ontario	Prince Edward Island	Quebec	Saskatchewan	Yukon & N.W.T.
D. PROVINCIAL COURTS													
Criminal	Provincial Statute	Provincial Statute	Criminal Division		Provincial Judges Court (Criminal) Division	Juvenile Court	Juvenile Court	Provincial Magistrates Court			Youth Court / Provincial Court		
Family			Family & Juvenile Division	Provincial Court	Provincial Judges Court (Family Division)	Provincial Court	Provincial Court	Family Court	Provincial Court (Family Division)	Provincial Courts	Social Welfare Court / Youth Court	Provincial Courts	Courts of Justices of the Peace
Civil			Small Claims Court						Provincial Court (Civil Division)		Small Claims Court		
Provincial and Municipal Offences			Criminal Division		Provincial Judges Court (Traffic Division)		Traffic Court (St. John's)	Provincial Magistrates Court	Provincial Offences Court		Municipal Court and Court of Justices of the Peace		

SOURCES

Gall, G.L., *The Canadian Legal System*, 2d ed. Toronto: Carswell Co., 1983, Chapters 5 and 7.

Bracken, Susan, ed. *Canadian Almanac and Director, 1984*, Toronto: Copp Clark Pitman Ltd., 1984.

Index